Knight Book of Easter Fun

Do you know how to make a monster Easter egg? This book will tell you, as well as describe how to make cards and decorations. It explains the Spring Calendar and provides lots of seasonal fun and games for indoors and outside with puzzles, quizzes and crosswords.

Knight Book of Easter Fun

Gyles Brandreth

Illustrations by David Farris

KNIGHT BOOKS
in association with
SCHOLASTIC
PUBLICATIONS

ISBN 0 340 19274 7

Text copyright © 1975 Gyles Brandreth
Illustrations copyright © 1975 Hodder & Stoughton Ltd

First published 1975 by Knight, the paperback division of
Brockhampton Press Ltd, (now Hodder & Stoughton Children's Books)
Second Impression 1977 for Scholastic Publications

Printed and bound in Great Britain in Knight Books for Hodder &
Stoughton Children's Books, a division of Hodder & Stoughton Ltd,
Arlen House, Salisbury Road, Leicester by Richard Clay (The Chaucer
Press) Ltd, Bungay, Suffolk

Contents

Happy Easter

If you want to know where I'll be on Easter Day this year
and next year and the year after that, just ask me and I'll
tell you. In fact, if you want to know where I'll be on Easter
Day in ten years or twenty years or thirty years from now,
ask me that as well because the answer will be just the same.
I'll be in Regent's Park, not far from the London Zoo. And
what will I be doing? I'll be hiding Easter eggs.

It's something we always do in our family. We go into
the park and hide eggs for one another. And once we've
hidden them we start to look for them. And we don't leave
the park until all the hidden eggs have been discovered. Of
course, we don't admit to one another that we've hidden
them. We pretend that the big eggs have been hidden by the
Easter Bunny and that the small ones have been laid by the
Easter Chick.

I know it sounds ridiculous, but that's because it is ridiculous. And it's because it's so ridiculous that it's such fun. And Easter is very much a time for fun. It always has been. It always will be. Long before the Jews celebrated the Passover in the spring, long before Easter became a Christian festival, the early pagans were enjoying special spring celebrations. They even gave each other Easter eggs!

This book is all about the fun that comes with spring. It begins with a special calendar explaining some of the important days that fall in February, March and April and describing a few of the traditions and customs associated with them. It includes ideas for making your own Easter decorations and for organising a glorious Easter picnic. It's packed with games and puzzles and jokes and riddles and springtime ideas for things to make and do.

I hope you'll like it and it will help you have your happiest Easter yet.

Spring
Calendar

Introduction

For thousands of years the spring has been a time for
celebrating all things bright and beautiful. Fresh flowers,
chickens bursting out of their eggs, bunny rabbits, new-born
lambs - they're all symbols of the feeling of rebirth and
renewal that comes when we begin to get the winter behind
us.

A long time ago, the month of April was called the
'Ostermonath' - the month of the east wind - and, way
before the days of Christianity, people who worshipped the
goddess of the east staged an eight-day festival at this time of
year in her honour. For centuries pagans celebrated the
arrival of spring in different ways and gave each other
presents, such as flowers and eggs.

Today, there are two principal religious festivals held
during the spring. In April the Jews celebrate the Passover
- when the Angel of Death passed over their houses and
spared everyone who did as they had been told by the
prophet Moses - and on some date between 22 March and
25 April - the precise day is different each year and has to
be worked out according to a special lunar calendar - the
Christians celebrate Jesus's rising from the dead on Easter
Day after his crucifixion on Good Friday.

Because Easter Day is what's known as a 'moveable feast',
so are all the other days related to it. In this Spring Calendar
these days - Shrove Tuesday, Ash Wednesday, Mothering
Sunday, Palm Sunday, Maundy Thursday, Good Friday -
are listed first. They are followed by the other special spring
days that fall on fixed dates and don't change from year to
year.

Shrove Tuesday and Pancake Recipe

Shrove Tuesday comes exactly forty-eight days before Easter. It is the day before Ash Wednesday, the first day of Lent, and it gets its name from the past tense of the old verb 'to shrive', which means to confess one's wrongdoings and to seek forgiveness for them from God. It was on Shrove Tuesday that good Christians would visit their priests in church to be 'shriven' and to prepare themselves for Lent.

It was traditional too to fast during Lent, to be very disciplined and to eat very little - sometimes only bread and water. That's how Shrove Tuesday has become Pancake Day. In order to get ready for the forty-day (the Sundays weren't counted) fast, families had to use up their supplies of food, so just before the first day of Lent they would mix all their eggs and flour and milk and fat in an enormous frying pan and make a special cake - the pancake. And once they had cooked one side of the cake in the pan, the only way to turn it over without breaking it was to toss it - which is how we get the tradition of 'tossing the pancake'.

And it's a tradition that's very much alive today. In homes and schools all over the country people still cook, toss and eat pancakes on Shrove Tuesday. At Westminster School in London they have an annual Pancake Scramble, when a giant pancake is tossed over a bar in the roof of the school's great hall and the boys scramble for a piece of it. The boy who manages to get hold of the largest piece is rewarded with a guinea - an old coin worth £1.05.

At Olney in Buckinghamshire on Shrove Tuesday they have a special race and ring a special church bell, known as the Pancake Bell. The race, in which women run the course wearing aprons and caps and have to toss their pancakes

11

three times as they go, has been held since 1445. The winner is given a prayer book by the vicar and a kiss by the bell-ringer. People come from all over the country to watch the race and its fame has spread around the world. At Olney in Texas, in the United States of America, they have even started a race of their own just like it.

In centuries gone by the tolling of the Pancake Bell was the signal for all sorts of special games to start. Shrove Tuesday was a day for playing football in the streets, for watching wrestling matches and cockfights. Most of these Shrove Tuesday traditions have now died out. The only one that hasn't is the Pancake tradition. It's as alive and well as ever it was.

PANCAKE RECIPE

If you feel like making your own pancakes on Shrove Tuesday, it isn't a difficult job.

You will need:

1 egg
½ pint of milk
¼ lb. of flour
lard or butter
salt
a frying pan
a mixing bowl
a wooden spoon and a palette knife

Method:

Begin by sifting the flour into the bowl and adding a pinch of salt. Break the egg into the middle of the flour. Add the milk, a little at a time, stirring it in all the while. Make sure there are no lumps and then beat well for roughly five minutes, until the mixture is all creamy and tiny bubbles appear on the surface. Now stand the bowl in a cool place for at least an hour.

As soon as you are ready to start cooking, beat the mixture again for three or four minutes. Melt a small knob of butter or lard in the frying pan and keep heating it until a very slight smoke comes from the fat. Pour in enough of the pancake mixture to cover the bottom of the pan and cook it over a low heat.

When the pancake mixture has set, lift it at the edge very carefully with the palette knife to check if the underside is a lovely golden brown. If it is, the pancake is ready to be turned over - or tossed. To turn it over, use the palette knife. To toss it, slide it backwards and forwards in the pan very quickly to make sure it isn't sticking and then flick it over boldly. If it lands in the pan, well done! If it lands on the floor, bad luck!

When the second side of the pancake is golden brown as well, turn it out on to a plate and sprinkle it with castor sugar and just a squeeze of lemon juice.

Ash Wednesday

Lent begins on Ash Wednesday, the day after Shrove Tuesday, and lasts until Holy Saturday, the day before Easter. It is a period of forty days (not counting the Sundays) during which Christians try to remember how Jesus fasted in the wilderness being tempted by the devil. It is a time when Christians try to learn self-control and discipline themselves by giving up something they really enjoy. There was a time when good Christians would simply live on bread and water in Lent. Now most people do little more than give up sweets for Lent - if that!

Ash Wednesday gets its name from the old custom of sprinkling ashes on the heads of certain people who had confessed wrongdoings and come to church on the first day of Lent to pray for forgiveness and to make amends for all that they had done wrong. Lent gets its name from the Saxon word for 'springtime'.

During Lent special hymns are sung in Christian churches and these three verses come from one of the most famous of them:

Forty days and forty nights,
   Thou wast fasting in the wild;
Forty days and forty nights
   Tempted still, yet unbeguiled.

Sunbeams scorching all the day,
   Chilly dew-drops nightly shed,
Prowling beasts about thy way,
   Stones thy pillow, earth thy bed.

Let us endurance share
   And from earthly greed abstain,
With thee watching unto prayer,
   With thee strong to suffer pain.

Mothering Sunday

Mothering Sunday, which used to be called Mid-Lent Sunday, comes three weeks before Easter and a fortnight before Palm Sunday. It gets its name in part from the tradition of visiting the 'mother church' (the local cathedral) to make an Easter offering, in part from the custom of allowing servants and working people to have this particular day off to visit their mothers.

When the servants did go home to their mothers on Mothering Sunday they would often take with them a Simnel Cake, a special cake made with spices, fruit and flour, and covered with a delicious almond paste, topped with eleven almonds as symbols of Jesus's eleven faithful disciples.

The word Simnel comes, in fact, from a German word for a kind of roll, but once upon a time people believed that the cake was named after a married couple called Sim and Nell who mixed a cake for Easter and then argued about whether to boil it or bake it. In the end they agreed to boil it first and bake it afterwards - which is what you must do to this day if you are following a traditional recipe.

People do still make and eat Simnel Cakes, but they have become more popular at Easter than on Mothering Sunday. On Mothering Sunday now children give their mothers cards and presents and flowers - and, if they're very thoughtful, give them breakfast in bed.

Palm Sunday and Maundy Thursday

PALM SUNDAY

Palm Sunday is the Sunday before Easter and commemorates Jesus's triumphant return to Jerusalem when all the people came out to cheer him and laid the branches of palm trees in his path. To this day, in most Christian churches, people who go to a service on Palm Sunday are given a small cross made out of a palm leaf. If you get one, you can preserve it by pressing it between the pages of a large book.

MAUNDY THURSDAY

Maundy Thursday, the Thursday before Easter and the day before Good Friday, probably gets its name from the Latin word for 'commandment', because it marks the day when Jesus washed the feet of his own disciples and said to them, 'I give you a new commandment: love one another'. For hundreds of years, on Maundy Thursday, in Christian countries, kings and queens, princes and lords would ceremoniously wash the feet of poor people and then give them food and clothes and money. The tradition survives in Britain with the ceremony of the Maundy Money, when the Queen, or another member of the Royal Family, distributes a few specially minted coins to a small group of elderly people chosen to represent the poor.

Good Friday

To Christians, Good Friday is the saddest day of the year. It marks the day when Jesus was hung on the cross to die. The cross you find on a Hot Cross Bun is a symbol of Jesus's cross. On Good Friday some people will spend the whole day in church, praying, listening to readings from the Bible and singing hymns - like this very famous one:

There was a green hill far away,
*   Without a city wall,*
Where the dear Lord was crucified
*   Who died to save us all.*

We may not know, we cannot tell,
*   What pains he had to bear,*
But we believe it was for us
*   He hung and suffered there.*

He died that we might be forgiven,
*   He died to make us good;*
That we might go at last to heaven,
*   Saved by his precious blood.*

O, dearly, dearly has he loved,
*   And we must love him too,*
And trust in his redeeming blood,
*   And try his works to do.*

Easter Day

To Christians, just as Good Friday is the saddest day of the year, Easter Day is the happiest - happier even than Christmas Day itself. On Easter Day Christians celebrate the moment when Jesus 'rose again from the dead'. The churches are given a thorough clean, the brasses are polished, fresh candles are lit, spring flowers are displayed everywhere. Some churches even have an 'Easter Garden', a model garden, made up from moss and grass and cut flowers, with a small cave built from stones representing the grave where Jesus's body was laid after it was taken down from the cross. The cave, of course, is always empty, because Easter is the celebration of Jesus's resurrection.

The world itself keeps Easter Day,
And Easter larks are singing;
And Easter flowers are blooming gay,
And Easter buds are springing.
Alleluya! Alleluya!
The Lord of all things lives anew,
And all his works are rising too;
Hosanna in excelsis!

It used to be traditional to wear new clothes on Easter Day and many girls and women still buy a new 'Easter bonnet' for the occasion. Easter Day is also the day for exchanging cards and Easter eggs. Some people still hide the eggs they are going to give in the garden or a wood and pretend that they have been brought by the benevolent Easter Bunny. Others still keep up the custom of rolling their eggs down a hillside. And if your egg wins the egg race, you'll not only get a prize: you'll have good luck for the rest of the year.

The day after Easter, Easter Monday, is a holiday and traditionally a day for going to a fair. On heaths and commons and in market places all over the country, the end of Lent and the arrival of Easter is celebrated with a fair on Easter Monday.

Saint Valentine's Day
14 February

Nobody knows very much about the original Saint Valentine, except that he was probably a priest who lived in Rome and was martyred for sheltering some Christians from the Romans. His feast day is 14 February and coming, as it does, right in the middle of the month it coincides with the date when, according to an ancient myth, birds begin to choose their mates. It's only this coincidence which has made Saint Valentine the patron saint of lovers and turned 14 February into the day when people 'send Valentines'.

People have been 'sending Valentines' to the girl or boy they love for over five hundred years. At first, only gentlemen would send them and the Valentine would consist of a short verse written down on paper and delivered by messenger or not even written down, but carried by the messenger in his head and recited by him when he reached the recipient.

In the last century, once the penny post had been introduced, the sending of Valentine cards became universally popular. Boys would send them to girls and girls would send them to boys. Some of the cards were quite simple, containing nothing more than a short verse like this very famous one:

> *Roses are red,*
> *Violets are blue,*
> *Carnations are sweet –*
> *And so are you!*

Others would be much more elaborate and would even involve pressed flowers and hand-embroidered lace!

Today, you can buy Valentine cards from all stationers and card shops or - and this is much more fun - you can make your own, drawing pictures of hearts and flowers on the card's cover and writing your own verse on the inside.

When it comes to sending a Valentine - and it doesn't matter if it's a home-made card or an expensive heart-shaped box of chocolates - there is one golden rule that must never be broken: the Valentine must be sent anonymously. Nobody must know you've sent it and you must certainly not sign it. The girl or boy who gets it can guess that it was you who sent it, but it's something you must never tell them.

29 February

It takes 365.2422 days for the earth to revolve round the sun, but since having 365.2422 days in a year would make life very difficult for everyone (especially the people who compile calendars), the ordinary Year as we know it consists of 365 days, while years where the date is divisible by four are called Leap Years and consist of 366 days.

In ordinary years the day of the month which falls on a Monday this year, will fall on a Tuesday next year and a Wednesday the year after, but in the fourth year - the Leap Year - it will 'leap over' Thursday to Friday. To make matters even more complicated the last year of a century is not a Leap Year unless its number is divisible by 400 - so, for example, 1900 wasn't a Leap Year, but the year 2000 will be.

In Leap Years the extra day is added on to the month of February, the shortest month of the year, and 29 February is a special day - particularly for girls. On the night of 28—29 February a girl will dream of the man she will marry and on the day of 29 February itself she can ask for a man's hand in marriage. Traditionally, boys propose marriage to girls, but on 29 February the rôles are reversed. Some people say that girls can do the proposing throughout a Leap Year, but this isn't really the case. According to the ancient custom, 29 February is the only day in the year when girls are allowed to enjoy that particular privilege.

Saint David's Day
1 March

The name 'David' is the nearest we can get to the Welsh name 'Dewi' and Saint Dewi or Saint David is the patron saint of Wales. Like so many saints, not much is known about him, but according to the legend he was born in the sixth century, the son of a Cardigan chieftain called Sant. He founded twelve monasteries, from Croyland to Pembrokeshire, went on a pilgrimage to Jerusalem and became a bishop, and was known as a great preacher with a wonderful speaking voice.

In Wales on Saint David's day the people all wear leeks. No one knows how this tradition arose, but one story has it that it all began during a battle when Saint David was called on to help the Welsh fight back an invading army. The battle took place in a narrow valley and so as to help the soldiers tell the difference between the enemy and the men on their own side, Saint David told them all to pick a leek from the nearby fields and stick it in their helmets as a means of identification. Of course, the story can't be true because Saint David died years before the battle took place, but all the same to this day soldiers in Welsh regiments of the British army are presented with leeks on 1 March.

If you are Welsh, but don't like the idea of wearing a leek on Saint David's day, you can always wear a daffodil instead. It is the national flower of Wales.

Saint Patrick's Day
17 March

Saint Patrick, the patron saint of Ireland, was born in Scotland around about the year 385. He was the son and grandson of clergymen and only went to Ireland because he was captured by raiders and taken there as a slave at the age of sixteen. Six years later he managed to escape and made his way to France, where eventually he became a priest. In the year 432 he returned to Ireland as a missionary bishop.

There were all sorts of unlikely stories about Saint Patrick, but the most famous is the one that tells how he rid all Ireland of snakes. One day, according to the legend, he went to the top of a high mountain and, with a miraculous power, drew all the snakes on the island up after him. Once they were with him at the top of the mountain, he drove them down the other side and into the sea where they drowned. Whether or not the story is true, one thing is certain: you will never meet an Irishman who will admit to having seen a snake on his native soil.

Just as the Welsh are supposed to wear a leek on Saint David's Day, the Irish are supposed to wear a piece of shamrock on 17 March. Shamrock - a kind of clover - is Saint Patrick's emblem because he used it to teach the people about the Trinity. 'God the Father', 'God the Son' and 'God the Holy Ghost' are the three parts of the Trinity, but they are all part of the one God - just as the shamrock has three leaves, but each leaf belongs to the same stem.

A three-leaf piece of shamrock worn on 17 March will bring you luck. A four-leaf piece of shamrock (if you can find one) worn on any day of the year will bring you more luck still.

Saint George's Day
23 April

April 23 marks the feast day of Saint George, as well as the
birthday, in 1564, of the greatest English poet and playwright
William Shakespeare. If we know very little about the
background of Shakespeare, we know almost nothing about
the background of Saint George. We don't even know why
he has become the patron saint of England.

He may have been born in Turkey in the third century
and have been a famous and valiant soldier, but we're not
even sure of that. The only thing we do know about Saint
George is that he slew the dragon - and, of course, that's
only a myth. But it's a popular myth that it would be rather
nice to be able to believe.

According to the legend, Saint George was riding
through a strange land one day when he came across a town
where all the people were in a state of great distress. They
told him that outside their town there lived a dragon who
every day had to be given one of their children to eat. On
this particular day the king's beautiful daughter was due to
go to the dragon, but bold Saint George rode there first,
wounded the beast and let the king's daughter lead it back
into the town in triumph. Saint George then killed the
dragon and saved the people, many of whom he later
converted to Christianity.

As well as being the patron saint of England and several
other countries, Saint George is the patron saint of soldiers
and boy scouts. On 23 April there is a special Saint George's
Day Parade of all the Queen's Scouts in the boy scout
movement at Saint George's Chapel, Windsor.

April Fools Day
1 April

Nobody knows the exact origin of April Fools Day - some
say it's a hangover from the time when New Year was
celebrated on 25 March and the revels ended six days later,
others say it dates back to the period when the court jesters
took the day off from their duties at court, others say it's all
to do with the pranks of the Greek goddess of Spring! - but
everybody knows it is the one day of the year when you are
actually encouraged to fool your family and friends.

Here are some popular April Fool tricks to try at home.
They must all be done before twelve noon and when
whoever you are trying to fool has been fooled you must
cry out loud and clear: 'April Fool!'

1 Just as your father's got into the bath go and tell him
   he's wanted urgently on the telephone!
2 Give everyone breakfast in bed as a special treat, but
   don't put boiled eggs in the egg cups: put in empty
   egg-shells instead!
3 Plant a Brillo pad in a small pot of earth and take it to
   your teacher as a present!
4 Give someone an enormous box beautifully wrapped.
   Inside make sure there are at least five layers of wrapping
   leading to an old potato.
5 Send someone a forged letter telling them they've won
   the pools or a prize with their premium bonds.
6 On a very crowded bus or in a very crowded train, say
   to your friend, 'Don't look now, but before you left
   home you forgot to put your skirt/trousers on!'

7 Ask someone to pop out to the shops for you to buy a pint bottle of gravy, a tin of bulls' eggs and a loaf of breadcrumbs.

8 Invite friends over to help with the gardening and take them out to prune the carrot bushes.

9 Ask your mother why she dropped that pound note at the bottom of the rubbish bin.

10 At five-to-nine in the morning tell everyone that you're awfully sorry but you've just remembered that the vicar 'phoned yesterday to say that he and his wife were planning to call that morning at nine.

11 Tell your best friend that there are details of a special competition with prizes for everyone who takes part at the back of this book. You'll find the details on page 129.

Easter
Decorations

Decorated Easter Eggs

You can buy all sorts of wonderfully decorated chocolate Easter eggs from the shops, but they are very expensive and not nearly as much fun as <u>real</u> eggs which you've decorated yourself.

PAINTED EGG SHELLS

Take a raw white egg and wash it carefully. With a pin make a tiny hole at the pointed end of the egg for blowing through and a larger hole at the other end of the egg for the inside to come out. Now very gently blow the egg out of its shell and into a cup. Keep the inside for making scrambled eggs and decorate the outside with pretty patterns and funny faces, as you please. When you've decorated your egg, put it in an egg cup so no one can see the end that has the larger hole.

COLOURED EGGS

It's traditional to eat boiled eggs for breakfast on Easter day and it's rather fun to colour the boiled eggs first. It's simple to do. Just boil the eggs in water that contains a small amount of vinegar and some cooking colouring: about a teaspoon to ¾ pint of water will do. When the eggs are ready and you take them out of the water, you'll find the shells have turned the colour of the colouring - but the eggs will taste just the same.

INITIALLED EGGS

To make your boiled eggs on Easter day very personal you can always initial them. Melt a little candle wax and use it to draw the name or initials you want onto the shells of each of the eggs. Let the wax harden and then soak the eggs in vinegar for roughly half-an-hour. Boil the eggs in water that has a little cooking colouring added to it, and when the eggs are ready and taken out of the water the name or initials you wanted will be clearly seen on the egg shells.

Easter Egg Bean-Bag

An Easter Egg Bean-bag makes a marvellous Easter present for anyone in the family or any of your friends or even for yourself. It's easy to make and enormous fun to play with.

Begin by collecting together some colourful material (you only need about a square foot), scissors, pins, a needle and thread, a packet of dried peas. Cut two egg shapes out of your material. The egg should be about six inches high and if you cut both shapes at the same time you'll be sure they're the same size. Pin the two shapes together all the way round the edge leaving a very small gap unpinned. Now sew neatly around the shape keeping your stitches about half-an-inch in from the edge. Don't sew over the small gap. Now take out the pins and turn the material inside out. Fill it with the dried peas and sew up the little gap, remembering to turn the rough edges of the material inside first. And there you are: in less than half-an-hour you've made a handsome Easter Egg Bean-bag.

Model Easter Chick

Trace or copy this picture of a little Easter chick on to a small piece of card.

Cut out the shape of the Easter chick and colour it bright yellow on both sides, shading in the wings and drawing in the eyes. Now make a stand for the chick by tracing or copying this illustration, cutting it out from card and folding it along the dotted lines.

Now stand the Easter chick in the cardboard stand and place it on the table as a special decoration.

Easter Nest

Another attractive decoration for the table is an Easter nest.
It makes a marvellous centrepiece and it isn't too difficult to
create. Begin by gathering a lot of green moss from the
garden or from a wood and by packing it firmly round the
edges of a saucer. Cover the moss with small spring flowers
(primroses look pretty) and fill the centre of the saucer with
those small chocolate Easter eggs that you buy wrapped in
coloured foil.

Once the nest is made, all you have to do is make a
chicken to sit on it. Cut out a circle of card about an inch
in diameter, fold it in half and glue it onto the chicken's
head, tail and wings. You can copy or trace these:

When you have glued the chicken together, colour it and it
will be all ready to perch on top of the nest.

Easter Card

Get a piece of white or coloured card, about ten inches wide and six inches deep, and fold it in half, so that it's now about five inches wide but still six inches deep. Now you've made you basic card, draw the shape of an egg on the front, making sure that the top and bottom and sides of the egg touch the edges of the card. Now cut around the egg shape <u>except</u> where the outline of the egg touches the edge of the card.

Inside the egg shape draw a jolly face like Humpty Dumpty's and colour it as you please. Inside the card itself write 'HAPPY EASTER'.

Giant Easter Egg

Begin by buying two feet of twelve-inch chicken wire. It isn't expensive and you can get it at a good ironmonger's or at a shop that sells gardening and farm equipment. Bend the wire round into a cylinder and then squeeze it in the middle and turn it into the shape of an egg cup. Now tear a newspaper into strips and paste the strips of newspaper over the wire. You can either use wallpaper paste or make your own mixing two ounces of flour into half a cup of water. Cover the wire with three layers of newspaper and a final layer of white tissue paper or kitchen roll. Leave it to dry for twenty-four hours and then paint it with a pretty pattern.

When the monster egg cup is ready, blow up a large white balloon and stick it round-end-upwards in the egg cup. Place it on the breakfast table and it'll look like a giant egg. If you've got the time and energy (and enough chicken wire), you can make a giant egg cup for the whole family and serve your parents and your brothers and sisters with monster eggs on April Fools Day.

Easter Fun and Games

Indoors

Bean-in-the-Bottle

What you need: Any number of players, a chair, a bottle and dried beans.

Place an upright chair in the middle of the room and behind it stand an empty milk bottle. The players then take it in turn to stand in front of the chair and drop beans (or peas) over the back of the chair into the bottle. Each player has ten beans to drop and after all the beans have gone, the player who got the most beans into the bottle is the winner.

SPRING RIDDLE

Question: Three fat men went out for a **walk underneath** a lady's umbrella, but none of them got wet. Why?

Answer: It wasn't raining.

Do-it-yourself Barometer

What you need: A bottle, a jar and some water.

In springtime the weather can be very changeable. If you want to be able to predict how it's going to change, you will need a barometer. And if you are going to make your own barometer, you will want a clear glass jar and a clear glass bottle which can be placed upside down in the jar so that the shoulders of the bottle rest on the top of the jar, with the top of the bottle just half-an-inch or so from the bottom of the jar.

When you have found the right jar and bottle, pour a little water into the bottle, place the jar over the top of the bottle and turn both bottle and jar upside down. Most of the water will now run into the jar, but some of it will stay in the neck of the bottle. When the weather is going to be fine, the water in the neck of the bottle will rise. When it's going to be wet, the water will fall.

If it sounds simple, it is simple. If it sounds a bit unreliable, it is a bit unreliable. All the same, it will give you some idea of what the weather prospects are - and if you get it wrong sometimes, well, so do the professional forecasters on the radio and tv.

SPRING RIDDLE

Question: Which travels faster, heat or cold?
Answer: Heat. You can catch a cold!

Empty Chair

What you need: Any number of players and chairs.

You need a circle of chairs facing inwards, with exactly the same number of chairs as there are players. All the players sit, except for one who stands in the centre of the circle. On the word 'Go!' he must try to sit down, while the other players try to prevent him from doing so by moving continuously round the circle from chair to chair. When he does manage eventually to hurl himself into an empty chair, the player sitting on his right moves into the centre of the circle and the game starts all over again.

SPRING RIDDLE

Question: Crocodile skins make good shoes, so what do banana skins make?

Answer: Good slippers!

Family Newspaper

What you need: paper, pencils, paste and photos.

Springtime is the best time for launching a family newspaper. What you do is find a large sheet of paper (about two feet deep and three feet wide) and make it look like two pages from a real newspaper by filling it with news about you and your family. You can write the items or type them on to separate pieces of paper and then paste them into position. Use photographs whenever you can and include your own drawings and cartoons. Here are some of the sections you can have in your newspaper:

NEWS STORIES

> Father Burns Scrambled Eggs - Fierce Row Follows
> Tim Buys New Shoes
> Aunt Jane Breaks Her Leg and Goes to Hospital
> Sarah Wins £10 With Her Premium Bonds
> Mother Wins Family Monopoly Championship
> Grandpa Flies to Canada on Business Trip
> Family Holiday in Cornwall a Success
> Family Car Breaks Down Outside Truro — AA to the Rescue
> Tim Comes Top of the Class in French

SPORTS NEWS

> Tim to Join School First Eleven
> Father Wins at Golf - Again!
> Flu Stops Sarah From Taking Part in Swimming Sports.
> Mother Joins Local Squash Club
> Tim's Football Breaks Neighbour's Kitchen Window

SOCIAL NEWS

Cousin Lizzie Christened at St. Mary's
Mrs Brown Comes to Tea
Happy Birthday Party for Sarah
Parents' Wedding Anniversary Celebrations
Bad Weather Spoils Picnic With Uncle Charles

FASHION

Sarah Gets New School Uniform (illustrated)
Father Given Birthday Bow-tie (illustrated)
Mother's Party Dress a Flop - To Be Changed Next Week
Granny Knits Cardigan for Tim (illustrated)
Sarah Wins Best-Dressed-Member-of-the-Family Award

COOKERY CORNER

First Taste of the New Home-Made Jam
Sarah Tosses the Pancake
Granny's Favourite Dish
Father's Recipe for Scrambled Eggs

PETS CORNER

Felix Has Fleas!
Bonzo Pictured in the Garden
Tommy the Tortoise Lost - then Found
Bonzo Visits the Vet

LETTERS TO THE EDITOR

Mother writes to complain that no one is helping her with the Spring cleaning
Tim writes to ask for more fish fingers for tea
Father writes a birthday poem for Sarah
Grandpa writes a letter home from Canada

CARTOONS

When you have written and collected all the items, got all the drawings and photographs you need, and pasted everything on to your large piece of paper you will have a newspaper to stick up on the wall for everyone to read. You can change it once a month or once a week or - if you're very keen and you've got lots to say - once a day! Make it look as much like a real newspaper as you can and before you start, think of a good name for the paper. Here are some different family newspaper names that may give you a good idea for yours:

THE SMITH NEWS
THE JONES GAZETTE
THE BROWN CHRONICLE
THE OSBORN ADVERTISER
THE WILKES WEEKLY
THE THOMPSON TIMES
THE ATTENBOROUGH TELEGRAPH
THE MITCHELL MIRROR
THE COHEN MAIL
THE NESBITT NEWSHEET

Find the Word

What you need: Any number of players and slips of paper.

This is one of those spring games that calls for a little preparation. Think of a fairly long word that has no single letter repeated in it - CORNFLAKES is a good example - and write that word in bold capitals on as many slips of paper as you will have players. Then cut all the slips up into single letters and hide the scraps of paper in different parts of the room.

When the players arrive, explain to them what you've done, tell them how many letters there are in the word (ten in the case of CORNFLAKES), don't tell them the word, of course, and then get them to look for the letters. Each player must find ten different letters and when he's found them must form the right word with them. The first player to find the letters and form the word is the winner and gets the prize - a packet of cornflakes, perhaps?

SPRING RIDDLE

Question: Where does Friday come before Thursday?
Answer: In the dictionary, of course!

Fooled You!

What you need: One player, one blindfold, an audience and a long piece of string.

Blindfold the player before you get ready to play the game. Once you are sure he can't see what you're up to, unravel the string and lay a trail with it that goes right through your home - round a chair leg here, behind the sofa here, under the kitchen table here, up the stairs there - and then tell the blindfold player that he has got to follow the string trail and when he gets to the end of it he will find a special prize. On the word 'Go!' the blindfold player starts out, following the string along its complicated route - but he never gets to the end, poor fellow, because you have joined the ends of the string together and formed one gigantic loop, so when the player gets to the end he starts all over again! He won't notice the knot that joins the two ends, because you will cleverly have tied lots of knots in the piece of string. Once the player has been around the circuit three times and still hasn't guessed why the piece of string doesn't come to an end, you can take off his blindfold and tell him the truth. If you're feeling kind, you can give him the prize as well.

This is a marvellous game to play on April Fools Day.

Hedgehog Potatoes

What you need: Any number of players, potatoes, pins and scissors.

The players all sit in a circle and each player is given a large potato, a saucer full of pins and a pair of nail scissors. On the command 'Go!' the players must pick up the pins with the scissors and stick them one by one into the potato. The pins must be firmly stuck into the potatoes and the use of fingers is not allowed. At the end of two minutes, the player who has stuck most pins into his or her potato is the winner.

SPRING RIDDLE

Question: What eight-letter word has only one letter in it?
Answer: Envelope.

Hobby Horses

What you need: Any number of players.

Each player has to think up a hobby - it can be as ridiculous as you like - that begins with their initials. The leader will then ask each player for his or her hobby and out will come the hilarious answers. Here are some examples to explain what happens:

Question: What's your hobby, Edward East?
Answer: Eating elephants!

Question: What's your hobby, Catherine Brown?
Answer: Collecting butterflies.

Question: What's your hobby, John Smith?
Answer: Jumping stiles.

Question: What's your hobby, Harriet Brown?
Answer: Hitting boys!

When everyone has given their own hobby, the players can take it in turn to think of the names of famous people and find hobbies for them. For example:

Florence Nightingale's hobby is fishing newts!
Robinson Crusoe's hobby is riding cows!
Winston Churchill's hobby is watering cress!
Jane Eyre's hobby is jumping everywhere!
Christopher Robin's hobby is crying rudely!
Bobby Brewster's hobby is bouncing balls!
Donny Osmond's hobby is drowning orang-utans!
Rupert Bear's hobby is riding bicycles!

This is a game that nobody wins and nobody loses, but hopefully one that everybody enjoys.

Hole-in-the-Sheet

What you need: Any number of players and an old sheet.

Hang an old sheet with two holes cut in it over the doorway - a small hole at about nose-height and a slightly larger one at about knee-height. Put half the players on one side of the sheet and the other half on the other side and make the players on one side take it in turn to stand behind the sheet with their nose poking through the top hole and their knee-cap poking through the bottom hole. The players on the other side have got to guess whose nose and knees it is.

This is one of those April Fools Day games that nobody needs to win or lose.

SPRING RIDDLE

Question: Why is it dangerous to put a clock at the top of a flight of stairs?

Answer: Because it might run down and strike one.

If I had a Million

What you need: Any number of players.

The players sit in a circle and one of them begins by saying 'If I had a million pounds I would buy......' And instead of saying what he would buy he <u>describes</u> it without naming it. The other players then have to guess what it is and the first player to do so then has his chance to describe what he'd buy if he had a million pounds.

SPRING RIDDLE

Question: What has a hundred legs but cannot walk?
Answer: Fifty pairs of trousers.

Last Word

What you need: Any number of players.

The players sit in a circle and the first player says a phrase or a short group of words that belong together. The next player then says a phrase that begins with the last word in the first player's phrase. The third player then begins his phrase with the last word in the second player's phrase. And so it goes on around the group, until one of the players can't think of a phrase beginning with the right word and has to drop out. The last player left in is the winner.

Here's an example of how the game might go with four players:

Player One:	Apple-pie
Player Two:	Pie in the sky
Player Three:	Sky high
Player Four:	High time
Player One:	Time-table
Player Two:	Table and chair
Player Three:	**Can't think of anything so he drops out**
Player Four:	Chairman
Player One:	Man and boy
Player Two:	Boy meets girl
Player Four:	Girl Guide
Player One:	**Can't think of anything so he drops out**
Player Two:	Guide dog
Player Four:	Dog's life
Player Two:	Life on the ocean wave
Player Four:	Waive the rules
Player Two:	Rules were made to be broken
Player Four:	**Can't think of anything so he drops out**
Player Two:	Broken-hearted
	Player Two is the winner!

Line Up

What you need: Any number of players and paper and pencils.

Give all the players three or four pieces of paper and ask them to write a line of dialogue on each sheet of paper. They can write anything they like on the paper and what they put on one piece doesn't have to be related to what they write on another. Just to prove that you can write what you like, here are ten examples:

'Will you walk a little faster?'
'I hate you!'
'The early bird catches the worm'
'Isn't it time for tea?'
'Have you ever seen the Leaning Tower of Pisa?'
'What made the lobster blush?'
'Stuff and nonsense!'
'Here we go gathering nuts in May.'
'I'm going for a walk.'
'This is the end.'

When each player has written a sentence on each of his pieces of paper, the pieces of paper are collected by the leader who sorts them out and then reads them out loud, as though they were all part of the same story. The results can be very, very funny. Nobody gets any prizes, but with a bit of luck everyone laughs a lot.

SPRING RIDDLE

Question: Why is tennis such a noisy game?
Answer: Because every player raises a racket.

Magic Carpet

What you need: Two players and a small mat.

The aim of the game is very simple: one player stands on the mat and the other player tries to get him off it. It's a rough, tough game, but it'll warm you up on a cold Spring day and shouldn't do anyone too much harm. Kicking and rugby tackles aren't allowed, but you can get away with anything else and may the best boy - or girl - win!

If you are playing the game in a room with a carpet, then any kind of mat will do, but if you want to play it on a slippery floor then you must only play the game if you have got a non-slip mat to use.

SPRING RIDDLE

Question: What is bought by the yard, but worn out by the foot?

Answer: A carpet!

The Memory Game

You will need: Any number of players, a tray of objects, and paper and pencils.

This is a well-tried game that never fails, but calls for a little preparation. Find a tray and place on it twenty different items. For example:

1. A bar of soap
2. A cherry
3. A pack of cards
4. A pencil
5. An Easter egg
6. A paper clip
7. A sponge
8. A potato
9. An envelope
10. A doll
11. An egg cup
12. A flower
13. A coin
14. A pair of scissors
15. A postage stamp
16. A ring
17. A slice of bread
18. A needle and thread
19. A pair of spectacles
20. A thimble

Now carry the tray round the room, letting each player look at it for exactly fifteen seconds. The tray is then taken from the room and the players have a minute in which to list all the items that they can remember having seen on the tray. The player with the longest accurate list is the winner.

Missing Letters

What you need: Any number of players and paper and pencil.

Supply each player with a piece of paper on which you have written a list of twenty or twenty-five words, with one letter missing from each word. The list might look like this:

T-RTOISE	P-OTOGRAPH
-MBRELLA	BATHTU-
SHEEPD-G	UNDER-ANTS
EA-TER	SU-SHINE
TRUM-ET	VEGET-BLE
POST-ARD	AIRCRA-T
ANGE-	P-INCESS
G-RAFFE	TOMAT-
BA-ANA	TOAS-
TELE-ISION	-RMCHAIR
ROB-ER	SCH-OL
DAFF-DIL	SPRIN-TIME
SANDW-CH	

The players then race to fill in all the missing letters and the first player to have completed the list correctly is the winner.

If you want to make the game more difficult and make it last longer, make out a list of words with _two_ letters missing from each word.

The Name Game

What you need: Any number of players and paper and pencils.

Give all the players a piece of paper and a pencil. Then give them one minute (or two if you're feeling generous) in which to write down the names of as many items or objects or people that could possibly come under a set heading. Here are some examples of headings:

Names of famous pop singers
Names of animals
Names of vegetables
Names of things you'd find in the kitchen
Names of television programmes
Names of flowers
Names of towns
Names of books
Names of things you'd find in a classroom
Names of birds

When the time is up, the players read out their lists of names and the player with the longest list of acceptable names is the winner.

SPRING RIDDLE

Question: What runs round a field, but doesn't move?
Answer: A hedge.

Pick-a-Match

What you need: Any small number of players and a box of matches.

This is a simple version of a famous and ancient game called Pick-a-Stick (which you can buy from most good games' shops). Pick-a-Match isn't as complicated and doesn't call for as much skill, but it still makes an absorbing game to play indoors on a cold spring day. You begin by emptying the contents of a box (or two boxes) of matches into a heap in the middle of the table. Players now take it in turn to remove a match at a time from the pile without moving any of the other matches. To get a match you can use your fingers or one of the matches you have already won. If, in trying to remove a match, you move any of the other matches, you leave the match you were after where it is and it's the next player's turn. Every time you manage to remove a match without disturbing any of the other matches, you get an extra turn. The winner is the player with the most matches at the end of the game.

SPRING RIDDLE

Question: What has many keys that fit no locks?
Answer: A piano.

Piglet

What you need: Two players, a balloon, a rolled-up newspaper, blindfolds.

Blindfold the two players and stand them face to face. Give one a rolled-up newspaper and the other a balloon. The player with the balloon must blow it up, but not tie it up, and on the word 'Go!' he must let little bursts of air out of the balloon to make a rude noise that will sound a bit like a piglet snorting. As the player with the balloon lets the air escape from the balloon, he darts around the room and does everything he can to escape from the other player who is chasing him with the rolled-up newspaper. The player with the paper has got to hit the player with the balloon over the head and as soon as he manages to do so the two players swap places - or another two players can join the game.

You must play this game indoors, but be sure to tidy away anything breakable before you start! If you play the game at a party with at least ten people, then the two players who are blindfolded can stand inside a circle formed by the remaining players holding hands. And before you start, get everyone to practise letting the air out of the balloon so that the noise is as piglet-like as possible.

SPRING RIDDLE

Question: What asks no questions, but gets a lot of answers?
Answer: A telephone!

Ping Pong Bucket

What you need: Any number of players, ping pong balls and a bucket.

Stand the bucket in the middle of the room and get all the players to stand in a circle around it, but as far away from it as possible. Players take it in turns to throw a ping pong ball into the bucket. It must land directly in the bucket, mustn't bounce out and mustn't even bounce on the way there. For every direct landing, a player scores a point. Each player can have five attempts at throwing the ball. The player with the highest score is the winner.

SPRING RIDDLE

Question: What bill never needs paying?
Answer: A duck's bill!

Ping Pong Goals

What you need: Four or more players and a ping-pong ball.

The players divide into two teams and face each other across the room. The wall at one end of the room counts as one team's goal; the wall at the other end counts as the other team's goal. A ping-pong ball is placed on the floor in the middle of the room. On the word 'Go!' the members of the two teams rush towards the ball on hands and knees and try to <u>blow it</u> towards their opponent's goal. Every time the ping-pong ball touches one of the walls a goal is scored and the ball is returned to the centre of the room. At the end of fifteen minutes, the team with most goals to its credit has won.

SPRING RIDDLE

Question: If two's company and three's a crowd, what are four and five?

Answer: Nine

Raisin Relay

What you need: Six or more players, raisins and toothpicks.

The players divide into two teams and each team elects a captain. The teams then line up side by side, with a bowl of raisins at the head of each team. Each player is given a toothpick. On the command 'Go!' the captain of each team picks up three raisins with his toothpick, feeds them to the player immediately behind him and runs to the back of the team. The second player now puts three raisins onto his toothpick and feeds them to the player behind him. And so it goes on until the team captain is back at the front of the team. The first team to finish wins the race.

SPRING RIDDLE

Question: Why do birds fly south in the wintertime?
Answer: Because it's too far to walk!

Rattling Boxes

What you need: Any number of players, prepared matchboxes and paper and pencils.

To prepare for this game you must find ten empty matchboxes and put into each one something that rattles. For example, you might fill your boxes like this:

1 Peas
2 Rice
3 Bread crumbs
4 Pebbles
5 Cork
6 Nails
7 Pins
8 Sugar
9 Tea leaves
10 Matches

Number each box and get every player to rattle each box in turn and then write down on a piece of paper what he thinks is inside each box. When all the players have rattled all the boxes and completed their lists, the player with the most accurate list is the winner. (To make the game easier you can always give the players the first letter of each lot of contents).

SPRING RIDDLE

Question: I haven't got it and don't want it, but if I did have it I wouldn't want to lose it for all the world. What is it?

Answer: A bald head.

Seat Swap

What you need: Any number of players and chairs.

All the players except one sit in a circle. The lone player stands in the middle and orders the seated players to swap seats. He can't name the players who have to swap seats, but he can describe them. For example he might say:

> 'All change those wearing glasses'
> 'All change those wearing shirts'
> 'All change those who didn't bath today'
> 'All change those wearing sandals'
> 'All change those wearing shorts'
> 'All change those who had bacon for breakfast'
> 'All change those who have had their birthdays this year'

And every time he says 'All change', the players who fit his description must get up and change places. In the scramble the man-in-the-middle must try to find himself a seat. Whoever's left standing after the change-over takes over in the centre of the circle and gives the new orders.

SPRING RIDDLE

Question: What letter is never found in the alphabet?
Answer: The one that's lost in the post!

Spinning the Plate

What you need: Any number of players and a tin plate.

The players stand in a circle, with one player in the middle who spins a tin plate. As he does so, he calls out the name of one of the other players who must rush to the centre of the circle and catch the plate before it stops spinning. If he succeeds, it's then his turn to spin the plate, while the first player joins the circle. If he doesn't get to the plate in time, he drops out of the game altogether and the original player has another go at spinning the plate and calls out another name. The last player left spinning the plate is the winner.

SPRING RIDDLE

Question: What kind of coat is made without buttons and put on wet?
Answer: A coat of paint.

Spring Cleaning

What you need: An apron, vacuum cleaner, broom, dustpan and brush, duster, cleaning cloths, bucket.

Spring cleaning has been a British tradition since Queen Victoria's day a hundred years ago. It's all part of the idea of renewal, rebirth and starting afresh that is associated with springtime and what it involves is simply house cleaning. If you decide to give your own room at home a thorough clean, here's a useful order in which to set about it:

1 Tidy up. Sort out your books and toys and belongings and put them away neatly.
2 Dust all surfaces. Begin with things that are high up: the tops of cupboards, window sills, mantelpieces. Brush the dust into a dustpan. When you can't use a brush, use a duster.
3 If there isn't a carpet in the room, sweep the floor thoroughly with a broom and gather all the dust in one corner. Then collect the dust with a dustpan and brush.
4 Wipe down all the visible surfaces that are painted. Use a damp cloth that's been soaked in a bucket of soapy warm water and squeezed dry. Wipe the surfaces firmly but not roughly and be sure to get off all the finger marks around cupboard doors, on doorknobs and on the skirting board.
5 Polish all wooden surfaces. Use a spray-on polish, but read the instructions very carefully before you start.
6 If there is a carpet in the room, run over it with a carpet sweeper or a vacuum cleaner.

Tiddly-Wink Golf

What you need: Any number of players and tiddly-winks.

The players all line up at one end of the race track - it can be a large room or a long corridor - and each is given a golf club (a tiddly-wink) and a golf ball (another tiddly-wink). They then take it in turn to flick their tiddly-winks across the room or down the corridor and the player who manages to flick his tiddly-wink past the finishing post with the <u>least number of strokes</u> is the winner. This isn't an ordinary race, so you don't need to hurry and the players should flick their tiddly-winks one at a time, with an impartial umpire keeping a beady eye on the proceedings and keeping count of the number of strokes.

SPRING RIDDLE

Question: What did the South wall say to the East wall?
Answer: Meet you at the corner!

Waiter, There's a Fly in my Soup

What you need: Any number of players and paper and pencil.

It's the oldest joke of all. We all know the first line. It goes like this: 'Waiter, there's a fly in my soup'. But do we all know the waiter's answer? There are lots of different answers, of course, and in this game, all the players have to write down the funniest reply they can think of. When they have all written down their answers they read them out and the one that everyone agrees is the wittiest is awarded the prize.

Here are some examples to get you going:

1 Don't shout about it, sir, or they'll all want one.
2 Of course, it's fly soup.
3 And it seems to be doing breast stroke.
4 I'll phone for the RSPCA at once.
5 Don't worry, sir, they don't drink much.
6 There's no extra charge, sir.
7 Hold on, sir, and I'll find the lifebelt.
8 Don't worry, sir, the spider on your roll will eat it for you.
9 Yes, sir, it's our speciality of the day.
10 Is it waving or drowning?

SPRING RIDDLE

Question: Why did the chicken cross the road?
Answer: For its own fowl reasons !

67

What's the Question?

What you need: Two players.

This is a game where two players ask each other questions all the time and talk sense while they're doing so. The first question has to be answered by a second question, the second by a third, the third by a fourth and so on. The first player who can't think of a question to ask or comes out with an answer that isn't in the form of a question is out. Here's an example:

Jack:	How old are you?
Jill:	Why do you want to know?
Jack:	Aren't you going to tell me?
Jill:	What do you think?
Jack :	Why don't you tell me?
Jill:	Why should I?
Jack :	Why not?
Jill:	When's your birthday?
Jack :	Don't you know?
Jill:	Yes.
	Jill's out!

SPRING RIDDLE

Question: What is everyone doing in the world at the same time?

Answer: Growing older.

ZYX

What you need: Any number of players and a stopwatch.

This is a very simple game that's enormous fun and not so easy to play successfully as it sounds. All the players have to do is recite the letters of the alphabet backwards. As each player goes from Z to A, he is timed and the fastest player is the winner - providing he gets all the letters in the right order.

The player who wins this game will probably be the one who has put the letters into rhythmic groups like this:

> Z Y X and W V,
> U T S and R Q P,
> O N M and L K J,
> I H G and F E D and C B A!

SPRING RIDDLE

Question: What sea has waves but no water?
Answer: The BBC.

Easter Fun and Games

Outdoors

Back-to-Back Race

What you need: Any even number of players.

The players divide into pairs and line up at the starting post. On the command 'Go!' they race down the course back to back with arms linked. The first pair past the finishing post wins the race.

SPRING ELEPHANT JOKE

Question: When do elephants wear busbies and carry bayonets?

Answer: When they're changing guards at Buckingham Palace, of course.

Centipede

What you need: Ten or more players.

Divide the players into two teams and line them up at the starting post. On the word 'Go!' the players go down on all fours and link up by holding on to the ankles of the player in front. They then move forward as fast as they can. The first 'centipede' to cross the finishing post in the winner.

SPRING ELEPHANT JOKE

Question: How do you fit four elephants into a Mini?
Answer: Two in the front, two in the back, of course.

Chaos!

What you need: Any number of players and slips of paper.

This is one of the few outdoor games that calls for a little preparation. Get as many slips of paper as there will be players and on half the slips write a special instruction (for example 'Do three somersaults and then a headstand' or 'Collect three other players and run round the oak tree and back bouncing a football between you as you go') and on the remaining slips write a different instruction that is the reverse of the first one (for example 'Don't let anyone perform a somersault or a headstand' or 'Don't let anyone run to the oak tree or touch a football). When the players arrive, give half of them one set of instructions and the other half the other set. Then on the word 'Go!' simply sit back and watch the chaos that follows!

SPRING ELEPHANT JOKE

Question: How do you get down from an elephant?
Answer: You don't, stupid! You get down from a swan.

Chinese Wrestling

What you need: Two players.

The two players stand back to back on either side of a marked line. They stand with legs astride and on the command 'Go!' bend down and grasp each other's hands through their legs. The aim of the game is to try to pull your opponent over the marked line. The first player to do so is the winner.

SPRING ELEPHANT JOKE

Question: What did the man say when he saw the elephants coming at him over the mountain top?
Answer: Here come the elephants, of course.

Clothes Horse Relay

What you need: Ten or more players, old clothes and two suitcases.

Prepare for this game by gathering together as many odd items of old clothing as you will have players. Anything will do: shirts, pyjamas, trousers, socks, pants, shoes, hats, coats, galoshes. Put half the garments in one suitcase, half in the other, and place the suitcases at the far end of the playing area. Divide the players into two teams and line them up at the starting post. On the command 'Go!' the first player from each team rushes forward, opens one of the suitcases, takes out the first garment he touches, puts it on and rushes back, touching the second player in line who then sets off to repeat the process. The first team to have donned all the old clothes and to be back at the starting line has won.

SPRING ELEPHANT JOKE

Question: How do you know you've got an elephant in the fridge?
Answer: Giant footprints in the butter, of course.

Donkey

What you need: Any number of players and a ball.

There's a splendid spelling game called Donkey that's great fun to play indoors. Outdoors Donkey has got nothing to do with spelling. Get the players well spaced out in a large circle and then have them throw a ball from one to another. Whenever a player drops the ball he takes on one of the letters in the word Donkey, so when he's dropped the ball once he's a D, when he's dropped it twice he's a DO, when he's dropped it three times he's a DON and by the time he's dropped it six times he's a DONKEY, by which time he's dropped out. The last player to become a DONKEY wins the game.

To make the game more difficult you can get the players to throw and catch the ball with their right hands only. To make it more difficult still you can get them to throw and catch the ball with their left hands. To make the game well nigh impossible, you can get the players to throw and catch the ball with their left hands while standing on just one leg!

SPRING ELEPHANT JOKE

Question: Why do elephants stand on one leg and drop every ball that's thrown at them?

Answer: Because they want to be donkeys, of course.

Elbow Power

What you need: Two players.

The players lie flat on their fronts facing each other. They place their right elbows on the ground and grasp hands. The aim of the game is for one player to force his opponent's hand down until the back of it touches the ground. The elbows must be kept on the ground at all times and no strength must be exerted until the word 'Go!'

SPRING ELEPHANT JOKE

Question: What did the grape say when the elephant stepped on it?

Answer: Why, nothing. It just let out a little whine.

Fill the Bottle

What you need: Any number of players, bottles, teaspoons and a bucket of water.

The players stand in a circle facing outwards, with an empty bottle in front of each one of them and a teaspoon in their right hands. In the middle of the circle is a bucket of water. On the command 'Go!' the players must turn round, run to the bucket, fill their teaspoons with water, run back to their bottles and pour the water into them. The first player to fill his bottle to the brim is the winner.

To make the game shorter use smaller bottles and larger spoons.

SPRING ELEPHANT JOKE

Question: Why are elephants grey?
Answer: Because they haven't washed in years, of course.

Hit the Bucket

What you need: Any number of players, a bucket, a bat and a ball.

One player balances on an upturned bucket and defends his bucket with a bat (a cricket bat, a rounders bat or even a sturdy stick would do) from the attackers who throw a ball at him. When the bucket is hit the thrower replaces the batsman. Batsmen score runs by whirling the bat round their bodies, one complete circuit counting as one run. Once everyone has had a turn to defend the bucket, the batsman who scored most runs is declared the winner.

SPRING ELEPHANT JOKE

Question: How can you tell when you're in bed with an elephant?
Answer: By the big 'E' embroidered on his pyjama jacket pocket.

Home-Made Skittles

What you need: Any number of players, bottles and tennis balls.

Find ten empty bottles, all of roughly the same size, and fill each of them with a little water to give them stability. Stand them at one end of the garden in a triangular formation like this:

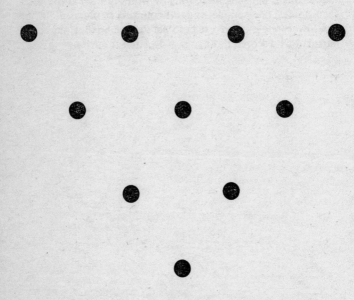

The lone skittle should be nearest the players who are equipped with three tennis balls and can each have three shots at the bottles. A player scores one point for every bottle he knocks over. He gets a bonus of one point if he has knocked down all the skittles by his third throw, a bonus of two if he has knocked them all down by his second and a bonus of three if he knocks them all down with his first. At the end of five rounds (by which time each player will have had fifteen shots), the player with the highest score is the winner.

SPRING ELEPHANT JOKE

Question: How does an elephant get down from a tree?
Answer: He sits on a leaf and waits till autumn, of course.

The Human Chair

What you need: Six or more players.

All the players form a circle and stand one behind the other. On the word 'Go!' everyone sits down on the knees of the player behind him, so that the whole circle forms a human chair. In theory, the players should be able to stay sitting like this for ever. In practice, the world record for a human chair is twenty-two minutes. Can you beat it?

SPRING ELEPHANT JOKE

Question: What would happen if you crossed an elephant with a kangaroo?

Answer: There'd be great big holes all over Australia, of course.

Ice Race

What you need: Ten or more players, two knives and ice cubes.

Divide the players into two teams and get them to stand in two rows facing forwards. Give the player at the back of the line a knife and the player at the front of the line an ice cube. On the word 'Go!' the player at the front must pass the ice cube over his head to the player behind him who must pass it to the player behind him and so on down the line to the last player who must take the ice cube, balance it on the side of his knife and run to the front of the queue. The first team to complete the task wins the round and another round follows with a fresh ice cube at the front of the queue and the knife returned to the back. There are as many rounds as there are players in each team and the team that wins the most rounds naturally wins the competition.

SPRING ELEPHANT JOKE

Question: What time is it when the elephant sits on the fence?

Answer: Time to get a new one.

Jellyfish

What you need: Four or more players and a bottle.

The players stand in a circle facing inwards and holding hands. In the middle of the circle stands a bottle. The aim of the game is to avoid knocking over or even touching the bottle, while at the same time trying to force a neighbour to do just that. If a player touches the bottle he drops out. The last player left in is the winner.

SPRING ELEPHANT JOKE

Question: Why do elephants have wings?
Answer: So they can fly south in wintertime, of course.

Orange Duel

What you need: Two players, four tablespoons, two oranges.

The players stand face to face holding an empty tablespoon in their left hand and a tablespoon with an orange balanced on it in their right hand. On the command 'Go!' the players use the spoon in their left hand to try to knock the oranges off the spoon their opponent is holding in their right hand. The first player to topple his opponent's orange has won.

SPRING ELEPHANT JOKE

Question: Why does the elephant go quack-quack?
Answer: 'Cos it isn't an elephant, stupid, it's a duck in fancy dress.

Orange Rolling

What you need: Any number of players and oranges.

This is a race in which the object of the exercise is for the contestants to push an orange along the course using only their noses! You can make the course as long or as short, as complicated or as straightforward, as you think the skill of the competitors will allow. Anyone caught touching his or her orange or seen pushing it with a forehead, a chin or a cheek is disqualified. The first orange past the finishing post is the winner.

SPRING ELEPHANT JOKE

Question: What do you use to shoot an orange elephant?
Answer: Why, an orange elephant gun, of course.

Pig-in-the-Middle

What you need: Three players and a ball.

Two players pass a ball between them, with a third player standing in between and trying to intercept it. When the 'pig-in-the-middle' manages to get hold of the ball, he changes places with the last thrower. This is a much more entertaining and exhausting game than it sounds and, played on the run, can be quite thrilling.

SPRING ELEPHANT JOKE

Question. What's the différence between a sneezing elephant and a spy?

Answer: None at all. They've both got a code in the trunk.

Quarter Staffs

What you need: Two players and two stout sticks about four feet long.

Robin Hood met Friar Tuck over a friendly bout of Quarter Staffs in Sherwood Forest. It's an ancient sport that tests the contestants' powers of balance and ingenuity as well as their strength. The players face each other holding their sticks firmly with both hands. They cross the sticks at right angles and the aim of the game is for one player to overbalance the other. It isn't easy, but it's enormous fun.

SPRING ELEPHANT JOKE

Question: Why is an elephant large, grey and wrinkled?
Answer: Because if he was small, black and wrinkled he'd be a prune, of course.

Roundabout Leapfrog Race

What you need: Eight or more players.

Divide the players into two teams and get the members of each team to stand in circles fairly well spread out and facing clockwise. The leader of each team then gets the players to get into the leapfrog position - bent forward, with hands on knees and legs rigid - and on the command 'Go!' leapfrogs over every member of the team in turn until he gets back to his own position where he taps the player in front of him on the shoulder and it becomes his turn to leapfrog round the circle. When every player has leapfrogged his way right round the circle, all the members of the team stand up straight. The first team seen standing straight has won.

SPRING ELEPHANT JOKE

Question: How do you know when an elephant's going on holiday?

Answer: Because he leaves his trunk in the hall, of course.

Scavenger Hunt

What you need: Any number of players and pieces of paper.

Supply all the players with a list of items that they have got to collect. The first player to return to base with every single item on the list is the winner. Here are some examples:

A flower pot
A stone
A dead daffodil
Some gravel
A pigeon's feather
A dandelion
A leaf from a particular tree
An empty cigarette packet
A trowel
A handful of mown grass

As well as getting the players to hunt for actual items, you can get them to collect information as well:

The time of the last bus to X
The name of the third shop in the High Street
The time of the last post on Sundays
The local vicar's surname
The number of the last house in Y Road
The number of the nearest call box
The number of the local constable

Obviously you will compile a list that suits the surroundings and the age and intelligence of the players. Naturally too, you will make sure that you know the answers to all the questions of information.

Three-Legged Football

What you need: Any large number of players and a football.

You play this game just like football, with two opposing teams trying to kick the ball into each other's goals. The only difference is that in this game the players pair off and have their ankles tied together! Ten minutes each way is quite long enough for this game - especially as you'll have to allow for plenty of injury time.

SPRING ELEPHANT JOKE

Question: Why did the elephant cross the road?
Answer: To get to the other side, of course.

Tossing the Bag

What you need: Two players and a large paper bag.

Blow up a large paper bag, but don't burst it. Instead, tie a bit of string or put a rubber band around the end. Now give it to the players who must toss it between them. The bag must never touch the ground. The first player to miss a shot and let the bag touch the ground loses the game.

A messier but more amusing version of the same game can be played with a plastic bag. But you don't fill it with air. You fill it with water instead! This version is only to be played well away from the house, in warm weather and in rough clothes.

SPRING ELEPHANT JOKE

Question: Why are elephants so wrinkled?
Answer: Have you ever tried ironing one?

Wheelbarrow Soccer

What you need: Four or more players and a football.

The players divide into pairs and the pairs divide into teams. And the two teams compete at ordinary football - ordinary football that is, with a slight difference. One member of each pair goes down on all fours while the other lifts him up by the thighs. The upright player pushes his partner and the partner uses his hands and his head to push the ball. The team to have scored most goals after ten minutes has won. At half-time partners change positions.

SPRING ELEPHANT JOKE

Question: What's red and grey and dangerous and lives up a tree?

Answer: A gun-slinging, tree-climbing elephant with bloodshot eyes.

Easter
Picnic

Introduction

There is something very special about eating out of doors and springtime is the time to start. Getting ready for a picnic is simple and enormous fun and you don't need to take anything fancy. Here, for example, is a straightforward picnic menu that would provide a feast fit for a king (well, for a prince anyway):

1 A flask of hot soup (out of a tin)
2 A selection of sandwiches (ideas on pages 98-99)
3 Cold meat or fish or cheese or egg and salad (ideas on page 100)
4 Fruit salad or fruit jelly (ideas on pages 102-103)
5 Chocolate Easter eggs
6 Something hot or cold to drink (ideas on page 104)

The secret of organising a successful picnic party is to make sure that you take _everything_ you need with you. There's nothing more annoying than getting to the picnic spot (five miles from home!) and finding you've forgotten the can-opener, the salt, and the sugar for the tea. Here's a list of picnic equipment to check before you set off:

1 Soup for starter
2 Second course
3 Pudding
4 Something to drink
5 Cold water
6 Hot water
7 Milk
8 Sugar
9 Salt and pepper
10 Mayonnaise and salad dressing
11 Soup spoons, knives and forks, dessert spoons, teaspoons

12 Soup bowls or mugs
13 Paper plates
14 Paper napkins
15 Can-opener and bottle-opener
16 Ordinary cups, paper cups or mugs
17 Paper or plastic bag in which to take all the leftovers
    and rubbish home

The only problem about a spring picnic is that you can never rely on the weather. Making the barometer described on page 40 might help, but if it does begin to rain just as you're about to set off, don't worry. An Easter picnic round the fireside can be almost as much fun as an Easter picnic out of doors.

Sandwiches

The sandwich is named after John Montagu, fourth Earl of
Sandwich, who lived in the eighteenth century and, on one
memorable occasion, spent twenty-four hours gambling with
nothing to eat but beef sandwiches. They have been popular
ever since and they make a perfect picnic food, because they
are easy to prepare, easy to carry and delicious to eat.

Here are the five rules of successful sandwich-making:

1　Spread thinly-cut slices of white or brown bread with
butter or margarine.
2　Cover half the slices with the filling of your choice.
3　Cover the slice with the filling with one of the slices that
has just butter or margarine spread on it and press the
two slices together gently.
4　Put the sandwich on the breadboard and, if you like, cut
off the crusts.
5　Cut the whole sandwich into four triangles.

When you have made all the sandwiches you need - and
for a picnic you are going to need at least three rounds per
person - pile them on top of each other and wrap them up
in tinfoil or grease-proof paper. If you can get hold of
grease-proof paper bags it is probably a good idea to put
each person's set of sandwiches into a separate paper bag
and mark the bag with their name. Then when you get out
to the picnic spot, no one can complain that they haven't
has as much as greedy so-and-so!

Sandwich Fillings

Here are some ideas for tasty, but simple, sandwich fillings:

1. Cold beef - the Earl of Sanwich's favourite.
2. Cold ham - with two or three slices of tomato.
3. Cold tongue - with a washed lettuce leaf.
4. Cold chicken - with a pinch or two of salt.
5. Sardines - open a tin, put the sardines into a bowl and mash them up, adding a pinch of salt, a pinch of pepper and a squeeze of lemon.
6. Tomato - slice the tomatoes, put them on the bread and butter or margarine and add a pinch of salt, a pinch of pepper and a shake of vinegar.
7. Salad - a slice of tomato, a lettuce leaf, two slices of cucumber and some pieces of watercress, with a pinch of salt.
8. Egg - hard-boil the eggs for ten minutes, lift them out of the water, tap the shells gently and put the eggs into a bowl of cold water to cool. When they're cold, take them out of the water, remove the shells, put the eggs into another bowl and chop them into tiny pieces. Add half an ounce of butter for every egg and mash it all up with a pinch of salt and a pinch of pepper. Now spread it on the bread and butter.
9. Grated cheese.
10. Cheese and chutney - a thin slice of cheese with some chutney from a jar spread over it.
11. Meat paste.
12. Fish paste.
13. Tomato ketchup.
14. Salad dressing.
15. Jam or Marmalade.
16. Honey.
17. Chocolate Spread.

18   Sugar - castor sugar sprinkled lightly over the bread
     and butter.
19   Chocolate - squares of black chocolate laid on top of
     the bread and butter. A French favourite.
20   Banana - either slice the bananas and put thin
     slivers on top of the bread and butter, or put the
     bananas in a bowl and mash them up, adding a pinch
     or two of castor sugar, before spreading.

Salads

On a picnic a salad goes marvellously with all sorts of things - cold meats (beef, chicken, ham, lamb, salami), cheeses, fish, even sandwiches. Here is how best to prepare some of the possible ingredients for a fresh picnic salad:

1 Lettuce - wash it carefully, pulling the leaves apart (don't cut them) and shaking them to get rid of the water.
2 Tomatoes - remove the stalks, wash them carefully and wipe them dry. If you like, cut them into halves or quarters.
3 Cucumber - leave the skin on, but wash it thoroughly, then cut the cucumber into wafer-thin slices.
4 Radishes - remove the stalks and wash and dry them thoroughly. Either slice them or leave them whole.
5 Spring Onions - peel off the outer skins and cut off the roots and green tops. Wash and dry thoroughly.
6 Watercress - wash it thoroughly and tear off any yellow or yellowing bits.
7 Mustard and Cress - with a pair of scissors cut it from the roots and wash it thoroughly.
8 Fruit and nuts - slices of banana, pieces of peeled apple, sections of peeled orange, peeled grapes cut in half with the pips removed, small squares of melon, well washed cherries, and even walnuts or hazel nuts, can make an original and very tasty addition to the salad.

Arrange all your ingredients as attractively as you can in a bowl and then cover the bowl with cellophane. If you don't think you can keep the bowl upright as you travel to your picnic spot, then don't bother about the bowl: simply put the salad into a cellophane or plastic bag and serve it from there. Don't 'dress' the salad before you set out, because different people may like it 'dressed' in different ways: some will want to eat it plain, some will want to add salt and pepper: some will prefer it with salad dressing, some with mayonnaise. If you take the different 'dressings' with you on the picnic, then your guests can choose what to have at the time.

Fruit Salad

Only make a fruit salad to take with you on your picnic if you have got a container in which to carry it. You can't expect to carry it all the way in an open bowl!

Preparing a fruit salad is easy and what you put in it depends very much on what fresh fruit is in the shops and what tinned fruit you've got at home. Here is a suggested mixture of fresh and tinned fruit that will make a very successful salad:

1 Take a small tin of pineapple pieces and empty it into a bowl.
2 Add a small tin of Mandarin oranges.
3 Peel a banana, slice it and put it in the bowl.
4 Peel an apple, cut it into sections and put them in the bowl.
5 Peel a pear, cut it into sections and put them in the bowl.
6 Take half-a-dozen grapes, cut them in half, remove the pips and put them in the bowl.

Gently stir the six ingredients and you will find you've created a delicious fruit salad that will serve at least four.

Fruit Jelly

This is the easiest picnic desert in the world. All you have to do is get hold of a packet of jelly and follow the instructions - adding the fruit (two sliced bananas for example or a small tin of mandarin oranges or some fresh sliced and washed strawberries) to the jelly mixture once you have dissolved the jelly itself and allowed the liquid to cool very slightly.

The joy of taking a jelly on a picnic is that though it will wobble inside its bowl, unless you're very careless it won't fall out.

Picnic Drinks

The easiest kind of drink to take on a picnic is a drink you can buy in a shop and to which all you have to add is cold water - if that. Here's a list of some of the drinks you can buy in a can or bottle. There should be something here to suit most tastes:

1   Milk
2   Orange squash
3   Lemonade
4   Lime juice
5   Blackcurrant juice
6   Apple juice
7   Grape juice
8   Pineapple juice
9   Tomato juice
10 Cola

If you take a bottle of something that needs to be diluted, whatever you do don't forget to take a flask of water. And if you're taking anything that comes in a can, be on the safe side and take a bottle opener that serves as a can opener as well.

If you want tea or coffee, then take instant tea (or teabags) and instant coffee, not forgetting the sugar and milk - either real or powdered - and a flask of boiling water.

If you want to spoil yourself and you've got a flask, you can always prepare a special picnic drink before you set out. A favourite for spring picnics - when the weather isn't always as warm as it might be - is a chocolate milk shake.

It's cold, but it's comforting. To make a glass, all you do is pour a glassful of milk into a mixing bowl and whisk in two heaped teaspoons of chocolate powder. Whisk the milk until it's fluffy, add a dollop of vanilla or chocolate ice-cream and pour it all into your flask. Delicious!

Easter Puzzle Pages

Easter Questions

EARTHY QUESTION

How much earth is there in a hole fifteen centimetres wide, sixteen centimetres long and seventeen centimetres deep?

JUMPY QUESTION

A man is travelling on a train that is travelling at exactly 100 kilometres per hour. He jumps one metre up into the air. Where does he land?

CLERICAL QUESTION

What's in the church, but not the steeple?
The parson has it, but not the people.

ANIMAL QUESTION

What do zebras have that no other animal has?

BASIC QUESTION

The more you take, the more you leave behind. What are they?

Answers on page 122

Crossword 1

Clues Across

1 You'll find plenty of these in the garden
5 You dip you pen into this to write
6 - - - constrictor
7 A negative word
9 You are descended from one of these
10 If you're naughty, this is what could happen to you

Clues Down

1 You'd be lost without these people
2 This is what an acorn can become
3 The opposite of flow
4 You will find it at the seaside - and in China and Japan they eat it!
8 You drink this in the afternoon - and in China and Japan they drink it all day long
9 Noah had one of these

Initial Quiz and 100 Plus

INITIAL QUIZ

What do these initials stand for?

1	AA	9	IOW	17	Q
2	BBC	10	JP	18	RAF
3	CBE	11	km	19	SW
4	DD	12	lbw	20	TV
5	eg	13	MFH	21	USSR
6	FBI	14	NZ	22	V & A
7	GMT	15	OK	23	WC
8	HRH	16	PM	24	YHA

Answers on page 123

ADDING UP TO 100

By putting plus or minus signs anywhere you like between the figures, can you make this sum work out correctly?

$$1 \; 2 \; 3 \; 4 \; 5 \; 6 \; 7 \; 8 \; 9 \; = \; 100$$

ADDING UP TO 100 AGAIN

How would you write the number one hundred with six nines?

ADDING UP TO 100 RATS

If three cats can catch three rats in three minutes, how many cats could catch one hundred rats in one hundred minutes?

Answers on page 124

Who is it?

Join all the dots from 1 to 60 and you'll find a familiar face.

Crossword 2

Clues Across

1 Easter - - -
2 Another word for present
4 In order to survive man - - - - and drinks
6 Belonging to yourself
7 The opposite of he
8 The opposite of far
11 This is something a bad workman will always blame
12 This is what a chicken turns into

Clues Down

1 Adam's companion
2 Another word for fetch
3 A city without a cathedral is usually just a - - - -
4 The opposite of odd
5 The opposite of sweet
7 It goes with pepper
9 Some people would eat this jellied
10 This is small and sharp and goes with a needle

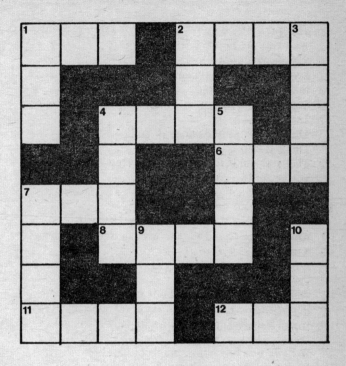

Answers on page 124

April Fools Day Quiz

1   What's the difference between twice twenty-two and twice two and twenty?

2   How many grooves has a gramophone record?

3   What can go up the chimney down, but can never come down the chimney up?

4   What's the difference between Noah's Ark and Joan of Arc?

5   What is worse than raining cats and dogs?

6   What has four wheels and flies?

7   What goes out black and comes in white?

8   You've got two coins in your pocket and together they add up to 55p, but one of them isn't a 50p, so what are they?

9   How many months of the year have 28 days?

10 Where can you build a house with all four walls facing north?

11 From what kind of tea-pot can you never get a cup of tea?

12 What do you get if you add one to thirteen four times?

13 What word do the English always pronounce badly?

14 If you were locked in a room with only a bed and a calendar, how could you survive?

15 What do you find in the middle of Cardiff?

16 What can run, but can't walk?

17 What's smaller than an ant's mouth?

18 What word of three syllables contains twenty-six letters?

19 What can speak in every language, but never went to school?

20 What do you lose every time you stand up?

Answers on page 125

True or False and Punctuation Puzzle

TRUE OR FALSE

Just one of these statements is true — which one?

1 One of these statements is false
2 Two of these statements are false
3 Three of these statements are false
4 Four of these statements are false
5 Five of these statements are false

PUNCTUATION PUZZLE

Punctuate this collection of words so as to make some sort of sense out of them:

That that is is that that is not is not is not that it it is

Answers on page 126

The Thirty~Nine Dots

Join up all the dots and see what you find.

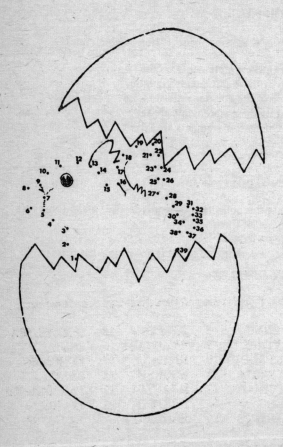

First Name Quiz and Easter Jumbles

FIRST NAME QUIZ

Here are the surnames of twenty-five famous people. What are their first names?

1	Bunny	10	John	19	Drake
2	Churchill	11	Nelson	20	Luther King
3	Wren	12	Washington	21	Dickens
4	Hood	13	Cavell	22	Keats
5	Sinatra	14	Columbus	23	van Gogh
6	Cromwell	15	Lennon	24	Kennedy
7	Shakespeare	16	Mouse	25	Bunter
8	da Vinci	17	Bonaparte		
9	Eyre	18	Menuhin		

Answers on page 126

EASTER JUMBLES

Unjumble these letters and turn them into proper words:

1	YBNNU	8	RFSLEOW	15	OOCCHLTEA
2	SATREE	9	EKACNAP	16	SNUB
3	FLFADOID	10	RPILA	17	KCHCNIE
4	EGNRDA	11	WSOREH	18	BALM
5	PPGNIARW	12	MEALYOP	19	TAECODRONI
6	SGEG	13	HRETMO	20	TBAIBR
7	NESTRPE	14	YADILHO		

Answers on page 127

Crossword 3

Clues Across

1 The Forsyte - - - -
3 A room in a prison
5 A form of Japanese theatre
6 This is what you would call people who are trying to get away from their situation
7 These will show you how much the things you want to buy will cost
9 The section of British Airways that flies to countries outside Europe
10 An anagram of ENDS and DENS

Clues Down

2 The opposite of Arctic
3 The day before Boxing Day
4 Plenty
6 Extra-sensory perception, in short
8 There's plenty of it on the beach, but don't get it in your eyes

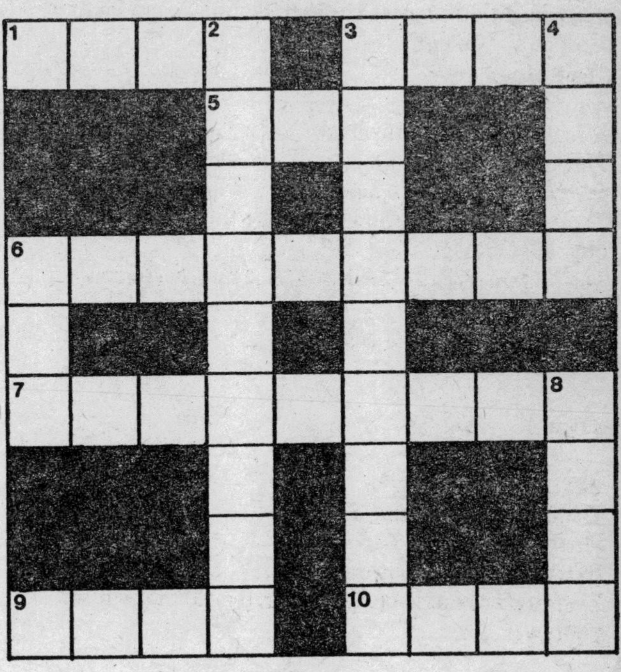

Answers on page 127

Spot the Difference

There are eight differences between Picture A and Picture B. Can you spot them?

A

Answers on page 128

B

Answer Section

EARTHY QUESTION
None

JUMPY QUESTION
On exactly the same spot

CLERICAL QUESTION
The letter R

ANIMAL QUESTION
Baby zebras

BASIC QUESTION
Footsteps

CROSSWORD 1

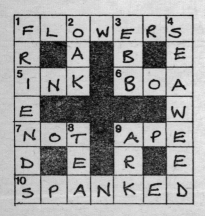

INITIAL QUIZ

1. Automobile Association or Architectural Association or Alcoholic Anonymous
2. British Broadcasting Corporation
3. Commander of the Order of the British Empire
4. Doctor of Divinity
5. exempli gratia, which is Latin for 'for example'
6. Federal Bureau of Investigation
7. Greenwich Mean Time
8. His (or Her) Royal Highness
9. Isle of Wight
10. Justice of the Peace
11. Kilometre
12. leg before wicket — a phrase used in cricket
13. Master of Foxhounds
14. New Zealand
15. Okay — meaning 'all right'
16. Prime Minister or post meridiem, which is Latin for 'after noon'
17. Queen
18. Royal Air Force
19. South West
20. Television
21. Union of Soviet Socialist Republics
22. Victoria and Albert — the name of a London museum
24. Water Closet
24. Youth Hostel Association

ADDING UP TO 100

There are several possible answers. Here are five:

$$123 - 45 - 67 + 89 = 100$$
$$123 + 45 - 67 + 8 - 9 = 100$$
$$123 + 4 - 5 + 67 - 89 = 100$$
$$123 - 4 - 5 - 6 - 7 + 8 - 9 = 100$$
$$12 + 3 - 4 + 5 + 67 + 8 + 9 = 100$$

ADDING UP TO 100 AGAIN

$99\frac{99}{99}$

ADDING UP TO 100 RATS

The same three cats.

CROSSWORD 2

APRIL FOOLS DAY QUIZ

1   Twice twenty-two is 44 and twice two and twenty is 24, so the difference is 20

2   Two — one on each side

3   An umbrella

4   One was made of wood; the other was Maid of Orleans

5   Hailing taxis

6   A garbage truck

7   A black cat when it's snowing

8   A 50p and a 5p piece. One of the coins wasn't a 50p piece, but the other one was!

9   All twelve

10   The South Pole

11   An empty one

12   14 every time

13   Badly

14   You would have the springs from the bed to drink and the dates from the calendar to eat.

15   The letter 'd'

16   Water

17   Whatever it is the ant puts into its mouth when it eats!

18   Alphabet

19   An echo

20   Your lap

THE TRUE OR FALSE PUZZLE

Number 4

PUNCTUATION PUZZLE

That that is, is; that that is not, is not. Is not that it? It is.

FIRST NAME QUIZ

1	Bugs or Benjamin
2	Winston
3	Christopher
4	Robin
5	Frank
6	Oliver
7	William
8	Leonardo
9	Jane
10	Augustus or Elton
11	Horatio
12	George
13	Edith
14	Christopher
15	John
16	Mickey
17	Napoleon
18	Yehudi
19	Francis
20	Martin
21	Charles
22	John
23	Vincent
24	John or Robert or Edward
25	Billy

EASTER JUMBLES

11	BUNNY	11	SHOWER
2	EASTER	12	MAYPOLE
3	DAFFODIL	13	MOTHER
4	GARDEN	14	HOLIDAY
5	WRAPPING	15	CHOCOLATE
6	EGGS	16	BUNS
7	PRESENT	17	CHICKEN
8	FLOWERS	18	LAMB
9	PANCAKE	19	DECORATION
10	APRIL	20	RABBIT

CROSSWORD 3

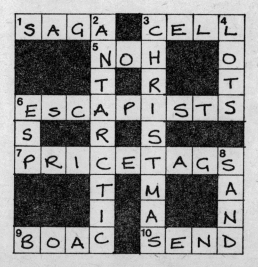

SPOT THE DIFFERENCE

1 The vertical stripes on the hat are in different positions in B
2 B has a different number of whiskers
3 B has only one tooth
4 B has a spotted bow-tie
5 B has only 3 buttons on the shirt front
6 B has no button on the shirt cuff
7 The coat-tail is different in B
8 The flower only has four petals in B

Goodbye!

WINGS OF DESIRE

"Linc, there's no reason why we can't make the best of a bad situation. It's obvious that we're attracted to each other . . . aren't we?"

"Very attracted," he whispered, his lips against her ear.

"And we're married now," she said, her voice slightly husky. "So there's no reason why we shouldn't . . . why we couldn't . . ."

He looked down at her, and his eyes were dark and glittering.

"It might not be that simple," he said tensely. "One of us might get hurt."

"You don't need to worry that I won't know what to do. I read a book."

"Good Lord." He straightened. "You're going to regret this. I'm probably going to regret this. But if you're willing to become lovers—Christ, *married* lovers—it would take a nobler man than I to turn you down, because I want you, Cassie Jones. I want you in the worst way. And I'm going to teach you things about love you could never learn out of any damned book . . ."

WINGS OF DESIRE

ELIZABETH LAMBERT

AVON BOOKS ◆ NEW YORK

AVON BOOKS
A division of
The Hearst Corporation
105 Madison Avenue
New York, New York 10016

Copyright © 1989 by Penelope Williamson
Published by arrangement with the author
Library of Congress Catalog Card Number: 89-91157
ISBN: 0-380-75599-8

First Avon Books Printing: September 1989

AVON TRADEMARK REG. U.S. PAT. OFF. AND IN OTHER COUNTRIES, MARCA REGISTRADA, HECHO EN U.S.A.

Printed in the U.S.A.

K-R 10 9 8 7 6 5 4 3 2 1

Chapter 1

Ｓhe flew. And the shackles that bound her to earth burst apart, setting her free. She soared high, and higher still, toward the sun, toward the very roof of the universe, and she laughed out loud. She lived for this, risked death for this. To touch the sky . . . to fly.

The control stick hummed in her hands, and the throb of the engine began to match the beat of her pulse. The machine was no longer a fragile contraption of wood and wire and fabric. It had become an extension of herself. Cassandra Jones had sprouted wings.

She banked the plane slightly and leaned over to see the earth she had left behind. The cold rush of air numbed her cheeks. Again she laughed.

From four thousand feet up in the sky, the broad, placid James River resembled a faded blue ribbon. It cut through fields of tobacco, wrapped around peach orchards, and outlined the spacious jade lawn of the Farrell plantation. The unusually bright February sun made the ribbon of water shimmer as if it were alive. But the land, a mottled palette of wintery greens and grays, looked strangely empty. It was the best way,

1

thought Cassie, the only way to view the world.

A dark shadow shaped like a giant bird with double wings crossed the earth below her. It took her a moment to realize it was not her own shadow she saw, but that of another airplane lower and to the right of her. Its sudden appearance in her piece of sky destroyed her mood of quiet exhilaration.

She reduced her speed and descended to get a better look at the intruder. It was a two-seater de Havilland, a biplane of British design. Two heads protruded one behind the other from the open cockpits. The name *Betsy* was scripted in fresh black paint on the olive drab fabric that covered the fuselage. A silly name for an airplane, Cassie thought with contempt. She had christened her own plane the *Pegasus*, after the winged horse in the Greek fable. No doubt Betsy was the name of the pilot's insipid little wife.

The pilot with the insipid wife must have spotted her because he rocked his wings in a friendly greeting. Cassie didn't return the gesture.

"Damn, damn, damn!" she shouted. It just wasn't fair. They were having a hard enough time lately, she and her Uncle Quigly, earning money for fuel and the maintenance of their expensive flying machine by staging stunt exhibitions and giving rides. During the summer they lived a gypsy's life, touring up and down the coast, but the winter months they spent here, in Kingly. Until now theirs had been one of the few airplanes in all of Virginia. There had always been plenty of skeptics and thrill-seekers willing to pay for the experience of watching an aviatrix perform impossible feats with her flying machine. A few were even brave enough to want to fly themselves. "Hoppers" they were called within the tight circle of men, and a very few women, who dared to pilot mankind's latest and most remarkable invention. Cassie had come to think of this as her territory, her hoppers. She didn't want to share them with anyone else.

She glared at the other airplane in hopeless frustration. Then she suddenly got an idea, and her mouth curved into a smile. She would do what any other animal did when threatened with the invasion of its territory. She would frighten the intruder away.

Cassie swooped down out of the glaring winter sun like a hawk from on high.

She held the dive until she was almost on top of him before she pulled out and whipped into a climbing turn—the tip of her lower port wing missing the invisible whirl of his propeller by inches. She had a brief, startlingly close view of a woman's white face, mouth stretched open in a scream, then she saw nothing but wide, cloudless sky. She glanced back for the briefest second and saw that the plane was rocking violently in the turbulence of her prop wash.

Her hands inside her fleece-lined gloves were sweating, and she licked her suddenly dry lips. God in heaven, she had almost killed two innocent people, not to mention herself, with her dangerous aerobatics. If the authorities heard of this, she would probably be grounded for the rest of her life. And it wouldn't be a worse punishment than she deserved.

She felt a tingling in her fingertips and realized she had been gripping the control stick so hard her hands had gone numb. Flexing her fingers, she sucked in a deep breath.

She made a wide, lazy circle, descending slowly, forcing herself to concentrate on the mechanics of her movements and the familiarity of her surroundings. Hazy smoke rose from the tobacco plant and textile mill that comprised the main industry in the town of Kingly. A toy train chugged along tiny silver tracks toward the bigger town of Lynchburg. Beyond rose the indomitable indigo humps of the Blue Ridge Mountains.

Late-afternoon shadows slashed across the fallow pasture she and her uncle used as a landing field. She made a low pass. As she had feared, the other plane had landed ahead of her. Its pilot—a tall, slender figure in whipcord pants, knee-high boots, and a brown leather jacket—stood with his fists on his hips, his head tilted back. She could actually feel the man's fury, like heat from a steel foundry, blasting up at her.

A girl dressed in bright orange was bent way over, peering into the tall weeds that filled the ditch beside the field. A small brown-and-white dog raced in circles around her. Even from this distance there was something about the girl that looked familiar to Cassie. She wondered what could be in the ditch to cause such concentrated attention, and then a tiny giggle erupted out of her tight throat. The girl in orange just had to be rich, spoiled Melodie Farrell, who had been frightened so badly she was losing her lunch.

Cassie cut off her engine as she banked around for her final glide. She slipped the aircraft a little sideways to see the ground, then the nose rose up to block her view as she eased up on the stick. Her wheels touched down gently, and she rolled to a stop at the far end of the field, as far away from the other plane as she could get. At least, she thought with satisfaction, she hadn't made more of a fool of herself by botching her landing.

She pulled down her goggles, leaving them to dangle around her neck, and yanked off her gloves with her teeth. She watched warily as the tall, slender figure marched toward her, his anger evident in every stride. Swallowing hard, she swung out of the cockpit and jumped lightly to the ground. She wiped her sweating palms on the seat of her greasy overalls and turned just as the man stopped in front of her.

"You damned idiot!" he roared—and socked her right in the jaw.

Gentle hands removed her leather helmet and smoothed the hair back off her forehead. Something rough and wet brushed her cheek, followed by a sharp, high-pitched bark in her ear.

"For God's sake, Patches," said a masculine voice, gruff with repressed laughter. "Don't you think enough damage has been done without your slobbering all over her and busting her eardrums to boot?"

Cassie opened her eyes and looked with bemusement at the face floating above her. It was a stunningly handsome face, with strong bones and smooth tanned skin, and a wide sensual mouth. She stared into eyes as vividly blue as a summer sky. But the eyes, unlike the mouth, were sad. The eyes spoke of hurt and bitter disillusionment, and she felt a peculiar need to comfort him. She reached up and gently stroked his cheek, smiling.

He smiled back at her, his whole face lighting up. "Hello," he said.

A shadow fell between them. "Why, if it isn't Cassie Jones," Melodie Farrell drawled in her syrupy voice. "Shame on you, Linc Cameron, for strikin' a woman."

Cassie's palm still rested against the stranger's cheek, but she snatched her hand back as the memory of what had happened came back to her. She felt for the first time a sharp stabbing pain that seemed to cover the whole left side of her face.

Fighting off her dizziness, Cassie struggled to sit up. He took her arm to steady her, but she wrenched it free. "I don't need your help!"

"Suit yourself." He had been crouched down on one knee beside her, but he now stood up abruptly, leaving her sprawled on the ground at his feet.

She flung her head up to glare at him. Pain sizzled in back of her eyes, making her wince. The afternoon sun, she noticed, was painting golden highlights on his nut brown hair.

"What are you, some kind of maniac? You almost knocked my head off."

His remarkable eyes darkened as if a layer of clouds had covered the sky. "*You're* the maniac. You almost flew right into us!"

Cassie got shakily to her feet. He watched her with a scowl on his face, making no further move to help her.

"You were never in any danger," she said, putting conviction into her voice to cover the lie. "It was a simple dive, and I was in perfect control the whole time."

"The hell you were. You left your recovery until way too late."

He had said the words not in anger, but as a rational observation, and they infuriated her because she knew he was right. Her jaw throbbed and tears crowded the back of her eyes, which infuriated her even more.

She bent over and snatched her helmet off the ground so she wouldn't have to look at him. "That didn't give you the right to hit me. Or do you always go around beating up on defenseless women?"

"I didn't know it was you. I mean, I didn't know you were you. Damn it . . ." He clenched his jaw tight and spoke between his teeth. "And something tells me you're not that damned defenseless."

Melodie, who to Cassie's disgust had been watching the stranger with a look of vapid adoration on her face, suddenly erupted into a fit of giggles. "If you didn't go around lookin' and actin' like a boy, Cassie, maybe you wouldn't get treated like one."

Cassie whirled on her. "Whereas no one could ever mistake you, Melodie Farrell, for anything but a poor, helpless female."

In fact, Cassie thought with contempt—and a rare twinge of envy—no one would ever mistake Melodie for anything but the epitome of expensively maintained femininity. Today she was wearing a voluminous barrel-shaped coat made of pumpkin-colored wool and trimmed in fur. It came to a fashionable three inches above her ankles and showed off her high-buttoned navy suede shoes. Cassie was suddenly aware of how ridiculous she herself must appear to the handsome stranger in her dirty, patched overalls and bulky man's tweed jacket.

Melodie was aware of her discomfort, and her smile was treacly sweet. "A man always likes to see a girl lookin' pretty. Something you obviously haven't figured out yet, since there aren't exactly a lot of fellas beatin' a path to your door."

"Hah! At least I'm not facing twenty-one and still unmarried."

Melodie's cheeks puffed and reddened. "Why, of all the nastiest, meanest things to say, when you know darn well that Monte and I planned to be married before he was killed in the war. Just 'cause you're still only nineteen—and *almost* twenty—that doesn't mean you're ever goin' to—"

"Get married," Cassie finished for her, putting a sneer into her voice. "No, but only because I refuse to enslave myself to some—"

"That's enough!"

The two girls jumped and looked at him, Cassie glaring and Melodie pouting.

"Quit clawing at each other like a couple of yowling cats."

"Cats!" Cassie exclaimed.

"Y-yowling?" Melodie sputtered.

"Yes, yowling. Something tells me you two have had this argument before, and frankly, I'm finding it a bit tedious."

It was the arrogant, condescending look on his face that did it, even more than what he had said. Cassie was so angry she thought steam must be pouring out of her ears. Obviously he was the kind of man who thought of women as nothing more than simpering ornaments whose sole purpose was to hang on the arm of some big, strong man and "do him proud" by looking pretty and suitably adoring. It made her so furious she wanted to scream.

Instead, she opened her eyes wide and batted her lashes. "Oh, *do* forgive us for boring you, Mister—"

"Linc Cameron. And the mutt's name is Patches," he

added, pointing to the little dog who sat at his feet grinning idiotically up at her with his tongue hanging out the corner of his mouth.

As Cassie struggled to come up with a thoroughly devastating retort, the stranger smiled broadly.

"We're pleased to make your acquaintance, Miss... Jones, is it?"

He really did have a beautiful smile, she thought— when he wasn't sneering in that infuriatingly superior manner. And he was probably well aware of the way that smile affected women. Well, he was about to discover that it had no effect on her.

She gave him an answering smile that bared her teeth. "As a solution to your ennui, Mr. Cameron, I suggest that you take yourself and Miss Farrell elsewhere. In fact, you happen to be trespassing on private property, and you have exactly one hour to get that piece of junk"—she waved her hand in the direction of the *Betsy*—"off my field!"

That, she thought as she stalked off, had certainly wiped the self-satisfied smirk off his face.

Unfortunately her exit was spoiled by his silly dog. Patches chased after her and darted ahead to plant himself directly in her path, barking at her excitedly.

"Go away," she whispered.

The dog gave her a beseeching look, cocking his head, and Cassie felt her hard resolve weakening. He was such an ugly little thing that he was almost cute, with a pug-nosed face and a dark brown spot directly over one eye, like a pirate's eye patch. He was aptly named, she thought, as he had the same brown patches all over his compact body.

"Get back here, mutt!" the stranger called out, laughter in his voice. "I don't think the lady wants our company."

The dog hesitated a moment longer, whining softly, before trotting back to answer his master's call. Cassie had to force herself not to turn around and watch him.

But Linc Cameron's eyes followed Cassie as she walked down the road toward a weathered, dilapidated barn. She resembled a circus clown in her baggy, ragged overalls, although they didn't quite disguise the feminine sway of her hips. Still, she looked hardly more than a child, he thought, with her wide gray eyes that were far too large for her pointed little urchin's face. And her hair was nothing but a long mane of tangled curls, although he had never before seen a warmer shade of gold. . . .

She was also about as friendly as a swamp snake.

"What the hell's the matter with her?" he asked.

"Oh, that's just Cassie Jones for you." Melodie Farrell thrust her arm through his and leaned against him. "Why, everybody in Kingly thinks she's crazy. She's always marchin' in those silly parades, demandin' us women be given the vote. As if we'd want it in the first place, I ask you. Lord, she even went to jail once. And then there's this airplane business. I mean, why would a girl want to wrestle with one of those monstrous, dirty ol' machines? One time I saw her—you will never believe this, Linc—but one time I saw her covered with grease, head to foot, like she'd been wallowing in it. Just like a pig in a mud hollow!"

Melodie laughed, but Linc didn't even smile. Melodie's laugh quickly died, and she shivered dramatically. "Can't we go back to the house now, Linc? I'm frozen right through to my bones."

At last Linc looked away from Cassie and glanced down at her. "Yeah," he said. "All right. Just let me peg down the *Betsy* first."

A tattered banner that said AIRPLANE RIDES in faded red letters was tacked onto the front of the huge barn, which Cassie used as a hangar for her plane and her Uncle Quigly used as his workshop. A small clapboard house with a tin roof leaned against the barn's side, as if it were too old and tired to support itself.

Cassie climbed the sagging front steps to the house, but she paused at the door and against her will turned around. The stranger was escorting Melodie to the Farrells' shiny green roadster, parked along the dirt road bordering the field. He had his arm around Melodie's waist, and she leaned against him, tilting her face up to laugh at something he said.

Cassie pushed the hair out of her eyes and glared at them. She told herself she wouldn't want to be in Melodie Farrell's expensive suede shoes for all the world. Melodie's brother might own the biggest tobacco plantation in all the county, but Melodie had grown up completely incapable of taking care of herself. She had not a thought in her head beyond trapping a man, any man, into marriage, and as each year passed she became more desperate. But then, maybe the stranger, this Linc Cameron, wanted to be trapped.

Cameron was helping Melodie into the passenger seat of the roadster with the careful tenderness of a man juggling a dozen eggs. Then he jumped behind the wheel in a showy leap that made Cassie utter a small, unladylike snort of derision. She was glad she'd told him to move his plane off her field. Since poor little helpless Melodie couldn't drive, he'd have to take her back to the Farrell plantation in the roadster and then walk back to get his plane. It would put him to some trouble, and it served him right.

Cassie waited for him to pull the roadster out into the road with a scattering of gravel, but instead he turned his head in her direction and whistled. For a moment she wondered if he was whistling at her, but then she realized that Patches still sat in the road, halfway between the automobile and the house. He was staring back at Cassie, a look of puzzlement on his face. When his master whistled he looked back and forth anxiously between the two of them. Then he took off running for the roadster, leaping into the rumble seat.

"Stupid dog," Cassie muttered, turning on her heel and going inside.

She hung her helmet and goggles on a peg beside the kitchen door and draped her heavy coat on top of them. The kitchen was chilly and she shook some coal into the mouth of the potbellied stove. She took a chipped enamel coffeepot off the cast-iron range and filled it with water from the old-fashioned hand pump at the sink. Glancing up, she caught her reflection in the window. There was a smudge of grease on her nose, and she rubbed it away angrily. She supposed it had been there the whole time she'd been acting superior and ordering *him* off her field. He and Melodie were probably laughing themselves silly about it right now.

She filled two buckets with water and emptied them into the tin bathtub that stood behind a paper screen in one corner of the kitchen. Then she went back to the sink to fill the buckets up once again.

After four more trips the tub was half-full. She pulled off her overalls and shrugged out of the worn flannel shirt she wore underneath, kicking them aside. So what if she looked ridiculous in her clothes; she liked to be warm and comfortable when she flew. If Linc Cameron was as good a pilot as he obviously thought he was, he ought to know it wasn't practical to go flying dressed as if you'd just stepped out of a fashion magazine.

She smiled to herself at the memory of Melodie throwing up in the weeds—a very unladylike thing to do. *That* certainly couldn't have made a good impression on him. And as for looking pretty, someone ought to do Melodie a favor and let her know how fat she looked in that huge orange coat. And while they were at it they might as well tell her that the hat perched on top of her bobbed hair looked like a mushroom growing out of her head. Why, Cassie suddenly wondered, was she wasting her time thinking about Melodie Farrell?

Because you're jealous, a niggling voice said.

"I am not!" she answered herself back.

Cassie stripped off her cotton camisole and drawers and stepped into the tub. She sat down, grimacing as the cold water lapped against her stomach. The tub was so small she had to fold her legs up under her chin. She pressed her mouth to her kneecap.

"Linc Cameron." She said his name, her lips moving against her knee as they formed the syllables. She wondered how well he knew Melodie Farrell.

She hoped he wouldn't blab all over Kingly about how she'd almost clipped him with her wing. She didn't want Quigly to find out about the collision she'd almost caused with her careless flying. Quigly wouldn't be angry—he never got angry. But he would be disappointed in her for deliberately endangering another aircraft. Flying was perilous enough without adding unnecessary risks, and Quigly was always lecturing her about her impulsiveness whenever she got her hands on the control stick.

And what was this Linc Cameron doing here in Kingly anyway? Cassie wondered, her thoughts running in circles. There weren't enough hoppers to support two airplanes in a small place like Kingly. Ward Farrell, Melodie's brother, had been a pilot in the war. Maybe the two men had met each other in France. Maybe he was here visiting Ward. Or maybe he had come to court Melodie.

The thought brought an unconscious scowl to her face.

Cassie suddenly felt chilled sitting in the tub. She washed quickly in the cold water and stepped, dripping, onto the floor. She dried herself off with a threadbare towel before wrapping it around her wet hair and padding naked across the worn linoleum and into her room. When she had appeared on her uncle's front stoop the day after her mother died, the house had consisted of only two rooms. Later, when they had both agreed she was here to stay, Quigly added a third room so she would have a place of her own.

Cassie reached for her wrapper just as a clattering knock shook the wooden frame of the screen door. That would be Wilhelmina Wright, she thought, come to sell eggs. Willie was the wife of a sharecropper who worked a small patch of Farrell land nearby, and she raised chickens to supplement her man's meager earnings.

Cassie pulled on her wrapper, belting it around her waist. She went to the window and opened it a crack. She couldn't see the front stoop from there, but if she yelled loud enough Willie was bound to hear her.

"Come on in, Willie. I'll be right out!" she hollered, and hearing the squeal of the door opening in reply, she pushed the window closed.

"There's coffee hot on the stove," she said a moment later, raising her voice loud enough to be heard in the next room. "Help yourself." She yanked the towel off her head and ran her fingers through her hair. She saw no need to get dressed; Willie wouldn't mind.

"Willie, you getting some coffee? Just wait till you hear about this incredibly gorgeous man I met today—"

Cassie stopped dead in the doorway, too mortified even to breathe. The stranger stood in her kitchen, leaning against the sink with a cup of steaming coffee in his hand, his long, booted legs crossed at the ankles. The brown-and-white dog had made himself right at home too, curling up nose-to-tail on the hooked rug in front of the stove.

"Hello, Miss Jones," Linc Cameron said, flashing her his dazzling smile.

He watched with amusement as she walked right toward him, her hands on her hips and fury in her eyes. The little wisp of a robe she wore flapped open down the middle to reveal a pair of very shapely legs. The deep V neck didn't cover a whole hell of a lot up top either, and it clung slickly to the moist skin it did cover. She had seemed to be a scrawny little thing in her overalls and thick woolen jacket. He could see now, however, that she wasn't the least bit scrawny where it counted.

She also didn't appear the least bit disconcerted to be confronting a virtual stranger in her kitchen while wearing only a thin cotton wrapper. She stopped in front of him, close enough for him to reach out and touch her. He swallowed a smile and concentrated on her face. It was not a happy face.

"Do you always come strolling uninvited into a strange house and help yourself to coffee?" she demanded, her eyes flashing.

"But I was invited. I distinctly heard you say come in."

"I said come in, Willie. Is your name Willie?"

"As a matter of fact I'm frequently mistaken for Willie. We're alike as two peas in a pod, Willie and I. As alike as two pumpkins on a vine, as alike as two, uh..."

"Kernels on a cob? It just so happens that Willie's skin is black as coal soot, and *she* weighs all of ninety pounds."

Linc laughed out loud, and Cassie covered her mouth with her hand to smother a giggle. It was a childlike gesture, and it reminded him how young she was. Then she said tersely, "What are you doing here?" in a tone of voice that reminded him how tough and gutsy she had to be to fly.

"You gave me one hour to get my plane off your property, remember?"

She looked around the kitchen with exaggerated surprise. "I don't see it parked in here."

He smiled and lightly traced the line of her jaw with his knuckles where a swollen bruise already discolored her skin. "Well, I was also wondering how your face felt."

Her whole body seemed to quiver at his touch, but she didn't back away. "How do you think it feels? It hurts."

"Honestly, Miss Jones, mad as I was, I never would have hit you if I'd known that—"

"I wasn't the man you thought I was."

"Something like that. Although that was a damned stupid stunt you pulled . . ." His voice trailed off.

"Who are you?"

Linc opened his mouth, but before he could speak she said abruptly, "I mean, where do you come from? What are you doing here in Kingly?"

"I come from nowhere in particular, and I'm here because a man I flew with in France is having a war memorial dedicated in his honor tomorrow. Maybe you knew him—Monte Lane?"

"Everybody in Kingly knows everybody else."

"Yes, well . . . they're breaking ground for the memorial tomorrow, complete with speeches and a band and God knows what all. It won't mean a hell of a lot to Monte, of course, since he's dead. But I was invited to stand around and look like a damned war hero, when after two bloody years of wallowing in heroics, I'd just as soon never have to—" He cut himself off, embarrassed at the bitterness he heard in his voice.

She didn't appear to have noticed it, however. In fact, his answer seemed in some obscure way to have relieved her. "Have you seen it yet?" she asked, actually smiling. He decided she had a delightful smile.

He grinned back at her. "Seen what?"

"The model for the memorial." Her eyes crinkled at the corners, as if with secret amusement. "It's going to be one of those pointy Egyptian things. It's very ugly."

Linc laughed. "An obelisk? Monte would probably have loved it. Are you going to the ceremony?"

Her lips curved into another smile. "I'll be there."

There was a long moment of silence. Cassie looked away and then back again, and their eyes met. Hers were the color of hot smoke, and their searing intensity seemed to be melting him, like a burning match held too close to thin silk.

"Cassie . . ." He breathed her name, his voice barely a whisper.

She jerked and turned away from him, pushing a wide sleeve up one arm and running her fingers through her hair. The movement pulled the cotton taut across her breasts.

"Would you like more coffee?" she asked quickly.

Linc let out his breath and looked down at his still-full cup. His mouth twisted into an unconscious grimace. "Uh . . . no, thank you."

She surprised him by laughing. "You don't have to be polite. I make the worst coffee in the whole state of Virginia. Quigly says I could sell it as weed killer and make a fortune."

"Who's Quigly?"

Cassie didn't answer. Instead she stepped forward and took the cup from his hand, pouring the coffee down the sink. Her fingers briefly brushed against his, and it was like two hot wires touching. Linc felt his stomach muscles tense. My God, he thought, this is crazy. No one falls in love in an instant.

She was standing close enough for him to smell the fresh scent of Pears soap on her skin. He studied her profile: the sharp curve of a cheekbone, the small bump on the end of her nose, the full mouth, with its slightly protruding upper lip. There was an air of vulnerability around that mouth that didn't go with her tough demeanor. She probably wouldn't admit to needing anyone or anything, he thought, but that mouth told him differently.

A cluster of blond curls clung damply to her forehead. Without thinking, he reached up and brushed them behind her ear with his fingertips. She turned to him, not in surprise but slowly, as if what was about to happen was inevitable. Her lips parted, and his mouth descended to cover them.

Her lips were even softer than they looked. There was a charming awkwardness to the way she kissed, as if she was unsure what to do but eager to learn. He moved his lips and she moved hers in sweet counterpoint. He pressed down harder and she pressed back, moaning softly deep in her throat. He was so lost in the exquisite feel of her lips that he didn't realize she had been holding herself stiffly until she relaxed against him. She felt warm and alive in his arms, and a sweet, pleasurable need began to build inside him. She sighed and rubbed against him, and he slipped his hand inside her robe, brushing the thin material aside.

Sucking in a loud breath, she pushed herself violently out of his arms. He stood still, waiting for the inevitable slap—which he supposed he deserved. He had come home from France to find the girls a lot bolder in their manners than they had been before the war. But that kiss, he knew, had come too fast and gone too far even for today's modern American girl.

But instead of slapping him, Cassie pulled the wrapper tight to her body and backed away, putting the kitchen table between them.

"Oh, God . . ." She brought a shaking hand up to her mouth.

"Cassie."

"Oh, God," she said again. "Please, don't . . . just leave. Please."

He didn't want to leave, not like this. Not without explaining that kiss, and not without knowing if he would even see her again.

"Listen," he said softly, "I don't want you to think . . . I didn't mean to . . . hell! I'm making a mess of this." He took a deep breath. "Look, Miss Jones, I know what you must think of me right now. First I hit you, then I come barging in here uninvited and try to . . . try to kiss you." He attempted a smile.

She said nothing, simply watched him with big, haunted gray eyes.

"Cassie . . . I'll look for you at the dedication ceremony tomorrow? Maybe we can have a cup of coffee afterward."

"No! I mean, no, thank you. I can't."

Linc shrugged. He snapped his fingers at Patches, who gave him a reproachful look before getting slowly up and following him to the door. Linc paused there, his hand on the knob, and looked back at her. She still hadn't moved.

"I am sorry," he tried once more.

Her head snapped up. "Fine. You're sorry. Now will you please leave."

The door clicked softly shut behind him. She heard the thud of his boots going down the steps and crunching across the gravel on the drive. For several interminable minutes while she stood unmoving, she heard nothing. Then there was the spit and rumble of an engine catching.

She ran to the door and flung it open, crashing out onto the front stoop. "Wait, come back! I didn't mean it!" she cried out as the plane taxied down the pasture, picking up speed. "I didn't mean it!"

Chapter 2

Linc Cameron, former captain in the Lafayette Flying Corps, leaned back against the side of a raised platform draped in red, white, and blue bunting. He decided that he felt like a circus freak on display. He was uncomfortable in his airman's dress uniform of red pants and a blue tunic, uncomfortable with the attention that was being paid him, uncomfortable with the whole damned thing.

And it was not exactly the most pleasant weather in which to have to stand outdoors and listen to a bunch of speeches. The dozens of tiny American flags that decorated the platform snapped in the sharp wind, and the bunting billowed, catching against the raw plywood. Nearby, a band tuned their instruments and blew on their hands to keep warm. Around them the grass of Kingly's town park was withered brown, and bare in places, like the pate of an old man.

Linc hunched his shoulders and stuffed his hands into his pockets, grumbling an oath.

"Hey, old man," a sardonic voice drawled in his ear. "You're scaring away all the pretty girls with that scowl of yours."

Linc glanced around at Edward Farrell, a tall, slender man dressed in a uniform identical to his. They had

19

flown and fought together in France, which in many ways made them close as brothers.

Linc made a face at his friend. "You know how much I hate this sort of shit, Ward."

Ward Farrell's whiskey-colored eyes narrowed as he smiled. "Well, you'd better get used to it. The war might be over, but the party's just getting started. And you're the guest of honor."

Someone climbed up onto the platform beside them and removed the white sheet that had been covering the clay model of the memorial. The two men turned to cast a critical eye at the sculptor's promised masterpiece. It wasn't quite an obelisk, Linc saw; it was thick at the base and rounded at the top. To Linc and Ward, conditioned by two years spent in the raunchy atmosphere of an aerodrome, its resemblance to a certain erect part of the male anatomy was instantly and blatantly obvious.

The two friends exchanged amused looks. Ward was the first to laugh out loud. "Christ, Linc, what were the town fathers thinking of? It looks like—"

"Yeah, I know," Linc said. "Like you after forty days and nights without a woman."

"I'll have you know," Ward retorted with feigned indignation, "that I've never gone forty days and nights without a woman."

Laughing, Linc looked around him. The park was small, only a square block in size. A weathered gazebo surrounded by elm trees sheltered the band, which had just launched into a mournful rendition of "Keep the Home Fires Burning." Beside the gazebo a red-and-white-striped tent had been set up for refreshments—iced cakes and cookies, a sickly-looking pink punch, and coffee and tea in silver urns.

Linc noticed a pair of young boys, dressed in identical sailor suits and straw hats, playing tag around the tent poles. He smiled to himself. He had been in hundreds of towns like Kingly—close-knit, peaceful, steeped in tradition—and he had always found comfort in their sameness. I could be happy settling down in a place like this, Linc thought. Settling down with a wife and getting started on having a passel of kids.

For at long last the war was over—it had ended three months ago—and Linc Cameron yearned with every fiber of his being for peace, for a normal life, so that he could forget about the death—and the killing.

Linc scanned the faces of the crowd. Although the occasion was a solemn one, people seemed to be having a good time, no doubt glad for the excuse to get together with friends and neighbors. Except for several young men who still wore doughboy khaki, everyone was dressed in their Sunday best. But February wasn't the most ideal time for an outdoor ceremony, and heavy winter coats covered the women's finery, so only a brooch at a lacy throat or the brief flash of a scalloped sleeve attested to what lay underneath.

Suddenly Linc realized that he was searching the crowd for one face in particular, and he cursed himself. After that kiss, the last person she would want to see would be him. And besides, a man like him, a man yearning for peace and normalcy ought to have enough sense to hightail it in the other direction when a girl like Cassie Jones headed his way.

But at that moment his eye caught a slender figure and the golden flash of blond hair, and in spite of his good intentions, his heartbeat quickened. But when the girl turned around it wasn't the right face.

The girl seemed to know him, however, for she raised her hand and waved. "Yoo-hoo, Mr. Cameron!" she called out, and started to stride purposefully toward him.

"Oh-oh. Better get all your defenses up, Linc, old man," Ward said, his narrow face alight with wicked laughter.

"Why?"

"'Cause you're about to be pounced on by the most

man-hungry female in all of Kingly. She even had her
claws into Monte for a while before my sister snatched
him out from under her nose." Linc groaned and Ward
laughed, clearly enjoying his friend's discomfiture.
"Why, I'll bet you she has that avaricious look in her
eye that says she thinks you're a prime catch."

The girl was still too far away to see her eyes, but
Linc felt a chill of apprehension nonetheless. Predatory
females always made him nervous. Then he saw to his
relief that the girl had been waylaid by two matrons
with tin collection cans—evidently doing some last-
minute fundraising for the memorial. The girl cast an
imploring look at Linc, but he turned his back on her.

"I'm no catch," he said to Ward. "Prime or otherwise."

"The hell you aren't. You're famous now, like it or
not. Ace fighter pilot, medals dangling off your manly
chest—the women love all that. Christ, they're already
descending on you like bees on a crock of honey."

Linc shook his head and grinned. "They're after you
as well, Ward."

Ward gave a self-deprecating smile in return. "Not
with my pathetic three victories." He shrugged. "Hell,
old man, you shouldn't be complaining. All this glory
and fame is going to make you rich."

Linc frowned. Ward was right—like it or not, he was
now famous. Only one other American, Eddie Ricken-
backer, had shot down more German planes than Linc
had. But he got no joy from all the adulation and attention. Deep down inside Linc felt a strange shame that
he possessed the ability to kill with such detached and
proficient accuracy. He certainly didn't want to be rewarded for bringing about the deaths of men who had
only been doing a job, the same as he'd been.

Melodie Farrell came trotting up to them with a tall,
thin woman in tow. Like Melodie, the woman was
clothed completely in black, but Linc had the impression that, unlike Melodie, this woman's mourning

dress was not simply being worn for effect.

"Why, aren't you two the most handsomest creatures alive!" Melodie exclaimed, kissing Ward on the cheek and looking at Linc as if she'd like to kiss him as well.

"Melodie, what—" her brother began, but she interrupted him with a squeal of delight.

"My, just look at this crowd! Monte would be pleased by the turnout, I just know he would." She pulled the woman forward by the arm. "Linc? This is Monte's sister, Janet. She's just been dyin' to talk to you—haven't you, Janet—you knowin' her brother over there in France and all. Oh dear," Melodie said, acknowledging someone's wave. "I've got to go get my instructions. I'm supposed to be pourin' coffee afterward. Lord, I hope I don't make a mess of things, like spilling it all over the mayor's wife!"

Melodie hurried off with a trill of laughter, leaving the woman behind.

"I'm sorry, Janet," Ward Farrell said. "Melodie isn't normally that unfeeling. She's just nervous, and when she gets nervous she babbles, and—"

The woman put a slender, black-laced, gloved hand on his arm. "I understand, Ward."

He nodded and sighed. "Janet, this is Linc. Linc Cameron."

A thin veil covered the woman's face, obscuring her expression. "How do you do, Miss Lane," Linc said somberly.

A sudden gust of icy wind sent dust rising around them and rattled the naked branches of the Dutch elm trees overhead. The woman pulled the collar of her coat tighter around her throat, and Linc saw a gold band winking beneath the thin black lace.

The woman noticed the direction of his gaze. "I lost a husband in France, as well as my brother."

"I'm sorry..." Linc said, knowing that any words would be inadequate.

Janet lowered her head. "Thank you. And thank you for coming here today." Then she looked up at Linc, and he caught beneath the veil the flash of what had been a charming smile before grief had touched it. "My brother's letters home were full of your dashing exploits, Mr. Cameron. I want you to know that you were very dear to him. He considered you his best friend."

Linc felt Ward stiffen beside him. Ward Farrell and Monte Lane had been friends for years—*best* friends—until he had shown up and made it a threesome. It wasn't until after Monte's death that it had occurred to Linc he might actually have come between the two boyhood pals. "We were very close," he said now to Monte's sister. "All three of us."

Janet smiled at him and then at Ward. "Yes, of course." She took a deep breath, as if girding herself for some unpleasant task. "Mr. Cameron, I understand you were there when...when my brother died. I was wondering if you could tell me if he...if he suffered...."

Suddenly the smell of burning flesh assaulted Linc's senses. So powerful was the memory that for a moment he couldn't breathe. He had to clench his teeth to keep them from chattering. He prayed for Janet Lane's sake that he was managing to control the look on his face.

"He didn't suffer. He died instantly," Linc finally managed to say, breaking the heavy silence. "There couldn't have been any pain." And he saw by the relief on Janet's face that his lie had been successful.

Just then a portly man waddled up to them, wheezing for breath and sweating in spite of the cold. Earlier he had been pointed out to Linc as the mayor of Kingly.

"If you could all please move to the platform," the mayor said. "The dedication ceremony is about to begin."

Linc helped Janet onto the platform and escorted her to a chair beside the model of the memorial. He and Ward took their places flanking her. The townspeople hurried to fill the wooden folding chairs that had been set out in rows before the platform. They sat stiffly, trying not to shiver in the cold, waiting politely for the ceremony to begin. For the first time Linc noticed that several people wore white cheesecloth masks to protect themselves from the virulent influenza that had already killed thousands across the country. They gave the scene a strangely macabre look.

Once again Linc felt uncomfortably on display. He wished he were anywhere else. Although he supposed if there were such a thing as heaven Monte was probably looking down on all this—the model of the statue, the band, he and Ward in their stiff dress uniforms— looking down on it all and laughing. But then, Monte had always loved dramatic exhibitions. It was what had gotten him killed.

Suddenly Linc thought he could see Monte's charred face floating out in the audience, mocking him. He squeezed his eyes shut as the band launched into a Sousa march and the audience applauded.

When the music died away, the mayor took his place before the speakers' dais and there was more applause. "We are gathered here today to honor these brave young men," the mayor began, and Linc smiled grimly to himself. He didn't think he was brave, and he certainly no longer felt young.

He had turned twenty-three the day he became a fighter pilot, over two blood-drenched years ago. America wasn't in the war yet, but when a French flying squadron of American volunteers, the Lafayette Escadrille, was formed, he had immediately signed up. In France he met Monte Lane and Edward Farrell, two friends from the same town in Virginia. Monte and Ward were everything that he was not—blessed with inherited wealth, while he had to scratch for every nickel; university educated, while he was self-taught; effusively friendly, while he was a loner. Yet Monte's and Edward's friendship had expanded to include him, and the three of them became inseparable. No, that wasn't quite true. Death had separated them easily enough when tracer bullets had blazed out of the blinding sun.

A commotion at the end of the park jerked Linc's mind away from the painful memories of Monte's death. A small band of suffragettes had turned the corner and was marching toward them down the middle of Main Street. Horns blared, police blew on their whistles, a mule pulling a vegetable cart balked, dumping tomatoes and heads of lettuce into the gutter.

The mayor's booming voice began to falter. "Men . . . who sacrificed so much . . . so much for, uh, democracy," he stuttered as the audience turned around in their seats to watch the parade. Linc exchanged grins with Ward; this was going to be interesting.

The women had brought their own music: tambourines and a pair of drums. They all wore sashes across their breasts that read VOTES FOR WOMEN, and corsages made of yellow paper. Their leader was a slender blonde wearing a big-brimmed picture hat with a wide, trailing yellow ribbon. Linc's smile faded. It had to be Cassie Jones, he thought. There couldn't be two blond female troublemakers on the loose in a town the size of Kingly.

The suffragettes had reached the fence that bordered the park. Linc wondered if they intended to climb over it. Then he saw one of the women loop the end of the thick-linked chain around a post and wrap the other end around her waist.

A patrolman ran up to the woman. He shouted at her and she shouted back, and then he tried to unwrap the chain. The woman pummeled his chest and kicked him in the shins. Even from where he stood, Linc heard the man's loud groans. Cassie Jones ran to the woman's assistance. She grabbed the man's wrist, trying to pry his fingers off the chain, and hung on even when his hand pulled loose so abruptly that she was lifted off her feet.

A second patrolman saw his partner under attack, and he wrapped his arms around Cassie's shoulders, trying without much success to pin her flailing arms to her sides. She struggled against him, flinging her head back. Her hat fell off, and a waterfall of golden curls tumbled down her back, becoming entangled in the man's cap and covering his eyes. She still clung tenaciously to the other patrolman's wrist, and in a desperate effort to break free of Cassie's grasp, he jerked his hand back. Cassie let go and his fist, flying up and out of control, landed square on her jaw.

"Cassie!" Linc shouted, leaping forward.

But the mayor had chosen that moment to try to get a better view of what was happening, and he stepped in front of Linc; so that the two men slammed into each other. For a second the mayor teetered and swayed on his feet on the very edge of the platform, and he grasped the lapels of Linc's uniform in a desperate effort to regain his balance. But it was no use. He fell head over heels overboard, taking Linc with him.

The mayor let go of Linc's coat with one hand and grabbed frantically for the bunting that was wrapped around the sides of the platform. He managed to clutch a handful of the thin, crepelike material, but it had only been tacked onto the plywood, and it pulled free with a loud rip. The two men, still arm in arm like lovers, hit the ground hard with Linc on top, and the air was driven from the mayor's lungs in a *whoosh* so loud it sounded like the stopper had been pulled out of an inner tube.

Most of the bunting had wound up wrapped around the mayor's portly body like a shroud. Linc, however, had only to disentangle one leg from the clinging crepe, and he yanked it free with a snarling curse, struggling to his knees. By now most of the audience had jumped to their feet, and some of the women were screaming.

Beside him the mayor, wheezing and gasping for breath, sounded as if he were suffocating, but Linc only had eyes for the slender blond-haired girl sagging unconscious in the burly arms of an angry cop.

"Let her go, you sonofabitchin' bastard!" Linc shouted. Then he was up and running across the broad lawn of the park, his hands clenched into fists and fury firing his blood.

Cassie opened her eyes to a familiar face, which seemed to go with the familiar throbbing in her head.

"You again!" she exclaimed, and then bit back a cry as a sharp stab of pain seized her jaw. She reached up and gingerly touched a new, rapidly swelling lump. She scowled at him.

Linc Cameron's dazzling smile lit up his face. "Hey, I'm innocent this time. I just happened to be in the neighborhood."

Cassie looked around, trying not to move her aching head. She saw the backyards of a line of row houses, a pair of stinking privies, someone's wash flapping loudly in the wind. Linc seemed to be half sitting on a pile of scrap wood and old bricks in the middle of a trash-littered alley. She lay partly across the scrap heap and partly on him—and her head was in his lap.

She sat up so abruptly that the world spun rapidly around her, as if she were riding a carousel that was out of control. Linc steadied her by grasping her shoulders and pulling her against his chest. She laid her cheek against the rough wool of his uniform tunic. His arms felt very strong and oddly comforting, and she could hear the measured beat of his heart beneath her ear.

"Darn you, you interfering brute," she said, her voice muffled by his chest. "You've ruined everything."

"And you're an ungrateful wretch. I saved you from being hauled off to jail. Which is where I'm likely to end up, since I just kicked a cop in the . . . uh, in a sensitive place and punched another one in the nose, and all this was after I had just sent the most important man in Kingly sprawling into the bunting."

Cassie couldn't imagine what he was talking about, but she didn't much care. She had her own problems, although it was hard to remember what they were given the way his hand was gently massaging the curve where her shoulder met her neck. The feel of his fingers on her bare skin was very ... nice. She sighed and snuggled against him, and Linc's arms tightened around her.

Cassie pulled away and got shakily to her feet. There was a rip in the jacket of her only suit, and somebody had opened the top three buttons. She glared at him as she fumbled one-handed to refasten them.

"You fool. I *wanted* to go to jail."

"You did?" He started to help her with the buttons.

Cassie shivered, remembering the awful month she had spent in jail. "No ... not really. But how else can we dramatize the plight of women in this country? This whole thing is all your fault."

"What whole thing is all my fault?" He gathered up her hair and pulled it back from her face. "No woman of mine has ever complained about her plight before."

"You're a man, so I don't expect you to understand," she said, ignoring the remark about his women, who probably numbered in the thousands. "You fought for democracy—Monte Lane died for it—yet you refuse to care that in the great democracy of the United States of America, only criminals, lunatics, and women can't vote."

"Well, at least you're in good company." He grinned at her.

Her treacherous lips threatened to turn up in answer. "That wasn't funny."

"I thought it was."

"I suppose you're opposed to giving women the vote."

Linc shrugged and got to his feet. "Considering the mess the world is in at the moment, you couldn't make things worse than they already are."

"What a typically shortsighted male attitude!" Cassie put her fists on her hips and lifted her chin into the air. "I suppose you're one of those idiots who'd like to see women banned from flying as well. I suppose you think we're too emotional to fly an airplane, that we'd go to pieces at the first sign of trouble."

His fingers cradled her outthrust chin. "You're doing a lot of unfair supposing. If a woman wants to fly, I say good for her. Only I do take exception when she's so irresponsible or careless that she almost flies her plane into mine."

Cassie flushed. Why did he have to be so infuriatingly right all the time? And why did she have to shiver and tremble at the merest touch of his hand?

Somehow he had maneuvered her so that she was leaning against a woodpile and he was in front of her, blocking off her escape. His fingers had left her chin and were moving gently down her neck, leaving a tingling sensation in their wake. His other arm encircled her waist, and she felt the pressure of his palm resting on her hip.

She couldn't seem to take her eyes off his face. Never had she seen eyes of such intense blue, but they were so sad. There was nothing, she thought, of tragedy and disappointment in the world that those eyes hadn't seen.

"I'm sorry," she whispered, not sure what she was sorry for, or if he had even heard her. Then she watched, mesmerized, as his lids came down and his finely chiseled lips descended slowly toward hers.

She turned her head away. "Don't," she said in a voice that had suddenly become breathless.

"What?"

"Kiss me," she said more loudly.

"That's just what I was going to do," he said, a little

breathless himself, and his mouth started to descend again.

Cassie pushed at him. "No, stop it. I mean it."

Linc raised his head, although he didn't let go of her waist. "I thought you liked me."

"Hunh. What gave you that ridiculous idea?"

"Oh . . ." He gave her an innocent smile that made him look like a little boy but didn't fool her for a minute. "Just something you said."

"Me? What? When?"

"You said I was incredibly gorgeous."

Cassie opened her gray eyes wide and even managed a convincing laugh. "You thought that was *you* I was talking about? It just so happens you weren't the only man I met yesterday."

"You met two incredibly gorgeous men in one day? How lucky can one girl get?"

She couldn't help it; she burst into laughter. Linc gathered her against him. "Ah, Cassie," he said, running his fingers through her hair and tilting her head back.

The first touch of his lips on hers sent an electric current through her body, and she shuddered in his arms. But this time she didn't pull away. His lips moved over hers as if he wanted to devour her. She had been kissed before and had found it pleasant, but this was . . . this was beyond anything she could even imagine. This was wonderful. This was ecstasy.

Linc deepened the kiss, running his tongue along her lower lip, across her teeth. Cassie felt herself opening up to him like a rare flower. The feeling was almost too intense, as if she would be turned inside out, would cease to exist altogether. She knew he would have to stop, but she wanted him to go on forever.

Eventually he did release her mouth, only to move his lips down the curve of her neck, blazing a trail with light, teasing kisses. She shuddered again and leaned into him.

"Linc." She sighed against his shoulder. "I want..."

He put his lips to her ear. "What do you want, Miss Cassandra Jones?"

She thrust him away and stepped back. Something strange was happening here. Her senses seemed to have suddenly flown away.

"I want you to leave me alone," she said, her voice trembling as she tried to force a tone of conviction into her words.

His blue eyes searched her face intently. "Are you sure that's what you want?"

"Yes!"

He touched the brim of his uniform hat. "Then good day, Miss Jones," he said. Turning abruptly, he sauntered down the alley, turned the corner, and disappeared.

"Damn!" Cassie kicked at a rusted milk can, stubbing her toe. "Damn you, Linc Cameron, that wasn't what I wanted at all."

Chapter 3

～⟠⟠～

Cassie pulled open the barn door and slipped inside. She paused, inhaling the heady odor that was unique to the world of aviation—the stink of castor oil and the bananalike smell of dope, the highly flammable varnish that coated the plane's fabric, creating a taut, durable surface.

Quigly was bent over his workbench, rummaging through his tools. The sight of him brought a fond smile to her lips. He was a small man, thin and wiry, with curly hair the color of wood smoke and a bristly gray mustache. Cassie guessed him to be about sixty, although she didn't know his exact age. But she knew he had been a young man already by the time his sister Sara, Cassie's mother, was born. In fact, he'd raised Sara after their parents had died together in a boating accident.

On a large wooden turntable sat the engine Quigly was working on. People called Quigly Jones eccentric because he lived in a shack and spent all his time and money inventing strange things like motorized bicycles, electric automobiles, and flying machines, but Cassie adored him.

Cassie's foot scattered a stone as she entered the barn, and Quigly looked absentmindedly over the rims of his spectacles as she came toward him. Then his pale blue eyes took in her bruised chin and disheveled appearance.

"What happened to you, kid? You look like you've been wrestling with a black bear."

Cassie laughed and kissed his whiskery cheek. "You should see the bear."

He rewarded her with a small, quick smile, the closest he ever came to showing amusement.

"Did you get the loan?" she asked him.

Quigly was gazing at his engine with a look of adoration most men reserved for a beautiful woman. As pioneer aviators sought to test the boundaries of their machines, flying ever greater distances, there was a need for more efficient, powerful engines to get the fuel-laden planes off the ground. Quigly Jones was convinced he had the solution in the engine he was building, and for the past week he had been in Richmond trying to get badly needed financing for his invention.

"Quigly," Cassie said patiently, used to her uncle's preoccupied dreaminess. "Did you get the loan?"

He looked up and shook his head.

"Damn!" Cassie exclaimed. They needed that loan badly. If they didn't come up with some money soon, they would have to give up their plan to produce the engine. Cassie figured they would need about ten thousand dollars to put Quigly's engine into full scale production, and they had maybe ten dollars between them. "Those fools in Richmond wouldn't know a good idea if it jumped up and bit them on the—"

"Nose," Quigly said, knowing full well that wasn't the word she had been about to use.

"Oh, Quigly, what are we going to do?"

He shrugged and stroked his mustache. "Something will turn up, honey. It always does."

Suddenly he snapped his fingers and pulled a rolled-up newspaper out of his back pocket. Spreading it open, he handed it to her, pointing at a headline with a grease-stained finger. "We could always have ourselves a go at that."

But Cassie wasn't looking at the printed words. A photograph had captured her attention. Linc Cameron's face stared up at her above a caption that gave his name in boldface type. Beneath that in smaller letters were the words: *Twenty-five victories*. Just looking at his smiling face caused Cassie's heart to do funny flip-flops.

"The race isn't until the first part of May," Quigly was saying, "so that gives us over two months to get ready for it. 'Course, we're expected to cover all our own expenses, which will be a hell of a lot for a race of that distance, and it's money down the drain if we lose —Cassie?"

"Um?"

He reached for the paper. "Are you feeling all right? Maybe we ought to talk about it later."

"No!" Cassie snatched the paper back out of his reach. "I'm feeling fine, or I would be if I wasn't always getting socked in the jaw by hot-tempered brutes."

She scanned the article rapidly. Leroy Irving Bean, the man who had made a fortune with a soda-fountain drink called Bean's cola, was sponsoring a transcontinental air race. Each entry was to be a single plane with a two-man crew. The race would consist of six legs, starting in Santa Monica, California, and ending in Long Island, New York, with official checkpoints in five other cities along the way. Each leg would be timed, and the lowest cumulative time would win. And the prize—

"Fifty thousand dollars!" Cassie exclaimed, looking up at Quigly.

He gave her his small smile and nodded. "Would buy us a lot of beans."

It would buy more than beans, Cassie thought, missing Quigly's pun in her excitement. With fifty thousand dollars they could build a prototype of the engine, then put on a demonstration—in England, perhaps. Her mind was racing ahead, already spending the prize money. Europe was well ahead of the United States in aviation design and manufacturing. And the demonstration would encourage other investors. She pictured a huge hangar filled with workers building model after model of Quigly's engine. . . .

Cassie raised shining eyes to her uncle's face. "Oh, Quigly, fifty thousand dollars. . . ."

"Yes, well, there is the minor matter of winning the race first."

Cassie laughed and shrugged, as if that were a minor matter indeed. She spread the newspaper out on the workbench so she could better study the article about the race.

Already several famous airmen had said they would enter the contest, including—and Cassie read this part more slowly—American war-ace Linc Cameron. The race was to be preceded by an air show where Cameron and others would put on an exhibition of death-defying stunts.

Cassie sniffed at this. She had suspected he was the type of man who couldn't resist showing off. Besides, just how death-defying could his stunts be if he had gotten so hysterical yesterday when they'd almost collided? Why, she had missed him by a good six inches at least! As for the race, if he thought he was going to fly off with that fifty thousand dollars, it was only because he hadn't seen his competition yet. Cassie Jones was going to meet Linc Cameron on equal terms—and beat him.

Quigly was again bent over his engine, working on the carburetor. Cassie picked up the kerosene lantern that sat on his workbench and held it over his head to give him better light. Without windows the barn was almost always dark.

"Quigly," she began, and was encouraged by an answering grunt, "have you ever been in love?"

He was silent for so long that she thought he hadn't heard her. Then she realized that he was giving his answer some thought.

"I think I was, once. A long, long time ago." He shrugged. "Nothing came of it though. It's a disease that generally afflicts the young."

"How do you know you have it—are, that is? How do you know when you're in love?"

"Well, for one thing, you can't stop thinking about the person in question. You spend all your time planning what you're going to do or say the next time you see them, which is a complete waste of time since when you do see them, you act like a damned fool anyway."

Cassie nodded knowingly. "And does your stomach get all fluttery when they're around, and your mouth dry up so that you couldn't even spit, let alone talk? And do you get so angry at them for making you feel that way that you say mean, stupid things and later wish you hadn't?"

Quigly straightened up and peered at her over the rims of his glasses. "You sound like you got it bad, kid."

"Oh, Quigly, I do. It snuck up on me all of a sudden. Is there a cure?"

Before he could answer they heard the purring sound of an automobile motor and the crunch of gravel under tires. Cassie jumped, then blushed.

"Now, I wonder who that could be," Quigly said.

She threw a panicky look at the barn door. "I . . ."

"Better go see who it is. Might be somebody important."

"I . . ."

Quigly took the lantern from her hands and gave her a gentle shove. "Go on, kid. There's no cure for what you got. You'll either fall in it so deep you won't want to get out, or you'll get over it naturally after sufficient exposure to the person in question. It's sort of like having the chicken pox. You might be left with a few scars, but you'll live."

Cassie nodded and swallowed hard. She turned and marched toward the barn door. Quigly smiled.

Edward Farrell jumped from the green roadster, his white silk scarf flapping in the wind. He wore a dotted bow tie, Norfolk jacket, and flannel trousers. There was a brown derby on his head, doeskin driving gloves on his hands, and a smile on his face. Cassie greeted him with a bright smile of her own, telling herself her old childhood friend was just the person she had wanted to see in the first place.

"Ward! I haven't seen you for weeks." She slipped her arm through his as he bent and gave her a light kiss on the cheek. "I've missed you. Where have you been?"

He looked at her in amazement, then laughed and shook his head. "You astonish me, Cassie. Really you do."

"Why? What do you mean?"

"The last time I was here I got down on my knees and asked you to marry me, and you turned me down flat. Didn't it occur to you that I might be too humiliated to come back again so soon? No one's that much of a glutton for punishment."

Guilt brought a poignant ache to Cassie's chest, for the last person she ever wanted to hurt was Ward Farrell. She remembered all those times growing up when he had been kind to her, times when it had seemed as if the whole world was against her except for Ward. But his marriage proposal at Christmas had shocked her, for she had never thought of their friendship—a friendship of childhood secrets and whispered dreams —as the sort of a relationship that would ever deepen into love. At least not sexual love.

Now she struggled to come up with something to erase the look of hurt that creased his narrow face. "We couldn't get married anyway, Ward," she said. "It's probably illegal or something. First cousins can't marry."

He shook his head. "Cassie, Cassie . . . everyone in Kingly knows there really isn't a drop of common blood between us. We could go down to the courthouse this minute and apply for a license, and no one would blink an eye."

She looked away, unable to refute his logic. Her dead mother's husband, Lawrence Kingly, might be the Farrell children's maternal uncle, but everyone in town knew that Cassie Jones was no child of Lawrence Kingly.

She sighed. "Oh, Ward, I thought we went over all this at Christmas. My refusal had nothing to do with my feelings for you. I like you, Ward—"

"Do you?"

"Of course, I do. And if I were ever to take a husband, I'm sure it would be you. But you know how I feel. I'm never getting married, Ward. Never."

He sighed as well. "I do know how you feel . . . and I suppose I can't blame you." He turned her around and began to lead her down the road along the field. "But you shouldn't judge the state of matrimony by your mother's experience. After all, it can't really be that terrible if mankind's been doing it for thousands of years."

"That's because *man*kind not only gets a mate when he marries, he gets an unpaid cook, washerwoman, maid, seamstress, and mother of his children. All womankind gets is a master. Why should I want to give some man the power to tell me what to do and when to do it?"

"Not to mention how to do it, why to do it, and who to do it with."

Cassie laughed. They had stopped beside an ancient, weather-beaten dogwood tree. Edward dropped her arm and leaned against the gnarled trunk. "As long as I can make you laugh, there's always hope. I'll never give up, Cassie. I don't merely like you—I love you."

He bent his head and kissed her. She let him, let him wrap his arms around her waist and pull her against him, for though they had kissed before, she had never thought of their kisses as having any serious meaning . . . until now. She wanted to compare how Ward's kiss made her feel to what she had felt this morning in the alley, when Linc Cameron had taken her in his arms.

And there was no comparison.

Cassie broke the kiss, pulling away from him. They stared at one another, and she saw the disappointment steal over his face. "I'm sorry, Ward," she whispered.

"Yes, well, I'm sorry too. Sorry about a lot of things." He looked away. Taking off his derby, he ran a hand over his slicked-down hair. "Do you know I'll probably have to take out another loan before I can plant next year's seedlings? Cigarettes are suddenly all the rage, and tobacco is more in demand today than it's been in over a hundred years. I've got hogsheads packed full of the stuff, and I still can't make the damned plantation pay for itself."

"But it's not your fault, Ward," Cassie protested. She knew the plantation was everything to Ward, for he had been raised believing he would be the salvation of the proud Farrell family's fortunes. Cassie had always pitied Ward for having such a burden placed on him so young. Now she tried to coax a smile out of him. "I thought you told me once the Farrell plantation has been a losing proposition ever since your family backed the wrong side in the War Between the States."

"Yes. But I seem to have made an even bigger mess of things ever since my father died. Everything I try just seems to put us deeper in debt."

"Then it sounds to me like you ought to be proposing to a girl with a rich daddy, not me."

He gave her a sad, crooked smile. "Maybe you're right."

"You could always enter that Bean's cola race," she said.

He looked at her blankly. "What race?"

She told him about the Bean's Cola Transcontinental Airplane Race and the fifty-thousand-dollar prize. "Quigly and I have decided to enter it, and the article said your friend Mr. Cameron is going to be flying in it too," she added.

At first Ward had seemed excited about the race, but now he shrugged and laughed. Cassie, who knew him well, could tell his laughter was forced. "In that case I won't bother to enter," he said. "Linc can fly circles around every other pilot I know"—he tapped her nose lightly with his finger—"except maybe for you."

Cassie smiled at his compliment, and a companionable silence fell between them. She wanted to ask Ward about Linc Cameron. She knew Linc was staying out at the Farrell plantation and that he and Ward had flown together in France. The whole town was talking about what a great ace he had been in the war, how he had shot down twenty-five enemy planes. Cassie wanted to ask Ward what the man was like. Where did he come from? How long did he plan on staying in Kingly? Did he have a girl somewhere? . . .

"Just what is Linc Cameron to you?" Edward asked abruptly, and Cassie was startled that he had so adroitly read her thoughts.

"Uh . . . nothing. I only just met him yesterday." She forced a smile. "And I suppose Melodie told you all about what happened. It wasn't the most auspicious meeting. Why do you ask?"

Edward studied her carefully, and Cassie began to fear that he could read her feelings as easily as if they were written on her face.

"You must mean something to him," he said. "Linc prides himself on his self-control, and I've never seen him lose it before. But when he saw you get hit by that policeman, he nearly went crazy. It was a pretty powerful reaction considering you two met only yesterday."

Cassie kicked at a tuft of grass and glared up at him. "You can just get one thing into your head, Ward Farrell. I don't like Linc Cameron, and I'm not ever going to like him. He might be your friend and a hero and all that, but I find him arrogant, overbearing, insufferable, and downright the most infuriating man I've ever met, and I don't care if you tell him I said so!"

Edward raised his hands in front of his face, laughing. "Hey, I'm the one who loves you, remember? And Linc's already got more than his share of adoring females. As far as I'm concerned you can go on disliking Linc Cameron till doomsday."

Cassie looked down the field, past where the *Pegasus* was tied near the barn. Edward had begun to tell her what he intended to do about the growing insolvency of his tobacco plantation, but she wasn't listening. The words to a silly song chased each other through her head: *I wonder when I shall be married, oh, be married, oh, be married. I wonder when I shall be married . . .*

She hadn't really lied to Ward. She did like him. But liking was not the same as loving. You could even hate someone while you went on loving them; they were two sides of the same thing. But the truly frightening thing about love was that it so often led to marriage. Then, before long, the love faded and turned dark, like tarnished silver, and all that was left was the marriage —two people trapped together, fighting each other, hating each other.

I wonder when I shall be married . . . oh, be married . . .

She would never be married, and she didn't care if one day she'd be pitied for being a spinster, an old maid. Unconsciously Cassie lifted her chin in defiance. She wouldn't be less of a woman simply because she chose not to be legitimized by a man's name, his support, his ring. And if love inevitably led to marriage, then she would have nothing to do with love, because she had seen what happened when shining love turned dark and bitter. She had seen the hell on earth her mother's life had become because of love and marriage, and she knew she wanted nothing to do with either.

Love and marriage—they were a woman's curse.

"It's a good thing Ward and the mayor are old friends," Melodie said to Linc, her cheeks dimpling with laughter. "Otherwise you'd be eatin' jail slop tonight instead of the delicious roast duckling Cook has fixed for us."

Linc lifted his glass of whiskey and soda in a mock toast to Edward Farrell and flashed a smile. They were sitting in a small, informal parlor within the spacious and elegant Farrell plantation house, indulging in one of the latest fads to sweep the country—predinner cocktails.

Ward returned Linc's toast. He didn't bother to disabuse Linc of the notion that he was responsible for encouraging the mayor to turn a blind eye toward Linc's assault on two Kingly policemen. But the truth was, Ward thought somewhat sourly, no one wanted to arrest a man who'd recently had a medal pinned on his brave chest by President Wilson himself.

Not that Ward begrudged Linc the glory that his courage had brought him. He just wished a little of that glory had rubbed off on him. He thought of what he had told Cassie earlier that afternoon, that he was going to have to take out another loan just to make it through the year. The trouble was, the plantation was already mortgaged to the hilt, and another loan might be hard to come by. On the other hand, a famous war ace like Linc Cameron would have bank officers falling all over themselves to lend him money. That reminded Ward of something. . . .

He got up and went to the desk in one corner of the small parlor. Picking up a copy of yesterday's *Richmond News* he unfolded it and brought it over to where Linc and his sister sat side by side on the sofa. Linc was telling Melodie his impressions of Paris, and she was listening to him, Ward saw with a twinge of disgust, with a moonstruck look on her face.

He shoved the newspaper under his friend's nose. "Why didn't you tell me about this?"

Melodie leaned over Linc's shoulder, and all three stared down at Linc's picture and the article about the Bean's Cola Transcontinental Airplane Race.

"Fifty thousand dollars!" Melodie exclaimed. "Did you see that, Ward? The winning prize is fifty thousand dollars!"

"Obviously," Ward said, not bothering to hide his bitterness, "Linc wanted to keep this news to himself. Maybe he's hoping that the less competition, the greater his chances will be of winning the race."

Linc looked up at his friend. "It never crossed my mind that you'd be interested, Ward. You always said that after the war was over you were never going to crawl into another cockpit." He shrugged. "To be truthful, the Bean's cola people approached me about entering only a couple of days ago. If it weren't for the fact that I'm flat broke and could use the money—"

Ward waved his arm dramatically, spilling some of his drink. "And you think I couldn't? Do you have any idea how much the operating expenses are on a place this size? Oh hell, I meant what I said about never wanting to fly again, but who can afford to pass up a chance at fifty thousand dollars?" He gave Linc a sudden smile. "That article said it's got to be two-man teams. You're going to be needing a copilot, so why don't we compete together?" He laughed. "It'll be just like old times, when you and Monte and I used to go hunting Germans together. We can split the expenses and prize money right down the middle, fifty-fifty. What do you say?"

For a moment Linc said nothing, then he sighed. "I'm sorry, Ward ... I already asked Pete Striker to be my copilot."

"I see. . . ." Ward struggled to hide his hurt. "Well, it was just a thought. Like you reminded me, after two long years of flying, I'm bloody sick of it." He forced a smile. "And besides, I've got a rich uncle who's apt to kick off at any minute. I've always maintained that the easiest way to come by money is to inherit it."

Melodie sighed loudly. "Oh, Ward, I hope you aren't goin' to go into all that again. Why, you know how Mama always said it isn't polite to talk about such things as money and inheritances in front of company."

"Ward doesn't need to stand on ceremony with me, Miss Farrell," Linc said. The smile he gave Ward was so warm and sincere that Ward's hurt and anger instantly evaporated.

Melodie laughed airily. "In that case you shouldn't stand on ceremony with *me*." She pouted prettily at her brother. "Ward honey, will you please give Linc your permission to call me Melodie. This 'Miss Farrell' business is making me feel positively old-maidish."

Ward's smile was teasing. "I think he's having a hard time adjusting to how much things changed back home while we were gone. You modern young ladies have got poor Linc positively terrified."

"Now don't you get me wrong, Linc," Melodie said. "I'm not really all that modern. I'm certainly no rabble-rousing suffragette like Cassie Jones."

Ward couldn't help noticing Linc's sudden interest at the mention of Cassie's name. "Has she always been like that?" Linc asked.

"Like what?" Ward said, pretending ignorance.

"I don't know. . ." Linc shrugged. "So fierce."

Ward studied his whiskey and soda. "I suppose fierce is an apt description of Cassie. And since we're on the subject, just what are your intentions toward Cassie Jones?"

Linc's head jerked up, surprise on his face. "I haven't known her long enough to have any intentions. Why? Are you—"

"Not in the way you mean," Ward said, hastily. The last thing he wanted was to have Linc find out he had proposed to Cassie—and that she had turned him down. "In a manner of speaking, except for that crazy uncle of hers, I'm her closest relative, and I feel sort of responsible for her. Cassie is . . . well, she's not like other girls. I'm afraid she could be easily hurt."

"In the first place, I wasn't aware you two were related," Linc said stiffly. "And, besides—"

"Oh, honestly, Ward!" Melodie chimed in. "What do you want to go givin' Linc the wrong impression for? Cassie's no relative of ours. Oh, *technically* I suppose you could say she's a cousin, but she isn't really. Our Uncle Lawrence was married to her mother, but everybody in Kingly knows that Cassie is a . . . well, I'm not supposed to use the word, but . . ."

"Bastard," Ward supplied. "And the whole town refuses to let her forget it. Which goes a long way toward explaining why Cassie is the way she is." A chime sounded within the house. Ward stood up and polished off his drink, glad for the chance to get Linc's mind off Cassie Jones. "Supper's ready."

Linc stood up and held out his arm for Melodie. She looked up at him with a smile sparkling in her light brown eyes. Ward followed them into the dining room.

It was obvious that his sister, like every other eligible female in Kingly, was attracted to Linc. Ward wondered if the interest was mutual. There had always been a competitive edge to his friendship with Linc Cameron, but because they had been through so much together, they were almost as close as brothers. Under normal circumstances, he thought, he wouldn't mind having Linc for a brother-in-law. But Linc had admitted that he was broke, and though he rarely spoke about his family, Ward had never gotten the impression that the Camerons, whoever the hell they were, were well-off financially. No, as much as he liked Linc, Ward de-

cided, it would never do for him to marry into the Farrell family.

Unless, of course, Linc managed to win that fifty
thousand dollars. . . .

Linc Cameron turned on the light in the guest bedroom and shut the door behind him. Patches, lying
stretched out before the fire, opened one eye, wagged
his tail lazily, and went back to sleep.

Linc took off his morning coat and tossed it on the
bed, tugging loose his tie and unbuttoning his high,
starched collar with a sigh of relief. Normally he would
have enjoyed the company of the Farrells—Ward could
always make him laugh, and Melodie was a delight to
look at—but he had spent the dinner hour yearning for
solitude.

He prowled the room, stopping beside a small
spider-leg table to pour a generous glass of whiskey
from a cut-glass decanter. The state of Virginia might
have voted itself dry before the war, but Ward obviously considered the Farrells above the law, for there
was no lack of first-class liquor in the house.

Linc savored the whiskey, rolling it around on his
tongue as he recalled his two brief meetings with Miss
Cassandra Jones. She had been on his mind all day, like
a nagging thought that refused to go away.

She was such an intriguing mixture of toughness
and sweet innocence. One moment she had been kissing him, rubbing her warm body against him like a
purring cat, and the next she was looking at him with
those damnable big gray eyes as if he had tried to . . .
hell! He shrugged. All women played at love. Perhaps
she was just more adept at the game than most.

Linc stretched out on the bed, resting the glass of
whiskey on his stomach. But within minutes he was up
and pacing the floor again. He opened the French
doors and stepped onto the veranda, which encircled
the entire second story of the plantation house. Below

him a rolling expanse of lawn spread down to the river, where the skeletal branches of sweet gum trees rustled in the wind. The crisp winter air cut through his thin shirt, and he shivered.

He was restless tonight, but in a strangely exhilarating way, and it was all the fault of those damnable gray eyes. If he had any sense—which he probably didn't—he would get as far away from those eyes as he could get. She was exactly the kind of woman he didn't like yet couldn't seem to stay away from. If he had learned nothing else from those years with Ria, he had learned all too well that a woman like Miss Cassandra Jones was pure trouble....

A rustling movement startled Linc out of his reverie. He glanced around him. The white wicker furniture looked like phantom shapes in the moonlight. One of the shapes moved suddenly and materialized into satin-clad flesh.

"Melodie!" he exclaimed, more sharply than he had intended. "What are you doing out here?"

"Same as you, I suppose," she said. "I heard a scratchin' noise and thought it was a coon. Those little critters come inside sometimes, lookin' for an easy supper."

"It was no coon, only me. I needed some air."

Melodie shivered and hugged herself. The moonlight glinted off her black hair and made her maple-colored eyes seem to glow in the dark. "It's cold out here."

Linc took a small quilt off a chair near the open door and draped it around her shoulders. He pulled the ends of it snugly under her chin, and she tilted her face up, expecting to be kissed. He started to lower his head to oblige her, then stopped. He released the ends of the quilt and turned away.

"Linc?" she said, a pleading note in her voice. "Is it because of Monte?" She laid her hand on his arm. "I know what you're probably thinkin', Linc. 'Cause Monte and I were engaged to be married, you think I belong to him. I can see you really have a strong streak of loyalty in you. But Monte is dead. He's dead and we're alive. He'd be happy to know we could find comfort in each other. Don't you think he'd be happy?"

Linc looked down into her lovely face and felt the familiar weariness come flooding back. "No, Miss Farrell. No, I don't think he'd be happy."

Her hand tightened on his arm, and she pulled him around to face her. "You're going to be leavin' us tomorrow, aren't you?"

"Yes."

Sighing softly, she traced his firm lips lightly with her fingers. "I can hardly believe a strong, brave airman like you would be runnin' away from little ol' me."

"Little ol' you has got me scared to death," he said, knowing it was a lie. It wasn't Melodie Farrell he was running from—it was a pair of haunting gray eyes.

Chapter 4

The dusty, battered Model T pulled up alongside the wrought-iron gates of the cemetery. "I won't be long," Cassie said, getting out the passenger side.

Quigly squinted into the afternoon sun as he peered nearsightedly over the radiator grill. "Take your time. I thought while you were here I might as well pay a little visit to the depot, see how they're coming with the loading. If those idiots drop even one of those crates . . ."

Cassie laughed and leaned over to pat the top of his balding head. "They wouldn't dare. Not after you threatened to boil them in castor oil if the *Peg* got so much as a scratch."

It was finally spring, and the *Pegasus* had been broken down and packed into crates for the long train ride to California and the start of the Bean's Cola Transcontinental Airplane Race. They would both be riding in the boxcar with it, leaving in the morning.

Cassie waved as Quigly put the flivver into gear and rattled out into the road. She had her hand on the latch to the cemetery gate when the clatter of wheels on stone caused her to turn around. An old-fashioned brougham rolled toward her, passing so close that she had to step back out of its way. As the brougham drove by she looked through the yellowed isinglass window and into a pair of familiar dark eyes. A heavy scowl twisted the man's shadowy face, and his eyes narrowed as they focused on her. Cassie stared back at him unflinchingly.

A pale, well-manicured hand grasped the window curtain and snapped it closed. The brougham passed through a pair of stone gateposts next to the cemetery and disappeared up a winding drive.

Cassie stared after it for a long moment. The hatred she felt for the man in the carriage showed plainly on her face.

Then she entered the cemetery, walking down a pebbled path to a plot marked by a miniature Grecian temple. The elaborate headstone was decorated with statues of chubby cherubs and fluted columns entwined with marble grapevines. Engraved on the false door of the temple were the words:

SARA, BELOVED WIFE OF
LAWRENCE KINGLY
1880–1913

Cassie knelt and laid a bunch of wild daisies tied together with a yellow ribbon on top of the grave. Daisies had been one of her mother's favorite flowers— daisies and buttercups. Then she noticed that someone else had visited the grave recently, for a large milk-glass vase filled with expensive hothouse roses had been placed on the roof of the temple.

For a moment she was bewildered, wondering who else besides herself would visit her mother's grave. Then she understood—and was filled with swift, hot anger. How *dare* he! she raged. How dare he pretend to grieve for her mother now, when he'd been so cruel to her while she lived.

Springing to her feet, Cassie turned and stared in the direction of a big old house, barely visible behind a veil of ivy and ailanthus. From where she stood all she could see was one tower of gray-slated gable with a single window that glimmered in the sunlight like a winking eye. But she knew *he* was looking down on her. Lawrence Kingly, her mother's husband, was watching her, and the hatred she felt for him made her tremble.

In fact, it was Edward Farrell who was at that moment looking out the tower window and down into the cemetery next door. He instinctively started to step back when he saw Cassie Jones stand up and turn to stare in his direction—almost as if he had a guilty conscience. Then he stopped and laughed at himself. He knew she wasn't able to see him from where she stood, and it wouldn't matter even if she could.

The door opened behind him, and Edward turned away from the window. Lawrence Kingly entered the room, leaning heavily on his cane. His graying hair lay in thin strands across the high dome of his skull, and the pale skin of his face was pulled taut over gaunt cheekbones. His black eyes were sunk deep and they glowed fiercely, the only thing about him that looked alive.

"How are you, Uncle?" Edward said, his hand stretched out in greeting.

"What in blazes are you doing here?" Kingly growled, ignoring his hand. He lifted the skirt of his old-fashioned frock coat and sat down stiffly behind a beautiful antique cherry wood desk that dominated the room.

"I've come to see how you are."

"Come to see how much closer I am to dying, you mean."

"You know that isn't true."

Kingly gave him an ironic look. "Well, I still am. Dying that is." He barked a laugh, then grunted in pain. "Pour me a glass of whiskey."

Edward went to a tea cart, which held a profusion of bootleg bottles, mostly empty, and poured a generous measure of whiskey into a large tumbler. He put it into Kingly's shaking hand. "I don't know why I can't simply come visit without you thinking—"

"Like hell! You're waiting for me to die so you can get your grubby hands on my money. I can smell the greed on you—it stinks up the room. Well, don't be in such a goddamned hurry, boy. It isn't polite. I've got six more months at the most, the doctor says, so you'll get my millions soon enough." He paused, and his lips stretched into a cruel smile. "Maybe I'll leave it all to you. Maybe. If you're humble enough."

Edward clamped his jaw against the prideful retort that threatened to fly out of his mouth and turned back to the window. He reminded himself that he was the only heir his uncle had to leave the Kingly fortune to. He was the only son of Kingly's only sister. There was no one else. Well, there was Melodie, of course, but the old man had always considered his niece an empty-headed fool. And there was Cassie. . . .

Edward swung his gaze around to his uncle, who was scowling down into the now-empty whiskey glass. No, Ward told himself, shaking his head. No, Lawrence Kingly would sooner leave his money to a dog pound than see it go to Cassie. Wouldn't he?

Frowning, he turned back to stare down into the cemetery below. Cassie, her head held high, strode briskly back down the path toward the cemetery gate.

"Is she still out there?" Kingly asked gruffly.

Edward turned slowly around again and looked at his uncle thoughtfully. "It bothers you that Cassie visits her mother's grave?"

An unreadable emotion flickered across Kingly's face. "I don't care what my wife's bastard does, as long as she stays away from me."

"And does she? Stay away from you?"

Lawrence Kingly's thin lips curled up, baring yellowed teeth. "She hates my guts. Always has."

"And how do you feel about her, Uncle? Your Sara's child? Now that you are about to die, are you perhaps regretting—"

"Shut up! I won't discuss it, or her." The old man blinked rapidly, then focused on Edward. His cackling laughter filled the room. "I could always leave it all to Cassie! Is that what you're thinking, boy? I bet you're just shittin' in your pants, worrying whether I'll up and get repentant and leave it all to my wife's bastard instead of to you!"

Edward tried to keep his face blank. He refused to be frightened by his uncle's empty threat. For it was an empty threat; it had to be!

"You must suit yourself, Uncle," Ward replied. "It is, after all, your money."

Lawrence Kingly laughed again. "So it is, so it is. And you'd do well not to forget it. Now, why don't you just quit pussyfootin' around and tell me how much you want this time?"

Edward turned away, unable to meet his uncle's penetrating gaze.

"Don't think I don't know why you're really here. You want another loan," Kingly said, sneering. "How much?"

Edward licked his lips and launched into his prepared speech. "There's this transcontinental airplane race. It offers a fifty-thousand-dollar prize. I thought I might enter it, but I need—"

"Never mind." Kingly opened a drawer in the desk and pulled out a leather-bound checkbook. "How much?"

"I thought . . . two thousand?"

The nub of the pen scratched across the paper as Kingly filled out the check. He blotted it and then held it out to Edward, waving it in the air. "Now take the damned thing and get out of my sight."

Edward plucked the check from his uncle's fingers

and backed out the door, mumbling his thanks while his uncle irritably waved him away.

The door closed behind his nephew. Lawrence Kingly sat alone behind his big desk in the heavy silence. Almost two hundred years ago the first Kingly—an indentured servant from the prisons of London—had come to this land, earned his freedom, and built this town. Generations of Kinglys had sat behind this desk, his father and his grandfather before him. But there was no son of his loins hovering anxiously over his shoulder the way he had hovered over his father's, waiting to take his place. Only his nephew, his greedy, profligate nephew, waited to inherit it all.

Yes, his nephew was the heir apparent to the town of Kingly, or at least to the parts of Kingly that counted—the textile mill, the tobacco-processing plant, the quarry. The thought made Lawrence Kingly laugh. There had never been any love lost between him and the town, so why should he care what happened to it after he died? If he did leave everything to Edward Farrell, the town would no doubt get the master it deserved.

He took a gold hunting watch out of his vest pocket, but he did not open it to read the time. Instead, he fingered the key that hung at the end of the fob before slipping it inside the lock of the upper desk drawer. He slid the drawer open; it was empty but for a photograph.

He laid the photograph on top of the desk. A young woman with dark hair and softly brooding eyes looked up at him. He felt all over again what he had felt twenty years before—the rage, the acrid, bitter disappointment.

"Slut," he said aloud. The word, full of hatred, reverberated across the room.

She had been a nonentity, a little bit of nothing from the wrong side of the river. He had plucked her from that shack she'd shared with her half-crazy brother and brought her here to his mansion, dressed her in furs and jewels, and married her. She had repaid him by spreading her legs for the first man who beckoned. She had shamed him before the entire town, the self-righteous folk of Kingly, who had snickered behind their hands that the great and mighty Lawrence Kingly couldn't keep his young and pretty wife satisfied after barely a year of marriage. He had wanted to kill her when he found out about it; he almost had killed her.

He laughed softly, bitterly. She had won in the end, though, his wife, his whore. She had felt the full brunt of his anger, but in the end she had defeated him by whelping her bastard. Always there was the constant reminder, the living proof in the blond hair and gray eyes of her daughter, her bastard, that she had been unfaithful, that although he had adored her, worshiped her, she had not loved him at all . . . not at all. . . .

He rubbed his fingers over the face in the photograph as if he could wipe out the derisive laughter he was sure he could see in those soft, dark eyes.

"Why?" he whispered, and felt the grief and pain pull at his chest. "Oh, Sara, Sara . . . why did you do it?"

Two weeks later and over three thousand miles away, the oceanside resort town of Santa Monica, California, played host to the biggest air show held in America since before the war. The airfield was located on grassy flatlands within spitting distance of the Pacific. Leroy Irving Bean had taken it over for his two-week celebration of flight—not to mention Bean's cola.

The grandstand was decorated with flags and streamers and giant banners shaped like soda bottles bearing the distinctive blue-and-yellow Bean's logo. A man in a red-and-white-striped coat was whipping up enthusiasm by shouting through a megaphone, dramatically describing the air stunts to come.

Cassie stood beside Quigly in the pilots' enclosure

and watched Linc Cameron's expert execution of barrel rolls, chandelles, and tailspins. He had just looped the loop five times in a row—"A remarkable feat," bellowed the man in the striped coat.

Hardly that remarkable, Cassie thought, although she had to admit she had never seen a prettier set of loops. She tilted her head back and watched mesmerized as Linc fell into a slight dive, then climbed to full power until he was flying completely upside down. At the top of the circle, instead of cutting his engine and diving down to complete yet another loop, he held full power and rolled a half turn to the left and back again into an upright position—a perfect Immelmann turn.

A man standing beside them let out a whoop. "Hot damn! Did you see that?"

Cassie and her uncle both turned to look at him.

Quigly smiled politely. "That fellow certainly does know how to fly."

Cassie sniffed. "Hunh. I've seen better Immelmanns." She neglected to add that the only time she had dared to try that stunt she had stalled out and scared herself half to death.

The man squinted back at them. He inspected Cassie carefully, taking in her overalls and boy's flannel shirt.

He grinned suddenly. "Hell, miss, that boy don't just fly an airplane, he *wears* it like a tailor-made suit."

"You know Mr. Cameron, then?" Cassie asked in a tone of complete indifference.

"We flew together with the Lafayette," he said. He was addressing Quigly now, as if only a man could understand the strong camaraderie forged by war. "And then after I got this"—he bent over and rapped his calf with his knuckles, and Cassie heard a hollow, wooden sound—"I was his chief mechanic. He's always had more guts than sense, that boy. He used to bring his Spad back—he flew a Spad in those days—he used to bring her back so riddled with holes, she looked like a duck full of buckshot."

Quigly looked impressed at this; Cassie pretended she wasn't.

The man pulled his cap off his head, ran a hand through a thinning thatch of ginger-colored hair, then yanked the cap back down to the tips of his ears. He peeled a cigarette off his lip, put it in his left hand, and stuck out his right hand. "Pete Striker."

Quigly introduced himself and Cassie, and the two men began to talk about the race. From the grandstand behind them, Cassie heard the spectators gasp in one loud hiss as Linc Cameron went into a long, controlled spin. Pete Striker, it seemed, was going to be Linc's copilot for the race. Cassie thought it would be a disadvantage to have a copilot with only one leg. Surely that was carrying friendship too far. Then she had to laugh at herself. Most people would probably think having a female for a copilot would be an even greater disadvantage.

Linc was holding the spin too long. Beside her the two men had fallen silent. Cassie dug her fingernails into her palms to keep from squirming with a sudden attack of panic.

"He's holding it too long," Quigly said, voicing Cassie's fear aloud.

The ginger-haired man didn't even bother to look up, as if by showing his lack of concern he could rob the stunt of its danger. "He always waits until the last possible second to pull out of a spin."

But Linc still hadn't pulled out, and he was running out of seconds. He needed at least two hundred feet of airspace to recover from the spin. He was close enough now for Cassie to see his head protruding from the fuselage—the brown blot of his helmet and the pale oval of his face. The scream of his engine hurt her ears.

Pull out of it, she cried out to him silently. She squeezed her eyes shut, unable to watch any longer. God, please, let him pull out of it now...please, Linc—

The shriek of Linc's engine suddenly changed pitch. Beside her Quigly breathed a huge sigh of relief. Cassie opened her eyes. The nose of the *Betsy* pointed skyward as its wings seemed to comb the long grass of the airfield.

Cassie turned on Pete Striker. She was so shaken she didn't know whether to scream or burst into tears. "That was . . . that was a *stupid* thing to do. He almost killed himself!"

Striker looked pale, and his grin was a bit lopsided. "He crash-landed over a half a dozen times in France, and each time he walked away without hardly a scratch. I suppose after a while danger becomes a spice you either get used to or can't live without—maybe both."

"Well I can certainly live without it!" Cassie said angrily, and strode off, but not before Quigly had seen the glaze of unshed tears in her eyes.

Striker asked him something about the *Pegasus*, but Quigly wasn't really paying attention to the conversation. He'd always assumed it was Edward Farrell who had inspired that little talk about love he and Cassie had had back in February. Now he wasn't so sure. He had always made it a point to allow Cassie a lot of independence and privacy in her life, and he was not about to start butting in now. But it wouldn't hurt to meet this Linc Cameron, he decided, and see for himself just what the fellow was like.

The man in the red-and-white-striped coat had once again picked up his megaphone and was addressing the grandstand. "And now, ladies and gentlemen, in just a few minutes Miss Cassandra Jones, America's prettiest aviatrix, will perform a feat so daring that you will not believe what you see with your very own eyes. She will stand erect on the upper wing of the airplane without any visible means of support whatsoever, while her pilot loops the loop, defying all the laws of gravitation!"

"Hey, is that you?" Pete Striker asked.

"What? Oh . . . yes, it is. I better go." Quigly shook Pete Striker's hand. "Say, d'you think you and Mr. Cameron would want to have a beer with me later on this afternoon?"

Pete struck a match on the seat of his pants and held it to a fresh cigarette he had clamped between his teeth. He grinned around it. "Hell yes, we would. Thanks."

Quigly found Cassie pacing back and forth alongside the *Pegasus*, waiting for him. As he walked up to her, he searched her face carefully but saw no sign of whatever it was that had so upset her earlier. He automatically began to inspect the aircraft, even though Cassie would have already done so. As he reached up to check the tautness of the flying wires, he was suddenly overwhelmed by an attack of dizziness. It was as if he'd suddenly had his head shoved underwater. There was a rushing sound in his ears, and darkness crowded his vision. He fell to his knees, nausea cramping his stomach.

Strong hands clasped his shoulders. "Quigly!" He looked up into Cassie's blurred face. "What's the matter?" she asked, the fear plain in her voice.

"Nothing. Just straightened up too soon," he lied. "Blood left my head too suddenly, and I got a little dizzy."

"Maybe we'd better not go up."

"No, no. I'll be fine."

Quigly stood up carefully and fored a smile, surprised that he could do it. He had to clench his teeth together to keep them from chattering, and cold sweat ran down his back. In the past he had occasionally been plagued by airsickness, but this was the first time he'd ever gotten sick *before* he went up. He looked at Cassie's concerned face and thought of how important this race was to her and to their future, how much she depended on him. And he hoped to God he wasn't losing his nerve.

Cassie fastened the chin strap of her leather helmet as the *Pegasus* trundled down the runway. She sat in the front cockpit, Quigly in the back. Quigly would do the piloting, while she performed the stunt.

The control stick moved between her legs as Quigly pulled back on it, and the plane glided smoothly into the air. They made a low pass over the grandstand, buzzing the spectators. Cassie looked down at the colorful sight—the flags and streamers and the sea of upturned faces. They all seemed to swirl together like streams of spilled paint.

Quigly banked the machine high on a climbing turn, and Cassie spotted a tall, familiar figure in a brown leather jacket standing and talking to a smaller man on the edge of the grandstand. As the *Pegasus* passed over their heads, the two men looked up. Impulsively, Cassie waved. But though the smaller man waved back, the tall figure in the brown leather jacket did not.

Cassie imagined the scowl that was probably marring that handsome face, and she smiled to herself. She would show Linc Cameron how to give the crowd a thrill!

At a thousand feet, Quigly leveled the *Pegasus* out, and the engine settled into a smooth, steady beat. They were over the pilots' hangars now, an area forbidden to the general public. Cassie turned around and gave Quigly a thumbs-up signal, and he nodded vigorously in response. The roar of the engine was so loud that they would have to communicate by hand signals and an instinctive understanding, honed by having done this stunt together dozens of times before.

Cassie stood up slowly, and climbed out of the cockpit and onto the wing. Through the leather soles of her boots she could feel vibrations from the engine drumming against the taut fabric of the wing, and she felt the inevitable rush of cold fear. She shut her eyes for a brief moment, taking a deep breath. Then she slowly let the air out of her lungs. Releasing her grip on the edge of the cockpit, she stepped out onto the wing.

Quigly was holding the *Pegasus* perfectly steady. Cassie stood in the middle of the wing with her feet braced apart, and the fear faded, replaced by an almost eerie calmness. To her right was the purple haze of mountains in the distance; to her left, the slate gray expanse of the ocean. Above her was the wide, empty blue sky.

Cassie looked at Quigly and smiled broadly, and he gave her a reassuring nod. Kneeling for a moment, she pulled out a pair of cables that were attached to a harness hidden beneath her heavy wool jacket. Working quickly, she hooked the cables into metal eyes at the base of the wing struts. She also fastened straps around her ankles and buckled them onto the surface of the wing. Standing up, she waved at Quigly to let him know she was ready, and he began a wide turn, heading back toward the grandstand, going steadily upward. When he had gained the desired altitude, Quigly looked at Cassie. She nodded—

And the *Pegasus* dived.

Cassie's stomach plunged to her feet, and the wind pressed against her face, pulling her lips into a skull-like grimace. The sky slid past her in a blue blur, and the blood roared in her head. Then she felt the straps of the harness straining against her body as Quigly put the *Pegasus* into a wide, magnificent curve. The earth spun around, the horizon rising up to meet her eyes.

By now, she knew, the crowd would be gasping aloud, trying to imagine how she could remain standing upright on the wing as the plane soared upside down. And indeed, she could feel the bite of the straps into her flesh as gravity exerted its inexorable pull.

The *Pegasus* climbed straight up toward the sky like

an arrow. It hovered an instant, as if standing still, and then plunged again, looping the loop. She was a bird soaring wild and free, and Cassie Jones laughed out loud.

Later, after they had landed and Cassie got a good look at Quigly's white, perspiring face, she sent him back to the huge hangar tent with orders to lie down. He didn't put up an argument, which told her more than anything else just how sick he must be feeling.

Chewing worriedly on her lower lip, Cassie walked around the *Pegasus* and stopped dead.

Linc Cameron was leaning nonchalantly against the end struts, a harness and a coil of cable dangling from his fingers. Patches lay in a spot of shade cast by the plane, his nose between his paws. His tail thumped the ground in greeting.

Cassie had forgotten how incredibly good-looking the man was. Her heart seemed to jump up and do a dance just at the sight of him, and the blood sang in her veins. He had taken off his leather jacket, and the breeze pressed the thin cotton of his shirt against his broad, muscular chest. The wind stirred his hair as well, tossing a sun-streaked lock across his forehead. His deep blue eyes bored into hers and did a funny thing to the muscles of her legs, making them go all weak and trembly.

Cassie stared at Linc, and he stared back. The look that flashed between them was as bright and intense as heat lightning.

It was too hot for her. She knelt on the ground as Patches trotted up. Linc Cameron had literally flown into her life over two months ago, kissed her twice, and casually flown away again. And although she had almost convinced herself that she didn't care, a part of her had missed him, missed perhaps what she had yearned for whenever they were together—that strange, compelling sexual attraction that seemed to flare up so easily between them.

She heard the grass swish against his boots, saw his shadow loom up, but she did not lift her head as he took two final steps and stood before her.

She had often wondered during the past three months what she would say to him when they met again here in California, and she had come up with several cutting remarks. Now, face to face with him, she couldn't remember a single one.

He swung the coil of cable before her face. "Isn't this cheating?"

Anger propelled her to her feet. "The man said no *visible* means of support. These"—she jerked the cable and harness out of his hands and tossed them into the cockpit—"aren't visible from the ground. You don't seriously think I'd attempt that stunt without them." She gave him a hard, measuring look. "Unlike some people, I don't feel compelled to take unnecessary risks. Poor Patches almost became an orphan today."

Patches whined pathetically.

Linc scowled at him. "Who asked for your opinion?"

"Don't take your nasty temper out on your poor dog. Just because you have a—"

"I don't have a death wish!" Linc snapped back so fast that Cassie guessed he had been subjected to a similar lecture from Pete Striker while she and Quigly had been flying.

"The hell you don't!" she shouted back at him. "You came within seconds of smearing yourself all over the airfield. And right in front of all those people—people who care about you, people like your friend Pete. People like—" She stopped herself just in time.

Linc sucked in a sharp breath. She met his stubborn, angry glare with one of her own.

Then his mouth twisted into an ironic smile, and he actually laughed. "There is one thing in your favor, Cassie Jones. You're refreshingly blunt." His smile faded. "Too blunt sometimes." He traced the line of her jaw with gentle fingers. "Maybe it's time I was equally blunt. Maybe I should tell you what I'd like to do to you . . . with you." He lowered his head and leaned closer to her, and his voice became a husky whisper. "Maybe I shouldn't even bother telling you. Maybe I should just go ahead and do it. . . ."

Cassie thought he was going to kiss her, and her lips actually parted in breathless anticipation.

Instead he turned away from her. Then he whipped around abruptly and seized her by the arm, his fingers biting into her flesh. "I might have known you'd turn up here. What the hell are you after? Besides making trouble and complicating my . . . complicating things."

Cassie stared at his hand until he let go. "You have a mighty high opinion of yourself if you think Quigly and I came all the way out to California just to watch you thrill the locals with your death-defying aerobatics. It just so happens we're—"

"Don't tell me." He gave her a smile so contemptuous that her palm itched to slap his face. "You and that crazy uncle of yours think you're going to compete in this race. Christ, you've no conception of how tough it's going to be. Right now the odds are that not even one of us who starts this fool venture will survive to see the end of it."

"Quigly and I will see the end of it. We're going to be the first in New York."

"Really?" Linc looked over the *Pegasus*, and his expressive mouth curved into a sneer of utter disdain. "Then you'll have to fly through me and the *Betsy* to do it," he said, sauntering off before she could tell him precisely what she thought of him and his damned *Betsy*.

Linc Cameron was, Cassie decided, absolutely the most infuriating man she had ever known in her life. She also thought that there had been something different about their encounter this time. Then she realized what it was.

This time he hadn't ended the conversation by kissing her.

The cavernous hangar was noisy with the drone of idling engines, the hiss of arc lights, and the laughter of men. The air was redolent of fresh sawdust and brewing coffee. Cassie sat on top of an empty oil drum, straining the impurities from a can of gasoline by pouring it through a chamois cloth.

"And this," said a voice behind her, "is going to be our toughest competition."

Cassie whirled around in surprise, almost knocking over the can. "Ward! What are you doing—" Her brows rose as she took in his outfit of tailored flannel overalls, jackboots, and a stiff leather jacket lined with fox fur. "You look . . . nice."

Edward Farrell held his arms out from his sides. "Like it? I want to look the part of the heroic airman when I land in New York to claim my prize. You didn't think I could really resist a crack at fifty thousand dollars, did you?" He gestured to the young man standing beside him. "Meet Gregory Pearce. He's going to be my copilot. Greg, this is Cassie Jones. She's got the best pair of hands of any flyer I've ever seen."

Cassie smiled at the man, who merely looked her over and then seemed to dismiss her entirely. He was extremely thin, with large, protruding ears and a prominent Adam's apple that bobbed up and down his throat like a fishing cork.

"But what are you doing here?" she said to Ward. "You kept swearing that you had no intention of entering the race."

He laughed. "Can't a fellow change his mind?"

"But why didn't you tell me before we left Virginia?"

"Well, it was really a last-minute decision, and I wasn't sure I could pull it off. I had to acquire a plane, and then talk Greg here into being my copilot." He looked around the hangar. "Quite a crowd, isn't there? Where's your uncle?"

"Lying down. He says he isn't feeling well, but I think he just wanted an excuse to take a nap." Cassie laughed to hide her concern. She had tried all afternoon to talk Quigly into seeing a doctor, but he kept insisting he was merely tired.

"Your friend Mr. Cameron is here," Cassie added sourly.

Ward grinned at her. "I know. I've seen him."

"Did you . . . did you bring Melodie with you?" Cassie asked, dreading the answer. She wasn't exactly sure why she cared so much—she only knew that she did.

He glanced around the hangar again. "As a matter of fact I did. Although I seem to have misplaced her at the moment."

At the mention of Melodie's name, Gregory Pearce had perked up like a bird dog smelling a pheasant. "You wouldn't have any idea where she might be, would you?" he asked Cassie eagerly.

Cassie shook her head, struggling hard to hide her treacherous feelings. For she would have bet her share of the prize money that she knew exactly where Melodie Farrell was, and the knowledge didn't please her one little bit.

For several minutes now Pete Striker and Patches had been watching the girl in pink silk daintily pick her way across the hangar, and it finally occurred to him that her ultimate destination was the *Betsy*. Patches seemed to be in agreement, for he growled a warning.

"Uh, Linc . . ." Pete said to Linc's back. Linc stood on a small ladder, bent over the engine, replacing a cracked cylinder.

The wrench slipped from Linc's fingers, and he scraped his knuckles on the crankshaft. He cursed loudly and profanely just as the girl approached them. Luckily he had chosen to swear in French, but Pete

Striker's already ruddy face grew even redder anyway.

"Uh, Linc . . ." he said again.

"What the hell is it?" Linc snapped, in English this time. He turned around, straightening, and barely missed banging his head on the engine cowling. His scowl deepened when he saw Melodie. "Miss Farrell. What are you doing here?"

Melodie pouted and batted her lashes. "Oh dear, I thought you would be glad to see me." Patches came up to sniff at Melodie's skirts. She shooed him away, then giggled. "Ward's decided to enter the race after all, and I'm goin' to be his advance man. Isn't that excitin'?"

Pete watched Linc leap gracefully off the ladder. He raised his brows expressively at the younger man. Some of the teams were sending what they called "advance men" ahead to various stopping points along the route with extra supplies of oil and gasoline and spare parts in case of a breakdown. Surely in this girl's case, Pete thought, her participation in the race would more likely be a hindrance than a help.

Patches had become fascinated with the tassels that dangled from Melodie's net overdress. He nipped at one, catching it between his teeth, and Melodie shrieked. Pete—who had been in the act of lighting a cigarette—jumped, dropping the burning match onto the sawdust-covered floor. He stomped on it quickly with his artificial foot. Linc was always lecturing him about the danger of smoking around the plane, and given the surly mood he had been in lately, if Linc had seen him drop that match he would have likely snarled Pete's head off.

"Oh, Linc!" Melodie wailed so loudly that Pete winced. "Your nasty ol' dog is eating my dress!"

"Stop it, Patches," Linc commanded.

"Oh, darn it all!" Melodie cried again. "Will you just look at that? I've gotten a great big ugly grease spot on my new dress. I can't be seen in public like this! I've got to go back to the hotel and change." She smiled up at Linc and brushed his cheek lightly with the tips of her fingers. "That Bean's cola fellow said there's goin' to be a big party Friday night before the race. If you're especially nice to me, Linc, I'll save one of my dances for you."

He smiled back at her. "I would be honored, Miss Farrell."

"Melodie. You promised you would call me Melodie."

He smiled again. "Melodie."

She laughed and backed up two steps, flashing Linc a final smile. Then she walked away, winding her way through the airplanes, toolboxes, and packs of equipment that filled the tent and leaving a wake of gaping men behind her.

Pete watched her disappear behind the wing of an Avro monoplane. "Forget about her Linc," he said. "La-di-da gals like her are all foam and no hops. What you want to do is get yourself hitched up with a gal like that Cassie Jones. Now Cassie's got more gumption in her little finger—"

Linc was wiping his hands with a rag. He flung his head up angrily. "Who asked you?"

Pete shrugged. "Patches don't like your la-di-da miss neither."

"Yeah? Well, I'm perfectly capable of choosing my own women. I don't need you and Patches doing any goddamned matchmaking. And I *especially* don't need you matching me up with Cassie Jones. She's trouble, and the last thing I need in my life right now is trouble!"

Chapter 5

~~~∽∽∽~~~

The sharp crack of an explosion ripped through the tent. Someone started screaming in terror as flickering shadows danced on the canvas walls, backlit by the flames outside. There was the pop and crackle of several smaller explosions, and the nauseating odor of burning castor oil filled the air.

Cassie leaped from her cot, instantly awake. Because she had been sleeping in her overalls, she was one of the first outside. Fifty yards from the tent an airplane was being consumed by fire, its silhouette blazing against the night sky like the mythical phoenix. Except that unlike the phoenix, this bird would never rise again from its ashes.

Linc Cameron stood before it, his head flung back, his hands clenched into fists at his sides. He was barefoot and wore only his pants. From the look on his face, Cassie knew it was the *Betsy* that was burning.

She watched alone with him, mesmerized by the horror of it. Then the others stumbled out of the tent, shouting questions and crying in alarm.

Linc turned slightly, and his eyes flickered briefly in her direction. The fire flared up brightly for a moment, shimmering in his dark pupils. Impulsively, Cassie

70

went to him, drawn by the unbearable sadness in those deep blue eyes.

"Linc," she began, but before she could say anything more, Pete Striker appeared from out of the darkness, swaying toward them unsteadily, dragging his wooden leg. Black scorch marks covered his face, and his hair and eyebrows were singed.

He stumbled over a clump of grass, and Linc flung out an arm to steady him. "Jesus, Pete! What happened?"

Pete wiped his mouth with the back of his hand. In the half-light cast by the dying flames, Cassie could see that his hand was shaking. He looked at Cassie for a moment, then his eyes settled on Linc's face.

"I got to thinking—" A pall of smoke from the burning plane drifted over them, making him choke. He sucked in a deep breath. "You know how I have trouble sleeping sometimes, Linc? When the pain in my leg gets real bad? Well, I got to thinking the valves and piston rings could use a good cleaning 'cause they've been sticking a bit. So I rolled her out here where I could work without bothering anybody, and I went back to the tent to get a lantern and some tools..."

Linc gave his arm a rough shake. "I know, I heard you. You woke me up. Pete, for God's sake, what happened?"

Pete's eyes shifted over to the *Betsy*, now a smoldering pile of twisted wreckage. "I was on my way back out to her when she just went up. Just burst apart like some damned...I don't know, Linc. It happened so fast—"

"You were smoking, weren't you?" Linc demanded, anger making his voice harsh. "Christ, Pete! Were you smoking?"

Pete hunched his shoulders and looked at the ground. "I wasn't, Linc. I swear it."

Linc said nothing more. He turned his back on what

was left of the *Betsy* and started to walk away.

Cassie stepped in front of him. "Mr. Cameron ... I'm so sorry."

He stopped and stared down at her, and his eyes narrowed. "Why should you be sorry? Now there's one less plane between you and fifty thousand dollars."

"It won't be the same! I wanted to beat you fair and square, not like this."

Cassie saw his chest rise and fall as he took a deep breath. The heat from the burning plane had coated his skin with a sheen of sweat, outlining broad, firm muscles that tapered to his slim waist and hips. A line of soft dark hair on his flat stomach seemed to point seductively downward, to the top buttons of his whipcord pants.

Cassie's head jerked up, and she met his eyes. The anger had left them, replaced by something else. Something that sucked the breath from her lungs and brought the blood rushing hotly to her face.

But then he turned back for one last look at the burning *Betsy*, and she saw his jaw clench.

"Oh, Linc ..." she said, aching for him. "This doesn't mean ... you could always get another plane."

His head whipped around. "With what? It took every cent I had just to get myself and that damned crate out here. Oh hell! Why are you looking at me like that? What do you care if—"

"Miss Jones!" A man ran up to them, his long shirttail flapping around his thin, bare legs. It was Gregory Pearce, Edward's copilot.

"Miss Jones, it's your uncle. I found him collapsed on the floor. He must have tried to get out of bed after the explosion and passed out. One of the other fellows has gone to telephone for a doctor." He looked at Linc. "And to get the police. I don't know ... we thought we should. Was it an accident?"

Linc ignored the question. "Wait, Cassie, I'll go with

you," he said, but she had already spun away from him, running for the tent.

Someone had picked Quigly up and laid him back on his cot. His face was pale and damp with sweat. He kept tossing his head from side to side. When Cassie knelt beside the cot and picked up his hand, his eyes flickered open, only to stare at her blankly before drifting closed again.

In the distance she heard the whoop of a siren. A hand touched her shoulder. "Cassie..." Linc said. "I'll ride with you to the hospital."

Quigly moaned loudly, and terror closed up Cassie's throat so that she could barely speak. "No...by myself. I'll go with him by myself."

"But you'll need—"

"No! I don't want you! Just leave me alone!"

His hand left her shoulder and she turned around, wanting to take back what she had said, but just then a pair of men carrying a stretcher pushed through the crowd.

Cassie rode with Quigly in an ambulance to the hospital. She felt so lonely and afraid. She wished she could have taken back the nasty words she had flung at Linc, but it was all too late. More than anything, Cassie realized, she wanted Linc Cameron to like her, but instead, everything she had done had been calculated to make him hate her. And now none of it mattered because Quigly was so sick. He might be dying, and he was all she had in the world—all she had.

She clasped Quigly's hand, squeezing it tightly. Oh, Quigly, don't die. Everything is all messed up. Help me, and please, *please*, don't die!

At the hospital they hurriedly wheeled Quigly behind a pair of swinging doors, making Cassie wait outside in a hallway that reeked of disinfectant. A few other people waited in the hall as well, sitting on wooden chairs that leaned against the wall. They nei-

ther spoke nor looked at Cassie. The hall was ominously quiet, but Cassie could hear noises from behind
the swinging doors—the clank of bottles on a tray, the
staccato murmur of a voice issuing instructions. It was
the first time she had ever been inside a hospital, and
she made a fervent vow never to enter one again if she
could help it.

After what seemed like hours, a doctor in a white
smock emerged from behind the swinging doors and
walked briskly up to her. The man had kind but tired
eyes.

"Are you the young lady who brought in Mr.
Jones?"

Cassie nodded, unable to speak.

"Your father?"

Cassie cleared her throat. "Uncle. My uncle."

"He has influenza, I'm afraid. Complicated by pneumonia. We're doing all we can, but..." He paused,
searching Cassie's face. "I don't like the sound of his
heart. Normally visitors aren't allowed in the wards at
night, but I'll tell Sister you may sit with him."

The ward they had put Quigly in was crowded with
beds. A nun in a stiff white uniform moved toward
Cassie on silent feet. She helped her place a chair beside Quigly's bed, then held her finger up to her lips in
a stern warning.

Cassie gazed down at her uncle's face. He seemed to
be resting peacefully. Except for his pallor, he hardly
looked sick. But a rubber tube had been inserted into
his nose, and the tube led to a metal canister that
hissed in time to the rise and fall of his breathing. Cassie would have liked to hold one of his hands, but they
were tucked tightly beneath the sheets.

Don't die, she cried out to him silently, over and
over. Don't die. She felt so alone, so terribly alone.

Once, toward dawn, Quigly opened his eyes and focused on her. "I never got to have that beer with your Linc Cameron," he said distinctly.

It was the only thing he said before he died.

Cassie sat on the rocks, watching the foamy tide curl up on the beach to deposit clumps of stringy seaweed and bits of shell before rolling back into the ocean. For some time now she had been aware of the man and dog walking toward her on the wet sand, but she would not look at them. Still, she thought, he must have had a hard time finding her, and the fact that he had gone to such trouble was oddly touching.

The dog reached her first, pushing his muzzle against her clenched hands. She rubbed the dog's ears but still wouldn't look at the man.

He stopped in front of her, thrusting his hands into the pockets of his leather jacket. "I heard about your uncle. I'm sorry."

Cassie watched Patches chase a sea gull into the surf. She tried to speak, to thank him for his sympathy, but she couldn't get the words out. She swallowed instead around the huge lump that had been stuck in her throat since Quigly died.

Linc dropped down beside her on the rocks. He leaned over, resting his elbows on his thighs. He exuded an air of solid, rugged strength, and she was filled with a sudden, fierce yearning to be held tightly against his broad chest and comforted by his hard arms.

"He was a great pilot," Linc said.

Cassie stiffened. "How do you know? You never saw him at his best."

"He had to have been good—he taught you."

A sob tore out of Cassie's throat, and she hunched over her bent knees. Linc gathered her in his arms, holding her tightly. She crushed her face against the smooth leather of his jacket as the tears poured from her uncontrollably.

He held her long after she ceased crying. Then she suddenly became aware of where she was, of what she was doing, and she pulled away from him. Linc released her gently and reached into the pocket of his pants for a handkerchief, handing it to her.

Cassie took it and looked up, giving him a trembling smile. "I've gotten tears all over your jacket."

He leaned over and gently brushed her tear-stained cheek with his knuckles. "It's been wet before. Tell me about your uncle. How did you two get involved with flying?"

Cassie shook her head, certain she couldn't talk about Quigly, but instead the words came tumbling out of her mouth. She told him about going to live with Quigly after her mother died. She had never been able to bring herself to speak to anyone—even her uncle—about Lawrence Kingly and the horror of her mother's marriage, and she glossed over that part now. Instead, she told Linc about the first time Quigly had taken her up in the flying machine he'd built himself, how she had sat in front of him in the cockpit, resting her small hands on his larger, experienced ones, for the first time in her life feeling a measure of peace and happiness.

"I wanted to stay up there forever," she said, laughing at the memory. And though the grief still tore at her heart, being able to remember and to laugh eased the pain somewhat. "Quigly practically had to pry me out of the plane with a crowbar after we landed," she finished, smiling.

Linc gave her an answering smile. "The first time I went up, I sorta stole the plane."

"You're making that up."

He smiled again, shaking his head. "I was in Hammondsport, New York, sort of passing through, and I came upon this plane just sitting by itself in a field with no one around. I decided to try her out."

"You went up for the first time all by yourself without anybody showing you how? I don't believe it!"

"Hell, I was only seventeen. At that age you think you can do anything. Although I do have to admit my landing technique left a lot to be desired. The guy who owned the plane, Glenn Curtiss—"

"*The* Glenn Curtiss? The Glenn Curtiss who manufactures airplanes?"

"The one and only. Anyway, he was waiting for me on the ground. After he got done chewing me out and threatening to have me arrested, he told me I had natural talent and hired me on the spot to fly exhibitions for him. He forgot to mention that the life expectancy of an exhibition flyer was about a month, tops. Or that most people wouldn't come out to watch us fly, but to watch us die. I almost got lynched once by a pack of skeptics because I refused to go up in a thunderstorm. They thought I was a fake, that it was impossible to fly a machine heavier than air."

Cassie nodded knowingly and smiled. "Even so, you could make good money flying exhibitions before the war."

Linc shrugged. "Sure. If you lived."

"I tried to get a job flying with the Curtiss Exhibition Company just last year. I figured they'd be short of pilots because of the war. But he laughed at me and told me to go home and take up knitting."

Linc laughed.

"Not you too. You men are all alike."

He picked up her hand, stroking the back of it with his thumb. "I'm sorry. I was only laughing at the idea of you knitting."

Cassie thought about it for a moment and then decided to forgive him. "Perhaps I'm unusually sensitive about the subject," she said, and Linc's lips twitched. "It's just that I've encountered nothing but obstacles since the first day I climbed into the cockpit. I had to fly ten perfect figure eights just to get my license!"

The injustice of this still rankled Cassie. Normally a pilot only had to fly two figure eights around a pair of pylons in order to earn a license. Suddenly she remembered how Quigly had stood beside her that day, insisting to the men administering the test that her sex had nothing to do with her ability to fly. Not only had he championed her before the world, he had instilled within her a belief in herself, a belief that she could accomplish anything if she set her mind to it.

But now he was gone, and somehow he had taken away a part of that belief in herself, that confidence, leaving her bereft and afraid.

Linc seemed to sense some of what she was thinking. His arm went around her waist, and he pressed her head back against his chest. "Your uncle must have been very proud of you."

Cassie swallowed hard. "We . . . Quigly and I . . . we were going to use the prize money to finance the production of the engine he's invented. I suppose I could still produce the engine for him, because I have the design patents. But I'll never get the financing, because no bank will lend me money. I won't be able to compete in the race now either. Of the handful of women pilots, no one else is interested. And no man will want to fly with me."

"I don't think Quigly would want you just to give up."

She pulled away from him. "You're a fine one to talk about giving up, Linc Cameron. What did you do last night after the *Betsy* blew up?"

"That's diff—"

"What's different about it? If you can quit, then so can I!"

He glared at her a moment, then let out an exasperated breath. "All right then, goddamn you, I'll fly with you!" He laughed at her stunned, suspicious look. "Why not? You need a pilot, and I need a plane. I am a pilot, and you have a plane. We can pool our resources."

"What do you get out of it?"

"Half of fifty thousand dollars. If we win."

Cassie studied his handsome face. He was trying to look guileless, but there was a glint of devilment in his eyes. "You're not after anything else?"

"Isn't twenty-five thousand dollars enough?"

"I don't know . . . I don't trust you. And if I decide to do it, the split will be sixty-forty."

"Now wait just a damned minute. It's fifty-fifty or the deal's off."

"It's my plane."

"Which isn't going anywhere without a copilot."

She glared at him, and he glared back. He really was the most infuriating man. . . .

"You win, damn you," she said. "I'll fly with you. But only because Quigly would have wanted me to."

"Fifty-fifty," Linc insisted stubbornly.

She scowled at him, but she nodded in agreement.

"Then it's a deal." He held out his hand, and she took it.

"Wait," she said, and this time the devil was in her eye. "We have to do this right, or it isn't any good."

She took her hand back and spat on her palm. Linc laughed and spat on his palm, then they pressed their hands together. "It's a deal," Cassie said, and they shared a slow smile.

Two days later, Cassie received a summons from the Bean's Cola Transcontinental Airplane Race Committee. It had been typed on stiff white paper and embossed with a seal. It looked terribly official and intimidating, as she supposed it was meant to.

Cassie put on her best outfit, a suit made of blue serge that was only a little over a year old. It had a narrow, pleated skirt and a plainly tailored jacket that dropped down low over her slim hips. The jacket had

military-style cuffs and collar, trimmed with black braid
and a matching black belt that cinched her small waist.
She pinned up her hair and covered it with her straw
hat with the yellow ribbon, then went looking for Linc.

She found him bent over a table made of discarded
packing cases, poring over an atlas. The race committee
had just that morning released the official list of the five
checkpoints that would mark the end of each leg of the
race, although the newspapers had already published
the same list weeks ago. Linc was obviously doing
some preliminary plotting of their course. Pete Striker,
who had agreed to join their team as the advance man,
was giving Linc his advice and jabbing at the map with
a nicotine-stained finger.

Cassie had been with Linc when he told Pete Striker
about the new flying arrangements. She had been worried at first that the older man would be angry or hurt,
but instead he seemed relieved.

"Suits me fine," he had said. "The damned leg's
been giving me hell lately, and I wasn't looking forward
to all them hours cramped up in a cockpit." Then he
nudged Linc in the ribs with his elbow. "You sly old son
of a gun."

"It isn't what you're thinking," Linc said, glaring at
him.

"Oh sure," Pete had answered, winking broadly.

Since then, Cassie had often caught Pete staring at
her with a funny look of proprietary fondness on his
face.

Patches announced Cassie's arrival by barking happily and padding over for a pet. Linc looked up and
saw her, and his face softened into a smile.

"You look nice."

"She sure does," Pete Striker said, and then chuckled.

Linc pressed his lips together and frowned at Pete,
then he glanced back at Cassie. "What's the matter?" he
asked, seeing the expression on her face.

She handed him the race committee's summons. Linc read it over carefully.

"They aren't going to let me race," she said.

"You don't know that."

"They're going to say it's too dangerous for a woman. Or that it's improper, or unladylike. Or someone's just passed a law that says women aren't allowed to fly in transcontinental races unless they have permission from the president of the United States and are absolved by the pope."

Linc laughed and laid his hand on her shoulder, squeezing it lightly. In spite of her preoccupation with the race, a part of Cassie couldn't help responding even to this casual touch. She had been feeling so miserably lonely and unhappy since Quigly's death that if anyone so much as gave her a sympathetic glance, she felt like bursting into tears. And both Linc and Pete had been kind to her, respecting her need to grieve alone, yet seeming to sense when she was ready for company.

Yet it was also true that Linc seemed to have erected some sort of invisible barrier between them. There certainly had not been a repeat of those passionate kisses they had shared in Virginia, and except when he forgot, like just now, he was careful not to touch her. Cassie told herself this was exactly the way she wanted things to be between them—friendly but strictly professional.

"I'll go with you to see them," Linc was saying. "They can't stop you from competing. You're my co-pilot—I need you."

She wanted to tell him she could fight her own battles, but in this case she knew it wasn't true. Bean's cola had invited Linc to compete in the race because he was a famous ace, and his participation gave the event prestige. Already his name was being connected with their product: boys across the country who wanted to be airmen like Linc Cameron were consuming gallons of Bean's cola. If Linc insisted that he fly with Cassie Jones or not at all, they would have to relent. If he did not insist, they could disqualify her, and there wouldn't be a thing she could do about it.

The race committee members had set up their headquarters in Santa Monica's elegant old hotel, ensconcing themselves in a ground-floor parlor with French windows that opened onto a veranda facing the ocean. They sat, five in all, behind a long table. Above their heads a ceiling fan whirled lazily, ruffling the papers before them. The entire scene reminded Cassie of a photograph she had once seen of a deserter facing a court-martial. The image didn't do much for her frayed nerves.

One of the men pointed to a chair that faced the table and asked her to be seated. He introduced himself as Phineas Barlow, Leroy Bean's secretary. He didn't act surprised to see Linc with her, although he had not provided Linc with a chair.

Leroy Irving Bean wasn't present, but then, Cassie had not expected him to be. A onetime chemist from Dayton, Ohio, Bean had gained a large fortune and some fame through the invention of a soda-fountain drink with a unique cinnamon flavor. With his money he had indulged his passion for speed and machines, collecting first automobiles and later airplanes. But although he had sponsored several airplane and automobile exhibitions and races, he had never tried to drive or fly any of his acquisitions; he had never even ridden in one. On the rare occasions when he chose to leave the mansion where he lived in palatial seclusion, he did so by horse and carriage. Whenever he had to deal with the outside world, he sent Phineas Barlow as his personal emissary.

In his late forties, Barlow was an imposing man with a full head of hair the color of iron filings. It was combed straight back from his forehead, displaying a prominent widow's peak. The widow's peak pointed like an arrowhead to a long, hooked nose, giving him the look of a ferocious eagle. He glared down at Cassie now, as if daring her to contradict what he was about to say.

"You are too small and too young to pilot an airplane," he said, and the other men nodded their heads in unison.

"I've been flying since I was fourteen. I have yet to have a serious accident."

"What's more," he went on, as if she hadn't spoken, "it's a proven fact that women are temperamentally unsuited to flying. They—"

Cassie leaped to her feet. "How do you know what sort of temperament I have? Who are you to—"

Linc grasped Cassie's shoulder and pressed her back into the chair, and the committee members exchanged looks as if to say she had just proved Barlow's point.

"Is there some sort of problem with my copilot's qualifications, gentlemen?" Linc inquired politely. "She has a license, and she has participated and competed in at least one other officially sponsored event. Those were, I believe—other than filing the entry fee—the only stipulations. . . . "

Cassie gave the men the full blast of her fiercest glare. "It's because I'm a woman—" she began, but Linc squeezed her shoulder in warning, so she glared at him as well.

"I can understand your concern, gentlemen," Linc said evenly. "Flying is dangerous under the best of circumstances. Which of us hasn't lifted the mangled body of a friend from a wrecked machine brought about by a single mechanical failure, a second of lapsed judgment?" Linc paused, and the men all nodded their heads in solemn agreement. "Nevertheless, I assure you I have satisfied myself as to Miss Jones's competence, as well as the safety of her aircraft." He smiled slowly. "It is, after all, my neck that's at risk here."

Cassie ground her teeth and rolled her eyes at the ceiling. His arrogance was beyond belief! He acted as if the risks were all his for taking on a female copilot. No one seemed to care that *she* was setting off on a four-thousand-mile flight with a man who flew as if he were tired of living.

The committee members conferred among themselves for a moment. Then Barlow leaned back in his chair, lacing his hands over his small rounded paunch.

"We sympathize with the loss of your own airplane, Mr. Cameron. And we understand how you might feel constrained to accept the offer of Miss Jones's services. However, as you are no doubt aware, Mr. Bean has a number of flying machines, and I can assure you that he would be happy to loan you any one you'd desire. You see, it is not simply a matter of the weaknesses inherent in the female sex—"

Cassie sprang out of her chair, so furious that she was sputtering incoherently. Linc shoved her back down again, and Barlow gave him a commiserating look.

"It's a question of propriety," Barlow continued. "You and Miss Jones have no legal, uh ... relationship, and yet you would be spending hours alone in each other's company. ... "

Cassie threw off Linc's hand and stood up. "Your implication is absolutely ridiculous! What do you think we could possibly *do* in separate cockpits, five thousand feet in the air?"

Barlow ignored her, continuing to address his remarks to Linc, who regarded the other man with a polite, almost sympathetic expression on his face. Cassie began to wonder whose side Linc was on. She might have known he'd desert her when things got difficult!

"There might even be an occasion, a breakdown for instance," Barlow was saying, "when you would have to spend a night alone together, away from the amenities of civilization. This race—a race crossing an entire continent—is the first of its kind in history. The whole world will be watching. I—that is to say, we—cannot afford to have any suggestion of impropriety, of immorality, associated with Bean's co—er, with the race."

Linc gave the man his most charming smile, which, as Cassie had reason to know, could be charming indeed. "I can understand your concern, gentlemen, but didn't you know? Miss Jones and I are getting married this Friday."

Cassie's mouth fell open. She was so shocked she could only get a tiny squeak out her throat, a squeak that turned into a yelp of pain when Linc stepped on her foot, hard, with his heavy boot. The brute probably would have done real damage if she hadn't been wearing her sturdy high-button shoes.

Then he actually had the nerve to take her hand and smile at her sweetly. "I'm sorry, my darling. I know you wanted to keep the ceremony strictly private, and I'm sure Mr. Barlow would understand your reasons. . . . " He turned and addressed the committee, a sad expression on his face. "She's in mourning for her uncle, you see. He was buried only yesterday."

"Damn you, Linc Cameron, if you think I'm going to let you—Ow! You're *mangling* my hand!" she whispered harshly.

"Do you want to race or not?" Linc hissed back under his breath.

Cassie's mouth clamped shut. She looked at the stubborn, doubtful faces of the committee members. It was obvious they didn't want to let her compete in the race, and they would seize any excuse to disqualify her. She found herself listening in a daze while Linc assured the men that their fears were groundless. That yes, he and Miss Jones were really getting married. That his future wife was an excellent pilot, and he had the utmost confidence in her abilities and the safety of her aircraft.

The next thing she knew, Linc had ushered her from the room. She was standing in the middle of the hotel lobby, looking at the impassive expression on his face, and she still couldn't believe any of it had happened.

"Are you crazy?" she exclaimed when at last she found her voice. "What are we going to do when Friday comes and goes and we aren't married? My God, you actually invited them to the wedding!"

"There won't be any need to do anything, because by Friday evening we'll be legally joined in holy wedlock."

Cassie stared at him. "You are crazy."

"Think about it a minute, for God's sake. There's no reason to get hysterical over the idea. It'll only be for appearance's sake, just for a few weeks, until we win the damned race and split the dough. Once the race is over, we can be legally unjoined."

"You are *crazy!* I have no intention of ever getting married. Not for a few weeks, not for a few minutes. And if I did, the last person I would marry would be you!"

He actually had the gall to look surprised. "Why not?"

"Why not? Why not!" she shouted, oblivious to the looks they were attracting from the other people in the lobby. "You are the most arrogant, infuriating . . . I don't even *like* you."

Linc gave her a cocky grin. "Liar. You not only like me, you're halfway in love with me."

"Why of all the monumental conceit!" She looked around for something to heave at his head, noticed the stares, and lowered her voice to a growl. "We are not getting married on Friday. We are never getting married, and you can just march yourself back in there and tell your fellow mighty males the truth!"

Linc's head snapped back, and the muscles tightened along his jaw. "You are the most ungrateful wretch it has ever been my misfortune to meet. You heard them in there. All I have to do is snap my fingers, and Pete and I would have a plane. I don't need you or the *Pegasus* to compete in this race, but whether you like it or want to admit it, you do need me. I only wanted—obviously during a moment of sheer insanity—to do you a favor."

As much as she hated to admit it, especially to him, Cassie was beginning to see his point. "I suppose we could go through some sort of ceremony," she conceded, "since that's the only way they'll ever allow us to race together. . . . "

Linc, however, was no longer in a conciliatory mood. "I'll have you know that under normal circumstances I wouldn't consider marrying you on a bad bet. You're not exactly my idea of the perfect wife. Christ, going through life hand in hand with you would be like doing a high-wire act with no safety net."

"Oh, really? And just what is your idea of the perfect wife? Some prissy-faced thing like Melodie Farrell who worships the ground you walk on?"

"I don't need to be worshiped, Cassie. Although some simple appreciation is nice now and then. What I want in a wife is quiet support and serenity—decorum."

"Decorum!" Cassie let out a mocking laugh. "She sounds boring to me."

"I *want* boring."

She gave him a sudden, impish smile. "That's too bad, Linc Cameron, because what you're going to get is this . . ." Cassie clasped the back of his neck with her hands and pulled his head down to meet her open mouth.

She felt his shock in the shudder that racked his body. Then he was kissing her back, pressing his lips hard against hers, grinding them against her teeth, and the passion she had stirred in him ignited her own. Her mouth opened beneath his as she kissed him with a fierce and surprising hunger.

Releasing him, she backed up a step. Then, without another word, she turned and walked away. He stared after her in stunned silence, the lingering trace of her kiss like a burning brand on his mouth. Not until the door to the hotel had closed softly behind her did he realize that at some point during that kiss he must have stopped breathing altogether.

He set off after her and tripped over a pair of suitcases that some idiot had left in the middle of the floor. He heard smothered titters as he picked himself off his hands and knees, feeling like a fool. Then he laughed and shook his head.

Kissing like that in public... they were lucky they hadn't been arrested.

Chapter 6

Cassie pulled the stopper out of the perfume bottle and held it up to her nose. She dabbed a little of the oily liquid behind her ears, then added a little more for good measure. The evocative scent, a subtle mixture of spices and orange blossom, brought tears to her eyes.

The perfume had been a present from Quigly, given to her last month on her twentieth birthday. It was so unlike her uncle, this frivolous and expensive gift, that she had puzzled over it for days, wondering if it was a hint that she should try to act more like a lady.

Finally she had asked him about it outright, for she knew she could ask Quigly anything.

He hadn't laughed, although he had given her one of his rare smiles. "Cassie, you don't need to change the way you are," he had said to her. "You are a woman—a beautiful, mature, and intelligent woman." He shrugged and blushed a little. "I don't know why, but somehow the perfume just seemed appropriate."

Now Cassie sighed. It was hardly a mature and intelligent thing to do—marry a man just to compete in an airplane race. She, Cassandra Jones, who had sworn up and down she would never get married. She told herself she was doing it for Quigly, so that she could carry on his dream and manufacture his engine with the prize money. But if that was true, why did she feel so confused and afraid right now, so completely unlike herself?

If only Quigly were here with his gentle and practical guidance. Suddenly the hollow feeling of loneliness that had shrouded her in the days since Quigly's death became so intense that she felt smothered by it.

Cassie started at a knock on the door. The perfume bottle slipped from her hands, shattering as it struck the floor and filling the air with its spicy bouquet. The door burst open, and Melodie Farrell flounced through it wearing a dress embroidered with silver thread and draped with fringed netting.

Melodie paused and looked around the room—the bridal suite—with just the hint of a smirk. "My, this is nice," she said, then she sniffed and wrinkled her nose prettily. "Oh dear, Cassie, I'm afraid you've overdone it on the scent. A little bit does go a long way."

Cassie knelt on the floor beside the shattered perfume bottle, struggling not to burst into tears. Her last gift from Quigly, and now it was gone forever.

She tried to pick up a piece of the jagged glass, only to slice open her palm. Pain seared her hand, and the tears, so near the surface, spilled over.

"Oh no, Cassie!" Melodie exclaimed. "Look what you've done. Be careful, you're bleedin' all over the place."

"There's a first-aid box in my flying kit,'" Cassie said between clenched teeth. "Will you get it for me, please? By the dresser next to the bed."

Melodie fluttered around the room, admiring the plush furnishings, while Cassie bandaged the cut herself. When she had finished tying off the piece of gauze, Cassie stood up and regarded the other girl with exasperation. Her hand throbbed with pain, she was getting married in five minutes to a virtual stranger, and here was Melodie, come to pay a social call.

"Melodie, what are you doing here?"

"What? Oh. I've come to see if you need any help getting dressed."

"I've been dressing myself since I was three."

"Don't be such an ol' sourpuss. One would think you were getting ready to attend a funeral, not your very own wed—oh dear, me and my big mouth. I completely forgot about your poor uncle. Why Cassie, you went out and bought yourself a new dress!"

Melodie walked in a circle around Cassie, making clucking sounds. Against her will, Cassie's eyes slid over to her reflection in the mirror that hung on the wardrobe. Her dress was made of pale peach silk, with a sleeveless overdress and a tasseled sash draped over the fashionably narrow hobble skirt. She wore matching court shoes with silver buckles, and she had fastened her long heavy curls on top of her head, holding them in place with a sequined bandeau and a single pink feather. The whole ensemble made her feel feminine and frivolous—and pretty. She knew it was a contradiction—wanting to look pretty at a ceremony where she would make vows she had no intention of keeping—but she didn't care.

Linc had forbidden her to tell anyone the truth about this farce of a wedding they were being forced to enact. He was right, as usual, but she really hated for anyone, especially Melodie, to think she was the least bit excited about this marriage. "It isn't new," she lied baldly to Melodie. "I've had this for months."

Melodie giggled. "Fibber! I've seen every one of your things a hundred times, and this is new."

Cassie bit her lip and cast an anxious look at the half-open door. "Melodie . . . is he down there yet?"

Melodie pursed her lips and widened her eyes. "Is who down where?"

Cassie started to clench her fists, but then remembered the cut on her hand. She had an overwhelming urge to punch Melodie Farrell right in the nose. "You *know* who."

"Don't be silly, Cassie. A man like Linc Cameron would never desert you at the altar, although there isn't an altar exactly. The hotel staff has set things up quite nicely in their front parlor, with vases of flowers and musicians and tables full of food. Really, everything is *so* romantic. . . . "

Melodie sighed softly and looked over at the bed. Cassie did the same, and she felt herself blushing.

"I don't mind telling you, I'm more than the teensiest bit jealous of you, Cassie Jones," Melodie said. "I've been longin' for a husband for simply ages now, and you always swore you never wanted to get married. Here you've gone and caught yourself just about the handsomest man I've ever seen, and tonight you're goin' to have him all to yourself in this great big bed!" She looked at Cassie speculatively. "Haven't you ever wondered how Linc Cameron makes love? I'll bet he's just divine." Then she giggled. "Or do you already know?"

Cassie's blush deepened. "I haven't . . . we aren't going to . . . oh, never mind! Let's just go down and get it over with."

But Melodie's question followed her out the room, and the answer leaped unbidden to her mind. For if Linc Cameron's kisses were any indication, she knew exactly how he would make love—the same way he flew an airplane—dangerously, impulsively, with skill and reckless abandon. And she knew something else as well. She might not want the marriage, but she wanted the marriage bed. She wanted it with the same hunger that took her up in the sky in a fragile machine made of sticks and fabric. Up in the sky again and again, in spite of the cost and the risk, and the fear.

Linc Cameron grimaced and ran a finger beneath his stiff collar. So many people crammed into one room had raised the temperature ten degrees. At least, he thought grimly, there would be no lack of witnesses for the ceremony. Every entrant in the race, and a good part of the town of Santa Monica, appeared to be on hand to watch him take a wife.

Linc had to admit Bean's cola certainly knew how to throw a party. If he hadn't in a moment of absolute insanity talked his way into getting married tonight, he might have been able to enjoy it. At one end of the long, narrow ballroom, a small orchestra played a spirited ragtime that had everyone tapping their feet. The women were all draped in spangles and sequins, and they shimmered in the soft light of the two large crystal chandeliers. The men, in their black cutaways, were more somber in appearance, but their laughter was just as loud and carefree.

There was a tinsel-bright gaiety to the crowd that had gathered to celebrate that night. Of course, it was the night before the race, and everyone, especially the contestants, was excited and maybe just a little nervous too. The hotel staff had set out tables of hors d'oeuvres —finger sandwiches and iced cakes—and tubs of champagne. But the corks wouldn't be popped until after the short marriage ceremony. Linc spotted several of the men drifting out the French doors and taking swigs from silver flasks. He didn't blame them. He longed for a drink himself. *I certainly deserve it more than the others*, he thought grumpily. *They* aren't getting married.

"Nervous, old man?" Edward Farrell said in his ear.

Linc scowled at him. "Where is she, for the love of God? This damned thing was supposed to start five minutes ago."

Edward straightened Linc's gray silk ascot, then brushed an imaginary spot of dust off the lapel of his cutaway. "Never has the course of true love been so bumpy. The way you two are acting, one would think you were being forced into this marriage at the end of a shot—" Sudden enlightenment filled Edward's face.

"God, no," Linc said, repressing a shudder. "You're wrong there."

"If I'm wrong it's only because Cassie's been playing hard to get—which wouldn't surprise me. Or that you're losing your touch—which would surprise me. I remember you showing up for a dawn patrol once, still in evening dress, a girl dangling from each arm."

"This is different . . ." Linc began, then he stopped as Cassie entered the room. He stood perfectly still, as if someone had just punched all the air out of his lungs.

"This is love," Edward said to himself.

Linc stepped forward and took Cassie's hand as she came up to him. He smiled to himself at the sight of the thick gauze wrapped around her palm. Lowering his head, he spoke softly, his breath caressing her cheek. "If you were trying to slash your wrist, you missed."

Cassie started to giggle, then she stopped abruptly when she realized that the entire room had gone silent, and everyone had turned to look at her. The blood rushed to her face, and her knees began to shake.

"Damn you, Linc Cameron. You said a quiet, simple ceremony. There must be two hundred people here!"

"I had nothing to do with it. This race is generating a lot of newspaper interest. Besides, as another famous lover once put it: 'Folly loves the martyrdom of fame.'"

"Who said that?"

"Lord Byron."

Cassie smiled in spite of herself. "You've read Lord Byron? You don't seem the type . . . oh, Linc, how are we ever going to get *un*married after all this?"

"Quietly, in a simple ceremony," he said, and she laughed.

He smiled down at her and, drawing her arm through his, began to lead her toward the front of the room, where a judge in solemn black robes stood talking with Phineas Barlow beneath a small latticed arch entwined with pink roses and ribbons. "Come on, my lovely and most unwilling bride," he teased. "Just grit your teeth and think of fifty thousand dollars."

In the end it wasn't nearly as difficult as Cassie had imagined it would be. She was even able to get her "I dos" out without choking over them. The one surprise came when Linc produced a ring to put on her finger. Somehow she had not expected that, and the sight of it—a heavy, plain gold band—made their vows seem suddenly serious and binding. But by then it was too late—the judge had pronounced them man and wife, and Linc was kissing her, his lips moving hard and warm over hers.

The band began to play a waltz. People crowded around them, separating them, and Cassie found herself face to face with Edward Farrell, who was looking slender and handsome in his elegant evening dress.

"You have an odd definition of 'never,'" he said, although his thin aristocratic face was expressionless. Even his whiskey-colored eyes were flat and blank.

A waiter walked by with a tray of fluted glasses brimming with an effervescent golden liquid. Cassie took one, assuming that it was champagne, which she had never tasted before.

She looked into Edward's eyes and smiled. "Please don't be angry, Ward. It isn't what you think."

"You didn't just marry Linc Cameron?"

"Yes, but—"

"Then it's what I think."

Cassie put the glass to her lips. The drink was fizzing, and it tickled her nose. She took a large swallow and almost choked at the sharp, tart taste. Tentatively, she took another swallow; it went down only a little easier. The band had abandoned the waltz for the more modern fox-trot, and people were dancing in a dizzying blur around them. Cassie blinked and looked at Edward, trying to remember what they had been talking about.

"Oh," she said.

Edward shrugged elegantly. "At least I can console myself with the thought that the better man won, and anyway, I'm used to it. Linc Cameron has always been somewhat daunting competition. He was the best we had in the Lafayette."

Cassie drank some more of the champagne, smaller sips this time. There was something strange about this drink, she thought. Quigly would share a bottle of beer with her from time to time, but it was nothing like this. This was making her feel tingly all over.

"I imagine Linc certainly thought he was the best." Then, because that sounded oddly disloyal, she added, "Well, he is good. I've seen him."

"You've seen the way he can fly stunts, but when it came to fighting, to 'dogfights,' as we called them, he scorned aerobatics. He would go on the prowl for enemy planes, and when he found one he would fly straight at it, almost to the point of collision, before opening fire. It was positively unnerving to watch." He laughed suddenly. "It was even more unnerving for the enemy. Killing people, narrowly missing getting killed himself—it takes nerves of iron to go up and do that again and again, day after day. It got to most of us after a while, but not Linc. He fought like beating death was just a game."

Cassie thought of the sadness she had often caught in Linc Cameron's eyes. "Maybe he was just better at hiding it than you—"

"Hot damn!" Pete Striker seized Cassie from behind and twirled her around, spilling the little that was left of her champagne and giving her a loud buss on the cheek. "I don't care what kind of nonsense Linc's been spouting about you being trouble, I knew you were the girl for him the moment I first clapped eyes on you." His eyes narrowed now as he watched Edward's retreating back. "What's Farrell been telling you?"

"Nothing. We were just talking about the war." She plucked another glass of champagne off the tray of a passing waiter. "What did you mean, you knew I was the girl for Linc? And what was that nonsense about trouble?"

Pete's eyes shifted evasively, and he busied himself with lighting a cigarette. Even Pete, Cassie noticed with a smile, had dressed up in a jaunty brown suit for the occasion.

"Nice wedding," he said. "Lotsa booze and grub. Must be costing a bundle. I thought Linc was broke."

"Bean's cola is springing for it all. They've even given us the bridal suite. It's got its very own bathroom, Pete, with this huge white porcelain tub." Cassie's laugh ended with a hiccup. "'Scuse me," she said, covering her mouth with her hand. "Where's Patches?"

"Back at the hangar with the *Pegasus*. Linc wouldn't let him come. Patches was mad at first, but he settled down after I explained how you and Linc were getting hitched. He approves of you. It's those la-di-da misses he don't like."

Cassie nodded seriously, as if this made perfect sense. She traded her empty champagne glass for a full one.

"Say," Pete said, suddenly worried, "you're gonna take Patches along on the race, aren't you? He went with Linc on every one of his missions. He's Linc's good-luck charm. If you left him behind Linc might take it into his head to . . . well, it'd be bad luck is all."

"If Patches doesn't go, I don't go," Cassie stated emphatically, and punctuated it with another hiccup.

Pete relaxed visibly. Then his eyes narrowed again, and he swore.

Cassie followed the direction of his gaze. Linc was leaning against the far wall talking to two tall, affable young men whom Cassie recognized as the Schmidt brothers. They were blond-haired, blue-eyed giants with square jaws and bulging biceps, and they were competing in the race with an Avro monoplane. After talking to them and checking out the sterling condition of their aircraft, Cassie had mentally marked them down as some of the toughest competition.

"Bloody Boche!" Pete growled.

"They're Americans, Pete. They were born in Dubuque."

"That's what they *say*. But if they're red-blooded American like they claim, then how come they got accents thick enough to choke a dachshund?"

"There was a family from Sweden living in Kingly, and all the kids had these Swedish accents, just like their parents. Probably the Schmidt brothers' family emigrated from Germany, and they grew up speaking German."

"Hah! I can believe they grew up speaking German, and that's about all of their story I do believe. They call themselves Hans and Werner Schmidt. Hell, that ain't no different than claiming to have a name like Smith or, uh . . ."

"Jones," Cassie said, and giggled.

Linc had spotted them. He waved and began to make his way toward them, weaving in and out among the twirling couples. Cassie watched him, thinking how austerely handsome he looked in his formal clothes. He really was incredibly gorgeous, and it just wasn't fair. It gave him a decided advantage in their contest of wills if she got all flustered and trembly just from looking at him. Sighing, Cassie quickly drained her glass of champagne and reached for another.

"Hey, you'd better go easy on that stuff," Pete warned her as Linc walked up.

Linc looked at Cassie's flushed face and shining eyes and laughed. "Are you getting drunk?"

"Of course not! This is only my fourth glass."

The band began to play a tango. Linc took Cassie's glass from her hand and gave it to Pete. "Let's dance," he said, pulling her into his arms.

"I don't know how to dance," she protested, although her feet seemed to be moving quite gracefully as they strutted across the floor to the tango's insistent beat. Cassie was in a wonderful mood. She felt as if she could do anything, risk everything. Linc's hand was at the small of her back, pressing her tightly against him. She could feel his hard body down the entire length of her, and she noticed with detached amusement how her heart quickened and her hand trembled in his.

"Linc, I've been thinking . . ."

"You've been drinking." He laughed softly and nuzzled her neck, sending chills rippling down her back. They did a smooth about-face and strutted in the opposite direction.

"*Thinking*. I've been thinking, that there's no reason why we can't make the best of a bad situation. Although it's silly to think we're in love with each other . . . isn't it?"

"Quite silly." His eyes roamed over her face and down her neck to her breasts. Her skin began to tingle as if he had actually touched her.

"But it's obvious that we are attracted to one another . . . aren't we?"

"Very attracted," he whispered, his lips against her ear.

His hand was caressing her back, burning through the thin silk of her dress. Her chest felt tight, as if she couldn't draw a deep enough breath. "And we're married now," she said, her voice slurred and slightly husky. "Legally, that is."

"For a few weeks, anyway."

"Right. So there's no reason why we shouldn't . . . why we couldn't . . ." Damn him! Was she going to have to be the one to say what they were both obviously feeling?

He leaned his head back and looked down at her. There was a wary, shuttered expression on his face. But Cassie had learned to look at his eyes, and they were dark and glittering, with a strange look that both frightened and fascinated her.

"It might not be that simple," he said, his voice tense. "One of us might get hurt."

She shook her head and stumbled slightly. His arm tightened around her waist, steadying her. "Not if we agree to certain condish-conditions ahead of time. No ties, no promises. And above all, no regrets. After it's over and the race is won, we split the money and go our separate ways."

"You don't know what you're saying. You're too drunk, and besides, I'd bet my last dime you're still a virgin."

"What does that have to do with anything?"

He laughed. "It is a minor . . . obstacle."

"I don't intend to remain a virgin forever, Linc Cameron. An.l you don't need to worry that I won't know what to do," she said as he twirled her around and bent her back over his arm. "I read a book."

"Good Lord." He straightened and stood still for two full beats of the music, until other couples started bumping into them. "What sort of book?"

"I went to the town library and asked to see a marriage manual. They had one hidden in a back room. They wouldn't let me check it out, so I had to read it right there, which meant I was a bit rushed. And that silly woman at the desk made such a big deal out of it, fluttering and blushing and twittering, as if no one had ever gotten married or decided to have sex before. Where did she think *she* came from, for heaven's sake? Anyway, the book was called *A Guide to Marriage,* and it was written by a doctor somebody-or-other in 1891, but things probably haven't changed all that much—what's so funny?"

Linc was laughing so hard that heads turned in their direction. "You are incredible, Cassie. Jesus . . . trust you to try to learn about lovemaking from a book!"

The music ended abruptly but Linc had already

stopped dancing. He cupped her cheeks between his hands and searched her face.

"How drunk are you? Don't answer that—I don't want to know. You're going to regret this. I'm probably going to regret this. But if you're willing to become lovers—Christ, *married* lovers—it would take a nobler man than I to turn you down, because I want you, Cassie Jones. I want you in the worst way. And I am going to teach you things about love you could never learn out of any damned book."

He seized her hand and pulled her toward the open door, where the crowd had started to spill out into the hotel's lobby. It was very noisy, and many were quite drunk. With the new constitutional amendment prohibiting liquor going into effect in a few months, it was as if everyone had decided to drink up all at once in preparation for the long, dry days ahead.

But before they could get free of the crowd, Edward Farrell stepped in front of them, bowing before Cassie. "May I have this next dance?" he asked.

"No," Linc replied for her.

Edward raised a quizzical brow just as Phineas Barlow walked up to Linc, laying a hand on his shoulder. "Mr. Cameron, may I have a word with you?" Barlow said. By the time Barlow was finished and Linc turned back to Cassie, she was gone.

He searched among the swirling dancers, but he couldn't find her. Then he spotted her across the room, talking to a pair of swarthy characters who had entered the race just that morning—Harry Ameston and Jim Morton. They flew an old, dilapidated Wright pusher biplane that looked as if it were held together with spit and string, and neither pilot seemed to know the difference between an aileron and an elevator. Linc had thought them harmless enough on first meeting them, but they didn't seem so harmless now. He didn't like the way Cassie was smiling and laughing up into their dark, handsome faces, and he didn't like the way they were eyeing her low neckline. And he particularly didn't like the way she was guzzling champagne as if it were lemonade. He cursed under his breath and started to push his way toward her, telling himself that he couldn't wring her neck if he wanted to make love to her, and he couldn't make love to her if she passed out before he could get her into bed.

But by the time he had fought his way across the crowded room, she had disappeared again. Linc grimly reminded himself that he shouldn't be surprised—this was exactly what you got when you married trouble.

A party of drunken revelers followed them up the stairs and almost into their room, laughing and shouting remarks that rivaled anything Linc had heard in Paris brothels. He shut the door on the noise and turned to look at Cassie. She stood in the middle of the room, swaying slightly and staring at him with smoky, heavy-lidded eyes.

Then she blinked and pushed back the tendrils of hair that had escaped her sequined headband. "I feel kinda funny."

Linc sighed. "I'm not surprised. You drank enough champagne to fill a bathtub." He went up to her and, turning her around, began unfastening the hooks on her dress.

"What are you doing?"

"I'm putting you to bed. Dawn, and the start of the race—remember the race?—is going to come awfully early tomorrow, and you're going to have one whale of a headache as it is."

He pushed the dress off her shoulders and down to her waist. The bare skin of her back looked temptingly smooth and golden in the soft light of the fire. He pressed his lips to the nape of her neck and then moved them slowly along the slope of her shoulder. But when she sighed and leaned against him, rubbing her firm round bottom against his thighs, he pulled abruptly away from her.

He pushed her dress down over her hips and let it fall in a puddle around her feet. She turned and encircled his neck with her arms, pulling his head down to within inches of her parted lips. "Kiss me," she sighed, and he felt her breath, moist and warm, caress his face.

He clasped her arms, intending to push her away, but his mouth wasn't paying any attention to his head. His mouth pressed down on hers, forcing her lips apart in a fierce, rough kiss that soon became gentle and deep. He slid his tongue over her lips and into her mouth, and although at first she stiffened slightly in surprise, she soon relaxed and met his intimately probing tongue with her own. Groaning, he threaded his fingers through her hair, ripping out the headband so that her heavy curls cascaded over his wrists like a golden waterfall.

His hands moved down her neck and across her shoulders until he found the straps of her camisole and eased them down, tracing the gentle swell of her breasts above the stiff edge of her corset. He marveled at the incredible softness of her skin. Releasing her mouth, his hands encircled her waist, raising her on tiptoe, and he lowered his head, bringing his lips down into the hollow between her breasts. He heard her quick gasp as she dug her fingers into his shoulders and arched against him, and desire flooded him as the blood pumped hot through his veins. His swelling manhood thickened and grew until he was so damn hard for her he hurt.

He told himself to slow down, to be gentle, but he didn't think he was going to be able to manage that. Never had he wanted or needed a woman as much as he wanted and needed Cassie. Scooping her up in his arms, he carried her over to the big canopied bed. She gave a tiny moan of protest as he released her and stood up to undress.

He pulled off his cutaway and vest and flung them across the room, then yanked at the ascot around his neck, sending the pearl stickpin he had borrowed from Ward Farrell rolling onto the floor beneath the bed. He sat down to pull off his shoes and socks, then stood up again to undo the buttons on his trousers. Then he glanced over at his bride and saw her closed eyes, and her steady, even breathing.

He stood beside the bed for several moments, glowering down at her supine form—provocative and alluring even in sleep, drunken sleep at that.

"Damn your eyes, Cassie Jones," he said, bending over and shaking her roughly, although he knew that even a forty-piece orchestra couldn't awaken her now. "I should have known you'd do something like this to me."

Sighing loudly, he sat down beside her and rolled her over onto her side. He pulled her camisole over her head and unlaced her corset, then removed the thin, underlying chemise. He paused to admire her naked breasts for a moment, until he realized he was making a big mistake and hastily averted his eyes. He then took off her shoes and peeled off her silk stockings. Her legs were surprisingly long for her small size, like a colt's, with muscles that were smooth and firm. He ran his palm up her calf to her inner thigh, to the lacy edge of—

Linc bolted to his feet, running a shaking hand through his hair. He was trembling all over, his mouth felt dry, and there was a rushing sound like roaring rapids in his ears. There was also a throbbing ache between his legs that wasn't going to go away any time soon.

Snapping back the bedspread and quilts, he quickly shoved her between the sheets, and then pulled the covers up tightly under her chin.

Weariness suddenly overwhelmed him, but he knew better than to lie next to her in the bed. Instead, he settled down into an easy chair that had been placed before the fire. He tried to get himself under some semblance of control—something that was becoming increasingly difficult to achieve whenever Cassie was near, whether she was awake or asleep, laughing with easy delight, or shouting at him in even easier anger, dressed in her boy's overalls or wearing nothing at all. . . .

Jesus. Linc felt flushed and awkward and about as desperate as a fifteen-year-old suffering the heat of his first passion. It shouldn't be so hard to exercise a little patience. With the zigzagging course they would have to follow to log in at all five checkpoints, they would wind up flying over four thousand miles between here and New York. Even flying from sunup to sundown, they could cover only between three and four hundred miles a day. They would have to stop at night, of course. And there would be other stops, too, for maintenance and refueling. Yes there would be plenty of other opportunities during the coming weeks to make Mrs. Linc Cameron his in fact as well as in name.

A shudder shook him, and he pressed the palms of his hands against his eyes. Cassie . . . his wife. How in God's name had he let this happen? She was too much like Ria. Ria, who scorned marriage and would never settle down to one place, one man. Ria, who would dare anything, risk everything, flaunt all conventions. Ria, who had smothered him with affection one minute, then locked the door in his face the next. Ria the unpredictable, Ria the impulsive, Ria . . .

Linc got up abruptly and went over to the bed. Frowning, he stared down at Cassie, at his wife. At least she didn't look like Ria. In fact, she looked more than ever like a child now, with her hand curled up into a fist beside her cheek, her breath sighing softly between her parted lips, her hair in wild and tangled disarray around her face.

I don't want this, Cassie Jones, he told her silently. I

don't want this because you're difficult and provoking
and aggravating. And you're trouble. You're trouble
spelled with capital letters and emblazoned with lights
and shooting stars. But mostly I don't want this because I'm afraid you're going to make me fall wildly in
love with you, and I don't want to be in love with you,
damn you. So don't go looking at me with those big
gray eyes of yours, wanting to hear me say I love you,
because it won't do any good. You'll never hear me say
those words, Cassie. Never.

He leaned over and took a handful of her hair and
brought it up to his lips before smoothing it out over
the pillow. Then he tenderly kissed her flushed cheek.

"Good night, my darling," he whispered softly, se-
cure in the knowledge that, since she couldn't hear
him, it didn't count.

Chapter 7

The airplanes were lined up in a row, looking new and shiny in their fresh coats of olive-drab dope. The wind ruffled the grass, and the flags fluttered in front of the grandstand. In spite of the early hour, curious spectators swarmed over the dark field. Cassie wondered how the officials would ever manage to clear it in time for the start of the race.

The rising sun was just beginning to glaze the sky a bright ceramic yellow when Phineas Barlow's voice boomed out, carried by a megaphone. "You may start your engines in five minutes, gentlemen. Would everyone else please get off the field. Please get off the field!"

Pete Striker hovered over the *Pegasus*, tightening already tight nuts and testing for the hundredth time the tension of the flying wires. Patches, wearing a silly look of excitement on his face, ran around barking and christening the wheels of the other planes until Linc ordered him up into the cockpit, threatening to leave him behind if he didn't start behaving.

Pete beamed a smile at Cassie as she came up to him. "You look kinda peaked this morning."

"I'm never going to drink champagne again in my life," she said, fighting a bout of nausea and trying unsuccessfully to ignore the pounding in her head.

Linc appeared from around the starboard side of the *Pegasus*. He ran his hand along the propeller blades, checking for nicks and dents.

"Who's piloting the first leg?" Pete asked.

Linc met Cassie's eyes with a warm smile. "America's prettiest aviatrix. After all, it's her plane," he said, and Cassie felt herself flushing with pride and a strange excitement.

She heard someone call her name and turned to see two young men coming toward her, bright smiles on their darkly handsome faces. She remembered meeting them last night at the party, wealthy playboys from somewhere on the East Coast who, as a lark, had entered the race with a borrowed plane at the last minute. They both had dark brown hair, parted down the middle and heavily brilliantined, and they dressed in the most modish of New York fashions. They were also both shameless flirts, but charming and funny, and Cassie had enjoyed their company.

She met the men halfway, giving them a bright smile and struggling to remember their names. Harry and Joe? . . . no, Jim.

"Hello, Cassie," the one called Harry said. He had a pencil-thin dark mustache that gave his smile a jaunty air. "You sure did look pretty last night. That new husband of yours is one lucky son of a gun."

"She looks darn pretty right now, Harry." Jim punched his friend in the arm and winked at Cassie. He was slighter of build than Harry, and was, Cassie remembered from the night before, a terrific dancer.

Cassie laughed at their ridiculous compliments. "Are you two ready for the race?"

"Ready as we'll ever be." Harry grinned and pulled a whiskey flask out his coat pocket. "We've remembered to pack the essentials."

"Warm up your engines!" Phineas Barlow shouted over the megaphone.

Cassie heard a footstep behind her and turned

around to see Linc striding toward her. His sky blue eyes, dark with thunderclouds, narrowed on her.

"Don't you have something else to do besides stand around and gossip, Cassie? This isn't a goddamned tea party." He gave Jim and Harry such a glowering look that the smiles slowly faded from their faces.

Harry glanced at Jim. "Uh . . . guess we'd better do like the man said and warm up our engine."

Ignoring Linc, Cassie gave Harry and Jim another of her bright smiles. "I hope we beat you, but good luck coming in second."

Jim laughed, showing a set of white, even teeth. "Don't count us out, Cas . . . er, Mrs. Cameron," he amended, his dark eyes flickering over to Linc, hovering at Cassie's elbow. "We'll make a race out of it. See if we don't."

The two men shook hands with Cassie and started to do the same with Linc, but were stopped by the look on his face.

As Harry and Jim walked back to their plane, Cassie turned on Linc in anger. "That was downright rude!"

He scowled down at her. "I would think you'd get tired of those two slobbering all over you like a pair of hungry pups."

"Don't be ridiculous. They were just being friendly."

"Yeah? Like they were being friendly last night—leering down the front of your dress and pawing all over you out on the dance floor?"

"They were doing no such thing! Just because we're married, Linc Cameron, that's no excuse for you to start acting like a husband!"

"Jesus!" Linc threw up his hands and strode back to the *Pegasus*. Cassie followed behind him, grumbling to herself about foul-tempered men who thought they *owned* a person.

Linc gave Cassie's bottom an intimate caress as he boosted her into the cockpit. She whipped around to glare down at him, and caught the flash of his teeth in the gray light as he grinned cockily back at her. They were sparring again, which meant, she thought, that at least things were back to normal between them.

She had awakened that morning with a throbbing headache, a mouth that tasted of cotton balls, and the sight of his scowling face looking down at her. At first she couldn't imagine what he was doing in her bedroom, and she sat up abruptly. Groaning, she held her aching head as pain lanced across her eyeballs. Then she noticed she was naked, at least from the waist up, and she snatched at the sheet to cover her breasts.

Her bloodshot eyes narrowed at him in suspicion. "Who undressed me?"

"I did." He flung her underclothes, flannel shirt, and overalls onto her lap. "But I hope you're capable of getting dressed again by yourself. And soon. We should have been out at the airfield ten minutes ago."

Cassie tried to put on her camisole and shirt while still holding the sheet up to her neck—not an easy feat. Naturally, Linc was not about to play the part of a gentleman by turning his back.

"Are you always this nasty in the morning?" she asked him.

He gave her a mean smile. "Yes. It's one of the few faults I allow myself. And I don't intend to give it up, so you'll just have to get used to it. Especially since we'll be sharing all our mornings together during the coming weeks."

Cassie was beginning to remember some of what had happened the night before, especially that she had come right out and practically begged him to make love to her. She felt a blush surge up her neck to her face, and she forced herself to look up and meet his eyes.

"Linc . . . last night, did we . . . ?"

"I didn't touch you except to undress you, if that's what you're asking. So don't go crying rape."

"I can't cry rape. We're married." The full meaning of her words suddenly struck Cassie, and panic filled her. She hunched her shoulders, covering her face with her hands. "Oh, God. . . . "

Linc hesitated a moment, then sat down beside her on the bed. He pulled her hands away, his fingers pressing into her wrists. "What's the matter now?" he asked, exasperation in his voice.

Cassie studied his face. She thought she probably shouldn't tell him, but she wasn't used to hiding her feelings. "It's not easy to explain."

"Try."

She took a deep breath. "I was arrested once during a suffragette parade, and I spent a month in jail because of it. It was a truly awful, filthy place—there were even worms in the food. Like a fool I thought it was going to be a big adventure, but when they actually put me in the cell and locked the door, I felt so cold and alone and afraid. I feel that way now, Linc. I feel as if I've been locked in a cell and can't get out until I serve my sentence. I feel so trapped, so . . . "

She saw the movement of his throat as he swallowed. "That isn't very flattering," he said, forcing a wry grin. "Comparing marrying me to a prison sentence."

"You don't understand. It isn't you. It's the idea of being married. It's . . . oh, I don't know. . . . "

He picked up her hand and rubbed her knuckles with the edge of his thumb. It was probably an unconscious gesture on his part, but it brought a strange warmth to Cassie's chest.

"There's no reason to feel trapped," he said. "This isn't meant to be forever, we've both agreed to that."

"But for now at least, and in the eyes of the law, we are *married*."

He cradled her face in his rough hands and stared deep into her eyes. "What is it you're trying to say, Cassie? Are you afraid I'll think yesterday's ceremony has given me the right to demand that you sleep with me?"

She tried to smile at him. "I'm not afraid of sex, Linc. Especially with you. It's just the idea that . . . oh, darn it all!" How was she ever going to explain it to him?

Linc released her and stood up. "God knows I do want you, Cassie. But when I make love to you, I want it to be with your willing and joyful participation—not because the law says I can take you now that you're my wife."

"Damn you, Linc!" she blurted out. "I *want* you to take me. I just don't want to be your wife. Or anybody else's wife!"

They looked at each other for a moment in silence, then Linc shrugged and ran his fingers through his thick dark hair. "We don't have time for this argument."

"I'm not arguing—"

"Conversation, then. We have to get out to the airfield."

"All right. But I want to say one more thing first."

Cassie got out of bed and stood before him. The tail of her big floppy shirt came down to the middle of her thighs. She saw his eyes flicker to her bare legs and watched his jaw tighten as he forced himself to look away. She wrapped her arms around his waist, pressing into him. Looking up at him, she watched the storm clouds of desire build dark and brooding in his sky blue eyes before she spoke.

"Last night, when I said I wasn't in love with you . . . I might have been lying. Just a little."

She felt the tight muscles of his back relax beneath her hands, and his mouth closed over hers in a kiss that was swift and rough with passion.

He tore his lips from hers, setting her decisively away from him, but there was laughter in his eyes. "Christ, Cassie, we don't have time for this either. We're going to have to hustle like hell, or we're going to miss the start of the race!"

* * *

Cassie squeezed into the front cockpit's worn wicker seat. Because she weighed much less than Linc, she would always, whether piloting or not, ride in the front seat to prevent the aircraft from being nose-heavy.

She pulled on her leather helmet, fastening the strap snugly under her chin, and adjusted the goggles so they rested more comfortably on the bridge of her nose. The engine of the plane parked next to them roared into life, and she started nervously.

Linc's head and shoulders came into view as he walked around to the front of the aircraft. She couldn't see Pete, who would be in back hanging onto the tail. Because the plane had no brakes, it was nice to have an extra pair of hands to hold the machine back once the engine was running, before the pilot was ready to gather speed for takeoff.

Linc put his palms on the propeller blade and gave Cassie a thumbs-up signal. She checked to be sure the ignition switch was off and that both the air- and gas-intake valves were open before she hand-pumped air pressure into the gas tank. Linc flipped the propeller four times clockwise, while Cassie slowly shut down the air valves. When Linc determined that the pistons had sucked in enough gas, he shouted: "Contact!"

"Contact!" Cassie shouted back, turning on the magneto switch as Linc gave the propeller a final heave and jumped clear of the flying blades. The engine coughed, sputtered . . . and died.

They tried it twice more without success, then Linc's head disappeared beneath the fuselage, and Cassie swung out of the cockpit, jumping to the ground. Linc and Pete checked the fuel tank, which was under Linc's seat. After a moment Pete straightened, wiping his hands on the seat of his pants. He turned to her, his face contorted with anger.

"Sugar!" he shouted above the other idling engines.
"Sugar?"
"Somebody poured sugar in the gas tank!"

Just then Phineas Barlow waved a giant checkered flag through the air, signaling the start of the race. The three of them stood frozen in place until the planes on either side started to hurtle down the field, blasting them with the wind of their prop wash.

Pete took off toward the hangar in his loping, awkward gait. They would need to drain the tank and flush it out before they could refill it with uncontaminated fuel, but that wasn't the worst of it. The engine would have to be completely overhauled, a good three-hour job. And from now until they logged in at the first checkpoint, every second would count against their cumulative time.

Cassie met Linc's eyes as the other planes took off around them and disappeared into the morning haze. They didn't need to exchange words to know what the other was thinking. It was not only that they would start hours behind the others for this first leg of the race. It was that somebody wanted to prevent them from winning so badly that he, or they, would go to the extreme of sabotaging their aircraft. As it was, the *Pegasus* was so fragile, her engine so unreliable, that with every mile they flew they risked death. They did not need an enemy who was determined to see them grounded at any cost.

In the end it took almost four hours to repair the engine and replace the contaminated gas. The motor caught on the first try, erupting into a welcome, shattering roar. Linc kicked the blocks out from in front of the wheels. Cassie gradually opened the throttle, and the *Pegasus* began to trundle down the bumpy field as Linc grasped the wing struts and pulled himself on board.

Then they were airborne, rushing out over the breakers of the Pacific Ocean. Cassie banked high on the turn and headed east. As they passed back over the now-empty grandstand and the airfield, she waved down at the tiny figure that was Pete Striker. She had grown quite fond of the old rascal; in some inexplicable way he reminded her of Quigly. Her eyes filled with sudden tears at the thought that Quigly would miss their greatest adventure. She would be doing it alone now. Then she smiled to herself. Not completely alone. She would have a little help from Linc and Pete. She was glad Pete had agreed to be their advance man, traveling by train to meet up with them at every other checkpoint along the route. Pete's casual, nonjudgmental affection and his hard-eyed, feet-on-the-ground approach to things seemed to offset the big hole Quigly's death had left in Cassie's life.

She chose her direction by following the golden gleam of the sun off the tracks of the Union Pacific Railroad. The checkpoint for the first leg of the race was the Saltair Resort, on the south end of the Great Salt Lake in Utah—over seven hundred miles away. They would navigate by using a magnetic compass and dead reckoning, so it was important to be alert for the prominent geographical and man-made landmarks that passed beneath them.

After considering the weather and the winds aloft, Cassie chose a cruising altitude of five thousand feet. She trimmed the aircraft, and the engine settled into a smooth, steady beat, a monotonous hum that was almost hypnotic. The familiar heady sense of freedom, of pulling away from the dragging, clutching bonds of the earth, began to steal over Cassie. Not caring whether Linc heard her, or what he would think of her, she laughed out loud for the sheer joy of it. Above the racket in the cockpit, she heard the faint sound of Patches barking in agreement.

They flew over the bleak, rugged terrain of the Mojave Desert, over salt flats and pale seas of sand mottled with shadows cast by skimming clouds. They stopped at the sleepy railroad town of Las Vegas for a brief rest and to refuel, then it was on to the red canyons, the pink-and-white-striped spires, and the rainbow-colored rocks of the painted plateaus. Cassie set the *Pegasus* down on one of these high, lonely plateaus just as the sun began to sink behind sheer lava cliffs, turning the sky into a shimmering sea of gold.

She climbed slowly out of the cockpit with muscles that were stiff from sitting and numb with cold. Her shoulders and wrists ached from the hours of fighting the controls. She pulled off her goggles and helmet, rubbing the sleeve of her jacket over her face. Her skin felt chapped from the cold and wind, and it was covered with a greasy film from the engine spewing oil.

Linc removed a canteen of water from the plane's locker and handed it to her. She looked up at him and saw her fatigue reflected in his face, but there was still magic in his smile.

She took the canteen and smiled back at him. "Thank you," she said, and her voice came out in a dry croak. They had said little to each other all day; it was too difficult to carry on any but the most necessary conversation above the noise of the vibrating engine and the wind rushing over the open cockpit.

He removed her helmet and smoothed back her hair with gentle fingers. He brushed his lips across the red imprints in her cheeks left by her goggles, and then his mouth descended to claim hers in a long, lingering kiss. His fingers moved up the column of her neck until his thumbs came to rest under her chin. Tilting her head back, he sought and captured her eyes with his.

"You are incredible, Cassie Jones," he said, his voice low and filled with awe. "I know few men and only one other woman who have the guts and strength for what you did today."

Embarrassed, she looked away, but he forced her head around and kissed her again, this time with less hunger and more tenderness. But when he at last released her mouth, she felt a stir of discontent beneath her happiness.

She wondered who the other woman was, this

woman with so much strength and guts? Whoever she was, Linc must have loved her—perhaps he still did.

They tied the plane down against the wind and filled up the fuel tank from the extra can of gasoline they carried. Linc had taken charge of provisioning the plane with supplies in case they had to spend the night in the open like this, and Cassie watched in silence as he began to set up a makeshift but efficient camp. He fed Patches a tin of cold boiled beef. Then he built a fire out of chaparral and set about making a stew out of two more tins of meat by adding a couple of fresh carrots and potatoes he had brought along, and putting it all together in a cut-off, scoured-out gasoline can. Finally, he placed a small pot of coffee on the fire to brew.

Cassie supposed he had gotten used to living in the rough during the war, but when she asked him about it, he laughed and told her that except for the few occasions when he'd crashed or been shot down, he had spent his nights at the Lafayette's home base at Cachy, near the Somme, where they even had a French chef who had once worked at the Ritz in New York. "Or I'd spend my leaves in Paris, raising hell," he added, giving her a delightfully wicked smile that made her heart miss a beat.

While the stew cooked they talked easily, mostly about the race and the route they would follow in the morning. When the food was ready, Linc produced a couple of tin spoons from his flying kit. "There wasn't enough room to pack plates," he said with a grin. "We'll have to share the can."

He had found room, however, for a pair of battered metal cups, and he produced these with a flourish, filling one with coffee from the pot. He put the cup in her hand, and the steam wafted up to warm her face and fill her nose with the pungent, rich aroma of brewed beans, making her sigh with pleasure.

They sat cross-legged on the ground, their knees touching, with the can of stew between them. Patches flopped down nearly on top of them, watching their moving spoons carefully for any stray bits that might fall off. They talked about the sabotage of their plane, but neither one could come up with any idea of who had done it or why.

Linc grinned at her around a mouthful of potato. "I've never seen anyone strip down an engine faster than you did this morning. Even Pete was impressed."

"Quigly always insisted I know more about how an airplane flies than how to fly it. He made me take an old engine apart and put it back together again and again until I could practically do it blindfolded. If it weren't for him..." A ridiculous lump clogged her throat. She raised her head, tears filling her eyes. "Oh, Linc. What am I going to do without him?"

Linc leaned over and tilted her chin up, pressing a light kiss on her lips. "You're going to win this race and build his engine."

Cassie nodded and gave him a watery smile. "What are you going to do with your share of the money if we win?" she asked him a moment later.

"I've always wanted to settle down in one place and run my own business. But since it has to be a business I know something about, and I only know two things, I suppose I'll go into airplane manufacturing of some form or other."

"What other thing do you know about besides flying?"

Linc pretended not to hear her question. Instead he described the idea he had for a larger, faster, aerodynamically designed plane that could be the foundation of an entire aviation industry. "Someday," he said, his eyes alight with excitement, "planes will be hauling not only freight, but passengers from city to city. Maybe even between America and Europe, although that's probably a good ways off yet."

Cassie thought it probably was, since the Atlantic was four times wider at its narrowest point than the longest distance that had yet been flown over water. She also thought that Quigly's engine and Linc's plane would probably make a good combination, but she was afraid that if she suggested continuing their partnership after the race he might get entirely the wrong idea. He might think she was trying to cling to the marriage, which was ridiculous, of course, since she felt practically claustrophobic at the thought of being married and could hardly wait to get unmarried. Besides, he had made it quite obvious all along that she was not what he wanted in a wife anyway. He hadn't even made love to her yet, even though she had been hinting; in fact, she had come right out and asked him, and yet he still... well, to be fair, it was her own fault that she had fallen asleep on their wedding night. She smiled to herself. Passed out dead drunk was more like it. But then again, even allowing for the possibility that he did want her, maybe he was reluctant to make love to her because he was being true to the other woman. She thought he was probably the faithful type, even if he was so incredibly gorgeous that any woman who saw him would want...

Damn, damn, damn! Who *was* this other woman?

A rustle of movement at the edge of the fire caught Cassie's attention. She saw the softly glowing eyes first and then made out the tall pointed ears and big hind feet. It was a jackrabbit, who had been attracted by the warmth of the fire.

"Look, Linc!" she exclaimed softly. "It's too bad we don't have a gun. We could have had fresh meat for dinner."

Linc looked at her as if she had just suggested committing murder. "How could you want to do such a thing? Look at that face, at that cute little button of a nose—what the hell's so funny?"

"You," she said, laughing and pointing at him. "You have such a woebegone look on your face at the thought of shooting that rabbit. It's hard to believe you just spent two years—" She stopped herself, but not in time.

"Killing people?" Linc snapped back.

Cassie said nothing. His face took on that shuttered look, and the sadness, the deepest she had seen yet, filled his eyes.

Linc flung the dregs of his coffee out into the night and stood up. "Let's get some sleep. The sky's clear, the moon's coming up late, and it's going to be full. We can make up some of the time we lost if we get up early and fly a couple of hours before dawn."

"But it will still be dark."

He gave her a dry smile. "It usually is before the sun comes up."

"Right," she said uneasily. She had never flown at night before; nobody she knew had. It was bound to be terribly dangerous.

She cleaned their few utensils with sand, then watched in silence while Linc pulled out a pair of blankets he'd wedged beneath his seat, spreading them out beneath the shelter of the starboard wings. He sat down on top of them and then took her hand, pulling her down beside him.

Cassie wondered if he was going to make love to her at last. She suddenly couldn't remember a thing she had read in that stupid book. What if she forgot what to do, or didn't do it right? What if she wasn't any good at it, wasn't as good as the other woman?

"Cassie . . ."

"What?" she asked nervously.

"Never mind. Get some sleep. It's been a long day, and it's going to be an even longer one tomorrow."

She felt both relief and disappointment as he stretched out on the hard stony ground, easing her down beside him. He wrapped the blanket tight around them against the biting wind, and slowly the nearness of his body began to warm hers. A strange lassitude drew all the strength from her muscles; exhaustion had seeped into the very core of her bones. She felt as if weights had been put on her eyelids.

Linc snapped his fingers, and Patches trotted over to lie obediently down against their feet.

Cassie yawned sleepily. "Now I see why you bring him along. Pete thinks he's for good luck, but he's really just to keep your toes warm."

She felt Linc smile in the dark, and his breath come soft against her cheek. "I have you to keep me warm now."

She snuggled up to him, laid her head on his chest, and let the soothing beat of his heart lull her into sleep.

Linc lay beside Cassie, wide awake. She was a restless sleeper, murmuring and rubbing against him, and it wasn't long before the tense ache in his loins that had been plaguing him all evening had grown into a full-blown erection. Another twenty-four hours spent in the company of his new wife had only made him want her all the more.

And still, Linc thought with despair, it would probably be a huge mistake to make love to her. He thought back to their conversation that morning. In the confused state she was in, she'd probably regret making love after it was over. And then there was the little matter of the marriage—something neither of them had wanted. An annulment, which they could get if the union remained unconsummated, would be a lot easier to come by than a divorce. Finally there was his own peace of mind to consider. Something told him that one night, even two weeks worth of nights, with Cassie in his bed was not going to get her out of his system. And yet if there was any woman who was absolutely not his type, it was Cassie Jones.

Cassie stirred, pushing her knee up into his groin, and Linc clenched his teeth. To hell with all good intentions, he thought. Tomorrow night he would have her . . . if he could wait that long.

Linc was all brisk business a few hours later when he

woke Cassie by gently shaking her shoulder. It only took a moment to pack their things back into the locker and coax Patches into the cockpit. Linc casually suggested that he take the controls, and Cassie breathed a little easier. This time it was she who spun the prop while Linc started the engine.

It was very cold aloft, but Cassie hardly noticed it, for she was spellbound by the eerie beauty of the desert landscape at night. The giant moon hung in the sky like a lone Christmas ornament, its half-light making weird specters of the rock formations and sand dunes. Mountains lurked to the east of them, hulking shapes against the smoke-colored sky. Beneath them stretched the plains, silvery smooth except where they were seamed by the black cracks of canyons and dry river beds.

Cassie had often watched the sun set from five thousand feet, but for the first time she watched it come up from this spectacular vantage point. The sight of the fiery orange ball blazing suddenly across the sky touched something primitive within her. She could see why there had been so many sun worshipers throughout the ages, for the sun was truly a symbol of birth, the renewal of life, and hope.

But soon the sun lost some of its splendor as it rose higher in the sky, and the desert landscape began to take on a monotone barrenness. As the hours passed and they flew along the edge of the Wasatch Mountain range to within sight of the Great Salt Lake, Cassie amused herself by mentally rehearsing conversations in which she subtly asked Linc about the other woman.

The Saltair Resort was built on pilings at the edge of the Great Salt Lake. The huge Victorian hotel had been painted a fanciful pink at one time, but over the years salt deposits had crusted it white, so that it glimmered and sparkled in the sun as if made of ice. The lake, gray as molten lead even beneath the bright blue sky, filled the horizon. Linc landed the *Pegasus* on a nearby field that had been cleared of rocks and brush and marked out by black arrows painted on a pair of boulders.

The race committee had set up a small pavilion at the end of the field where the contestants could check in. Cassie was relieved to count only seven other planes tethered in a row beside the pavilion. Since fifteen teams had started the race, they must already have made up a lot of the time they'd lost because of the sabotage to their fuel.

Linc went right away to log them in, while Cassie— with Patches running between her legs and getting in the way—refilled the tank and checked the plane for any damage that might have been caused by the stress of the flight. She was sitting on top of the upper left wing, mending a tiny rent in the fabric, when she heard Patches's warning growl and the crunch of footsteps on the gravelly dirt. She looked down to see Edward Farrell and his copilot coming toward her. She noticed with amusement that Ward's dapper new flying suit was already stained and coated with dust.

Edward stopped beneath the wing and tilted his head back, staring up at her. "Linc must be out of his mind to bring you along on this madcap adventure. Are you all right?"

Cassie removed the thick needle she had stuck between her teeth and glared down at him. "Why shouldn't I be?"

"Linc said you've been plagued by sabotage too."

"Too?" Cassie grasped the leading edge of the wing and swung down onto the ground before them. "You also were sabotaged?"

"We think someone might have poked a hole in our radiator," Gregory Pearce put in, his large, protruding ears seeming to twitch with indignation. "We showed it to Mr. Cameron, and he agrees it could have been done with an ice pick." He sighed. "It could also have been an accident."

"Since it didn't show up until this morning, it had to

have been done last night if it was sabotage," Edward said. "A group of about ten of us wound up together at dusk near some godforsaken town south of here. It must have happened then. The hole was so tiny that the water leaked out slowly, but by the time we got here we'd been reduced to pouring a jug of cold coffee —which we just luckily happened to have along with us—into the radiator to keep the engine cool."

"We didn't want to land beforehand, of course," Gregory added. "Especially not after we had used up all our water."

Cassie thought of the desolate country they had flown over and repressed a shiver. "Who's doing it?" she wondered aloud. "And why?"

Edward gave her his elegant shrug. "The why is pretty obvious I should think. As for the who, we'll just have to keep watch. Maybe we can catch him in the act."

Edward invited her and Linc to join them for supper, and then he and Gregory set off for the hotel. Cassie picked a wrench out of the toolbox and walked around the plane to the other pair of wings, intending to tighten the cables. Then she spotted the Schmidt brothers at work on their aircraft, trying to fit a new propeller to the engine shaft. She wondered if they, too, had been the victims of sabotage. She was just about to go ask them when Linc suddenly appeared before her.

When he spoke his voice was hard with a strange anger that bore no relation to his words, and his expression was harsh. "Bean's cola has reserved a room for us at the hotel," he said, plucking the wrench out of her hand. "Why don't you go get cleaned up and get some rest while I finish this."

"But—"

"Don't argue. You piloted most of this leg, it's only fair that I do the maintenance."

Cassie shrugged. "I'll take Patches with me then,"

she said, and Patches thumped the ground with his tail.

"No," Linc said curtly, and Patches's head drooped dispiritedly. "I want him to guard the plane when neither of us is around."

Cassie pulled her flying kit out of the locker and started to turn away, then she turned back again. "The engine was knocking a bit just before we landed. Why don't you—"

"Damn it, Cassie! Can't you credit me with having just a little ability in this venture?"

"I do," she said, backing up. "I didn't mean to... I'm sorry." She turned and walked stiffly toward the distant hotel. She heard Linc call after her, but she ignored him. She had only tried to be helpful; he certainly didn't need to snap her head off.

The hotel had a broad veranda filled with wicker chairs and tables. A gramophone blared out a tinny rendition of "Alexander's Ragtime Band," and several couples were attempting to do the turkey trot around the furniture. A fitful breeze carried the smells of popcorn and cotton candy from a concession wagon that sat at the lake's edge.

As she waited for the desk clerk to produce the room key, Cassie spotted a brightly colored poster perched on an easel in the middle of the lobby. The poster advertised a circus and its coming attractions—including elephants, a lion tamer, and clowns. In the bottom right-hand corner, a pair of figures swung from a trapeze above the bold red words: FEATURING THE FLYING CAMERONS. The coincidence made Cassie smile. She would have to ask Linc if they were any relation. Unfortunately, the first performance wasn't until tomorrow night. Too bad they would miss it.

Cassie was shown into a room on the ground floor that opened onto the veranda and faced the lake. The hotel had yet to be modernized with electricity, but it did have individual bathtubs in every room. Cassie took a long, hot bath and washed her hair.

Because they needed to fly as light as possible in order to maintain a good steady speed and conserve fuel, she had not been able to bring many clothes with her. She had managed, however, to stuff her wedding dress into her kit, although she had waited until Linc's back was turned because she hadn't wanted him to think she was being sentimental or anything ridiculous like that. She had also brought along a plain, black gabardine skirt, with a matching, semistiff underskirt and a white shirtwaist with a falling collar of crocheted lace. She started to put on the peach silk, and then decided it was a bit too fancy for the Saltair Resort. She put on the black skirt instead.

She left off a corset, however. She never wore one flying—it was too uncomfortable and constricting, and besides, the hateful thing always made her skin itch. But lately she'd been discarding it altogether and wearing only a camisole, even under her regular clothes. The corset was a ridiculous item of clothing that served no useful purpose she could think of. If men were forced to wear them for even one hour, Cassie thought, they would pass a law the very next day banning the corset's existence—something they could do since they had the *vote*, which women still didn't have, almost a hundred and fifty years after the Revolution. But once women did get the vote, one of the first things to go, Cassie vowed, would have to be those damned corsets. . . .

It had been a long time since breakfast, and Cassie's stomach started to grumble in protest. She decided she wouldn't wait for Linc any longer and set off in search of the restaurant by way of the veranda. As she rounded the corner, she spotted Linc standing at the bottom of the steps that led to the front of the hotel.

He was talking to the most beautiful woman she had ever seen.

As Cassie paused to watch, Linc said something.

The woman threw back her head in laughter, and Linc laughed too. Then the woman leaned forward and kissed him on the cheek. Cassie felt a stab of pain in her chest that was as real as if someone had thumped her with a hammer, for even from where she stood she could see the years of easy intimacy that lay behind that kiss.

And Cassie knew she didn't need to ask Linc about the other woman now. She was about to meet her.

Chapter 8

The woman was still laughing as Cassie walked up. She was not as young as Cassie had first supposed, although she was even more beautiful up close. Her skin was a dusky rose color, and she had high, sharp cheekbones and eyes that tilted up at the corners, giving her face an exotic cast. She had sleeked her chestnut hair back from her broad forehead and twisted it into a tight roll, and she wore a plain, high-necked, black taffeta dress that ought to have looked severe but instead clung to her body, emphasizing her sensual curves.

Linc saw Cassie first. When the woman noticed his expression, she turned her head sharply around and fixed Cassie with a hard, chilling blue stare.

"Hello, Cassie," Linc said with a sigh.

The two-timing wretch, Cassie thought. He didn't look at all happy to see her. He looked, in fact, as if he hoped a hole would open up beneath her feet and swallow her.

"So this is Cassandra!" the woman exclaimed in a sultry voice. She had a foreign accent, and her eyes sparkled with sudden mischief. "Linc told me you were sleeping. I think he had some foolish idea he could keep us from meeting." She paused and looked back and forth between the two of them. "Darling, have you married this poor child without telling her a thing about yourself? He can really be so provoking at times," she said to Cassie. "I had to find out about *you* by reading a newspaper. I am Ria, of course."

Cassie turned on Linc, feeling embarrassed and jealous and furious. She glared at him, and he glared back. "You rotten bastard!" she cried, loud enough to stop conversation on the veranda and make the dancers pause. "You might have told me you had a mistress."

"Mistress!" The woman threw back her head and let out a rich peal of laughter, while Linc made a sound that resembled one of Patches's growls. "Oh, Linc darling, it quite serves you right," she said. Then she turned bright, laughing blue eyes onto Cassie. "My son likes to pretend he descended to earth fully grown, like a god from Greek mythology. The truth is that he came into the world the same way all mortals do—squawking and bloody and—"

"Ria, for God's sake," Linc hissed around clenched teeth.

Cassie's eyes had opened wide in astonishment. She stared at Linc, whose face was flushed a bright red. "Son? Linc is your son?"

"Yes, my dear. " Ria smiled. "As I said, Linc hates to admit it, but he does have a mother." She took Cassie's shoulders, holding her at arm's length and scrutinizing her from head to toe. "Let me look at you. What sort of girl are you? The newspaper account had you piloting airplanes. Surely that can't be true—you're so small!"

Cassie felt herself smiling broadly, and she realized that it was due more than anything else to relief. This beautiful, exotic woman was not Linc's mistress after all. She was his mother!

"Linc and I are copilots in the transcontinental race, Mrs. Cameron," she said. "It's how we met . . . sort of."

"No, no, no. You must call me Ria, or else I shall feel like an old crone." She slipped strong fingers over Cassie's arm and waved the other hand in Linc's face. "Go play with your airplanes, darling boy. Cassandra and I are going to have a cup of tea and a woman-to-woman talk."

Linc tried to get between them. "Cassie isn't thirsty."

Cassie stepped around Linc and slipped her arm through Ria's. "Cassie is so thirsty," she said, so emphatically that Ria punctuated it with another one of her rich laughs.

As they mounted the steps, Cassie cast a quick look over her shoulder. Linc stood ramrod stiff, watching them with a look of pure terror on his face. Ria glanced back too, and then her eyes met Cassie's and they traded smiles.

In the lobby Cassie paused before the circus poster. "Is this you?" she asked Ria. "The Flying Camerons?"

"Yes, I am an aerialist. My younger son, Tommy, and I are the only true Camerons left in the troupe now, but we've kept the name. It goes back some years and was quite famous at one time. We have nothing to be ashamed of, in spite of what that foolish boy must have told you."

Cassie didn't know what to say, since Linc had neglected to tell her that he even had a living mother—and a brother. She continued to study the poster, although she could feel Ria's eyes on her.

"Perhaps instead of taking refreshment here," Ria said, "you would prefer to come to my caravan. We'll walk through the lot, and you can see them putting up the big top for the performance tomorrow night."

Cassie's face lit up. "I would like that very much."

During their days of flying airplane exhibitions, Cassie and Quigly had often hooked up with traveling shows of one sort or another to take advantage of the large crowds the bigger events attracted. What she remembered most about the circuses were the exotic smells—fresh sawdust and roasted peanuts, and the more potent elephant dung.

This company was larger than the ones she and Quigly had traveled with. She counted three tigers, two lions, and a giraffe among the wild animals caged in ornately painted parade wagons. There were numerous sideshows as well, including a tattooed lady, a contortionist, and an Egyptian mummy. Several of the men unrolling the canvas for the big tent called out to Ria as they walked by. Another young man with one arm in a sling was tuning the calliope. He looked up, saw Ria, and waved them over, but Ria ignored him.

It had always amazed Cassie that circus caravans, which appeared so small from the outside, were actually quite roomy. Ria's caravan was divided into a sleeping alcove, a sitting area, and a galley with a wood-burning stove. Her few pieces of furniture were old but valuable and well cared for, and the ornaments had obviously been selected to pleasure both the eye and the soul. Cassie sucked in her breath with delight at the Persian carpets covering the walls in shades of scarlet, gold, and midnight blue.

Ria turned on an oil lamp with a pink shell shade. It cast a soft, flattering light on everything, especially Ria herself. "It occurs to me that this is an occasion for a celebration," she said. "And tea does not strike the right chord." She disappeared behind a tasseled velvet curtain into the sleeping alcove. Cassie fervently hoped she wasn't going to produce a bottle of champagne.

She came out with a plain, unlabeled bottle and two small glasses, which she set on a brass-topped table. She motioned Cassie to sit on a nearby settee while she filled the glasses. She handed one to Cassie.

"Prosit," she said, and drained hers in one swallow before sitting down in a facing chair.

Cassie looked into her glass dubiously. "What is it?" she asked. It looked like water.

"It is called vodka. A Russian drink, distilled from wheat."

Cassie took a tentative sip and gasped. "My God! It tastes awful!"

Ria laughed. "Do you always say precisely what you are thinking?" Her laughter quickly wound down, and she looked searchingly at Cassie.

"I'm sorry," Cassie said. "I didn't mean to be rude."

"Nonsense, child. I was simply wondering how Linc ever managed to find you—and how he had the wisdom to marry you once he did."

Cassie decided it was not her place to enlighten Linc's mother with the truth about their marriage. "Did Linc train to be an aerialist along with his brother?" she asked instead.

Ria refilled her glass, then held it before her face, cupped between her two palms. Unlike the rest of her, her hands, Cassie noticed, were large and big boned and somewhat ugly.

"Linc wanted nothing to do with the trapeze," Ria said. "I always assumed it was because he was afraid of heights." She lifted her shoulders in a tiny shrug. "Obviously that proved not to be true. But then, Linc has always been full of contradictions. On the day he left home—he was sixteen at the time—he informed me that he despised the circus life. The next time I saw him, he was touring the country performing aerobatics with one of those frightful flying machines. I couldn't see much difference between the life he was leading and the one he claimed to despise."

Ria started at a sharp knock on the caravan's wooden door, and Cassie jumped, spilling half of her drink. The two women looked at each other. "Linc," they said simultaneously.

Ria's eyes danced with mischief. "I knew he couldn't bear to leave us alone together for long. He's terrified I'll reveal all his dark secrets."

Cassie was dying to hear about Linc's dark secrets. "Go away, Linc!" she shouted.

The door flung open and Linc stormed in. "Cassie . . ." he growled ominously. He spied the glass in her hand. "What are you drinking?"

"Something Russian. It's—"

"No, you're not." He pried it away from her, sniffed it, then set it down out of reach. "You're staying sober tonight if I have to gag you."

"Linc!" Ria exclaimed. "You're being perfectly dreadful. You shouldn't let him get away with it," she said to Cassie.

"He won't—isn't," Cassie said between her teeth.

"What are you doing here at Salt Lake anyway?" Linc said to Ria. "You're supposed to be in Texas this time of year."

"Tommy will explain," Ria said.

"Tommy! What does he have to do with it?"

Ria said nothing. Mother and son glared at each other, and Cassie saw two strong wills clashing in a battle that had been going on for years. She understood a lot about Linc Cameron in that moment, more than he would have liked.

A muscle throbbed in Linc's jaw. "Where is he then?"

"Are you looking for me?" The young man with his arm in a sling, the one who had been tuning the calliope, entered the caravan.

He nodded at Cassie, mumbling a shy greeting. His face was badly battered and bruised, but even so his resemblance to Ria was marked. Except for his dark hair, he looked nothing like Linc. He was slighter of build and not nearly as tall, but he moved with the controlled athletic grace of an acrobat.

The two brothers stood looking at each other in silence. There was, Cassie was glad to see, no clash of wills here, but rather a genuine fondness.

Linc stepped forward and gave the younger man a brief, rough embrace. "Tommy . . . how are you? Christ, what a stupid question. Did you take a bad fall?"

Tommy's eyes flickered over to his mother.

"I haven't told him," she said. "You must do that yourself."

"Tell me what, for Christ's sake?"

There was a long silence while Tommy studied the floor. Then he said, "We have a new calliope, Linc. I was remembering how much you used to like the old one when we were kids. I thought maybe you might like to see it. The new one, that is."

Linc's eyes narrowed as he regarded his brother. "All right," he said. "Let's go then."

Ria's face was motionless as she watched them leave. Cassie was filled with an almost unbearable curiosity, but she doubted Ria would reveal to a stranger what she had been unwilling to discuss with her own son. And Cassie wouldn't dare ask Linc; he was so suspicious and secretive, he would only accuse her of acting like a wife.

The door shut behind the men. "Now," Ria said. She kicked off her shoes and tucked her feet up under her like a little girl. Her eyes had regained that child's spark of mischief. "Shall I tell you about the time Linc took a lion for a walk down Broadway?"

Shrill music piped out of the steam whistles of the calliope, echoing up into the lofty ceiling of the empty big top. Linc seized Tommy's wrist, stilling his hand. There was a loud, grating crash of notes, then silence.

"Out with it," Linc said.

Tommy's hand clenched into a tight fist. "You're not gonna like it, Linc."

"I don't like it already. Why don't you start with the reason you're here at Salt Lake?"

"Sure." Tommy breathed out a sigh at this temporary reprieve. "I don't suppose you know that Cal Dobbins sold the company a couple of years ago? To a Mr. Bartinelli from New York. A few months ago Ria and Mr. Bartinelli became . . ." Tommy looked up from the keyboard.

Linc's face was perfectly blank, even his eyes. "So Ria has taken a new lover. It's hardly the first time, Tommy, and it doesn't explain a thing."

Tommy plucked one of the instrument's keys. A shrill note bounced mournfully off the canvas walls. "She read about this airplane race in the newspaper a while back. She found out you were going to be in it and where the stops were likely to be, and she got Mr. Bartinelli to book us on a run out west here this spring."

Linc frowned. "She got the besotted fool to divert an entire circus of thirty-four wagons just so she could meet me here? Why?"

Tommy grinned weakly. "She wanted to see you?"

"Hogwash."

Tommy fumbled in his pocket for a cigarette and matches. He had a hard time lighting up one-handed, so Linc did it for him. "Go on," Linc said.

Tommy took a deep drag on the cigarette, then blew smoke out into the shadowy tent. "Mr. Bartinelli's a big-time gambler, and he's got a lot of friends who are gamblers too. None of us, not even Ria, figured out until it was too late that they were all with the Black Hand."

"Jesus," Linc said softly. The Black Hand was a secret society composed mostly of Sicilian immigrants who operated as extortionists, blackmailers, and killers-for-hire.

"It gets worse." Tommy looked at Linc, and his olive complexion slowly turned a dark red. "Mr. Bartinelli started taking me with him to a few poker games during the off-season. Christ Linc, the cards were hot—I couldn't lose. Course, no lucky streak's gonna last forever, and I started to hit some cold spells now and then. But not a lot—at least, not at first. And then I got stuck in this real bad patch. Nothing was turning up right, you know? So I started to play for even higher stakes, hoping to recoup. But by then I was playing with markers instead of cash, and it didn't even seem like real money to me. I just sort of lost track of how deep I was getting in... until one day Mr. Bartinelli told me I had to settle up."

"And when you couldn't, they gave you that"—Linc gestured at Tommy's broken arm—"to teach you a lesson and maybe convince you that you could come up with the money after all."

Tommy's lips twisted and he nodded. "They gave me a month to pay up. They said if they had to come around asking again, they'd bust my kneecaps next time and put me in a wheelchair for life."

"Why didn't Ria get her latest lover boy to let you off the hook?"

"She asked him to, and he said he'd consider it. But only if she would agree to marry him."

Linc let out a short, harsh bark of laughter. "I can just imagine what her answer was to that." Ria would never give up her independence, Linc thought. She had never once put his or Tommy's needs ahead of her own, even when they were kids. She wasn't likely to do so now that they were grown and, theoretically at least, able to take care of themselves. And all this was mostly Ria's fault to begin with. Bartinelli had set Tommy up with the Black Hand as a means of getting control over her. He couldn't have known, of course, that nobody got control over Ria.

"They got in a big fight over it," Tommy was saying. "Now they're not even talking to each other, so there's no hope of her talking him out of calling in the markers."

Linc leaned his shoulder against the side of the calliope, thrusting his hands deep into the pockets of his whipcords. "You've wasted your time coming to me, Tommy. I doubt I could scare off the Black Hand, and every cent I had went up in smoke in Santa Monica last week."

"Yeah, we read about that in the paper." He paused,

clearing his throat. "This is the part you're really not gonna like, Linc. . . . I told Mr Bartinelli you've promised to make good on my markers with the prize money you're going to get out of this airplane race."

Linc felt his chest tighten with helpless rage that his crazy family had once again entangled him in their messy lives. He wished he could just turn on his heel and walk away, but he knew that if he did and Tommy suffered because of it, he would never forgive himself.

"I see," he said finally, winning for the moment the struggle to control his temper. "How much do you owe these guys anyway?"

Tommy couldn't meet his brother's eyes. He pulled the sling that cradled his broken arm tight against his chest, hugging himself. When he did speak, it was in a voice barely above a whisper. "Thirty-three thousand dollars."

All the blood drained from Linc's face. "Jesus God!" He flung himself away in a violent movement, then he whipped back around, and Tommy flinched from the raw anger he saw in his brother's eyes.

"I've still got over three thousand miles of flying left between me and that money," Linc said, "and there's no guarantee that I'm going to get there first. What'll they do to me if I lose—smash *my* kneecaps?"

Tommy licked his lips and swallowed. "I'm supposed to tell you . . . they've said you gotta make good on my markers or . . . or they're going to kill me." He tried to pull off a wry grin but couldn't quite make it. "At least they didn't threaten to kill you."

Linc shook his fist in his brother's face. "I ought to kill you myself and save them the trouble. Even if I do win the damned thing, only half the money is mine. The rest belongs to Cassie."

"She's your wife, isn't she? So it'll all wind up as yours anyway. Look, Linc, I'm sorry I got you involved with this, but what else could I do? The trapeze is my life. I'd die as a cripple. When they showed me a way outta this mess, I grabbed it. I've never had your kind of guts."

The rage slowly drained out of Linc. He rubbed his hands over his face and through his hair. "Hell, I don't know, Tommy," he said, and briefly closed his eyes.

For some reason a vision of Cassie's face flashed behind his shut lids, so clear that she might have been standing before him. He felt a strange, compelling need to unburden himself to her, to go to her as a husband to a wife, in need of comfort and understanding and advice. But the thought was surely absurd, wasn't it? What sort of advice could she give him? She was hardly more than an inexperienced child herself. And she had made it quite plain that, beyond sharing his bed, she had no desire to play the part of a wife. He certainly couldn't ask her to contribute a portion of her prize money to bail out his brother, especially when he hadn't even bothered to tell her of the boy's existence.

"Let's go back to the caravan," Linc said to Tommy. "We both could use a drink. And I can't afford to let Cassie out of my sight for too long. She and trouble gravitate to one another like drunks to a saloon."

"You know, Linc, that wife of yours is really pretty. And I bet she's one hot little tomato in, uh . . ." Tommy's voice trailed off at the look on Linc's face. "Sorry," he mumbled.

They walked back through the lot, mostly empty now that the day's work of setting up was done. A fitful breeze carried the smell of brine from the lake, and the late-afternoon sun bathed the encircling mountains in a hazy yellow light.

"There's something else you ought to know," Tommy said, breaking the silence between them. "Mr. Bartinelli told me he was going to send a couple of his boys along on the race—to keep an eye on you and look after his interests."

Frowning, Linc considered the list of contestants. The suspects that leapt immediately to mind were those damn pups, Harry and Jim. They certainly *looked* Sicilian, and it would explain why they constantly seemed to be hovering around the *Pegasus*. He had thought they were interested in Cassie, who had—he ground his teeth at the memory—certainly been encouraging them. But now he wasn't so sure. . . .

Linc stopped, grasping his brother's arm. "Those boys of Bartinelli's, are they a couple of swarthy-looking characters with a Wright pusher biplane who know damn-all about flying it?"

Tommy shrugged. "I don't know what they look like, or what kind of plane they fly. I don't even know their names."

"Wonderful," Linc said, and Tommy cringed at the tone in his brother's voice.

They entered the caravan to find Ria and Cassie in the galley, convulsed with laughter over a pot of something spicy that was bubbling on the stove.

"Linc darling, you've married a girl who doesn't even know how to boil an egg," Ria said. Then she looked at Cassie, and the two of them went off into more gales of laughter.

Linc scowled at them. He should have known they would take to each other; they were two of a kind. And he certainly should have had more sense than to leave Cassie alone in Ria's company. God alone knew what sort of trouble they'd been brewing up, and one thing he didn't need more of right now was trouble.

"Linc?" Cassie said, giving him an incredibly sweet smile. "I told your mother we would love to stay for supper." She leaned into him, pressing her breasts against his arm, and a sudden jolt shot through him.

He stopped himself just in time from crushing his mouth down over hers in a passionate kiss. "Fine," he gasped instead, setting her away from him and backing up two steps. He glanced up to catch Ria's speculative eyes on him, and he blushed guiltily, feeling like a kid who had just been caught looking at pictures of naked ladies.

Later that evening, Cassie and Linc walked hand in hand along the lake's edge, their feet crunching on the putty-colored mud, which was crusty with salt deposits. They watched the silvery gold sun sink into water that reflected the light like polished metal.

Cassie rubbed her thumb along Linc's callused palm. "Isn't the lake beautiful? It's such a strange color."

He stopped and pulled her around. Threading his hands through her hair, he tilted her face up. "Like quicksilver," he said, his voice rough. "The color of your eyes."

She waited for his kiss, but instead he released her and resumed walking, although after a while he again reached for her hand. She sensed that he was troubled about something, no doubt the mysterious problem that his brother had confided to him that afternoon. She wanted to tell him they would have a better chance of solving it, whatever it was, if they worked at it together, but she was too afraid he would think she was intruding on an area in his life where she had no right to be.

"I like your mother," she said when she could no longer bear the silence between them.

He squeezed her hand and smiled. "She likes you. And that's some sort of compliment, I guess. Ria likes very few people."

"Who was your father? Was he a trapeze artist too?"

Linc didn't answer for so long that Cassie suspected the conversation had already wandered onto forbidden territory. He stopped again and put his hands on her shoulders, then worked them up over her lacy collar until the tips of his fingers touched the bare skin of her neck. Cassie sucked in a deep breath and held it.

"I never knew my father," he said. "He was just one of the many men who passed in and out of Ria's bed.

Tommy and I had different fathers, and I don't think either of us was a planned or blessed event. Ria never has liked children much, and she particularly didn't like being pregnant because it prevented her from performing. She also didn't like having us kids because we got in the way of her life . . . and her lovers."

Cassie wanted to tell him how strangely similar her own lonely childhood had been to his before Quigly had come into her life, but she couldn't seem to get the words past her tight throat. There were secrets that she needed to keep from him, and the story of Lawrence Kingly and her mother was one of them.

Linc brushed his thumb along the edge of her jaw. "Don't look so sad. I had a lot of what I suppose you could call stepfathers over the years, and a few were quite good to me."

"But most weren't?"

"Most were merely indifferent . . . what's the matter?" Tears had welled up in Cassie's eyes, spilling out the corners. "Cassie, sweetheart. Why are you crying?"

"I'm not," she said as the tears poured down her face.

He kissed her wet cheeks, then held her tightly against him, stroking her back. The tears dried up as quickly as they had appeared. Ashamed now, she pulled away from him.

He sensed her embarrassment and gave her a sudden, brilliant smile. "Have you ever gone swimming in a salt lake?"

"Is it different than the ocean?"

"Let's find out." He laughed and, to Cassie's astonishment, began pulling off his clothes.

"But we haven't any bathing costumes," she said.

"So?" He laughed again. "Who wants to go swimming in ten yards of wet flannel anyway?"

They were at the remote end of the lake, out of sight of the resort and the more popular lakeside paths. The sun had sunk below the horizon now, although a touch of daylight still tinged the dusky sky.

Linc had already pulled off his boots and shirt and was unbuckling his belt. He noticed her watching and paused a moment, then flashed her a cocky smile and began unfastening his fly buttons. When she realized he was actually going to pull his pants right off without turning his back, she looked quickly away. But some demon in her made her look back again.

One summer when she was seven, while swimming in the river, Ward Farrell had dared her to take off all her clothes. She had refused—until he did it first. She remembered studying his skinny ten-year-old body with avid curiosity, comparing it to her own and deciding she liked hers better. But a boy's body, she thought now, was far different from a man's. The sight of Linc Cameron's blatant and obvious masculinity made her heart beat fast and caused a hard knot of heat to burn deep in her belly.

Linc stood straight and tall before her, unashamed in his nakedness, and let her look her fill. Then he turned and waded out into the water. She stared at his smooth, lean back, her eyes tracing the clean lines of the muscles that tapered to his hard buttocks and thighs.

He stopped when the water had strategically reached his waist and turned around. Putting his hands on his hips, he called out a challenge. "Are you coming in, Cassie Jones? I dare you!"

"All right, all right . . . but close your eyes while I get undressed."

"No," he said, and she wanted to stamp her foot in frustration over his stubbornness. He really was the most infuriating man alive.

She sat down on a rock and unbuttoned her shoes, pulling them off, and then removed her garters and stockings. She stood back up and unhooked her skirt, stepping out of it. Her fingers hesitated for a moment at the buttons on her shirtwaist; she could feel his eyes on her like steam bubbling up from a caldron, moist and hot against her flesh.

Cassie looked up and defiantly returned his look. Slowly, her eyes on his face, she began to undo the buttons, slipping the soft material down over her shoulders and sending it fluttering to the ground. Then she unfastened the waistband of her taffeta underskirt and let it slide in a crackly whisper to her feet. The breeze caressed her bare limbs, making her acutely aware of her near nakedness. She tilted back her head and let it cool her flushed face.

"Don't stop," Linc said, and his voice broke.

Her soft teasing laughter echoed out over the lake as she waded in, still wearing her camisole and drawers. The water was warm and light against her skin, and strangely buoyant. Her feet kept wanting to float out from under her. It had grown darker, and she could no longer distinguish Linc's features. He was merely a black shadow, looming out of the water in front of her.

She stopped while they were still several feet apart. "Come here," she said.

She heard the sharp hiss of his indrawn breath, and then he was suddenly in front of her. He reached for her, but she pressed her palm against his chest, holding him at arm's length. She could feel the rapid beat of his heart. Slowly, she began to move her hand across his finely toned muscles, brushing against his nipples and lower, down across his ribs to the hard slab of his stomach. He was breathing fast now, as if he had been sprinting, and she heard him stifle a groan. Her roaming fingers reached the waterline, where the arrowhead of hair pointed down between his thighs, and she stopped. He took her by the wrist and started to bring her hand lower still, but in a sudden movement she pulled away from him. She rolled onto her back and kicked hard with her feet, hitting him with a shower of water.

She heard his yelp of surprise amid the loud splash and then a sudden silence. She thought he would want to pay her back for that trick, and she tried to swim away, but the buoyant water kept lifting her feet higher than her head. The salt burned her eyes and stung the tiny scrapes and cuts on her body that she hadn't known she had. Once her head slipped completely under, and she almost gagged on the briny taste that flooded her mouth.

She gave up swimming and drifted to her feet. The water lapped gently against her breasts as she looked around. The lake was empty. "Linc?" she called out softly.

She sucked in a sharp breath, stifling a scream as his hard arms encircled her waist from behind, pulling her back against him. "I want you, Cassie," he said, his breath hot on her neck, and she felt his manhood, thick and hard, press against her bottom. "Feel how much I want you."

She swayed back against him as his hands moved up to cup her breasts. He massaged them gently, his fingers teasing her nipples through the slick wet cotton of her camisole, pulling them into hard, quivering points. His lips were moving up and down the cords of her neck, igniting a feeling so exquisite that she had to grit her teeth to keep from crying out loud from the pleasure it brought her.

"Ah, God, Cassie..." He sighed and pulled her around to face him. His eyes were as hard and glittering as glass, reflecting back the silver water. Her breath caught, and the muscles low in her stomach clenched into a tight ball. It was the way she felt just before attempting to do a dangerous stunt for the first time— terror, yes, but also a dizzying excitement, an irrepressible desire to risk it all.

He lifted her up in his arms and waded toward the shore. Wrapping her hands tightly around his neck, she pulled his head down to her eager mouth. His lips were warm and firm and slightly salty. They pressed down on hers with a bruising, passionate intensity that drew the breath from her lungs and sent the earth whirling around her as if she were spinning through the sky in the *Pegasus*.

Their mouths were still locked together when he set her down on the shore. He ended the kiss with a groan, pulling away from her. He searched the dark ground for their scattered clothes while she stood in silent shock, her lips still tingling from the pressure of his kiss.

"Hurry," he said breathlessly, shoving her shirtwaist and skirt into her arms. Cassie struggled to put them on over her wet underclothes while Linc disappeared into the darkness, muttering to himself. "Damn it to hell. Where are my pants?"

He found them caught on a clump of sagebrush. He looked endearingly clumsy as he hopped around from one foot to the other, pulling them on.

Cassie sat down on the rock, fumbling with her shoes, but her fingers were trembling so much she couldn't seem to manage. Linc knelt beside her and impatiently tried to push the stiff leather over her wet, sticky feet. Looking down at his bent head, she was seized with a sudden need to run her fingers through his thick, dark hair.

Linc had also been distracted by this new and close-up view of Cassie's bare legs. His hand encircled her ankle and began a slow journey up the inside of her calf, stopping to fondle the back of her knee. Her fingers tightened in his hair, pulling his head back. He stood up, bringing her with him, and his lips were on hers again in another crushing kiss.

His hands moved up her back and down over her shoulders, scorching her skin. His fingers slid under her collar, and he yanked her shirtwaist open, then pulled at her camisole, impatiently pushing the material aside. He rubbed and caressed her breasts, first one and then the other, his fingers searching for and finding her nipples.

"Linc," she breathed, her lips teasing the side of his mouth, her voice soft with laughter. "You're undressing me again."

"Jesus." He released her so abruptly that she almost fell. But then he grasped her wrist and started to pull her with him toward the path that led back to the hotel.

"Wait, my shoes!" Cassie cried out. "And your boots, and the rest of our clothes."

Linc rolled the clothes, shoes, and boots up in a ball and stuffed it under his arm. Then he grabbed her hand and took off running. Cassie struggled to keep up with him. She didn't remember there being so many rocks and thistles the first time they had trod this path, but her bare feet found each one of them now. While they ran, she tried to rebutton her shirtwaist, wondering how they were ever going to make it unnoticed to their room wet, half-dressed, and looking crazed with lust.

At last the hotel came into view, but by now the salt-water had dried on their skin, causing it to itch and burn.

"Linc!" Cassie gasped, slowing him down. "My skin is on fire!"

"I thought I saw some outdoor showers around by the bathing beach."

He led her down a pebbled path, back to the lake. The showers were simply two rough wooden cubicles marked MEN and WOMEN in faded white letters. Luckily the place was empty, and Linc didn't hesitate. He pushed Cassie through the door marked MEN and came in with her.

They didn't bother to remove their clothes, which stuck to their sticky bodies as if they had been smeared with paste. Linc turned on the single faucet, and they stood beneath it together, letting the cold water pour over them.

Cassie started to laugh, but Linc stopped her with a

kiss that drew her up on her toes. He thrust his tongue past her teeth and deep into her mouth, and she met it with her own. He pressed the length of his body to hers, grinding and rubbing his hips against her stomach so that she could feel the full strength of his male hardness through their clothes.

She wondered what it would be like to feel him inside of her, and she said so. "I want you inside of me, Linc. I want you."

Linc trembled at her provocative words. He took her hand and rubbed it against his erection, teaching her the first of many ways in which she would come to please him.

But he only did it for a moment, and then he abruptly pulled away from her. "We better slow down," he said, his breath ragged. "I'm already too close to completely losing control."

Cassie wasn't sure exactly what he meant, but he went back to kissing her and that was fine with her. There was nothing so wonderful in this world, she decided, as Linc's kisses.

When the last of the saltwater had been washed away, they emerged from the shower, laughing and clinging tightly to each other. They raced, hand in hand, up the hotel's front steps and around the veranda, dodging the wicker chairs and tables. Linc bumped a potted geranium and sent it skidding over the wooden floor and splashing into the lake below. He rounded the corner, stopping suddenly, and Cassie caromed into him. She laughed and then tried to stifle the sound by pressing her mouth into his shoulder.

"Ssshh!" He wrapped his free arm around her and covered her mouth with his hand. She kissed and nibbled at his palm, and then she saw Edward Farrell's slim, elegant figure emerge from his room and step onto the veranda. Edward's eyes seem to pierce the darkness, seeking them out.

"Linc? Cassie? Where have you two been? We looked for you at supper."

Linc swore softly under his breath as Edward strolled toward them. Cassie made a smothered sound, and Linc released her mouth.

"How about joining me in the bar for some brandy?" Edward said, coming up to them. "Good Lord, what have you two been doing? You're half un—you're soaking wet!"

"We were just going to bed," Cassie blurted out unthinkingly. Linc made a strangled noise deep in his throat, and she thought her own face must be glowing in the dark from her sudden embarrassment.

There was a long, awkward silence.

"I beg your pardon," Edward said stiffly, then he turned on his heel and strode toward the open door to his room.

They managed to walk sedately the rest of the way to their own room, but the moment they were inside Cassie flew immediately into Linc's arms. He slammed the door shut with his foot while his hands were busy almost ripping off her wet clothes in his desperate haste to get her undressed.

"Cassie, Cassie," he whispered. "I thought I'd go mad with wanting you, wanting to make love to you, to have you, to make you mine."

His hands and lips seemed to be everywhere at once, setting her bare flesh on fire. She didn't realize he had been slowly backing her up to the bed until her knees hit the edge and she fell back, bringing him with her. He rolled her onto her back and leaned over her, his chest rubbing against her tender, sensitive nipples. Their eyes locked, and she watched as his slowly darkened until they were almost black with desire.

"Cassie . . . honey." His voice throbbed with emotion. "I don't want to hurt you. I'll try to be slow and gentle, but I am so desperate for you I don't know how long I can hold back."

She put her fingers to his hard lips and felt them soften and part with a sigh. "Don't hold back," she said "Love me."

He did, covering her face and throat with kisses, cupping her breasts so that they seemed to swell and fill his hands. He lowered his head, taking each of her nipples in turn into his mouth and rolling it around his tongue. He stroked the length of her, his hand gliding over her hipbone and down to the soft triangle of hair between her thighs. He moved his fingers up and down, sliding into her and then out again, rubbing against this sensitive, secret part of her until her whole body started to sing like a wire strung too tightly. Her head fell back, and she pressed up against his probing fingers, trying to draw him even deeper inside of her. She wanted him in her; she wanted *all* of him.

Suddenly she felt him pull away from her and leave the bed. Surely this wasn't all . . . She opened her eyes and reached for him. "Linc?"

"Right here," he said, giving a final tug on his pants and flinging them across the room.

He started to slide back into her arms, but she stopped him, putting her palm against his chest. She stared boldly at his engorged manhood. The very act of her looking caused it to swell even more and surge upward, and a deep groan tore out of Linc's throat.

Instinctively, Cassie's hand closed around his hard shaft, and a violent shudder coursed through Linc's body. The feel of it surprised Cassie. It was so hard and yet so soft and silken, like a sword sheathed in satin.

"Oh, Linc," she sighed. "It's so . . ."

"Big?" he supplied hopefully.

She laughed deep in her throat, and her fingers tightened around him. She stroked him the way he had shown her in the shower, and she was rewarded by his deep sighs of pleasure.

He parted her thighs with his knee, and her legs fell open to receive him. He entered her slowly, and she stiffened with sudden fear at the sharp stab of pain. But Linc kissed and stroked the tenseness from her, and the pain and fear floated away like wisps of morning mist. He began to move inside her then, with deep, slow strokes that grew in intensity until this time the vibration was not only in her muscles, it sang in her blood. Her limbs trembled and she was flying, climbing higher than she had ever been before. She couldn't breathe, and her vision darkened as she hovered for an instant on the brink of oblivion. And then she was falling, falling, falling back to earth. . . .

Cassie felt a sudden lightness as Linc rolled off her. She lay stretched out flat on her back, one arm flung up as if to shade her eyes, although the room was lit only by a single lamp. Slowly their harsh breathing quieted and he stirred, groping for her hand.

Cassie raised herself up on her elbows and leaned over him, peering down at him intently, unaware of the serious expression on her face.

He gathered her hair off her neck, wrapping it around his fist. "I didn't hurt you too badly, did I? It should be better for you the next time."

"Oh, Linc, it was wonderful. Better than flying!" She blushed, burying her face in his neck. She loved the way he smelled—a tangy male scent now with a hint of saltwater. After a while she raised her head and searched his face again. "But I suppose it's all old stuff to you. You've done it hundreds of times before."

"Hardly hundreds of times, and never with you. And never like that," he added with feeling. He rolled her onto her back and rose above her. His eyes roamed over her, lighting upon her breasts, and he traced a finger down her cleavage.

"We must not have done it the way the book said to," Cassie murmured somewhat breathlessly, for Linc was now planting light, nibbling kisses along her collarbone.

"Umm?" he mumbled, as his tongue licked at the hollow between her breasts.

"The marriage manual. In the part where it described the act of sexual congress—"

Linc flung his head up. "Sexual *what?*"

"Congress. Well, that's what the book called it anyway. Only I think we must not have exactly followed the steps the book set out, because the way the doctor described it, it sounded rather messy and sort of ridiculous even, and—don't laugh!"

"I can't help it." He pulled her to him, giving her a swift, hard kiss on the mouth. "You're incredible, Cassie. I doubt there's another woman like you in the world."

She buried her head in his shoulder to hide the pleasure she felt. If he thought that, then surely he must love her . . . just a little.

Chapter 9

Two days later, Cassie sat in Billings, Montana, with her feet dangling over the edge of the wing, sharing a can of water and some beef jerky with Patches and throwing pebbles at the cows that strayed too close to the plane. Cows seemed to love the taste of doped fabric; she had heard of a whole plane being eaten to the bare ribs in five minutes.

She wondered what was keeping Linc. She was anxious to get started on the five-mile hike into town, but she didn't want to leave until Linc returned from logging in with the race committee. They had flipped a coin to see who would get to go into town for supplies and who would be stuck with the greasy job of overhauling the engine, and Linc had lost. He had then tried to talk her into making it two tosses out of three, but she told him to go whistle "Dixie"—a favorite expression of Quigly's that for some reason had struck Linc as particularly funny. But now he was obviously trying to avoid his end of the deal by hanging around the nearby ranch house, where the committee had set up its headquarters, and no doubt whistling "Dixie" with the other pilots.

Not that there were many other pilots here yet. The *Pegasus* had been the second plane to land, behind only the Schmidt brothers. Edward Farrell had arrived not long after them, followed by four more planes. Cassie thought she and Linc were probably in fourth place now, maybe even third.

A gust of wind rocked the *Pegasus*, whistling through her bracing wires and pulling at the ropes that tethered her to the ground. Cassie looked to the west, where trumpet-shaped clouds with blackened bottoms obscured the mountains. She had never been blessed with Quigly's weather sense, but even an amateur could see there was a bad storm brewing. She shivered and hunched her head down into the collar of her wool jacket; the wind was cold.

This certainly was beautiful country, Cassie thought as she stared out over the miles of open, grassy plains that stretched to the peaks piercing the distant horizon. The air was thick with pollen and smelled of wood smoke, and the cottonwoods and willows that grew along the pasture groaned as they bent with the wind. But she wondered why Bean's cola had chosen such a remote place as Billings, Montana, for this second checkpoint. Only a few ranch hands and Indians from the nearby Crow reservation had been there to watch them land. Out here, at least, the race could hardly be generating as much interest as Bean's cola had hoped.

The sound of an automobile engine interrupted her thoughts. It was a Model T, and new by the looks of it. Linc was in the passenger seat, and a girl was driving.

Cassie jumped down from the wing and trotted forward, Patches at her heels. The automobile jerked to a stop beside her with a squeal of brakes. "Where have you been?" she said to Linc, ignoring the girl.

He swung easily out of the seat. "The race committee is debating whether to start the next leg in a couple of hours instead of tomorrow morning. The old-timers are predicting that storm's going to bring snow with it. If they're right, we could get stuck here for days."

"Surely it wouldn't snow this late in the year!"

"We got over a foot in June last year," the girl said. She had emerged from behind the wheel and walked around to Linc's side.

Cassie gave her a long, cool look. She was dressed for riding and looked to be about Cassie's age, but she was dark and tall, and, in Cassie's opinion, downright skinny. During the last two nights, Cassie had become very knowledgeable about the part of a woman's anatomy that Linc liked best, and this girl had nothing to offer in that department.

"Cassie," Linc said. "This is Miss—"

"What's happened to Pete?" Cassie asked. Pete Striker was supposed to have met them there with the extra supplies.

"He sent a telegram from Butte. A bad rock slide buried the rail tracks over the pass. It looked like it was going to be closed down for a while, so he decided to go on ahead when it's cleared up. He hopes to beat us to Kansas City. But if not, he'll catch us in Baton Rouge instead. Cassie, this is Miss—"

"Well really, Linc. What good is having an advance man if he's forever *behind* you?"

Linc gave her a furious look, and she matched it. They traded glares for several seconds, and then Linc said in a voice that was practically a growl, "Cassie. This is Miss Gallegher."

The girl smiled tentatively at Cassie, but she didn't bother to smile back.

"This is all so exciting," the girl said, giving Linc an uneasy glance. "All these flying machines landing on my pa's ranch. When Linc told me he had a girl for a copilot, I just didn't know whether to believe him or not."

"Linc does lie sometimes," Cassie said.

Linc took her arm and pulled her over to the *Pegasus*, out of the girl's earshot. "What's gotten into you? There's no reason to be so rude. And besides, Miss Gallegher has offered to give me a lift into town. It'll save us time, and we may only have a couple of hours now."

"It was nice of her to offer, Linc. I'm sure she won't mind when she finds out that it's me she's going to take and not you."

Patches, who had gone up to sniff at the girl's riding boots, suddenly backed up and bared his teeth in a low-voiced growl. Linc angrily called him over, and Patches padded up, not looking the least bit contrite.

Linc scowled at him. "And what in blazes has gotten into *you*?"

"He doesn't like your la-di-da misses," Cassie said.

Linc gave her an affronted look. "She isn't mine, and I'm not the slightest bit interested in making her mine. This week I happen to be a happily married man."

"Hunh." Cassie pulled the toolbox out of the locker and thrust it into his hands. "You'd better get started on the engine, Linc. It'll take a good hour."

"You have a heart made of stone, Cassie Jones. A heart made of arctic ice. Glacial, arctic ice—" The rest of Linc's words were drowned out by an arriving plane. It was the old pusher biplane piloted by Harry and Jim, those two charming but somewhat inept young men Cassie had met on the night of the wedding.

The ground wind had picked up considerably during the last few minutes; it whistled loud and shrill through the *Pegasus*'s bracing wires. It was going to be a tricky landing even for experts, and Jim and Harry were no experts. As the plane came in low for its final approach, Cassie could see they were going way too fast for the gale-force winds.

The plane landed heavily, hurtling wildly down the field. It hit a stone or a rut and tilted sharply, skimming the ground and ripping a huge hole in the belly of the fuselage before spinning to a stop. People started to run toward the fallen plane, but Linc grabbed Cassie's arm, holding her back.

"Don't," he said.

"Why not?"

A stubborn look crossed his face. "Because I sa—because I'm asking you not to."

"That's not good enough," Cassie retorted, knowing exactly what he had been about to say. She wrenched free of his grasp and followed the others out to the plane, which now lay on its side in the middle of the field like a bird with a broken wing.

Harry and Jim were a bit shaken up, but neither was seriously hurt. Their plane, however, was going to take hours to repair. Everyone commiserated with the unlucky pair while feeling secretly thankful that it hadn't happened to them.

Cassie helped some of the men drag the plane off the landing field. Linc was already working on the engine when she returned, and Miss Gallegher hovered at his elbow, asking stupid questions.

"They're all right, in case you're interested," Cassie told him.

"I'm not," he snapped back.

Cassie decided that if he was going to sulk she would simply ignore him. She picked up the old ten-gallon milk can they used to hold the extra gasoline they carried. Turning to the girl, she inquired with bright heartiness, "Did Mr. Cameron explain that I would be the one going into town?"

The girl threw Linc a quick look. "I was thinking, maybe you could borrow the Lizzie and drive yourself in? That is, if you don't mind."

"Why, I do thank you for your kindness, Miss Gallegher," Cassie said, her voice as honeysuckle sweet as Melodie's at her best. "And I'm sure my husband thanks you as well."

The girl's mouth fell open. "Husband?" she squeaked. "But he never said you two were married!"

Cassie gave her a brilliant smile. "I told you he lies," she said. As she walked off she heard the sound of Linc's smothered laughter.

Cassie tossed the milk can into the back of the Model T, cranked up the engine, and climbed behind the wheel. She whistled for Patches, who came bounding over and jumped into the passenger seat, wearing his idiotic grin of excitement. Patches loved going places, it didn't much matter where; he was a dog with itchy paws.

She bounced across the field, spewing dust in her wake as she followed the wagon tracks that led away from the ranch. Before long she spotted a small hand-lettered sign that pointed down a badly rutted dirt road to Billings. As she drove she wondered if Linc ever got tired of being chased by women. Not that she was really worried he would succumb to Miss Gallegher's dubious charms while she was in town. For one thing, he would be too busy; and for another, he wouldn't have the energy.

They had made love that whole night at the Saltair Resort, drifting to sleep just about the time they had to be up again to resume the race. The next night they stayed in a seedy old hotel in the town of Whiskey Peak, Wyoming. But they had hardly noticed their surroundings, being engrossed instead in discovering the thousand and one ways to bring each other to mutual rapture with lips and hands and tongues, with loving and teasing words, with bodies that gave and took, conquered and surrendered.

That morning, after they had dragged themselves out of the narrow bed with its sagging mattress, Linc had looked at her with bleary eyes. "Cassie, we've got to stop doing this for a while," he said. "Take separate rooms tonight or something, because I can't get near you without wanting to make love to you. But if we both don't get some sleep soon, we're going to wind up flying into a mountain."

Cassie told him he was absolutely right—they shouldn't forget that the most important thing was to win the race. They decided to celebrate this rare moment of agreement with a kiss. One thing soon led to another, and they were forty-five minutes late getting started.

She was in love with him—there was no use denying it. And although he had not actually said so, she thought he might be in love with her. He loved *making* love to her, at least, and that was something.

It was like living in a dreamworld, and she wished it could last forever. Days together in the sky, meeting danger and challenge with a common purpose; nights spent seeking tender solace and abandoned passion in each other's arms. But, win or lose, the race would end someday—someday soon. And then real life would intrude on their dreamworld, and their love would fade away, like snow melted by the spring sun. Because from life, real life, they both wanted different things.

The morning they left Salt Lake, Ria had come to the airfield to tell them good-bye. Mother and son had stared at each other in silence a moment, and then Linc had spoken. Cassie heard real anger in his voice, and underlying it was something else—something akin to despair.

"I'll do it," he said, although Cassie had no idea what he was promising to do. "If I can. But only because, between the two of you, you've left me little choice."

Ria's lean cheeks looked hollow as she sucked in a deep breath. "Thank you."

"Just try in the future to leave me out of your problems. Stay out of my life, Ria. That's all the thanks I want." And then Linc turned his back on his mother and strode off toward the *Pegasus*.

When Ria turned around to Cassie, tears were sparkling in the older woman's eyes.

"Promise me . . ." Ria said. "Promise me you'll never stop loving him. He does so need to be loved."

"I love him," Cassie said, unable to promise more.

"When he was a child—" Ria's eyes gazed at something far away, some place in the past—"we would pull into a new town at dusk. They were all the same to me, so boring with their steepled churches, corner groceries, and solid, respectable-looking banks; their white houses, each with a swing on the front porch. But Linc would wander the streets, looking in the windows at the families sitting around big mahogany tables set with linen and china. He would peer in the kitchens at the mothers in their starched white aprons taking pies out the oven, and there would be... there would be such a *yearning* in his eyes..."

Cassie had been filled then with a feeling of such utter loss and hopelessness that it was all she could do not to weep. For though she loved Linc Cameron with her whole heart and mind, she knew with despair that what he wanted most she would never be able to give him.

Just thinking about that last, unsettling conversation with Ria brought fresh tears to Cassie's eyes. Rounding a bend in the road, she almost smacked into a large band of men on horseback. She swerved to the side and watched as they thundered by her. They were all heavily armed with rifles and shotguns, and they looked angry, intent on a serious mission.

She drove slowly down Billings's main road. It looked deserted, which was not surprising since most of the inhabitants had apparently galloped out of town. She pulled up in front of a livery stable where an old man with luxurious muttonchop whiskers sat on a barrel, whittling a stick. She asked him where she could buy some gasoline, shouting above the wind.

He had to spit around the huge tobacco plug he had stuck in his cheek before he could answer her. "Richere," he said, or something that sounded like that.

Cassie ordered Patches to stay with the car while she followed the old man around to the side of the stable. He had just finished filling her milk can from a large barrel of gasoline when another pack of riders hurtled by them, stirring up a cloud of choking dust.

"You all here in Billings know something I don't?" she asked the old man.

"Eh?"

"How come everyone's riding out of town like their tails have caught on fire?"

He spat a brown bullet out the side of his mouth. "Reckon they be formin' themselves a posse. The Jasper Mining Company payroll was done robbed this mornin'. Over five thousand bucks worth, folks're sayin'."

The old man helped her carry the now-heavy can back to the automobile. Cassie paid him and then set off for the grocery store she had spotted across the street. She felt a few pairs of curious eyes on her as she climbed onto the plank sidewalk and went through a door whose awning creaked mournfully in the wind.

Inside, the store smelled wonderfully of cinnamon, freshly baked bread, and apples. Cassie's stomach let out a low growl—she had missed breakfast that morning because she and Linc had been in bed when they should have been eating. She asked the grocer for a pound of coffee and got him to grind it for her. While he was doing that, she walked around the store selecting jerky and cans of biscuits, smoked salmon, and some more of the boiled meat. She debated whether they would have a chance to eat the fresh bread before it grew stale, decided they would, and plucked a loaf out of the bin. Putting her selections on the counter, she asked the grocer to weigh up a couple of pounds of the mixed dried fruit and selected a fresh apple to munch on right now.

A pair of grizzled old codgers sat on either side of a checkerboard which was spread out on an upside-down cracker barrel. They were discussing the robbery. Cassie listened with idle curiosity while the grocer totaled up her purchases.

There had been six in the gang in all, one of the old

men said, jumping two red checkers with a black one and causing his opponent to let out a groan or a belch, Cassie wasn't sure which. But one of the robbers had evidently been shot during the getaway, he went on. The sheriff's men had found him later, abandoned by his fellow thieves but still breathing.

"The rest of 'em ain't likely to get fer, Dish," his crony replied. "Not with that payroll bein' mostly in silver dollars. All that weight's bound to slow 'em down."

"That's jest what I been tryin' to tell you, you blamed fool," Dish growled goodnaturedly. "The feller they done caught started bleatin' to Sheriff Beechum after they threatened to hang 'im 'bout how they up and hid the loot somewheres along the road outta town."

The other old man hacked a laugh. "Now what do you wanna bet that if ol' Beechum and his boys find that payroll stash, the Jasper Mining Company never comes to hear of it—damn it, Dish, I gotta watch you ever' second else you try an' cheat!" he exclaimed as two more red checkers disappeared off the board. "When was the last time you ever played me a game fair and square?"

"If you knowed as much about trackin' as you claim to know about checkers, Nash, we could have a go at findin' that payroll ourselves and die rich men. Maybe I'll jest take a ride out anyways. I was a fair scout in my day."

Nash snorted. "What day was that? Hell, Dish, you couldn't find your way from here to the shithouse if there weren't a path already worn—"

Dish cleared his throat loudly and nodded his head at Cassie. Nash flushed a bright red and studied the board between his knees, mumbling something about how the world was going to rack and ruin if a man couldn't enjoy a simple conversation without worrying if there was a member of the opposite sex hovering in the background ready to take offense.

Cassie smiled to herself as she left the store with her box of groceries. She paused on the sidewalk to look around her. Being raised in Virginia, she had grown up with a romantic view of the West. She had been excited at the prospect of taking a stroll around Billings to explore the foreign atmosphere. But she could see now that except for the fact that the buildings were made of wood instead of brick, and many had false fronts to make them look taller, the town didn't appear to be much different than Kingly. A payroll robbery wasn't all that remarkable an occurrence either in Cassie's opinion. The First Mercantile Bank of Kingly had been robbed one Sunday when she was ten, and she had seen the whole thing. She'd been playing right across the street when it happened, and she had enjoyed a spell of notoriety as the town's only witness to the event.

Pushing aside the memory, Cassie decided she would go back to the airfield early and help Linc with the overhaul. Patches greeted her return to the car as if she had been gone for twenty years, and she gave him a piece of jerky to chew on. She was two miles shy of the Gallegher ranch when the Model T chugged to a stop, the motor dead.

She pounded on the steering wheel in vexation, then got out and spun the crank again and again with no success. She checked the engine carefully, but she could see nothing wrong. It was only then that she thought to check the fuel tank. It was empty.

"You idiot!' she berated herself. At least she had plenty of gasoline with her. Grunting, she lifted the milk can out of the back and then searched the flivver's toolbox for a funnel.

Meanwhile, Patches had spotted a prairie dog and took off after it. Cassie yelled at him not to get lost, but she doubted he heard her. The wind was blowing harder now, flattening the goldenrod and prairie grass in rippling waves.

She had just finished screwing the cap back onto the tank when Patches returned. "A lot of help you've been," she chided him, glancing down. Something fluttered out the corner of his mouth. She hunkered down beside him. "What have you been getting into?"

It was a piece of paper of some sort. She pried open his jaws. No, it wasn't a piece of paper; not an ordinary one, anyways. Cassie's heart did a flip-flop. It was a dollar bill!

"Patches, where did you get this?" The dog cocked his head at her. She scrambled to her feet. "Come on, boy! Show me where you got this."

Patches ran around her in circles, yipping excitedly, then made a beeline for a nearby pile of rocks choked with brambles and milkweed. He pawed frantically at the ground. There was a sudden flash of silver, like a mirror reflecting the sun.

The outlaws hadn't done a very good job burying their loot, Cassie thought—although they *had* been in a hurry. Patches must have seen the freshly turned dirt and thought he had discovered a gopher hole. One of the partially uncovered sacks had burst, spilling paper currency and silver dollars onto the ground.

Cassie was never able to explain later—not to herself and certainly not to Linc—what demon had seized her. She could only guess that it had been some sort of trance brought about by physical exhaustion and the same mental collapse that was causing her to be in love. One moment she was looking at a scattered pile of dazzling coins, and the next she was gazing down at all five of the payroll sacks arranged in a nice neat row along the backseat of the flivver.

At that moment she spotted a big roan trotting down the road toward them, carrying a double load. It was Linc, riding in back of Miss Gallegher. Cassie hurriedly tore off her coat and tossed it over the bags of money, dumping a bewildered Patches on top of it all.

"Finders keepers," she told him, giving his head a

couple of pats. "If that posse were to find it, they'd only divvy it up among themselves anyway."

Patches cocked his head and gave her what she swore was a look of disapproval.

"If you had stumbled upon some other dog's bone buried out here, you'd keep it," she told him defensively.

Patches sniffed with disdain.

"All right, all right." Cassie sighed. "I know we can't keep the money. But if we deliver it safely back to the mining company, they might give us a reward, so keep your muzzle shut for now, and let me do the explaining to Linc."

"Cassie!" Linc called out to her as he dismounted. "Where the hell have you been? The race started twenty minutes ago. Did you get a flat?"

"It's all right now. Crank her up and let's go," she said, nervously wiping her sweating palms on her pants.

Linc, thank heaven, had walked to the front of the car to work the crank, but the girl, still mounted on the roan, was sidling too close for Cassie's comfort.

"Better not get too close," Cassie said to her. "That crank's got a powerful kick to it. It's liable to come flying off." And to Cassie's relief, the girl backed her horse up.

Cassie climbed behind the wheel, shivering as a gust of wind blasted through her shirt.

"Where's your coat?" Linc asked her.

"In back. I got hot, uh . . . changing the tire."

The flivver's motor purred to life. Linc had started to walk around to the passenger side when the girl let out a piercing scream. Her horse reared, whirled around on its haunches, and galloped off while bullets rattled on the ground like hailstones, followed by a crackling noise like a string of firecrackers going off at once.

Linc dove headfirst into the car, banging his nose on

the dashboard. This struck Cassie as quite funny, and she laughed out loud.

"Christ! They're *shooting* at us!" she heard Linc yell over the noise of the motor, the wind, and the gunfire.

Cassie hunched over the steering wheel and pressed down hard on the pedal. The flivver jerked forward, tires spinning in the dirt. It lurched and bounced over the ruts, banging her and Linc against one another like beans in a Mexican gourd. She risked a look over her shoulder and saw five men on horseback bearing down on them. Then a movement above and to the right caught her eye, and if she had been the fainting type she would have passed out right then.

More riders galloped along the ridge beside them, many more. It was the posse from Billings. The men had spotted them or the outlaws or both, and more gunfire flashed as bullets pinged into the sturdy metal body of the Model T.

"Why are they shooting at *us*?" Linc yelled.

Cassie was pressing down so hard on the pedal that she thought she would push her foot through the floorboard. Steam began to curl out of the radiator. "We've got something they want!" she shouted to Linc, not daring to take her eyes off the road.

"What? Got what? Christ!" he exclaimed as more bullets whizzed over their heads.

Patches chose that particular moment to start howling. Linc thought he had been shot and practically fell out of the automobile trying to get to him in the backseat. Cassie cringed, expecting a bellow of rage when Linc discovered the money. But she heard nothing—if you could call a shrieking wind, a howling dog, and dozens of rifles and shotguns blazing away at you nothing.

She glanced behind her and saw to her dismay that Linc was calmly tossing the bags of money, one after the other, out the back of the flivver. The bags split open when they hit the ground, sending silver dollars rolling out in rivers and currency bills swirling up to be caught by the wind. This was greeted by cheers and bellows of rage and intermittent gunfire.

"Don't give them all of it!" she wailed, twisting around in her seat and unintentionally jerking on the wheel. The flivver skidded on the loose dirt and bounced over several ruts. If it hadn't been seven feet tall and bottom-heavy, it would have flipped over like a turtle onto its back.

Cassie wrestled the wheel back under control. She glanced around again and almost screamed as Linc shoved his face so close to hers she could feel the heat of his breath.

"If we get out of this alive, I'm going to kill you, Cassie Jones! I'm going to strangle you with my bare hands, and I'm going to smile while I'm doing it."

Cassie swallowed hard and turned back around to stare straight ahead. She supposed he had reason to get a *little* angry, but that didn't give him the right to threaten murder.

She suddenly realized they were no longer being chased and shot at. Her fingers relaxed their fierce grip on the steering wheel, and she slowed down a bit. The makeshift airfield was in sight now, the *Pegasus* looking lonely all by itself in the empty pasture.

Sometime during the last half hour the black clouds had moved in overhead, and they now started to spit out an icy rain, which made a hiss as it landed on the flivver's overheated radiator. Cassie stood on the brake, and the automobile came to a shrieking halt. The radiator boiled over and the engine coughed and died, but Cassie was already out and running for the *Pegasus*. She wanted to be the first in the cockpit so that Linc would have to spin the prop.

She scrambled on board. Patches followed, carrying her coat between his teeth and dragging it in the dirt. Linc shouted something that she couldn't hear above the wind as he tossed in the supplies and extra gasoline and sprinted around to the propeller. The engine started up immediately. Linc jumped back, and Cassie sent the *Pegasus* forward so fast she was thrown back against the seat. The plane rocketed down the pasture. She glanced over her shoulder and saw Linc running along behind her, his face red and contorted with effort and rage. She opened the throttle, and the plane began to lift.

She had to have been five feet off the ground when she looked back a second time. Linc put on a burst of speed, springing forward and up, higher than she would have ever thought possible, and just managed to grab onto the trailing edge of the lower wing. He hung from his fingertips, suspended in the air as the plane climbed higher, then jackknifed his legs and pulled himself on board. She felt the pull of his weight as he walked across the wing and adjusted for it automatically until he was safely in the cockpit.

She expected any minute to feel a pair of strong hands wrapping themselves around her throat. Even so, it was too bad her plan hadn't worked. That arrogant, interfering man needed to be taught a lesson. Although he probably really *would* have strangled her if she had succeeded in taking off without him. Not that she had intended to desert him completely—only long enough for him to get good and worried that she wasn't coming back.

Summoning up her courage, she twisted around to look at him—and saw to her astonishment that he was laughing.

Chapter 10

Cassie sucked in a sharp breath at the sight of the deep, ugly crack that ran the entire length of the propeller blade. She reached out to touch it, then superstitiously pulled her hand back. "My God, Linc. We were..."

"Yeah," Linc said. "I know. We were damn lucky it didn't break apart while we were over that timberland."

Cassie pushed her wet hair out of her eyes with a shaking hand. The rain was coming down hard now, and its icy slashes stung her face like needles. Even riding a whistling tail wind they had been unable to pull ahead of the storm. The cloud level had begun to get dangerously low, but the terrain had turned heavily forested and rocky, with no place to land. Cassie's worry had almost reached the level of honest-to-God fear by the time she spotted an open meadow and thankfully set the *Pegasus* down. It was while landing that she had begun to suspect that something was wrong with the propeller.

Linc was now staring at the damaged blade, frowning. He ran his fingers along the crack, then leaned forward to peer at it through the driving sheets of rain.

"What is it?" Cassie asked.

168

He straightened and stepped back. "Look for your-self. This split in the wood wasn't any accident. It was made with a chisel probably, then camouflaged with putty and varnish so we'd be less apt to notice it during the preflight check."

Especially, Cassie thought guiltily, since they had been so preoccupied with each other that they'd grown lax with routine things such as preflight checks. She started to ask him who could have done it, then snapped her mouth shut on the useless remark. "At least we're carrying a spare," she said instead.

They looked at each other . . . and shared the same, simultaneous thought.

Cassie whirled around so abruptly her heel slipped in the mud, and she would have fallen if Linc hadn't reacted with his lightning reflexes, grabbing her arm and holding her, one-handed, in the air until she could gather her feet back under her.

They carried the extra propeller lashed beneath the fuselage. At least, Cassie saw with relief, it was still there. But they had to shove Patches, who had bur-rowed under there to get out of the rain, out of the way to get at it. Linc soon became impatient trying to untie the taut, slick knots and cut the rope with his pocket-knife instead. He brought the propeller out and propped it up against the wing struts. Cassie looked it over quickly and started to let out her breath in a sigh of relief. And then she saw it—a slight bulge in the varnish where the extra coat had been applied to cover the putty.

She wrapped her arms around herself, shivering in her rain-sodden coat. You could walk for miles before you stumbled across another human being out here. And when you did he wasn't likely to be carrying a spare airplane propeller in his pocket. She watched Linc's long fingers play over the surface of the blades, looking for more cracks. His lips were set in a tight line, and they looked blue against his white face. It made her realize just how cold and wet and miserable she felt.

"What are we going to do?" she asked, surprised at the fear she heard in her own voice.

He turned and gathered her into his arms, pressing her head against his chest. "I don't know yet, but there's no sense in worrying about it now. No one else is flying in this weather anyway, so for the moment we aren't losing any time. It gives us a chance to"—he brushed her cold lips with his and then flashed her his dazzling smile—"to get caught up on some of that sleep we've been missing."

Linc made a cozy shelter by hanging a pair of tarps down from the fore and aft wing edges. He cleared away most of the rocks and spread blankets over the floor of their makeshift tent. They wouldn't be able to have a fire, but two people and a dog would soon generate enough heat to make the enclosed space comfortable.

They ate a cold meal out of the canned food and dried fruit that Cassie had bought earlier that afternoon. Above their heads the rain drummed steadily on the wing fabric. Blessed warmth began to seep beneath Cassie's soaked clothes, and she felt her eyelids grow heavy.

Linc lay stretched out, propped up on one elbow. Cassie sat at his feet with Patches's head in her lap. "Come closer," Linc said. His face was impassive, but his voice sounded stern to Cassie's sensitive ears.

She eyed him warily. He had yet to confront her over all the trouble she had caused back in Billings, and she wanted to be a little farther away from him than this when he did—like maybe across the country.

She shifted so that Patches lay between them. "I thought you said you wanted to get some sleep."

"I do." He grinned at her a bit sheepishly, and Cassie's fears abruptly vanished. "It hurts my pride to admit this, but I'm too plain exhausted to do anything now *but* sleep. I just want to hold you in my arms while I do it."

She lay down beside him, and he pulled her close against his chest. But after a moment she raised up so that she could see his face. "You really aren't mad at me?" she asked. "I wasn't really going to keep that money, Linc. I thought if we turned it in, we might get some sort of reward. I didn't mean to get you shot at."

The arm that he had wrapped around her waist tightened. "I might have been a little angry at first—"

"A little! You threatened to strangle me."

"A lot, then. But I learned long ago that it's pointless to get mad over something you can't change, and trying to keep you out of trouble would be like trying to empty the ocean with a thimble. You are yourself, Cassie," he said, but his eyes were so sad Cassie felt her own eyes well up with tears. She buried her head in his chest so that he wouldn't see them.

Sometime later Cassie awoke to a shower of light, teasing kisses on her face. She opened her lids to look into eyes that were a depthless, cerulean blue.

"It's tomorrow morning, and it's still raining," Linc said before his mouth lowered and moved over hers.

Cassie sighed softly and closed her eyes. Then one lid popped open, and she stiffened.

Linc released her mouth. "What's the matter?"

"Patches is watching."

"Patches," Linc said, "go outside."

Patches gave Linc a look that said, You must be out of your mind. I could drown out there.

Linc raised a flap of the tarp and pointed. "Go!" he said in a voice that brooked no argument. Patches slinked out with his tail drawn up tightly under his belly, a look of such misery on his face that Cassie had to stifle a laugh. She wasn't being completely heartless though, as there was plenty of dry shelter under the fuselage.

Linc lowered himself back down beside her. "Now, where were we?"

They began slowly undressing each other, stroking bare skin with featherlike caresses, licking and kissing all the tender, sensitive places until their bodies became slick with sweat. The air was filled with their hot, harsh breathing, and Cassie thought she would die if he didn't take her soon.

"Linc..." she pleaded, arching up to rub her pelvis against him.

Linc released her nipple from between his lips. He raised his head, weighing the fullness of her breasts in his palms. "I love your breasts, Cassie. Of all your delectable parts—and you do have some delectable parts..." He pointed out a few with his fingers and his lips and his tongue. "I think I love your breasts the best."

"I hadn't noticed." She laughed softly until he smothered the sound with a kiss.

He whispered teasingly against her open mouth, "And which of my delectable parts do you love best?"

Cassie gasped. "Really, Linc! I can't say that word *out loud.*"

"Why not? No one's around to hear you but me. And it's my part."

Cassie's blush spread all the way down her neck. She turned her head, bringing her lips close to his ear, and whispered it.

"My big toe!" Linc exclaimed, momentarily shocked. And then he laughed. "I ought to make you pay for that," he growled, and he began to do things with his fingers that he knew would drive her almost wild, while his searching, restless tongue moved down to the pulse in her neck.

He straddled her, bracing himself on his hands, and they watched the hard length of him enter her, fill her. He looked up and caught her eyes.

"Is this what you love, Cassie?"

"Yessss . . ." she said on an hiss of indrawn breath as he pressed deeper into her.

"Is this what you love?"

"Yes!" she cried, and her hips lifted to meet his hard, piercing thrust.

He arched back, putting his weight on his knees and lifting her pelvis to meet his long strokes. He drove into her fast, then slow, then fast again. Drove into her until his muscles froze and his head flung back, and she saw the first shudders begin to rack his body. Then she, too, was lost to the vibrating, pulsing hum, the spinning sky, and the long weightless fall.

"It couldn't have been done in Billings," Linc said much later, as they lay snuggled close in each other's arms. Cassie knew he had been thinking about the sabotaged propellers. "There wasn't time."

"It must have been done at Salt Lake then." She burrowed deeper into his arms. "But Patches was on guard."

"He's seen us being friendly with most of the other pilots. We're always hanging around each other's planes, swapping stories, even helping out with maintenance now and then. So if whoever's been tinkering with the *Pegasus* is familiar, a friend, Patches isn't apt to perceive the danger. He's only a dog, Cassie. He can't read minds, or motives."

"I wasn't criticizing him," Cassie said defensively. "I only meant . . . oh, I don't know what I meant."

He kissed her. "Never mind. I was just thinking— they did such a good job of making the split undetectable that the putty and varnish acted like a sort of glue. That's why the blade held together so long. I wonder what they thought when they saw us show up, dumb and happy, in Billings."

"You keep saying 'they'. What makes you think it's more than one person?"

"I don't especially. It's just a figure of speech."

Linc's face was perfectly blank as he spoke, but he

had taken a few seconds too long to answer, and Cassie had seen something flicker in his eyes. She pulled away from him and sat up, giving him the full force of a ferocious glare.

Linc threw up his hands in front of his face as if she were about to spit bullets at him instead of words. "My God, Cassie. You could freeze a man's blood looking at him like that."

"Damn you, Linc Cameron! Whatever, *whom*ever you suspect, you have no right to keep it from me. My life is at stake here too."

"You're crazy. I don't suspect anybody. You know as much about what's going on as I do."

There was a ring of conviction in his voice, even a hint of hurt feelings. But when she looked into his eyes, she knew he was lying.

"It's a risk, Cassie," Linc said. "A big one. It might hold up for a hundred miles, or fall to pieces on takeoff."

Cassie looked up at the bright blue sky, at the fleecy, fair-weather clouds. "What other choice do we have?"

"None, I guess. Except quit and admit defeat."

She gave him a teasing smile. "Then what are we doing standing around here talking and wasting time when we could be flying?"

They had finished fitting the spare propeller onto the engine shaft that afternoon just about the time the weather cleared. They hadn't really discussed it, but when the rain started to let up, Linc had left the shelter and Cassie had gone with him, knowing exactly what he was going to do. The varnish and putty did act as some sort of adhesive agent—they had probably flown a good eight hundred miles on the other doctored propeller. The next checkpoint was Kansas City, Missouri, about eight hundred miles from where they were now. They couldn't count on the spare to get them that far, but it might hold together long enough for them to get to a major town where they could pick up another propeller in a hurry . . . if they were lucky.

Ironically, they had been so preoccupied with the propeller they had a few unexpected anxious moments when it looked as if the meadow might be too short for takeoff, especially with the mud sucking at their wheels, slowing them down. But Linc expertly held the *Peg*'s nose level to gain more speed and then lifted her gently, clearing the treetops by a bare, breathtaking foot.

It was a perfect afternoon for flying. The winds aloft were light, the sky a clear pristine blue that went on forever. The engine throbbed steadily, and Cassie began to think they would make it after all.

She was wrong.

They had just spotted the distinctive shape of Chimney Rock, Nebraska, a pointing finger on top of a giant, up-ended cone, when the *Pegasus* gave a mighty heave and started to shudder and yaw. A fragment of propeller blade sliced through the air, barely missing their heads, followed by a sudden, whistling silence as the engine cut off.

They went down fast, faster than Cassie would have liked. She knew Linc was a good pilot, but until that moment she hadn't known how good. There hadn't been time to size up a field for rocks, stumps, or ditches, yet he held the plane steady on a long sweeping glide, riding the wind currents toward an expanse of black earth. It was a recently plowed field, and Linc set the wheels down precisely in the furrows, so that the plane rolled to a smooth, graceful stop.

He had made it look easy, Cassie thought as she sat in the cockpit, stunned, and tried to stop shaking.

Linc jumped down and stood grinning up at her. "Let's try that again. With a bit more practice we could turn it into a stunt and charge people two bits to see it."

Laughter bubbled up in Cassie's tight chest. She descended into his waiting arms, feeling wonderfully snug and safe in his strong embrace. Patches ran in a circle around them, yipping excitedly.

A man who had been working a nearby field with a team of oxen and a bull-tongued plow turned the plow on its side and came running across the freshly turned furrows. He skidded to a halt a few feet away from them. In his early thirties, he had a stern, weathered face covered with a ragged black beard. He regarded them warily out of earth brown eyes.

"You folks all right?" he asked after a moment.

"We busted a propeller," Linc said, giving the man an easy smile. "I don't suppose you've got a spare."

The farmer shook his head. He took a few tentative steps closer to the plane, looking at it with awe. "I seen a picture of these newfangled machines in one of those magazines my Maisie's always reading. I didn't rightly believe it could fly, though." He grinned suddenly at Linc. "Still don't know for a fact that it does."

Cassie laughed. "Where's the nearest town? If we can get her fixed, I'll take you up for a ride and prove it to you."

The farmer looked Cassie up and down, taking in her masculine clothing, and his mouth tightened into a line of disapproval. "I thought you were a boy," he said. "Until you spoke up, that is. The Lord don't hold with women who forget their place. You'd do well to remember that, miss, and dress accordingly."

Cassie stared at him, shocked into speechlessness. Then the anger came, and she opened her mouth to let him know just what *place* she would like to send him to, but as usual Linc was too quick for her.

"You were saying something about the nearest town?" he put in smoothly.

"I wasn't, but it's no secret. The nearest town is Bridgeport. About sixteen miles from here, smack dab on the Platte River. It's no more'n a wide spot in the road. You won't find no spare whatchamacallits in Bridgeport. We got a prime cabinetmaker in Hank

Mason though. Might be he could make you one of them things you busted."

"Sixteen miles is a bit far to walk," Linc said. "Do you have an automobile or a buggy we could rent?"

"Yep, got me a buckboard. And I won't charge you nothin' to borry it neither, if you've a mind to, but it won't do you no good to go into town this afternoon. Hank went up to Scotts Bluff for his niece's wedding. He'll be back tomorrow, though, most likely. Never did get along too good with his sister."

Cassie wanted to curse in frustration at this further delay, but she thought the farmer would probably faint from shock. She heard a shout of excitement and turned around to see a boy racing barefoot toward them across a field of sprouting corn. A woman lagged farther behind the boy, for she had a baby balanced on one hip.

The boy's breath was coming in great gasps as he stopped before them to dance up and down, first on one foot and then the other. "Lookit, Ma! Lookit, Ma, it's a airplane! It plumb fell out of the sky!"

The woman laughed and looked at the *Pegasus* with shining eyes. She was younger than the farmer by a few years. Though the hard work and life on the plains had already begun to fade the bloom of her youth, she was still pretty, and her smile was broad and friendly. Cassie warmed to her immediately.

"It didn't fall out of the sky, Josh." The woman laughed again. "It was *flown* here."

"Actually, your boy's more than half right," Cassie said. "We did sort of fall out of the sky. Our propeller broke, and we had to make a sudden landing in your field. We'll pay for any damage to your crops."

"She's a girl," the farmer said, nodding at Cassie, his stern disapproval of her still very evident.

"I can see that, Seth." The woman gave Cassie another one of her broad smiles and switched the baby to her other hip. "I'm Maisie Turner, and this is my husband, Seth. Knowing Seth, I imagine he got so busy jawing at you he forgot to introduce himself properly."

To Cassie's amazement the harsh-faced farmer blushed at his wife's words. He held out his hand to Linc, who took it, smiling brightly in turn. "I'm Linc Cameron. And this is Cassie, my, uh . . . wife."

Cassie fought down an almost irrepressible urge to copy one of Melodie's favorite mannerisms and hold out her hand palm down to the disapproving Seth Turner, showing him that she could at least act the part of a lady, no matter what she was wearing. She settled instead for a halfhearted smile.

Patches suddenly barked sharply, reminding everyone that he had been left out of the introductions.

"What's your dog's name, mister?" the boy asked, kneeling down to shake Patches's paw.

"Patches."

"Can he fly the airplane, too?"

"No, but he always comes along for the ride."

"I told them they could borry the buckboard," the farmer explained to his wife. "They think Hank could maybe make 'em a new part for their machine to take the place of the one that busted. Now you stay back out of the way, boy," he said sharply to his son, who had sidled up for a better look at the wounded *Pegasus*.

"Oh Seth, let him be. It's likely the closest he's ever going to get to an airplane." Maisie Turner beamed at Cassie and Linc. "You'll stay the night then. We don't have any extra room in the house, but you can bed down in the hayloft. Please say you'll stay. Joshua here is likely to burst if he don't get a chance to ask you all the questions he's got humming in his head."

Linc accepted the invitation, explaining that he had to tie the *Pegasus* down first in case the wind picked up during the night. Then they collected their flying kits and followed the Turners across the fields just as the sun was beginning to set behind them.

The farm consisted of a sturdy barn painted a bright

red that dwarfed the sod house beside it. In back of the barn was a windmill that turned lazily in the evening breeze. A couple of toddlers, both girls, were playing in the puddle around the base of the water pump that stood in the front yard, and Patches immediately loped over to join them. Cassie noticed the farmer give the muddy children a disapproving scowl, though he said nothing. Another pigtailed girl of about six stood in the doorway, watching them with round, solemn eyes.

"Are all these children yours?" Cassie blurted out, and Maisie laughed.

"Every blessed one of them!"

The house consisted of an all-purpose living room and a kitchen, with a divided sleeping loft above that was reached by a ladder. The floor was bleached plywood; the furniture roughly made. But every surface sparkled, and there was a cheerful air to the house, as if it had taken on Maisie Turner's own personality.

Seth Turner paused behind them in the doorway. "Airplanes or not," he said diffidently, "I still got work to do before supper. Joshua, you fed them chickens yet?"

"But Pa . . ."

"You do your chores," Maisie said, ruffling her son's hair. "The Camerons will still be here when you're done."

The boy shuffled out the door dejectedly, and Maisie grinned suddenly at Linc and Cassie. "If the truth be told, mostly it's me who's dying to hear all about what you're doing here and where you're going, and how you get one of those flying machines up in the air in the first place. But I imagine you'd like to clean yourselves up a bit before we start wearin' you out with all our questions. You can use Seth's and my room for now to freshen up whilst I start supper. It won't be much more than a mess of snap beans and sweet corn, I'm afraid. But I'll beat up a batch of buttermilk biscuits. Peggy"— she turned to the older girl, who had followed them inside—"go fetch these folks a bucket of fresh water, and then clean the mud off those girls before your pa has a fit."

Linc poured water into an enamel basin and rinsed the soap off his face. "You couldn't find a friendlier person than Maisie Turner," he said. He rubbed a towel over his damp hair, pausing to peer at Cassie. "What are you doing?"

She had dumped her flying kit out into a pile on the floor. "What does it look like I'm doing? I'm changing into my skirt for supper. Otherwise that infuriating farmer will likely want to feed me out in the yard with Patches and the chickens."

Linc tossed the towel aside and pulled her into his arms, trying to kiss away her scowl. "There's one good thing about Seth Turner—he puts me in a good light. I don't mind your overalls. Although I do have to admit I like you best wearing nothing at all."

Cassie wriggled free of his grasp and stepped back, glaring at him with her hands on her hips. "Linc Cameron, you are even more infuriating than that farmer!"

He gazed at her, completely bewildered. "What did I do?"

"You're acting so...so damned *cheerful*. As if we hadn't a care in the world. Doesn't it even matter to you that we've lost the race?"

"The race won't be won until the plane with the best time lands in New York, and that hasn't happened yet. A thousand things could go wrong with the other leaders between now and then. We still might be able to make up for the time we're losing here later on down the road."

Cassie had to admit that any number of things could certainly go wrong for the others. They had yet to speak of it between them, but two of the original entrants had never arrived at Salt Lake—lost somewhere in the desert, perhaps forever. And the accident that had occurred at Billings with the pusher biplane was more proof that things besides weather could delay a team. And if Ward Farrell's radiator leak really was caused by an ice-pick puncture, then they probably weren't the only ones suffering unexpected break-downs along the way.

"Maybe we won't be the only unlucky ones on this leg," she said, putting her thoughts into words. "But what about the saboteur? It makes me furious to think he's gaining all this time on us by cheating."

For a moment Cassie thought Linc was going to say something, something important, but the moment passed and he shrugged instead. "Let's wait and see how things stand in Kansas City before we give up." He gave her a cocky grin. "Hell, you and I can fly cir-cles around anyone else in this race. It's going to take more than sugar in our gas tank and a busted propeller to hold us back. We're going to win this, Cassie. You and I—together."

Cassie was filled with sudden joy at his words. Not only did he refuse to give up, to be beaten, but most astonishing of all was the faith he seemed to have in her ability to persevere at any cost. She had thought that Quigly was the only man on earth willing to think of her not as a fragile and brainless female, but as an individual—as capable as any man and more capable than most. But Linc had not spoken only of himself, he had included her as well. *We are going to win this, Cassie,* he had said. *You and I—together.*

She felt a curious constriction in her chest. If she had not been madly in love with him already, she would have fallen in love with Linc Cameron for that one thing alone: he believed in her and was not afraid to tell her so.

"Why are you looking at me like that?" he said.

"I was thinking . . . that I love you very much."

She saw the surprise on his face, then watched as it turned to joy. She thought for a moment that he would say he loved her in turn, but he did not. Instead, he reached for her, pulling her into his arms. He kissed her, a kiss that began gentle but soon turned hard and demanding. She pressed against him, running her palms up and down his back, and felt him tense with mounting excitement.

He groaned and tore his mouth from hers, giving her a ragged smile. "We'd better go downstairs and help Mrs. Turner with supper before things get out of hand up here. Somehow I don't think this was quite what she had in mind when she offered to let us freshen up."

Cassie laughed low in her throat and brushed his cheek with her lips. "We've made love in some odd places so far, but we've yet to try a hayloft."

"When this is over," Linc said, "I'm going to rent us the biggest, softest bed in all of New York City, and we're going to wear that bed out making love night and day, every which way it can be done and a few ways that haven't even been invented yet."

All of which made Cassie flush furiously with embarrassment—and happiness.

Chapter 11

Cassie had all the Turners, even the dour Seth, convulsed with laughter as she related the story of her part in the Billings payroll robbery. Linc watched her from beneath carefully lowered lids, marveling at his fortune in having found this rare woman. And the greater fortune that somehow, against all his expectations, she had come to love him.

As she talked and laughed, her eyes would come occasionally to rest on him, eyes that were a mysterious, smoky gray, hinting at depths Linc knew he could never fully delve, not in a lifetime of loving her. And her hair, shining in the soft light of the kerosene lamps, seemed woven with every shade of gold from taffy to ripened wheat. He thought of taking her in his arms and burying his face in that hair, pressing his lips to her mouth, tasting deeply of her erotic essence—like biting into a sun-ripened peach on a hot summer day. He had a sudden, breathless image of her lying naked beneath him, of plunging his hardness into her softness, and he felt a surge of desire so strong that he almost gasped in pain.

He shifted uncomfortably in his chair, smiling wryly to himself. It was a good thing he was sitting down, and that the kitchen table discreetly hid the lower half of his anatomy. Then he looked up to find Maisie Turner's soft hazel eyes resting on him with a secret knowledge that brought a blush to his cheeks.

And yet in spite of what her nearness was doing to him, he could not stop looking at Cassie. His wife. She had surprised him earlier with her declaration of love. She had made it so solemnly, so honestly. And he was ashamed that though he loved her in return with every fiber of his being, he hadn't yet found the courage to tell her so.

"I wasn't *really* going to fly off without him," Cassie said, finishing her story and giving Linc a smile of such sweet tenderness that it almost brought tears to his eyes. "I just wanted to scare him a little."

Linc laughed at this. "You didn't think being shot at by a thundering herd of outlaws and a posse was frightening enough?"

Seth Turner harrumphed. "I can't believe you'd allow her to operate that contraption of yours in the first place," he said to Linc. "It isn't a proper occupation for a woman."

Linc stifled a groan, waiting for Cassie's inevitable eruption of fury. But she merely replied in a mild tone, "The *Pegasus* belongs to me."

"Does it really!" Maisie Turner exclaimed, casting a look of triumph at her husband.

Seth in turn gave Linc a skeptical look. "But if you're married"—he cocked one brow and raised his voice with doubt until Linc nodded—"then the machine's yours by conjugal right. A wife ain't entitled to hold property separate from her husband. And besides," he said, pronouncing his final word on the subject, "if the Lord had meant for mankind to fly, he'd have given us wings."

To Linc's surprise Cassie reached over and tweaked Seth Turner's beard. "But God did give us wings," she said, laughing as Seth blushed and then pretended to scowl. "The *Pegasus* is proof of it. And after we get the new propeller on tomorrow, I'll take you up in her. I'll take you up and show you God's domain from the best vantage point there is: the sky."

Seth stared at Cassie with such astonishment that Linc had to stifle a laugh. "You couldn't get me in one of them things," he stated emphatically. "No, ma'am. Not if you was to offer me a million bucks."

"I should like to go for a ride," Maisie said softly. "I shall go for a ride," she added more emphatically, meeting her husband's startled, disapproving look and forcing his eyes down. "If you'll take me, that is," she said to Cassie.

Cassie smiled. "I'd love to."

The Turner children had been raised to keep silent during the supper hour, but Joshua was finding it impossible to contain himself any longer. "How old were you when you first learned how to fly, Mr. Cameron?" he burst out, casting a swift, anxious look at his father, who to his astonishment gave him an indulgent smile.

"I was seventeen," Linc said. "But Cassie—Mrs. Cameron—was only fourteen the first time she went up."

Joshua's eyes opened wide. "Honest? But I'm ten already! Pa . . . ?"

"Absolutely not," Seth said.

Joshua's face crumpled with disappointment, but he knew better than to argue. "Ma said she read all about you in a newspaper. That you were an ace in the war," he said to Linc, his young eyes shining with blatant worship. "I bet you had hundreds of kills!"

It always happened sooner or later; they always wanted to know about his part in the war. Usually Linc reacted to this probing, no matter how innocent, with a snarling surliness. But because he liked the Turners, he had steeled himself so that he would be able to meet their inevitable questions with the proper degree of nonchalance. Yet he knew that something of the jumbled mixture of terror and self-loathing and pervasive weariness that he still felt about the war showed in his face despite all his efforts.

When he spoke, though, he was pleased to find that his voice was light and even. "I was credited with twenty-five victories, but they weren't all 'kills' in the sense you mean, Joshua. Some of the enemy pilots I shot down walked away from their planes and lived to fly another day. There was one man... Karl Schumacher. He was a *Kanone*. That means 'top gun' in German—the same thing as our word 'ace.' He and I must have met each other in a good dozen dogfights." Linc smiled wryly. "And he won most of them as I recall."

"But you got him in the end, I bet?" Joshua said, not wanting to believe that his hero could be defeated by anyone.

Linc repressed a shudder. "Yes..." he said slowly. "I got him in the end."

Suddenly the smell of burning flesh assailed Linc's nostrils, and he thought he might be sick. He pushed his plate of half-eaten food away and reached almost blindly for his cup of coffee. The coffee was black and hot, and it burned the roof of his mouth, but the feeling of nausea passed.

"How is it done?" Joshua asked eagerly. "A dogfight, I mean."

"Joshua, I don't think Mr. Cameron cares to talk anymore about the war," Maisie said.

"That's all right, Mrs. Turner." Linc knew he had to force himself to come to terms with the war so that he could get on with a normal life. In a way it seemed he had come back from France as crippled in spirit as Pete Striker was physically. Everyone kept insisting he was a hero, but he could dredge up little pride in his twenty-five victories. Strangely, all he could feel was guilt—guilt that he had survived while so many others had died, and guilt that he had actually enjoyed the hunting and the killing while he was doing it. He knew it was not a manly thing, this guilt. And he was ashamed of it, ashamed that he had somehow failed himself or the expectations he had of himself as a man.

So he made himself speak of the war, although for the boy's sake—and his own—he talked only of the early months when they truly had been like knights of old, riding forth to do battle, and chivalry had ruled their actions.

He talked about the pair of lion-cub mascots they'd had in the Lafayette called Whiskey and Soda; about the gramophone that played ragtime and fox-trots day and night; and about the Indian rain dances they used to do as a joke, but for fair weather, not foul, so that they could go out on the prowl for enemy planes. "Our emblem was an Indian head. We painted it on our planes so that we could tell friend from foe."

"What was Schumacher's emblem?" Cassie asked. She had been listening to Linc with her chin resting on her fist, as intrigued as the boy.

"A black cross. Now, there are certain cardinal rules you must remember if you ever find yourself in a dog-fight, Joshua," Linc said, giving Cassie a quick grin. "Keep the sun at your back, and strike your opponent from behind. Fire only at close range, and always carry through the attack once you've started it. If the enemy dives on you, don't try to evade his assault—fly straight at him to meet it. And above all, pray that your gun doesn't jam."

To Linc's amusement Cassie had listened with fierce concentration, as if this advice would come in handy someday. "And did your gun ever jam?" she asked.

"Once. But I remembered the rule about always carrying through with the attack. So I flew right at the enemy and rammed him with my undercarriage." Linc laughed suddenly. "I think I surprised him right out of the sky, but I can't be sure since I went down so fast myself I didn't see what happened to him. That was one crash I almost didn't walk away from."

"I'm going to be a fighter pilot when I grow up," Joshua stated emphatically.

"So am I," Cassie said, and they all laughed.

After a moment's silence, Seth cleared his throat and shoved back his chair. "It's time you children were in bed," he said.

Joshua heaved a dramatic sigh, but he rose obediently from the table. The baby was already asleep in a cradle by the stove, but the oldest girl helped shoo the two smaller ones up the ladder to the loft. Linc saw the boy scoop Patches up into his arms and struggle up the ladder with him, all the while trying to appear nonchalant. At least Patches would have a soft bed to sleep on. Linc caught Cassie's eyes, and they shared a secret smile.

After the children were settled in bed, Seth went to a set of shelves above the stove and took down a square wooden box. He gave the box a stroke of almost reverent affection before holding it out to Linc. "Would you care for a cigar?"

"Seth Turner," Maisie said, "if you men are going to be smoking those smelly old things, you'll be doing it outside, not in my house."

Seth and Linc took their cigars and a pair of chairs out into the yard, while Cassie helped Maisie clear up the supper dishes.

"How long have you and your man been wed?" Maisie asked as she handed Cassie a dish towel and showed her where to stack the clean plates.

Cassie counted backward mentally. "Five days."

"My!" Maisie exclaimed, laughing. "But then, I didn't think it was too long. Not the way he's been lookin' at you all ev'nin'."

"What way is that?" Cassie asked, amused.

"Sort of hot like. As if he was burning up inside with a fever. I know that look. I've seen it often enough on my Seth, especially in the early days." She grinned suddenly. "I still catch that look in his eye, come an evening, and it's going on eleven years."

Cassie sighed inwardly. She wondered if Lawrence Kingly had worn such a look in the early days of his marriage to her mother. Certainly in the later years the only look in his eyes had been one of pure hatred.

"Of course, the children are a joy and blessing," Maisie was saying. "But it's hard to concentrate on your man when you have a handful of young ones all pulling on your skirts, demanding your attention. And this farm. Seth says the devil must have emptied his pockets onto this land. It takes a powerful lot of hard work to make it pay. We forget sometimes, Seth and I, that we used to use that bed upstairs for other things besides sleeping."

Linc came in just then, saying that he knew how farmers liked to go to bed with the sun, and that he, too, was ready to call it a day. Maisie gave Cassie a knowing look and smothered a laugh with her hand.

A flash of heat lightning streaked across the sky, and the chirr of crickets followed Linc and Cassie as they made their way by lantern light across the yard. At the door to the barn Linc stopped and, setting the lantern down, pulled Cassie into his arms. He kissed her.

He sighed against her hair. "I've been wanting to do that all night."

"Your breath smells all smoky," she said.

"Sorry."

"No, I sort of like it."

"Cassie?"

She pressed her lips against the pulse in his throat. "Um?"

"Never mind." He released her, reaching down to pick up the lantern.

The barn smelled of horses and freshly mown hay. A cow mooed once as they entered and then began to chew loudly on her cud. Linc hung the lantern from a hook on the wall, then carried the ladder over from where it leaned against a pile of hay bales and propped it against the opening in the loft.

He grinned at her and made a sweeping bow. "After you, madam."

Cassie began to climb the ladder, raising her skirt much higher than was absolutely necessary and giving a seductive view of her legs. She felt his hand roam up her calf as he started up the ladder after her, and she smiled to herself.

Linc's fingers slid under the leg of her drawers, brushing lightly against her sensitive skin. Laughing softly, Cassie paused to let his hand slide up her thigh. His gentle exploration went higher still, and she sucked in a sharp breath, trying to squirm out of the way of his suddenly tickling fingers. Linc's head then disappeared beneath Cassie's skirt, and the ladder began to sway.

Linc found the button fastening her drawers, popping it open, and the soft cotton slid down around her knees. His fingers probed intimately between her legs, and she felt the shock of his lips on her bare flesh. "Linc!" Cassie gasped, jerking reflexively, and the ladder tilted alarmingly.

"Christ!" Linc exclaimed, and threw his weight sideways. But he was too late. The ladder came crashing down, taking them with it.

Linc's head popped up from between two rungs, and he blinked straw and dust out of his eyes. Cassie had been thrown free, and she lay facedown on the barn floor in dreadful stillness, and Linc's heart stopped.

He flung off the ladder and crawled on his hands and knees toward her, thinking that if she'd broken her neck he would hang himself here and now from the rafters. As he got closer to her he saw with piercingly sharp relief that she was alive, for she was shuddering. He thought she must be suffering some kind of shock.

He touched her back, and the shuddering increased. "Oh, God, please," he prayed aloud. "Cassie..." He tentatively rolled her over and saw to his horror that her face was contorted with pain. Then she sucked in a deep, wheezing breath and drew her knees up against her stomach. He suddenly realized that she wasn't hurt at all. She was laughing!

The terror he had felt left him in a rush of breath, leaving him angry. He grasped her shoulders, intending to shake the life out of her, but crushed her against him instead. He showered her with kisses, kissing her eyes, her mouth, and her hair, while she laughed and cried out that he was smothering her. And he thought that he wanted to do just that. He wanted to smother her with love, so that she would always be his—so that she would never leave him.

And yet, later, as they lay in each other's arms in the hayloft, hot and sticky with sweat and clinging bits of hay, he knew with a terrible sadness that in spite of all her protestations of love, he would end up losing her after all.

It began innocently enough, with one of those light, teasing conversations they so often shared after an intense bout of lovemaking.

"Tell me about Betsy," she said as she leaned over him to brush the damp hair back from his face.

"Who?" he asked absently, more interested in the breast that swayed tantalizingly before his eyes.

She punched his chest, and he grunted. "Don't try to act stupid on me, Linc. I want to know everything about this Betsy person."

"I don't know any Betsy . . . oh, Betsy!" He grinned at her.

"Well?"

"I don't know."

She swung at him again, but he grasped her wrist, laughing. "I honestly don't, Cassie. The plane was named the *Betsy* when I bought her. You know it's bad luck to change a plane's name."

She studied his face, trying to decide whether to believe him or not.

"It's nice to know you can be jealous," he said. "And totally unnecessary when a man is as besotted with a woman as I am with you. Making love with you like this, tonight, drives the thought of all other women—past, present, and future—completely out of my head."

Cassie scowled at him. "What other women?"

"I just told you, I can't remember."

"You're such a liar, Linc Cameron." She fondled his limp manhood until it started to stir again, then planted a loud kiss on his chest.

He twisted a piece of her hair around his finger. Desire was a warm, sweet ache building inside of him. It was insatiable, this desire, and he was surprised himself by his sexual stamina. Would there ever come a time, he wondered, when he wouldn't feel the want, the need of her, so soon after having her?

"But what about you?" he asked casually, delaying the moment when he would begin making love to her again. "Is there anyone in your past I should be jealous about?"

"Ward Farrell asked me to marry him once."

"The hell he did!" Linc grasped her hair, pulling her head up so he could see her face. "You told him no ... didn't you?"

"Of course. I told him I was never getting married, and I meant it then. I still mean it now." She pulled away from him and sat up, wrapping her arms tightly around her. He thought he could see the pulse beating nervously in her throat. "I didn't want to fall in love with you, Linc. But even though I have, you needn't worry that things have changed as far as I'm concerned. I have no intention of trying to hold you to this marriage, because I know how things will be. You'll become just like Seth Turner. You'll want to have a passel of kids and settle down on some farm—"

"Farm! I know damn-all about farming."

"You must know damn-all about babies, too, if it hasn't occurred to you that without taking precautions, babies are generally the end result of all this..." She waved her hand at the mussed pile of hay.

"Naturally it's occurred to me, and I admit that having a kid right now would complicate things, so—"

"I don't want children *ever*."

"Fine. No kids. I'll pay a visit to the drugstore tomorrow and buy us a package of precautions."

"And when this race is finished, this ridiculous marriage ends right along with it."

"Fine. No marriage, no kids, no farm. Is there anything else you'd like to add to the list while you're at it?"

She waved her hand at the hay again and said tentatively, "No more this?"

"Oh no, my tempting, temperamental, temporary wife...." Laughing softly, he traced a finger between her breasts. "*This* is nonnegotiable."

Her lips trembled into a smile. Then she grew serious again. "You've said often enough what kind of woman you want in a wife. I am not that woman, Linc. I never will be."

"You're swatting at ghosts with a baseball bat, Cassie," Linc said for the sake of his pride. "I haven't forgotten our deal. No ties, no promises. And no regrets. Wasn't that what you said, Cassie Jones? No regrets?"

A strange expression flitted across her face. He supposed it was probably relief. He wanted to ask her if she would feel differently if she knew that he had fallen in love with her. But he didn't dare. He was too afraid of the answer.

Seth Turner stood beside the buckboard in the dawn light looking like both a country bumpkin and a city sophisticate, wearing his Sunday coat, vest, and tie, and his work pants and heavy field shoes caked with dry mud. While Linc finished hitching the team to the wagon, Seth copied down on a catalog page a growing list of things his wife wanted brought back from town.

"And we could do with a new garden hoe," Maisie was saying. "The blade's rusted out on our old one."

"Shucks, Maisie," Seth said with a huge sigh. "Where'm I goin' to put all this stuff? That watchama-callit these folks're going to get Hank to make could wind up bein' a full load."

Maisie stood on tiptoe to kiss her husband's bearded cheek. "It's called a propeller, dear. And if things get too crowded in the buckboard, you can always hold it in your lap."

Seth looked so appalled at this that Cassie and Linc both burst out laughing.

A gust of hot dry wind flattened the women's skirts against their legs and sent Seth's hat sailing off his head. Joshua, with Patches yipping at his heels, chased it across the yard, sending the chickens squawking and flapping their wings. Cassie looked to the west, where the sky was a dark, smudgy brown, the color of river mud.

"Sandstorm's coming," Seth said. "And it's going to be a doozy by the looks of it."

Cassie caught Linc smiling. The high surface winds were already too hazardous for takeoff, and these mid-west dust storms were known to cover hundreds of square miles. With luck the other planes would all be grounded this morning, too.

After the two women waved their men off, Cassie offered to help Maisie with her daily chores.

Maisie smiled her thanks. "It's real nice of you to offer, Cassie, but I'm not working today. I've declared it a holiday. I plan to set ourselves down over a pot of coffee and have a good gossip."

Cassie was amused to discover that Maisie's idea of a holiday was first to do a load of washing. "If I can get it lone before this storm hits," she said, "with this hot vind it should be dry in no time."

The washing was done in the yard with a scrub)oard and a wooden tub that had a hand wringer fas-ened to the rim. After the clothes were on the line, hey went inside "to rustle up a batch of pies while the hubarb is fresh picked." Cassie wondered what Maisie Turner did on days when she really put her mind to loing some work. She felt as useless as Patches, follow-ng Maisie around and mostly getting in the way.

"How I do envy you, Cassie," Maisie said as she olled out a circle of freshly kneaded pie dough. "Trav-ling clear across the country like you're doing, seeing o many different sights, meeting different people and eeing how they all live. I was born right here on the North Platte, and the farthest I've been is Scotts Bluff one summer when I was twelve. I'm not really com-olaining, mind you, but I read some of an evening, when I get the chance. There's things I've read of that 'd dearly love to see."

Cassie looked at Maisie's slender figure bent over the kitchen table. She noticed for the first time a few strands of gray in her chestnut hair and the crow's-feet around her cheerful eyes. Five children in eleven years of marriage, long days of baking, canning, and preserv-ng; milking the cows and slopping the hogs; plowing and hoeing and weeding, only to begin the endless cycle again. Cassie wondered what dreams Maisie Turner had had eleven years ago, and whether any of them had been realized.

"How can you stand it?" Cassie blurted out.

Maisie looked up at her, surprised. "Stand what?"

Cassie waved her hand around the kitchen. "This. This lonely, endless work. The farm . . ." she trailed off. And Seth, she thought, although she didn't say it. How do you stand Seth?

Maisie brushed a strand of hair off her face, leaving behind a smudge of flour. "Maybe I wouldn't be able to stand it if I was to have to do it alone. But I have Seth."

"But you're like a slave to him. He's so—"

"I am not! How dare you even think that!"

Cassie bit her lip. "I'm sorry. I . . . I don't think sometimes before I speak."

All the anger left Maisie. She even managed a smile. "You're young yet, so you think love should be all sunny days and spring flowers and pretty speeches. You'll come to see after a while that marriage, like life in general, I guess, has its ups and downs. A man and wife, they come to settle into a way of living together, and what works for one couple doesn't necessarily work with another. Maybe, looking in from the outside, you don't see how Seth and me are much of a match. I'll admit to you that he has some narrow-minded, stubborn ways that rub me so raw sometimes I could just scream. But in the end I'm sure of one thing, and it's the only thing that matters to me. I love Seth, and I know he loves me. Loves me and respects me too, and that's more than a lot of wives get from their man."

Cassie felt a hard wrenching deep inside where something made of despair and fear, something that had put down long, strangling roots, started to tear free. She realized that there was something vital she had to understand, and Maisie Turner could explain it to her. She opened her mouth to speak. . . .

A blast of wind suddenly shook the house, plastering sand against the sod walls with a sound like a thousand glasses shattering at once. A scream came from outside where the children and Patches were playing.

Cassie got the children and Patches safely inside and then went back out to help Maisie bring the wash in off the line. The wind drove the dirt and sand against their faces, lacerating them like tiny knives. It got under their eyelids, and into their mouths. When they got back inside Cassie had to rinse her mouth out several times with water, and even then it still tasted like she was eating dirt every time she swallowed.

Maisie sat the younger children on a braided rag rug before the stove to play with her button box, then set the older ones to doing sums out of an old schoolbook. The baby, undisturbed by the storm, continued to nap in his cradle. At last the promised coffee was put on the stove, but when Maisie sat down, it was to ask Cassie whether it was true that ladies in the big cities had taken to wearing an undergarment called a brassiere in place of a corset. Cassie realized then that the storm had driven their earlier conversation from Maisie's mind, and Cassie was reluctant to bring it up again.

And the thing of despair and fear that lived deep inside her stretched out its roots and took hold again.

"What is it?" Maisie exclaimed, her eyes sparkling with childlike excitement as she studied the large cardboard box wrapped with a big red satin ribbon that sat in the middle of her kitchen table.

"It's a box," Seth said, and grinned at Linc. His beard was coated white with dust, and dirt caked the seams of both their faces. Every time one of them moved, fine sand drifted onto Maisie's immaculate floor.

But Maisie didn't notice. "Oh, Seth! I can see it's a box," she said. "Open it."

"You open it. It's a present to you from Linc. It was his idea," Seth said gruffly. "So if you've got to blubber all over somebody's chest after you get a look at it, do it on his."

Maisie's fingers were shaking so badly that Cassie had to help her untie the bow. Cassie wondered what Linc had done: he hadn't mentioned to her that he was going to buy Maisie a gift in town. His impulsive generosity both surprised and pleased her.

Maisie opened the flaps of the box, and her hands flew up to her mouth, stifling a gasp. Cassie saw the rounded edge of what looked to be a big brass horn, and she leaned over for a closer look. It was a slightly battered secondhand gramophone.

Maisie wiped at her tears with the edge of her apron. "I told you she'd blubber," Seth said.

"How could you know how much I've longed for one of these talking machines?" Maisie said, sniffling and beaming at Linc.

"I was given a hint."

Maisie looked at her husband. "You said it was his idea."

"It was his idea to get you a surprise. He asked what you'd like, and I told him."

Linc lifted the gramophone out of the box. "I'm afraid they only had one disk to go along with it." He cranked the handle and the scratchy, tinny strains of "Little Brown Jug" filled the kitchen.

Maisie laughed with delight and, to his profound shock, seized Seth by the waist and began to dance around the kitchen table. Cassie went into Linc's arms and they danced too, twirling around and around the room until their laughter drowned out the music and the moaning wind outside. The children stood in silent shock in the doorway. Never had they seen their parents act so silly, and they didn't know what to make of it.

Then Patches threw back his head and began to howl. He hated music almost as much as he hated to get wet. The gramophone began to wind down, but Patches's howls only got louder.

"Patches!" Linc bellowed. "Shut up!" Silence suddenly descended upon the kitchen. Even the wind outside seemed to have cooperated, dying down to a rustling whisper.

"Storm's passing," Seth said, clearly making an effort to reassume his dignified, sober demeanor.

Cassie had kept her arm around Linc's waist, and

she leaned into him. "What about the propeller?"

He grinned at her and kissed the top of her head. "You ought to see it. It's a work of art." He turned and faced the Turners. "If the wind's let up enough for take-off, we have to be getting on. There's still a good three hours of daylight left and, well . . ."

Seth harrumphed. "I still say that if the Lord—"

"Don't you say any such thing, Seth Turner," Maisie put in. "And if you do, you shouldn't." She flashed her broad, friendly smile at Linc and Cassie. "I hope you win your race. I'll be lookin' for word of it."

Seth grumbled. "Now she'll be sendin' me into town every week for a blasted newspaper."

The Turners accompanied them out to the field and watched while Linc, with Cassie's help and Patches's interference, fitted the new propeller onto the *Pegasus*. When they were almost finished Cassie spoke to him softly, and Linc nodded his head in agreement.

Cassie went up to Maisie Turner. "Do you still want me to take you up for a ride?"

"Oh Lord!" Maisie's hand flew to her cheek, and she looked at her husband.

"Go on ahead, Maisie," Seth said. "If you're kilt, I'll marry me Parsons' oldest girl. She's young enough so's I can still train her not to give out any sass, which is something I neglected to do with you."

The wind still ruffled the grass a bit as Linc helped Maisie get settled in the cockpit. He lent her his helmet and goggles. She suddenly felt a bit scared, but he gave her an encouraging grin. "You're in good hands," he said, patting her on the shoulder.

Maisie looked around the cockpit at the bewildering array of gadgets, which both baffled and intrigued her. There was a greasy, oily film over everything, and its smell permeated the air. She jumped at the sudden shattering roar as the engine ignited, then tensed as she felt the plane begin to move.

To Maisie, the plane whipped down the field at an incredible speed, and the wind rushing over the mud-speckled windscreen seemed to press the flesh right against the bones of her face. They went by Seth and the children in the wink of an eye, so that they were merely a blur to her. She felt a sudden sinking sensation in her stomach, and she looked down to see that they had left the ground—they were flying! She looked up then, and there was nothing before her but the wide blue sky. She thought this must be what a cathedral was like—open and limitless and silent.

Of course, the silence was only in her imagination, for in reality the noise of the vibrating engine was so loud it seemed to tickle her blood, and the air as they blasted through it whistled in her ears in spite of the thick leather helmet she wore. She began to notice a feeling of strain in the muscles of her face, and she laughed when she realized it was because her mouth was stretched open in a huge grin of pure joy.

Cassie banked the plane into a wide turn, and Maisie saw the earth below her, the house and barn and windmill looking so tiny she thought they could fit in the palm of her hand. And Chimney Rock and the North Platte—those significant, dominating landmarks of her entire life—had been reduced to mere specks on the face of the wide, beautiful world she saw stretched out before her.

Too soon, they came back down to earth. As they rolled to a stop Seth came running up, and she saw a mixture of love and worry and pride on his face. She jumped down, throwing herself into his arms.

"Well?" he said, and she knew he was afraid that in some way she had been seduced away from him.

She smiled into his eyes. "I thought the world looked to be a mighty big place from up there. So big, in fact, that a woman needs an anchor to hold her down or she'd just up and float away and disappear. . . . You are my anchor, Seth."

She could see from the look on Seth's face that he had no idea what she was talking about. But Cassie had heard it all, and Maisie knew that her words had reached the heart and mind of the person they were meant for.

Chapter 12

~~~~~⌒○○⌒~~~~~

A s the *Pegasus* rolled to a stop, a crowd of people surged up to the plane, wrapping around it like surf around a pile of rocks. They were cheering and shouting, and Cassie heard her name and Linc's. Several men held cameras up in the air, pointing their dark, blank eyes into the cockpit.

Cassie began to feel the first flutterings of a claustrophobic panic. She turned around to Linc, fighting a mad impulse to crawl over the fuselage and into his lap for protection. "Linc, these people!" She practically had to shout to make herself heard above the noise. "What's happening?"

"Looks like somewhere between here and Billings we suddenly got famous." He started to swing out of the cockpit.

"Where are you going?"

"I got to log us in." He grinned and leaned over to chuck her lightly under the chin. "It's you they're mostly interested in anyway—America's prettiest aviatrix. Just flash them a big smile and say something quotable." He turned to jump out of the plane.

"Linc!"

"What?"

Don't leave me, she wanted to say, but she knew

202

that was silly. "I don't want to be famous!" she wailed.

He laughed and stepped onto the wing, then leaped gracefully to the ground. The crowd opened and seemed to swallow him up. Cassie wondered if she would ever see him again.

She folded her arms across her chest and hunched down in her wicker seat. Patches had curled himself into a tight whimpering ball at her feet. Cassie felt like whimpering with him. She heard the drone of an engine and looked up to see Edward Farrell's plane, a Curtiss "Jenny," pass over the airfield. She watched it bank to make its final approach before landing.

Perhaps if I ignore them, she thought, they'll all go away and bother Ward instead. There was a thumping noise, and the *Pegasus* rocked. She glanced down to see a hand with a knife trying to saw through the fabric on one of the wings.

"Hey!" she yelled, scrambling out of the cockpit. She swung down from the wing, batting at the arm with her foot and knocking the knife to the ground. She got a brief glimpse of a boy's frightened face before he backed up, melting into the crowd. Men with press cards stuck through their hat brims hurled a barrage of questions at her, grasping at her sleeves and her coat to get her attention.

"Please," she said. Then louder, "Please, stop!"

A hush fell on the crowd. They all looked at her expectantly, waiting for her to speak. She couldn't think of a thing to say.

"Mrs. Cameron?" someone called out. "Is there a secret to flying?"

"Getting off the ground," she said unthinkingly, jerking with surprise at their burst of laughter. Then she realized what she had said and laughed too.

"Mrs. Cameron, are you ever frightened up there?"

"Only when Mr. Cameron has the controls," she answered, and they laughed again.

"What are you going to do with the fifty thousand dollars if you win?"

"Spend it," she shot back, enjoying herself now.

Several people at the edge of the crowd had turned to watch Edward Farrell's plane touch down at the end of the field. There was a growing murmur of excited voices, then someone screamed. Cassie whirled around and almost screamed herself.

The Jenny was ripping down the tarmac, its nose aimed right at the *Pegasus*. Several more people screamed, and soon everyone was running, scattering toward the open field that stretched away from the runway.

All but Cassie. She stood frozen in place as the other plane bore down on her and the *Pegasus*.

Then the plane began to veer away, but slowly, too slowly, and Cassie thought it couldn't possibly miss them. It would shear off the *Peg*'s port wings and hit her at the same time. She told her legs to get out of the way, to run, but she couldn't move. Then the angle between the two planes began to widen, and it looked as if maybe it would miss them after all. She tensed, clenching her fists.

The Jenny streaked by, so close that a blast of air slammed Cassie's eardrums and set the *Pegasus*'s wires to vibrating. She sagged against the wing struts, her heart beating so loudly it sounded like a bass drum in her ears. Then Patches crawled out onto the wing and started to howl, and she let out a hysterical burst of laughter.

Catching a flash of movement out the corner of her eye, she flung her head up to stare into a gaping black lens. She gasped, throwing her arms up in front of her face.

The man with the camera laughed. "You stand there cool as a polar bear in January while an airplane bears down on you at thirty miles an hour, and then you

jump a mile when somebody takes your picture. . . .
Miles Terrance, the *Kansas City Star*."

Cassie glared at him.

He folded up the camera and slung it over his
shoulder, taking a pad of paper and a pencil out of his
breast pocket. "Is it true you're just along for the ride,
that Linc Cameron does all of the piloting?"

"Of course not!" Cassie responded, stung at the injustice of his accusation.

"Is it true you were a Ziegfeld chorus girl, and were
hired to go along on this race, a pretty face to help
drum up publicity for Bean's soda pop?"

"That is the most ridiculous—"

"Is it true that you and Cameron aren't really married, that you are, or were, in fact, Leroy Bean's mistress?"

A big hand landed on the reporter's shoulder, jerking him around. Pete Striker shoved his ruddy face up
under the man's nose.

"Would you ask your sister a question like that?"

"I don't have a sister."

"Your mother, then. Would you ask your mother a
question like that? Or do you even got a mother?
Maybe you were whelped in the gutter by a stray
bitch."

The reporter's face paled, then grew red. He opened
his mouth, then shut it. He backed up a step, and his
eyes shifted over to Cassie. "If you're a phony, I'll find
out," he sneered. "Read about it in the *Star*." Then he
brushed by Pete and strode angrily down the runway.

Cassie flung herself against Pete, pressing her face
into his chest. "Oh God, Pete. They were trying to cut
her up. They were cutting up the *Peg!*" she cried, still
not able to believe it.

"After souvenirs, probably." He patted the top of her
head. "We'll get her patched up, Cassie, honey, don't
worry."

She pulled away from him. "Where have you been? Some advance man you are!"

Grinning sheepishly, Pete rubbed a hand over his chin, grating against his whisker stubble. "You think flying across this blasted country is hard, you ought to try doing it on the ground."

Cassie spotted Linc coming toward them with his distinctive, long-legged stride. "There's Linc. Have you seen him yet? Did he tell you what happened? If he tells you I robbed a bank, don't believe him. Who's winning?" she asked as Linc walked up.

"Pete, where the hell have you been?" Linc clapped Pete on the back, shaking his hand. He gave Cassie a relaxed, easy smile. "The Schmidt brothers are in first and with a comfortable lead, I'm afraid. Ward Farrell's second. Even though he came in behind us on this leg, his cumulative time's still forty-six minutes better. I heard there was almost a collision on the runway, did you see it?"

Cassie waved a dismissive hand. "Oh, it was nothing. So, where are we, fourth?"

"Third."

"Third!" Pete spat out in disgust. "The race is close to half over, and we're no better than *third*. What the hell's the matter with you all? This ain't no la-di-da fly across the country and have ourselves a picnic thing we're doing here."

Linc looked so hurt that Cassie had to choke back a laugh. "We're doing our best, Pete," she said. "We've had a bit of trouble."

"What sort of trouble?"

Linc told him about the doctored propellers.

"Bloody Boche!" Pete exclaimed. "The bastards!"

Linc and Cassie stared at him.

"Well, it stands to reason," he said defensively. "I mean, they're in the lead, aren't they?"

"There isn't a shred of evidence that points to the Schmidt brothers," Linc said. "And their accent doesn't prove a thing," he added when Pete opened his mouth.

"Yeah?" Pete growled. "Then if it ain't them doin' it, who is it?"

"Linc thinks it's Harry and Jim," Cassie said.

Linc's head flung up and he stared at her in astonishment. "How did you . . . ?"

"You get a murderous look on your face if anyone even mentions their names."

"Who the hell are Harry and Joe?" Pete demanded.

"Jim," Cassie said.

"Couple of swarthy characters with an old Wright pusher biplane," Linc said by way of explanation. "And I don't think it's them."

"Yes, you do," Cassie said.

"I don't."

"You do."

"Damn it!" Pete roared. "Why couldn't it be Harry and Joe?"

"Jim," Cassie corrected. "And they aren't swarthy, they're nice."

"Because it doesn't make any sense," Linc said, answering Pete but glaring at Cassie.

"I didn't say it made sense," she retorted. "I said that's what you thought."

"I don't. I only *considered* the possibility, all right? But there's no reason for them to pick on the *Peg*, especially when it's in their best interest for us to wi—" He cut himself off.

"To what?"

Linc set his jaw. "Nothing. Let it go."

But Pete wasn't willing to let it go. "What you said don't make any sense, Linc. They're tryin' for the fifty thousand bucks just like everybody else, so why would they want to see us win?"

"Forget it, Pete, will you for Chrissakes!"

Pete snapped his mouth shut. He stared at Linc a moment, then shrugged. He reached into his pocket and pulled out a box of cigarettes. He shook one out and tapped it on the back of his knuckles.

Cassie tried to hold Linc's eyes, but they shifted away from her. "Be like that then," she said, giving him one of her fiercest glares.

He glowered back at her. "Just quit putting words into my mouth."

"I'm not. You're the one who—"

"The hell you aren't!"

"Oooh, you are so infuriating!" she raged at him, then stormed off, leaving Linc staring after her, breathing heavily and clenching his jaw.

Pete chuckled.

"What are you laughing at?" Linc growled at him.

"Me? Nothin'," Pete said, and chuckled some more.

The race committee had set up its headquarters in a large, corrugated-iron hangar owned by a company that flew the mail service between Kansas City and Chicago. The committee had decorated the rounded roof with blue and yellow flags and slapped up dozens of advertising posters on the walls. Galvanized tubs filled with chipped ice and bottles of Bean's cola stood outside the hangar's wide, open entrance.

Cassie was walking at a brisk, stiff pace toward the hangar, muttering to herself about a certain lying, secretive man, when she heard a familiar voice call out her name.

She whipped around. "You!" she exclaimed. "You almost ran right over me!"

Edward Farrell came up to her, smiling weakly. "My rudder cable broke." He shivered. "Lord, Cassie, it was bad enough to find myself hurtling out of control down the runway, bearing down on another plane, but when I saw you just standing there, I almost . . . why in God's name didn't you get out of the way?"

Cassie gave him a disgusted look. "And desert the *Pegasus*? How could I ever tell Linc that I let someone run right over our plane?" A moment later she added,

"You said your rudder cable broke. Do you think it was more sabotage?"

He shrugged. "With something like that it's hard to tell one way or the other."

She was about to tell him what had been done to the *Pegasus*'s propellers when a group of men spilled out the hangar's wide doors. Cassie tensed, afraid she was about to be assaulted by more intrusive journalists, then realized the men's attention was focused upon something in the center of their group. Cassie got a glimpse of cornflower blue, accordion-pleated crepe de chine moments before she heard the distinctive airy laugh of Melodie Farrell.

The group of men rippled and parted, and Melodie emerged sandwiched between the Schmidt brothers, her dainty lace-gloved hands clinging to their brawny arms. The other men let out a collective, good-natured groan at her choice before trooping faithfully behind as the brothers led her toward their Avro monoplane parked across the field.

All but Gregory Pearce. He stared after her a moment, his leprechaun's face woeful with dejection. Heaving a huge sigh, he hunched his skinny shoulders and turned—falling right into a tub of Bean's cola.

Cassie laughed out loud as she watched the man haul himself out of the tub, dripping rivulets of water. "Poor Mr. Pearce," she said to Edward. "Does Melodie even know he's alive?"

"We can't always choose the person we fall in love with," Edward replied, though with a teasing note in his voice. "You haven't said, Cassie... how are you and Linc finding the life of wedded bliss?"

Cassie pulled off her helmet and slapped it against her thigh to knock off some of the dust and sand. She avoided Edward's eyes. "We've been pretty preoccupied with the race."

"But you can't be flying every minute of the day.

And then there are the nights. How do you spend your nights, Cassie?"

Cassie felt her cheeks grow hot. "Sleeping."

He grasped her chin, pulling her head around, and she stared up at his weary, brooding face.

His lips twisted into a bitter smile. "And *before* you sleep? Does he make love to you, Cassie? Do you enjoy it, Cassie?"

"Ward, don't do this."

"Would you rather I did this instead?" And he ground his lips down on hers in a hard, brutal kiss. She struggled a moment, then stopped resisting altogether, simply standing there unmoving until he had finished.

When he released her, she wiped at her mouth with her hand but said nothing.

"So it's true then," he said. "This marriage isn't just some publicity stunt arranged by Bean's cola. Or maybe it was in the beginning, but somebody forgot to tell you not to fall in love with him."

Cassie sighed. "Very well, Ward, since you insist upon hearing it, I'll say it—I love Linc. I'm not ashamed to admit it."

Edward's face tightened. Then he laughed abruptly. "Oh, but what about him, Cassie? Do you mean anything to him at all, or are you just a pleasant diversion to while away the hours when he isn't flying? There've been a lot of diversions in Linc Cameron's life, because he likes to amuse himself with girls like you. But when it comes to happily ever after, he'll be looking for someone a little more . . . *conventional*, shall we say."

Cassie pushed by him, but he grabbed her arm, his fingers digging in so hard she felt their pressure through the thick material of her coat.

He stared at her with bright, hurt eyes. "You fell in love with the wrong man, Cassie Jones. I hope you won't come to regret it someday."

* * *

Linc entered the hangar with Patches, docile and obedient for a change, following at his heels. They paused together in the entrance, and Linc looked around for his errant wife. The large hangar was filled with pilots, race officials, and sightseers, their loud talk and laughter bouncing off the metal walls and echoing in the lofty ceiling.

Linc bent over and tugged gently on one of Patches's ears. "Do you see her?" Patches whined softly. "Then go track her down for me, will you, boy? Before she gets into trouble." And Patches trotted happily off, tail wagging.

Linc spotted Melodie Farrell, flanked on each side by a Schmidt brother. Melodie waved at him, and he strolled over. "Hello, Miss Farrell," he said. "I'm happy to see you've arrived here safe and sound."

Melodie laughed and blinked her wide, long-lashed eyes. "Why, it wasn't difficult at all, Mr. Cameron. I simply got on the train in Los Angeles and got off right here in Kansas City. It's what you and Ward and the misters Schmidt here"—she bestowed a dimpled smile on each brother in turn—"it's what you all are doing that's so frightfully dangerous." She shivered prettily. Linc and the Schmidt brothers exchanged self-congratulatory smiles.

"They were showing me their flying machine, Mr. Cameron," Melodie said. "And I was quite horrified to see there was a *huge* rip in one of the wings."

"Did you run into some trouble?" Linc asked casually.

"That sandstorm. She very bad," Hans, the younger and more effusive brother, replied in his thick accent. "The wind, she snapped our cables, allowing the ailerons to flap and damaging the airplane's right wing."

"Are you sure it was an accident?"

The brothers exchanged puzzled looks. "Accident? Yes, yes, of course. The wind."

Patches raced up, barking, and Melodie shrieked,

snatching up her skirt. "Oh, it's that nasty old dog! Keep him away from me. He bites."

"No, he doesn't," Linc said, although he bent over and grabbed Patches's collar. Then he heard Cassie's throaty laugh and turned around with relief.

Cassie came toward him, smiling and linked arm and arm with a formidable-looking matron wearing a severe military-style suit. She towered over Cassie and marched beside her with an awkward, rubber-boned gait. A man followed a step behind, by contrast appearing small and dapper in a fashionable lounge suit, homburg hat, and spats.

"Linc!" Cassie exclaimed. "Look who's here to see me. It's Tessa, Tessa Pernell, a very dear friend of mine. We went to jail together."

"And it was the most peaceful month this country had seen in over fifty years," the dainty little man said with a quirky smile.

"This is her husband, Anselm," Cassie said. "He's always talking nonsense. Tessa, Anselm, this is my— this is Linc Cameron. My, uh, copilot."

"So you're the young feller who had the guts to marry Cassie Jones." Anselm Pernell shook Linc's hand while his wife looked Linc over with blatant curiosity. Linc put a lot of voltage into his smile. He sensed uneasily that it was important to Cassie that he meet with this woman's approval, and that it wasn't going to be easy to do so.

In her midfifties, Tessa Pernell had a plain, flat-nosed, sallow-skinned face that had probably never been pretty, not even at the peak of her youth. She wore her coarse gray hair pulled into a tight bun, and she had topped it with a boxy hat that reminded Linc of the kepi he used to wear with his airman's uniform. Yet there was something compelling about the woman's small dark eyes, where deep fires fueled by a quick mind and a fanatic zeal glowed from within.

The woman nodded sharply at Linc, as if he had just

passed inspection, and Linc had to resist an urge to snap his heels together and salute. "I understand this race won't be reconvened until tomorrow morning," she said. "Since you'll be spending the night in Kansas City, I insist you spend it with us."

"That's very kind of you, Mrs. Pernell—"

"Not at all. Anselm, darling, where have you parked the Daimler? You'll need to collect your things, of course," she said to Linc. "Anselm can go with you. Cassie and I will wait here. But don't let Anselm get to dawdling over the airplanes. There's a frightful crush in here, and Cassie abhors crowds."

Linc and Anselm exchanged looks. Then Anselm shrugged and Linc laughed and they went off obediently to fetch the flying kits.

Cassie watched Linc's retreating back a moment, then she turned to her friend.

Tessa's thick gray brows rose dramatically. "Cassie, he is . . ."

Cassie sighed, then laughed. "I know, it's so infuriating. He's so incredibly gorgeous it just isn't fair. Pretend you don't notice."

"Don't notice! Absolutely impossible, my dear. My lord, that smile of his!"

"He's a darn good pilot too, only don't tell him I told you so. He's convinced he's doing me a favor, taking me, a mere female, on as his copilot."

Tessa sniffed. "If he didn't feel that way, he wouldn't be a man. . . . Cassie, when you wrote me about this race, you said you would be flying with your uncle. Has something—"

Sudden tears filled Cassie's eyes, and she blinked them away. "He died, Tessa, of the flu. In California."

Tessa squeezed Cassie's arm. "Oh, my dear . . . I'm so sorry."

Cassie sucked in a deep breath. "It happened so fast, I'm still not used to it. Every time we land I keep expecting to see him waiting there for me. Remember that engine I told you he'd invented? If we win, I'm going to manufacture it with my share of the prize money."

"Your share?" Tessa asked, but before she could question Cassie further, the men were back with the flying kits. As they followed the Pernells to the Daimler, Linc told Cassie that Pete was already at work overhauling the engine and that he would stay with the *Pegasus* all night.

"Do you think there'll be another attempt to sabotage her?" she asked, and Linc said he didn't know what to think. Cassie, looking carefully into his eyes, saw that this was true. Whatever his suspicions had been earlier, he had evidently changed his mind. But it still hurt more than she cared to admit that he wouldn't share his thoughts with her.

Anselm Pernell drove the long black touring car over rolling hills and down sun-dappled streets lined with poplars and cottonwoods. He turned into a graveled drive and glided to a stop before an elegant three-story house. The house was painted white with dark green shutters at the windows and fronted by a large wooden porch. On the porch sat a wicker swing rocker with blue-flowered cushions.

As they mounted the steps, Cassie saw Linc's eyes alight with pleasure on the swing, and she felt a poignant tug in her chest. She hoped that someday he would have a house like this, with a swing on the porch. And she was surprised at the feeling of loneliness that squeezed her heart at the thought that she wouldn't be there to share it with him.

As Cassie stepped aside to allow Anselm to open the door, her eyes fell on the gold star pasted in the front window, which meant a loved one had been lost in the war.

She turned and seized her friend's hands. "Oh, Tessa, your son . . . I'm so sorry."

Tessa nodded and squeezed Cassie's hands tightly. "It seems somehow against nature to find yourself alive after your child has died. That's why it's more important than ever for the Senate to pass our suffrage bill. Once women are given the vote, we'll have the power to see that political evils like war never happen again."

There was a small, sad silence, then Anselm said to Linc, "Were you over there?"

"Yes. First with the Lafayette Escadrille, and then later with the Lafayette Flying Corps."

"Todd was with the marines. It happened last June at a place called Belleau Wood. So many hundreds of our boys died that day, so many thousands died in all, in a way it seems selfish to dwell on our own personal grief. I suppose you know..."

"Yes," Linc said quickly. "I know."

Linc took one look at Tessa's gleaming entryway, with its potted plants and large Chinese vases, and ordered an unhappy Patches back onto the porch. Tessa gave them a quick tour of the ground floor and then led them up a walnut staircase to one of the guest rooms. It was a calm, comfortable room with a large bed covered with a chenille spread. Lace curtains framed a pair of windows that faced the street, and a woven rug covered most of the parquet floor.

"Please make yourselves at home," Tessa said. "No doubt you'll want to remove some of the grime from your journey. Tea will be served in the library in a little over an hour at four o'clock sharp. We'll see you there."

Later, as Cassie sat at the dressing table trying to comb the wind-tangled knots out of her hair, she covertly studied Linc's reflection in the mirror. He lay stretched out on the bed, looking darkly handsome in his white linen shirt and braces. But the old, brooding sadness was back in his eyes. She wondered if it was the talk of the war that had caused it, or if it had something to do with her.

She went to sit down beside him on the bed. Leaning over, she kissed him lightly on the forehead. "Tired?"

"A little."

She caressed his neck, playing with his hair where it curled down over his collar. "You need a haircut," she said.

"I'll get one this afternoon after tea. That is, if your Mrs. Pernell grants me permission to leave the house."

Cassie laughed.

"Is she always so bossy?" Linc asked her with a grin.

"She doesn't mean to be. It's just that she's so used to running things. Not only has she been able to combine marriage and a career as a lawyer, but she's so involved in the movement too. She's president of the Equal Suffrage League, and on the board of directors for the National American Women's Suffrage Association."

Linc made a face. "I suppose that's how you wound up going to jail together."

"Two years ago we marched in a big parade in Washington. There were thousands of us, Linc. The feeling was so . . . so electric. I knew then that we were going to win the vote, even if it took years, because so many of the leaders were like Tessa, so *committed* to winning at any cost." She leaned over to rub noses with him. "We burned President Wilson in effigy, and that's when we got arrested. Are you scandalized?"

"Horribly. You admire her very much, don't you?"

"Yes," Cassie said. "Yes, I do." Then she gave him an impish grin. "Tessa's a worse troublemaker than I am; poor Anselm lives in constant terror of what she'll do next. But you can tell he adores her."

Linc's thumbs caressed her ribs through the thin material of her camisole. His mouth twisted into a funny smile. "When it comes to women, we men are but helpless slaves to our passions. You demand that we adore you, and we have no choice but to obey."

She laughed. "Oh, Linc, you're as bad as Anselm. You spout the most ridiculous nonsense sometimes."

He glanced at his airman's wristwatch. "You'd better

hurry and finish dressing. It's ten to four."

She kissed him again, this time on the mouth. But his lips felt cool and unyielding beneath hers. After a moment, when she felt no response, she released him and stood up. "Why don't you go on down and join Anselm in the library," she said. "I'll be along in a few minutes."

Linc took his time wandering through the house on his way to the library. He ran his palm over the smoothly polished banister, looked up at the sun shining through the beveled glass of the rose window, listened to the tap of his footsteps on the gleaming wood floors. He felt a sharp stab of nostalgia, as if he really had spent his youth in a house like this and not in a nomadic circus caravan following the gaudy big top.

Linc found Anselm Pernell alone in the library reading a newspaper. Anselm laid the paper down and stood up as Linc entered, and his face broke into a conspiratorial smile. "Well, young feller, shall we have ourselves a nip of whiskey before Tessa descends on us with her pots of tea?"

"Yes, I'd like a drink. Thank you."

Anselm produced a bottle and a pair of smudged glasses from the bottom of a desk drawer. He poured a measure into each and touched the rim of his glass to Linc's in a toast. "To flying. And winning."

They drank in silence for a moment, savoring the taste of the whiskey. Then Anselm said abruptly, "What do you think about giving women the vote?"

"I'm in favor of it," Linc answered honestly. He felt Anselm's eyes on him, then heard the older man let out his breath in a soft sigh.

"I just thought I'd give you fair warning. Tessa is bound to try to pin you down on the subject. She's always been involved in the women's suffrage movement, as Cassie has no doubt told you. But since Todd was killed it's become a crusade to her. She's changed . . . hardened. She didn't used to be so intolerant."

"It's understandable," Linc said.

"Yes. Yes, I suppose it is. More whiskey?"

"Please."

"We'd better enjoy this while we can," Anselm said as he refilled their glasses to the brim. "Do this a few months from now, and we'll be breaking the law." There was a rustle in the hall and the sound of soft feminine chatter. Anselm winked at Linc and raised his voice. "You notice how it's been mostly women in back of this temperance movement? The dear ladies won't be satisfied until one by one they've denied us men all of life's little pleasures."

"Oh, for heaven's sake, Anselm. Whiskey gives you gas anyway," Tessa said as she strode into the room. Cassie followed, along with a servant wheeling a tea cart, which Anselm eyed with a look of weary tolerance.

"I've been hearing all about this race," Tessa said to Linc as she poured the tea. "I think it's a fine opportunity for Cassie to prove to the world that a woman can compete successfully in a masculine arena. But in some ways it's probably been harder for you, Mr. Cameron. You're to be congratulated for having the courage to fly in the face of tradition, if I may be forgiven the pun, by accepting a female, even though she is your wife—perhaps especially *because* she is your wife—as your copilot."

Linc smiled at Cassie. She smiled back at him nervously. She obviously hadn't confided to her good friend Tessa the real reason behind their marriage. He wondered why she hadn't. And why he was so glad she hadn't.

"It doesn't take courage to want to fly with the best, and Cassie is one of the best," he said. "Speaking of breaking traditions, I understand that you're a lawyer, Mrs. Pernell."

"We both are," Anselm interjected. "I prosecute and she defends. She wins and I lose. We have a city full of murderers and thieves running around loose, and it's thanks to that woman." He pointed a finger in his wife's face.

"At least we are spared having prisons full of innocent men, thanks to you," Tessa countered testily.

The older couple exchanged such glowering looks that Linc struggled to hide a smile. He glanced over at Cassie and saw her lips twitching. Their eyes met, and they both looked quickly away again, fighting down laughter.

"Tessa has written a book," Cassie said after a moment.

"What about?" Linc inquired politely.

Anselm shuddered and rolled his eyes at Linc, and Linc suddenly wished that he had kept his mouth shut.

"The subject of the book is the advocacy of free love," Tessa said. "And before you expire of shock, let me explain that I do not mean that women, any more than men, should hop from bed to bed like rabbits. I only mean that, married or not, a woman's body is her own, to give to a man or not, when she so chooses and as she chooses." She paused, smiling a bit triumphantly at Linc. "You appear surprised, yet you shouldn't be. For hundreds of years now women have considered themselves owned by their men, and men have gladly assumed the role of master."

Linc thought of Ria, who had so often shamed him in the past by changing lovers almost as often as other women changed sheets. She had never read a book in her life; didn't, in fact, know how to read. Yet she would have laughed at the preposterous idea that her body—her finely trained, carefully preserved body— was not her own, that she must choose some man as her master. He felt a jolt of fierce pride that his mother had flaunted her independence and refused to change to please any man . . . even when it had been her own son who demanded it of her. He remembered Ria's face the last time he had seen her, full of hurt and anger and pride, and he wished suddenly that he had left things better between them.

Tessa stood up abruptly. "We must be leaving, Cassie."

Linc's head jerked up. "Where are you going?"

"Just to a little meeting," Cassie said with a falsely bright voice that made Linc's nerves tingle with warning.

"What sort of meeting?"

Cassie started backing out of the room. "I won't be long. And I'll take Patches with me," she added, as if Patches could somehow prevent her from getting into trouble. Hell, he was more apt to lead her right into it, Linc thought.

"You look worried, young feller," Anselm said after the women had left.

Linc forced a smile. "Do I?"

"Uh-huh."

Linc sighed, rubbing his hand over his face. "Where do you think they're really going?"

Anselm shrugged and reached for the bottle of whiskey. "I don't know. But I'll give you a bit of unsolicited advice from an old hand at this game. Never ask a woman a question if you don't think you're going to like the answer."

Chapter 13

"It's scandalous," Tessa Pernell said, shaking her head and pursing her lips in disgust. "There ought to be a law against it."

Cassie looked with fury at the sign with big bold print in the window of Jonathan Gunther's Fine Cigars. NO WOMEN OR DOGS ALLOWED, it said. She pointed it out to Patches, who wagged his tail and gave her his idiotic grin. Since he couldn't read, he didn't know that he was being insulted.

"And that establishment is even worse," Tessa said, pointing down the street to the red-and-white-striped pole next to the entrance to Rudy Sloan's Barber Shop. "I once tried to go in there to speak to a colleague about a very important court case, and I was practically ushered bodily from the premises. And when I tried to explain the urgency of the situation, that . . . that *barber* had the nerve to *snicker* in my face."

"I'm used to getting snickers," Cassie said. "At least he didn't try to pat you on the head like a child or a dog—sorry, Patches—and call you a 'dear girl.' That's what they're always doing to me."

The other women murmured sympathetically. Besides Cassie and Tessa, there were three other women —all friends of Tessa's, and ardent suffragettes.

"I'm frequently called a 'girl,'" said a petite, round-faced woman with doll-like eyes. "And I'm thirty-three."

"Disgraceful," Tessa said. "And then there is that establishment." She wrinkled her nose, pointing across the corner to the Crystal Palace. Its window advertised billiards and Gold Bond beer, and it directed the ladies to use a separate entrance in the alley. "We are banished to a cramped little back room, of course," Tessa said, "where the food is quite inferior. I, personally, would never wish to patronize the place, nevertheless..."

"It's the principle of the thing," Cassie said.

"Unfortunately, we can't attack them all," another woman said. "There aren't enough of us."

"I say we pick on Jonathan Gunther and his fine cigars," Cassie suggested, looking down at Patches. The other women looked at Patches too, and they exchanged smiles.

"I agree," Tessa said. "There is something particularly mean about a man who doesn't like dogs."

Tessa led the attack, with Cassie and Patches close behind. As they approached the painted wooden Indian that guarded the front door, Cassie pointed her finger like a gun at his noble nose. "Bang!" she said, and heard the women behind her laugh.

Jonathan Gunther was leaning on the back counter, poring over a pipe catalog, when the bell above the door tinkled softly. He glanced up, a look of inquiry on his face that froze into shock when he saw the women.

"Ladies, what...what...?" Gunther stuttered, coming out from behind the counter. He was a big, broad-shouldered man, with thick curly black hair that no amount of brilliantine seemed able to control.

"I should like," Tessa said with a wide smile, "to purchase a box of cigars. Do you have a particular brand you recommend? Something with a pleasant aroma."

As she spoke, the other women spread themselves around the shop, glancing with apparent interest at the display cases and shelves of tobacco cans and humidors.

Gunther fluttered his hands and stuttered some more. "But...but..."

"And I," Cassie said, "am interested in looking at your pipes." She walked over to a set of racks containing pipes in various shapes and sizes. "However, I haven't much money to spend. Which of these are the least expensive?"

Gunther was flapping his arms like a chicken now. "This is not allowed!" he bellowed.

"What does it mean when it says 'wrapped in specially cured Sumatra leaves'?" Tessa inquired brightly.

"Out, out, out!" Gunther shouted, arms waving wildly, and Patches growled.

Gunther froze, arms in midair, and looked down. "A dog!" he roared, advancing on Cassie because she happened to be the closest. "Get him out. Out!"

Snarling, Patches launched himself at the man's legs.

Gunther kicked out in anger and fear, and the toe of his heavy brogue landed a glancing blow on Patches's ribs. Patches howled with pain.

Cassie howled as well and swung her purse, aiming for the man's head. But Gunther ducked and the purse went sailing out of her hand. The strap hooked around the brass hat rack like a lasso. The hat rack teetered, then crashed through the front window, sending cigars, pipes, and cans of tobacco spilling out onto the sidewalk. A crowd immediately gathered outside.

"Police, police!" Gunther shrieked. "Vandals, thieves! Get the police!"

"How dare you kick my dog!" Cassie screamed, and aimed a punch at Gunther's face.

Gunther knocked her fist aside easily and grabbed her, hugging her arms to her sides to keep her from swinging at him again. She kicked him instead, and he roared in fury and pain.

Tessa, fearing that Cassie would be seriously hurt, dumped a box of cigars over Gunther's head. "Murder!" she shrieked. "Police, help!"

Linc Cameron had left Rudy Sloan's Barber Shop feeling like a new man. There was nothing, he thought, like a professional shave and haircut to put a man in a good mood. He sauntered cheerfully down the street, pausing to stop at the window of the Crystal Palace, where he studied his reflection, straightening his tie and adjusting the angle of his straw boater.

The first time he heard the whistle, he thought it came from the peanut wagon parked along the curb. Then he heard it again, too shrill and loud for a peanut wagon, and he noticed that there was a lot of shouting going on as well. Curious, he glanced around—and saw the love of his life struggling in the arms of a muscular, black-haired man.

Linc shouted Cassie's name and sprinted into the street, dodging a bakery wagon and barely missing the cowcatcher of a trolley car. He arrived at the same time as the police.

The patrolman had seen the same thing Linc had—a tiny, blond-haired girl struggling to fight off the attack of a hefty brute—and he charged to the rescue, swinging his club. But Linc, conditioned by past experience, thought he was after Cassie instead. He bunched up his fist and plowed it right into the policeman's nose.

The man staggered back, wrapping his arms around the wooden Indian to keep from falling to the ground. He shook his head, spraying the blood that poured from his nose, and bared his teeth in a snarl. Linc grinned and pulled back his fist.

"Linc!" Cassie cried, bursting free of Gunther and grabbing onto Linc's arm. "Don't!"

Three more policemen came running up.

"Get him!" their fellow officer roared, fighting his
way free of the Indian's wooden embrace and pointing
his club at Linc. And then he swung the club with all
his might into Linc Cameron's unprotected face.

Linc looked out at a blurry world through the swollen slits of his eyes. He saw bars, and through the bars,
a faded Liberty Bond poster taped to a concrete wall.
Since he didn't like the view, he closed his eyes again
and drifted back into unconsciousness.

The clank of a key in the lock jerked him awake. This
time when he opened his eyes the world looked less
blurry. He saw a policeman standing in the open door
to his cell. The policeman pointed at Linc and cocked
his thumb. "Out."

Linc rolled off the slab of concrete he'd been lying on
and got stiffly to his feet. He picked up the jacket that
he had been using as a pillow. His face throbbed, and
he explored it gently with his fingers. He realized that
his tie seemed to have disappeared somewhere, and he
started to look around for it.

"You putting down roots in there or what?" the policeman barked.

Linc slung his jacket over his shoulder and stepped
out into the hall. Anselm Pernell stood there, leaning
nonchalantly against the wall.

"Thanks," Linc said to him, and his voice came out a
hoarse croak.

"It helps if you go fishing with the judge every other
Sunday," Anselm said with a shrug and a grin. "We've
all agreed that you were trying to protect your wife and
merely got carried away."

Linc tried to smile back and opened the cut on his
lip. He winced, dabbing at the blood with the back of
his hand. "What about damages? I saw—"

"Taken care of," Anselm said. "Come on, let's get
out of here. They need this cell. It's Friday night, and

they round up more drunks than they know what to do with on Friday nights."

Outside it had grown dark, although the night air still retained the sun's heat. Linc heard a thrush singing somewhere and the hum of insects. He sucked in a deep breath and turned to Anselm.

"Where is she?" he growled.

"Cassie? At home, getting dressed for dinner. Tessa and I have had words, and we are no longer speaking. No doubt you and your wife will exchange words as well. It could turn out to be a rather quiet meal."

"I'm not going to say a thing," Linc said matter-of-factly. "I am merely going to wring her neck."

Anselm chuckled. He led Linc to the Daimler, which was parked at the foot of the precinct steps. "Oh, your dog was wounded in the fracas, I'm afraid," he said as he pulled open the passenger door.

"Patches? What happened?"

"A cracked rib, I believe. The vet has seen to him. Nothing too serious, I'm happy to report."

They rode in silence back to the house. But as Linc started to get out of the automobile, Anselm held him back.

"From what I could gather from Tessa when we weren't shouting at each other, they didn't expect things to degenerate into violence quite the way they did. I think your Cassie got the fright of her life." He laughed. "Actually, I think she's even more frightened of what's going to happen. While they were hauling your unconscious body off to jail, all she could say was: 'Linc is going to kill me, Linc is going to kill me.'"

"I *am* going to kill her. The only question is whether I do it before or after I wring her neck."

Anselm brushed these obviously hollow threats aside with a wave of his hand. "This was nothing compared to some of the things Tessa has done in the past. Or some of the fights we've had as a result of them. Life with that woman has never been what you'd call

sy. I guess I've probably left her a dozen times in the
irty-odd years we've been married." He smiled rue-
lly. "I got as far as the corner once."

"Maybe the trick is not to look back." Once more
inc started to get out of the car.

Anselm touched him lightly on the arm. "Linc...
ave you ever asked yourself what it would be like to
ave been born a woman? Imagine if you were a
oman like Cassie—intelligent, strong, talented—and
et everywhere you looked there were fences hemming
ou in or keeping you out, signs posted forbidding you
o do the things you love and ordering you down roads
ou have no desire to take. What would you do?"

"I don't know," Linc said. Then he sighed. "I sup-
ose I can sympathize with Cassie's battles, but I don't
ant to join them. It seems as if I've been fighting my
ntire life, and I'm tired of it. I want some peace and
erenity for a change."

Anselm cocked an expressive brow. "Peace and se-
nity, huh? You'll get precious little of that married to
assie."

"Christ, I haven't had a minute's peace since the day
met her," Linc said with feeling. "I suppose I should
ave known better than to let myself fall in love with a
oman like Cassie in the first place. I *did* know better,
ut like an idiot I went ahead and did it anyway."

Leaving Anselm to garage the car, Linc ran up the
orch steps and flung open the front door. Tessa stood
1 the hall, guarding the stairs.

Her eyes widened slightly at the sight of his battered
ace. "Oh dear... are you in a temper?" she asked him.

"Yes," he said.

"It wasn't her fault, Linc. To begin with, it was en-
irely my idea, so shout and rail at me if you must.
lthough nothing like this would have happened if
hat odious man hadn't assaulted your dog."

Linc took a step toward the stairs. "Excuse me," he
aid, but Tessa held her ground.

"What are you going to do to her?"

"Don't worry, Mrs. Pernell," Linc said with a straight face. "If I murder her, I can always hire you to defend me."

Tessa bit her lip to hide a smile and stepped aside. "Linc?" she called out softly when he was halfway up the stairs. "You're exactly what Cassie needs. And I told her as much."

Linc scowled to cover his surprise. "What Cassie Jones needs is a keeper."

He threw open the door to the guest room so hard it banged against the wall, rattling the Currier and Ives print that hung over the bed. Cassie, sitting at the dressing table, jumped up so fast she knocked over the stool. Fresh from her bath, she wore only her thin cotton wrapper. The sight of her, looking so small and vulnerable, and staring at him with those big, haunted gray eyes, knocked what little anger Linc had left right out of him, and for a moment his face softened. Then he noticed Patches, curled in a ball in the middle of the rug and looking up at him with frightened, pain-drugged eyes, and he became incensed all over again.

He slammed the door shut and flung his jacket onto the bed. "I must have been out of my ever-loving mind the day I married you, Cassie Jones. You're trouble with a capital T!"

"I know," she said meekly. "Linc, I'm sorry. I never meant for—"

He took a step toward her, and she backed up, her hand clutching the front of her robe between her breasts.

Linc continued to advance, and his voice dropped to a menacing growl. "You've been ripping through my life like a tornado ever since the first day I met you, leaving nothing but disaster in your wake. But this latest, Cassie...damn it this was too much. It wasn't enough that you had to get me beaten up and tossed into jail, but to drag a poor, innocent dog into..."

Cassie's face crumpled and she started to cry, and Linc stopped.

"Ah, Cassie...don't..." He raised his hand, and she flinched, as if expecting a blow. "Jesus, Cassie. I'm not going to hit you, for God's sake."

He took her in his arms. She tried to pull away, but he tightened his grip, pressing her head against his chest. He thought he would never understand women. Normally Cassie was as tough and prickly as a nettle, and he had to tiptoe around her for fear of getting scratched. Now, when he wanted to have a good knock-down-drag-out fight, she had burst into tears, making him feel like the biggest brute alive.

He pressed his lips to the top of her head. His hand stroked her back, moving down over her round, firm bottom. He felt himself becoming aroused. He gathered up her hair and started to nibble on the exposed skin of her neck. "Cassie," he sighed.

She pushed away from him, flinging her head up to give him a typical Cassie glare, although her cheeks were streaked with tears. "You are so infuriating, Linc Cameron. What are you yelling at *me* for? I told you not to punch that policeman."

Linc blinked. "Huh?"

"Who asked you to come charging to my rescue like some blundering, quixotic knight?"

"Cassie—"

"And I told you in the first place that it was a stupid idea for us to get married, so you have some nerve blaming that on me."

He seized her shoulders and brought his mouth down on hers in a crushing kiss, forcing her lips apart.

She slammed her fists against his chest, then sighed in surrender, grasping his shirt and pulling him to her as he slid his tongue along hers, probing her mouth. Keeping his lips locked on hers, he pulled at her wrapper, pushing it down to her waist, and his hands went immediately to her breasts. He cupped them in his palms, weighing their fullness, then rubbing his fingers against the hard buttons of her nipples while his lips left her mouth to explore the taut curve of her neck and shoulder.

She struggled awkwardly a moment to free her arms from the clinging material of her wrapper, letting it fall to the floor. Then she wrenched open the buttons of his shirt, pressing her breasts against his chest, rubbing her soft, naked flesh against his. Her hands glided down his side to his waist, finding what she wanted. She fumbled with the buttons until he opened them for her, pushing his hardness into her hands.

"Linc..." she groaned, her breath hot and moist against his neck. She grasped him firmly, almost roughly, pushing him between her thighs and into the silky, curly hair. His hands clamped her waist, lifting her until he slid within her, and they fell backward onto the bed, locked together. He rolled her over until he was on top, driving into her.

But as he felt the pressure building inside of him, demanding release, he slowed, then stopped. He fitted himself firmly into her, luxuriating in the feel of being deep in the hot, pulsing core of her, while his mouth searched out her pliant lips again, and his hands made love to her breasts.

He pulled out of her to bring his mouth lower, circling her nipples, tracing each rib in descending order, dipping his tongue into the hollow of her stomach, then moving his lips lower, following the ridge of bone to the treasure between her thighs. He plunged his tongue into her, sucking, licking, tasting of her secrets until she arched her back, pressing against him, and her fingers grasped his hair.

"Oh God," she moaned, then stifled the rest of it with her fist.

Her muscles seemed to hum and vibrate beneath his touch as he slid his hands under her bottom, lifting her. She draped her legs over his shoulders, and he thrust into her again. He looked down at her—at her bare skin, rosy in the lamplight and sleek with the sweat of desire and fulfillment; at her hair spread out like a veil around her, gossamer strands of gold; at her mouth, parted and moist, lips tender and swollen and beckoning him still—and he felt the coming explosion building inside of him. He thought he would not survive it this time, it would be too much, and then he stopped thinking at all.

When the last of the shock waves passed, Linc found himself lying flat on his back with Cassie leaning over him, her compelling gray eyes fastened on his face.

He was still so short of breath, and it was a moment before he could speak. "Damn it all . . . we forgot to use one of the precautions."

She smiled teasingly. "Never mind. If I have a baby I'll blame it all on you." She traced his bruised, swollen lips with her fingers. "Linc, I meant what I said."

"About it being my stupid idea to get married?"

"About being sorry for what happened—Patches getting hurt and you winding up in jail. . . ."

He slid his hand under her hair to caress her neck. "Does this mean you're going to try to stay out of trouble until we get to New York?"

She thought a moment, then sighed, resting her head on his shoulder. "No."

He laughed, nuzzling her with his chin. "What am I going to do with you, Cassie Jones?"

She raised her head, pinning him down with those damnable, haunting gray eyes. "You could try loving me," she answered solemnly.

He rolled her over, burying his face in her hair. He held her tightly against him. Ah, God help me, he thought, but I do, I do, I do.

Cassie traced her and Linc's initials in the morning dew that glistened on the fuselage, drawing a heart around them. Then she heard footsteps on the tarmac and hastily wiped out the drawing with her sleeve. She whipped around, feeling the flush of guilt on her face, then smiled when she saw it was Pete Striker.

"Where's Linc?" Pete asked around the cigarette that dangled from his mouth. The next leg of the race was due to start in thirty minutes. Several of the other teams were already warming up their engines.

Cassie nodded toward the hangar where Linc leaned against the fender of the Daimler, talking with Anselm Pernell. Tessa had an early meeting with a client and had been unable to come to see them off.

"Did anything happen last night?" she said to Pete. "Did you catch any suspicious-looking characters lurking around the *Peg*?"

Pete ground the butt of his cigarette into the tarmac before bringing his head closer to Cassie's. "Not a blasted thing," he said, his voice low. "And what's more, I had myself a word or two with most of the other pilots . . . there's been no sabotage done to their planes."

"But—"

"Breakdowns and failures, sure. Clogged carburetors, broken oil lines, all the usual stuff. But no obvious sabotage like what was done to your propellers."

"What about Ward's radiator? And the broken rudder cable. Couldn't those have been sabotage?"

Pete shrugged. "Maybe. But I don't think so. Those sorts of things happen on any flight, especially on a grueling haul like this one."

"Then you're saying it's a personal thing. That somebody's trying to stop us, and only us, from winning."

Pete looked up and met her eyes. "Maybe he's just trying to stop you . . . period."

"Kill us, you mean?" she said bluntly. "That's silly, Pete. No one has a reason to want us dead."

His eyes flickered away from hers. He looked down to the ground, then off across the airfield into the distance. "Cassie . . . you aren't going to like hearing this.

Christ, I don't like saying it. It has to do with Linc, and the war."

Cassie thought of the sadness she would so often find in Linc's eyes. "What really happened to him over there, Pete?"

"The same thing that happened to a lot of us. Too much death and too much killing. It was all so personal, Cassie. It wasn't just shooting randomly at some faceless enemy. We got to *know* those Boche pilots. It got so we knew their faces, sometimes even their names, and still they were the enemy. Day after day we hunted each other, fought, killed, died..." He shuddered. "God, did we die. Some days thirty men would go up, and only half of us would come back. First you would start to avoid looking another man in the eye in the morning, in case you would have to bury him that afternoon. After a while you got tired of losing friends so you stopped making them altogether. And the fighting affected every man in different ways. Some men became cold-blooded killers—one guy who had a fancy for silver cups went out and bought himself a new one every time he shot down an enemy plane. Others it broke, turned into cowards. You want to know what happened when they told me they'd had to cut off my leg? I bawled like a goddamned baby, but not out of grief. I was *relieved*, relieved that I wouldn't have to fly again."

Cassie blinked back hot tears. "Oh, Pete . . ."

"For the longest time I thought Linc was magic, that he alone of us all had discovered a way to maintain his sanity. He was like two people—a ruthless but careful hunter in the sky, and a carefree, almost gentle man on the ground. But toward the end, especially after Monte was killed, he found it harder and harder to keep the two Lincs separate. He became even more of a ruthless hunter and started taking risks, big risks. If was as if all this time the death and the killing had been eating him up inside until he wanted . . ." Pete stopped, but Cassie said it for him.

"Until he wanted to die himself."

Pete tugged at his cap with a shaking hand. "Yeah."

And Cassie knew then what he had been trying to tell her. "You think Linc still wants to die? That he's deliberately sabotaging our plane?"

"Not deliberately. I don't think he knows he's doing it when he does it."

"He has to know!"

Pete grabbed her shoulders, giving her a rough shake. "No, he can't know. Because if he did it would mean he was—" Pete cut himself off, letting her go.

It would mean he was trying to kill me as well, Cassie silently finished for him. She turned toward the hangar, her eyes searching automatically for Linc. He was still with Anselm, but bent over now, fondling Patches's ears. He straightened up and saw her looking at him. He raised his hand in a wave and she waved back.

"No," she said. "Not Linc. I don't believe it." But she could hear the doubt in her voice.

Pete took her helmet and goggles from where she had laid them on the lower wing and placed them in her hands. "I hope to God I'm wrong. But just in case I'm not . . . don't leave him alone anymore with the *Peg*, Cassie. For his sake as well as yours."

Chapter 14

They followed the rail tracks out of Kansas City, heading southeast toward the brown, docile Mississippi and the next checkpoint: Baton Rouge, Louisiana. They spent the night in a small town on the Arkansas side of the river, renting a room from a widow who occasionally took in boarders. The room smelled of violet sachets and had pots of geraniums on the windowsill. Cassie went into Linc's arms convinced that if she loved him hard enough she could save him from himself.

Afterward, Linc cradled her face with his hands and stared deeply into her eyes. "For so long I've thought I could never believe in anything, find joy in anything again, but now I've discovered you," he said. It was the closest he had come to saying that he loved her, and Cassie would have felt relieved if she hadn't seen the sadness lurking in his eyes.

Linc's side of the bed was empty the next morning when she awoke, and Patches had disappeared. They had tied the *Pegasus* down in a pasture on the edge of town the evening before, and she found Linc there, wiping his hands on a wet rag. A lantern sat on one of the wings, and tools were scattered on the ground at his feet. Patches chased a dragonfly in the grass. The sun was just beginning to light up the eastern sky.

"What have you been doing?" she demanded, running up to him.

He looked up in surprise. "I thought the engine sounded a bit rough yesterday."

"It didn't sound rough to me."

He shrugged.

"Linc..." she began, then stopped. What was she going to do, demand to know if he had just sabotaged their plane? "You should have asked me to help you," she said instead.

"I thought I'd let you sleep." He put his palm against the side of her face, tilting her head back to meet his eyes. "You've already done more than your share of the maintenance work. Have I told you yet that you're the best copilot a man could have?"

Cassie nodded and forced a smile. She thought of Pete's warning not to leave Linc alone with the *Pegasus*. She glanced at the engine, hidden now beneath its cowling. Had he done something to it while she was sleeping? There was no way of knowing, short of taking the whole thing apart and putting it back together again herself. She could do that, of course, but it would take hours. And what explanation could she give him without arousing his suspicions if he were guilty, or hurting him terribly if he were not. No, she would just have to trust him—trust him with her life.

Yet the memory of the sadness haunting Linc's eyes was with her as they flew across an azure sky lashed with mare's-tail clouds. Cassie had the controls as they followed the Mississippi south, but it was one of the rare times when she found no pleasure in flying. It was very cold aloft, the sharp wind chafing her cheeks, cutting through her heavy coat. Her hands, even in their fleece-lined gloves, soon grew numb.

She tried to understand how it would be possible for a man to methodically arrange for his own death and not be aware that he was doing it. He would have to be insane. But then, the war had driven some people crazy. Shell-shocked, they called it. She had seen a man suffering from shell shock once; he was a loose-jointed skeletal figure with twitching nerves. Yet, except for Linc's propensity to fly into a rage every time she got into trouble, he was the steadiest man she knew. She remembered how he had so calmly brought the *Pegasus* down after their propeller had shattered and the engine had cut off. If he wanted so badly to die, that certainly would have been the moment to do it, she thought wryly.

Linc's hand fell on her shoulder, startling her into awareness so that she jumped, jerking on the stick and causing the plane to bank sharply. The front of a squall suddenly appeared like the sheer face of a cliff in front of them, and she had but a few seconds to adjust the controls before they plunged into the clouds.

It was as if a damp white sheet had been flung over their heads. Then the air seemed to literally drop out from under them as they hit a downdraft. Rain splashed against their faces as if squirted from a giant hose, and Cassie had to ride the elevator hard as they were buffeted by the wind. Pitching, yawing, and rolling in the violent gusts, the plane felt as helpless as a piece of driftwood tossed on a hurricane-ravaged sea. She glanced quickly back at Linc and pointed upward. Linc nodded; they would try to get above it.

The rain froze into a glaze on her goggles as she climbed, and fierce winds continued to batter the plane. Fearing carburetor icing, she kept her eye on the altimeter, her ear tuned to the sound of the engine. Even as she thought it she began to hear the rough, uneven pulse that indicated a loss of power. Her eyes flickered over to the airspeed indicator, and she saw it wasn't registering. She rapped it hard with her knuckle, but it still read zero.

She had been plunging about for too long in the dense grayness, and she knew that she had lost her equilibrium. She had no physical feeling of what was up or down, right or left, and her hands froze on the controls in indecision. Without the airspeed indicator to warn her, she didn't realize that she was flying slower and slower, too slow for her sharp rate of climb, approaching the speed at which the plane would no longer be able to remain aloft until—she stalled.

The plane shuddered and whipped into a high-speed, spiraling dive, plunging through the darkness. Helpless, Cassie watched the sinking altimeter and revolving compass, trying desperately and blindly to stabilize the controls. Burning pain from the rushing air pressed against her ears, and the blood left her hands and feet. Darkness began to creep around the edge of her vision.

Then there was a sudden, contrasting flash of brightness as they burst through the clouds, dazzling Cassie's eyes. She blinked and saw that the world had been turned upside down. Where the sky should be was the ground—green earth and brown river—rushing at them with dizzying speed.

They had only seconds to live, but it was all Cassie needed. With the sight of the ground, her equilibrium returned. She shoved the throttle forward and snapped the plane out of its spin with a jerk that jarred her teeth. The propeller bit the air fifty feet from the surface, so close it sent up spray from the river beneath them.

The storm still raged around them, sharp, crooked bolts of lightning doing a dance above their heads like marionettes jerking on a string. Cassie had only one thought left in her numb, frightened mind—to put the *Pegasus* down, *now*.

Running along the river was a long expanse of green field, and she guided the *Peg*'s nose straight toward it. The plane landed hard, its wheels plowing a furrow in the soft earth and throwing up a spray of water.

It wasn't until she had climbed out of the cockpit and

felt the ground real and solid beneath her feet that Cassie experienced the full depth of her fright. She went into Linc's arms on legs as stiff and awkward as stilts, collapsing against him and shuddering uncontrollably.

"Oh God, Linc. I stalled. The airspeed indicator jammed or something, and I stalled. Oh God, I almost got us killed. . . ."

The rain poured down, and the wind lashed them. He pulled her over to the lee side of the fuselage, pressing her tightly against him. "Cassie, you were incredible. That was the most magnificent piece of flying I've ever seen in my life."

"No, no, no." She shook her head wildly back and forth. "I panicked. You should have taken over the controls, Linc. Why didn't you take over the controls?"

He unstrapped her helmet, pulling it off along with her goggles. He kissed her cold, wet cheek. "Honey, I was so completely disoriented I—"

She punched him hard in the chest. "You bastard!" she screamed.

He was so stunned he simply stood there and let her hit him again. But when she pulled back her fist a third time, he grabbed her wrist, deflecting the blow.

"Cassie! What is the matter with you?"

"You! You're the matter!"

"What have I done now?"

She wrenched her wrist free and backed away from him, rubbing the spot where he had bruised the skin. "You know," she said coldly.

"Know what? Christ, living with you is like having a scorpion by the tail. You never know when it's going to turn around and sting you."

She laughed hysterically. "And what do you think it's like trying to live with you? You might want to die, Linc Cameron, but I don't!"

"What the hell are you *talking* about?"

"It was bad enough making me fall in love with you, making it so that I can't live without you. Now you've decided you've got to die, and you're trying to take me with you."

He said nothing, simply stared at her. She felt the wetness on her cheeks and knew that it was more than just the rain. She hated the way he always managed to send her emotions into tailspins more violent than any she had experienced in the *Pegasus*. It seemed that *he* was always calm, collected, in control. Yet lately all she had to do was think about him, especially how much she loved him and how frightened that made her, and she would start gushing like a geyser.

"I think you had better explain what you meant by that remark," he said at last, still calm, controlled, and collected, of course. The shuttered look she had not seen in a long time was back on his face.

She summoned all her courage, unconsciously thrusting her chin in the air. "You want an explanation, I'll give you an explanation. I don't think the instrument failure was an accident. I think that if we look we'll discover it was more sabotage. . . ."

"And?"

"And you did it."

There, she had brought it out into the open. Now it was up to him, except that he was doing nothing, just looking at her. Then he turned abruptly and walked away.

"Linc!" she called after him.

He didn't even pause.

"Linc!" She ran up to him and, digging her fingers into the sleeve of his leather jacket, pulled him around to face her. She had expected anything—anger, derision, disgust—anything but what she saw. Hurt, bitter and furious, blazed in his eyes. In one blinding, painful instant she knew that she had been wrong—incredibly, stupidly wrong—and that there was nothing she could do or say that would ever make it up to him. She had lost him forever.

He pried her fingers loose from his sleeve, then

dropped her hand. He walked off, and this time she let him go. He followed the bank of the river, and before long he had disappeared into the rain and brush.

She went back to the *Pegasus* and crawled under the wing to get out of the rain. She leaned back against the wheel and drew her knees up under her chin, wrapping her arms around her legs, and she cried.

A cold nose nuzzled her hand. She pulled Patches into her lap, burying her face in his damp fur. He licked the tears off her cheeks, whining softly.

After a while the rain stopped, and the sun broke through the clouds, bringing with it a soft, damp heat. Cassie had pushed Patches off her lap and started to get up when she noticed that the far wheel was half-buried in black, sticky mud. Worried, she made a quick exploration of the field; the *Pegasus* seemed to be sitting in some sort of depression, which was both good and bad. It was good in that the entire field wasn't a quagmire, so once free of the mud they shouldn't have much trouble taking off. The bad part would be getting free of the quagmire in the first place. Of course, if Linc didn't bother to come back . . .

Cassie shut her mind to the thought. With Patches's exuberant help, she started to look the *Pegasus* over carefully to see what damage it had sustained during their violent plunge through the storm-tossed sky. Overall the *Peg* wasn't in bad shape, Cassie quickly decided, although they would need to put in a lot of hours on maintenance work once they arrived in Baton Rouge. She had saved examining the airspeed indicator for last. She stared at it now for a long time, then went to the locker and removed the toolbox.

It didn't take long to figure out what had happened. The connecting line to the gauge had been severed just enough so that any violent, sudden movement—the heavy pitching they had experienced flying into the squall, for instance—would cause it to snap apart. It was sabotage—there could be no doubt of it.

She took a walk down along the river, hoping to see Linc on his way back. There was little river traffic, only a fishing skiff and a rusty towboat hauling an empty barge. Close to the water the air smelled of mold and dampness. The riverbank was edged with a silt beach covered with trash left by the last high water. Cassie came upon a big turtle sunning himself on a log, but as she got closer he slid off his perch and into the muddy river. Patches spotted a water turkey and chased it into a tangled mess of nettles and blackberry vines, stirring up a cloud of gnats and mosquitoes. Cassie had to get down on her knees and haul him out of the brush by his hind legs.

"Look at that." She pointed to a clump of shiny, distinctively shaped leaves. "Do you know what that is, you idiot dog. That's poison ivy." She picked the burrs out of his fur. "If I'm all blotchy and red and itchy tomorrow, I'll know who to yell at."

She looked once more upriver and then, sighing, headed back to the *Pegasus*. Linc was there waiting for her. As she came up to him she thought she saw relief flash across his face, but when he spoke his voice dripped icicles.

"There's a small town about a half hour's walk from here," he said. "I'll try to hitch a ride going south. You can fly the *Pegasus* on to Baton Rouge, and I'll meet you there when I can."

"If . . ." Her voice cracked, and she had to clear her throat. "If we don't arrive at the checkpoint together with the *Pegasus*, we'll be disqualified."

He gave a short, bitter laugh, shaking his head. "You have more guts than sense, Cassie, still wanting to go up in an airplane with me. Here I am liable at any minute to go off the deep end and send us crashing into a mountain. Of course, there aren't any mountains around here. But there are a lot of swamps and water. I can send us into the drink, Cassie, and then if the crash doesn't kill us we can die by drowning. We can sink nto the murky depths together, arm in arm—"

"Stop it!" she shouted, covering her ears. "I know
you're hurt, and I—"

He seized her wrists, pulling her hands down.
"Hurt! You're damned right I'm hurt. How do you
think it feels to discover that the woman you love
thinks you're some sort of lunatic bent on killing not
only yourself, but her as well?"

He probably wasn't even aware he had said it. But
Cassie heard it, and she seized on that one word,
seized on it as if she really were drowning and it was a
lifeline.

"You love me?"

He went perfectly still. It got so quiet that Cassie
could hear the fishermen calling out to each other on
the river.

He drew in a deep breath. "I love you. All right, I've
said it. I love you. I hope you're satisfied. We're wrong
for each other, wrong in every way, yet you've gotten
me so damned much in love with you that you've managed to ruin me for any other woman." He put his
hand over her mouth as she started to speak. "No,
don't. Don't say anything. We made a deal to end this
once we get to New York, and I intend to stick with it.
For my own sake as much as yours. So don't say anything, just . . . kiss me. . . ." And his mouth crushed
down on hers with a desperate, hungry need that told
her even more than his words the true depth of his
feelings.

Cassie felt something tear loose inside her, something that had been bound and weighted in chains. She
had given him her body days ago, but with this one
kiss she gave him herself, and if she could not belong
to him forever, at least she belonged to him for now.

He ended the kiss by moving his lips up to her eyes,
where he kissed each lid in turn. She felt the brush of
his mouth against her temple. "I love you," he said,
then laughed. "It's funny how the more you say that,

the easier it gets. I love you, I love you. You're probably going to be sick and tired of hearing it by the time we get to New York."

New York. Cassie felt a coldness seep over her. Nothing had changed. He had said he loved her, but a part of her had known that all along. He had said they were wrong for each other, and she knew that too. He wanted peace, a wife, children, a porch with a swing. And she wanted . . . what did she want? She was no longer sure. All she knew was that Linc wanted and needed a *whole* woman, a woman to be all his. But there was something empty inside of her, a part of her that seemed to be missing, and until she found it she knew she could never give him all of herself.

She slipped out of his arms. "Linc, I have to talk to you about something else. Do you promise not to get mad?"

"What is it?"

"Promise you won't get mad first."

He let out an exasperated sigh. "I hate it when you do this, Cassie."

"Promise," she said mulishly.

"All right, damn it, I promise. But if—"

"I examined the airspeed indicator," she said quickly. "It was sabotage. And we're the only ones, Linc, the only ones being sabotaged. Pete asked around. Someone's trying to kill us."

Linc studied the ground, lost in thought. "Well, we've decided it isn't Harry and Jim, and we've decided it isn't me—we *have* decided it isn't me, haven't we, Cassie?"

She nodded seriously.

"Then there's only one suspect left."

"Who?"

"You."

"Linc!" Cassie gasped. Then she saw the corner of his mouth twitching, and she aimed a mock blow at his head. "That wasn't funny, Linc Cameron!"

"It serves you right." He draped his arm across her shoulder. "Come on, let's get out of here. We're losing this race."

"Uh, Linc . . . there's something else."

"What?" he asked warily.

"Do you promise not to get mad?"

He flung his arms up in the air. "Cassie, you are driving me crazy!" he bellowed. Then he heard what he'd said, and he started laughing. "Jesus. What is it? I promise not to get mad."

She swallowed hard and lifted her chin. "I, uh . . . put the *Peg* down in a mud hole."

Linc walked around the *Pegasus*, looking at the situation and struggling manfully not to swear. "Well, things were a bit hectic at the time," he finally said. "It wasn't your fault."

"Yes it was."

"Yes it was," he agreed. "But we all make mistakes." He grinned at her. "I, on a very rare occasion and at some point in the far distant past, have been known to make one. We'll have to jettison everything that isn't nailed down and hope the wind kicks back up."

Linc started to toss things out of the cockpits and locker. While his back was turned, Cassie took the peach silk dress and the matching shoes that had been rolled up in a ball in the bottom of her flying kit and stuffed them between her shirt and overalls. It made her look as if she were six months pregnant, but she thought Linc would probably be too preoccupied with getting the *Pegasus* off to notice. Patches, meanwhile, climbed into the front cockpit and burrowed under the seat.

Linc calculated how much fuel would be needed to get to Baton Rouge, then drained off as much as he dared. With his pocketknife he cut some brush and wedged it under the wheels to give the tires something to bite into. Luckily they were already pointed into the wind. Cassie spun the prop while Linc started the engine, then she scrambled quickly on board.

It felt at first as if the *Pegasus* had been glued to the earth, then with a mighty groan she began to lumber down the field, straining against the pull of the sticky mud. As he felt her tail begin to rise, Linc struggled to keep the nose up. Then suddenly the wheels pulled free with a loud, sucking pop, and they were airborne.

He made a wide half turn, gaining altitude, and pointed the *Pegasus* toward Baton Rouge.

Cassie broke off a section of orange, popping it into her mouth. The wet tartness exploded against her tongue, and she leaned back against the wing struts, sighing with pleasure. Closing her eyes, she turned her face toward the late-afternoon sun, basking in its warmth. She could still feel a tingling numbness in her cheeks from the hours of being buffeted by the cold winds aloft.

There were even more journalists waiting for them in Baton Rouge than there had been in Kansas City. Bean's cola had at last managed to ignite the country's interest in the race. Bets were being placed on the outcome, and even those not of a sporting nature were at least choosing their favorite teams to cheer on. One of the reporters had confided to Cassie that she and Linc appeared to be the people's choice. "Young couple like you, just starting out in life," the man had said. "Folks want to see you wind up with that prize money." But another reporter had again asked her if it was true that she was a Ziegfeld chorus girl and Leroy Bean's mistress.

Still, Cassie was beginning to lose her fear of the press, with their intrusive notebooks and cameras. She answered most of their questions cheerfully, ignoring the nasty ones, but she was relieved when the next plane landed and they all trooped off to shout their questions at someone else.

One of the reporters had lingered behind to toss her

the orange with a wink and a grin, then laughed off her thanks. "Just remember who fed you when you were tired and hungry, when you're livin' in one of those fancy mansions on Fifth Avenue," he had drawled with a charming and inviting smile.

She felt the brush of cool lips against her cheek, and her eyes flew open. "No rest for the weary, my sleeping beauty," Linc said. "We've got a lot of maintenance work to do."

She straightened up, stretching. "We left our tools somewhere along the Mississippi."

He dropped a heavy chamois bag at her feet. "I borrowed some."

She pressed a section of the orange against his lips, and he opened his mouth, sucking it in. "So where are we?" she asked. "Still in third?"

"Uh-huh," he mumbled around the orange. He chewed and swallowed. "That was good. Give me another one."

She snatched what was left of the orange back out of his reach. "Trade you for a kiss."

His lips tasted of orange, tangy and sweet, and the rough masculine smell of him was making her feel a bit giddy. She clutched the sleeves of his leather jacket and held on for dear life while he kissed her.

"So, have we closed the gap any?" she asked, a bit breathlessly, after he released her.

"The cumulative time intervals have tightened up all the way down the line," he said. "Most of the teams who were still in it in Kansas City have made it here by now. All except Harry and Jim."

"Oh. Poor Harry and Jim."

Linc grinned. "Yeah. Poor Harry and Jim."

"Why don't you like them? I think they're nice."

"Cassie, I'm not going to have this argument again."

She put her hands on her hips. "You want to know what I think?"

"No."

"I think you're just jealous because I happen to like them."

"Hunh! You want to know what I think?"

"No."

"I think you need another kiss," he growled, and lunged for her.

She shrieked and took off running. Ducking arround the *Peg*'s tail she smacked hard into Edward Farrell's chest.

"Hey!" Edward steadied her by grasping her shoulders. "What's the matter?" Then he saw Linc and released her. He cocked a sardonic brow. "Well, well, old boy. Troubles with the little woman already? What is that little ditty: 'A wife, a dog, and an olive tree, the more you beat them the better they be'?"

Cassie opened her mouth to set him straight.

"My experience has been something like this," Linc said with an easy grin. " 'You may beat the devil into a wife, but you'll never beat him out of her.' "

"Oooh!" Cassie exclaimed. "I don't know which one of you is more infuriating!"

She turned on her heel, intending to stalk off, when she heard the hum of an approaching aircraft. She looked up to see the distinctive silhouette of the Wright pusher biplane, black against the setting sun.

"It's Harry and Jim!" she announced triumphantly.

Linc muttered something under his breath, and she smiled to herself. They stood watching the plane land, and afterward no one was able to explain how it happened. The aircraft seemed to be coming down fine, when all of a sudden it slammed into the ground and burst into flames.

A blast of heat from the explosion washed over them as if they were standing in front of a giant furnace. Cassie pressed her hands against her mouth to stifle a scream. Beside her Linc made an odd noise and jerked, and she turned to see his face was deathly white and covered with glistening sweat that seemed to mirror the flames. And his eyes...his eyes were filled with stark terror.

"Linc..." She touched his arm, and he flinched as if she had struck him, then stumbled away from her. She started to go after him when Edward held her back.

"Leave him alone."

"But—"

Edward's fingers tightened, digging into her flesh. "It's how Monte died, burned to a cinder in his plane. Monte was like a brother to him—more than a brother, actually. And Linc saw it all. He saw Monte go down, saw the flames. Linc went down after him, but it was too late. An hour later the rescue crew found Linc curled up in his cockpit, sobbing like a child."

There was a tinge of contempt in Edward's voice as he said this, and it angered Cassie. She didn't see how Linc Cameron's manhood was diminished just because he had allowed himself to care so deeply for his friend that he'd wept at the man's death.

A fire wagon had been summoned to put out the flames, but it was too late. Cassie thought she saw the blackened shape of a body sitting in the front cockpit, and she turned quickly away.

Edward gathered her into his arms, and she pressed her face against his chest. "Oh Ward, what can I do? I love Linc so much, I can't bear to see him suffer."

The hand that had been stroking her back stilled a moment, then resumed. "There isn't anything you can do for him, Cassie. A man never gets over something like that. Never."

Cassie was halfway through the overhaul when Linc finally returned. The plane wreckage had been cleared off the field, and the bodies removed. It was the first serious accident thus far in the race, and it had sobered everyone, reminding them that what they were doing was dangerous—fatally dangerous.

Cassie felt unsure of what to do or say as Linc

walked up to her. He met her eyes but said nothing. After a moment she turned back to the engine. They worked on it side by side in silence, although several times Cassie had to bite her tongue to keep from blurting out questions she knew he couldn't bear to answer.

She didn't speak until they were cleaning up and putting the tools away. "I suppose we'd better take turns staying awake all night to be sure no more sabotage is done to the *Pegasus*," she said. She didn't mention that the prime suspects, at least in Linc's mind, were now dead.

"No need," Linc replied. "I had a talk with the race committee this afternoon about what's been going on. They were scandalized, outraged, et cetera, and they promised to put a guard on her tonight." He cocked his head toward a barn that had been converted into a hangar. "We're to lock her up in there. There'll be a man armed with a shotgun posted outside to make sure that no one comes near her until we show up tomorrow morning."

Cassie chewed on her lip. "I suppose that'll work."

"It'll work. We need our sleep, otherwise we'll wind up killing ourselves through fatigue and carelessness." He forced a weak smile for her benefit. "Right now I'm so beat I feel like I just went fifteen rounds with Jack Dempsey."

Cassie's answering smile was only a little better. "Fifteen rounds? Who are you kidding? I saw you take on those policemen, remember? You wouldn't last fifteen *seconds* in a ring with Jack Dempsey."

Linc felt as if his muscles had indeed been beaten to a pulp, yet as he lay on the bed later that night and watched Cassie undress in their tiny rented room, the fatigue slowly began to melt away from him. Her sun-kissed hair glowed golden in the soft light of the kerosene lamp; her smoky eyes obscured her thoughts, beckoning him to try once more to delve her mysteries. She was beautiful and she was his, and he waited for her, naked and hard with desire, to come to him.

She came at last. He tangled his fingers in her hair as, leaning over him, she began to rub her breasts in slow and sensuous circles on his chest, and Linc felt the muscles tighten deep in his gut. Her hands found his erection, stroking along his hard length, while her lips made their way down his chest until they joined her caressing fingers, and he clenched his jaw to keep from groaning out loud as she took his shaft into her warm, moist mouth.

She made love to him with her lips and throat and tongue, and the explosion when it came obliterated everything. There was nothing in the universe but her and his need for her, igniting into a raging fire, burning bright and hot and hard, until it consumed them both.

Much later, as she lay sleeping in his arms, Linc stared wide-eyed up at the ceiling and thought about all that had happened that day. Bartinelli's watchdogs were now dead, but it wasn't much of a reprieve. He had no doubt there would be another pair from the Black Hand waiting for him in New York to collect the thirty-three thousand. He wondered if Bartinelli's boys had been the saboteurs. It had never made much sense, and it still didn't. Unless the *Pegasus* landed in New York with the best time, Bartinelli would never see any of that money, and putting Tommy in a wheelchair was going to be small consolation. As for himself, he had made one bad mistake in not telling Cassie about all this at the very beginning. It was too late now; she would never forgive him for the deception. They had only one week left, one week before New York, when she would walk out of his life forever. He wanted to spend those days loving her, not fighting with her. One week . . .

You liar, he told himself with an inward, self-depre-cating laugh. There was no way he was going to be able to give this woman up once they got to New York. If she wanted to spend the rest of her life tramping arround the country flying airplanes and marching in suffragette parades, he was doomed to follow along after her. Hell, she would need somebody on hand just to rescue her from the all the trouble she was bound to get into. No, she didn't know it yet—and she wasn't going to like it when she found out about it—but Miss Cassandra Jones had herself a husband for better and for worse, and forever.

That settled, he turned his head and gave her one last kiss before closing his eyes and drifting off to sleep.

That night he dreamed about Monte's death.

Chapter 15

*H*e watched the enemy plane spin toward the earth trailing a gray plume of smoke, and he wagged his Spad's wings at Monte in a victory salute. Monte, flying wing to wing with him, waved back.

They headed for home. The joy of victory was so strong he wanted to throw back his head and laugh out loud. But it wasn't just from the success of the day's hunt. The war would be over soon, they all knew it. Even the Germans knew it. A month ago, even two weeks ago, he would have thought he stood a better chance of surviving standing up in front of a firing squad than he did of enduring this hell. But it was different now. He would have shouted it aloud if Monte could have heard him: "We did it, old man, mon ami, old sod. We did it! We've lived through the war!"

He suddenly heard the familiar tack-tack-tack of a machine gun and saw holes appearing in his right wing. He went into an immediate dive, glancing over his shoulder through slitted eyes to protect his vision from the glare of the blinding sun. He caught a glimpse of the single-winged silhouette of a Fokker fighter, a black cross on its red nose. He felt rather than saw Monte peel off to the left away from him.

They had hunted as a team hundreds of times, he and Monte, so they both knew instinctively what the other would do. Their styles complemented each other; Monte often joked *that they flew fighter planes the way they pursued women. "I dazzle the enemy with the brilliance of my aerobatics," Monte would say, "while Linc flies straight in for the attack, holding his fire until he gets within point-blank range."*

Linc did this now, circling around, playing hide-and-seek in and out of the clouds, closing in on the enemy from above. He recognized the plane now, it was Schumacher, damn Schumacher. He attacked the German, coming straight out of the sun just the way the Fokker had done moments before. His fingers tensed on the triggers of his guns, but he held his fire in the instant before Monte burst out of a cloud in front of him, banking so sharply he seemed to be skimming along on the tip of a wing, his guns hacking bullets—and missing.

The Fokker returned fire. He saw the flash of the tracer bullets, followed their yellow arc, saw them rip into Monte's Spad. The Spad shuddered once as if it were a living thing in pain, and then it fell. It simply fell out of the sky trailing bright orange flames. Monte! Linc's mind screamed in agony, although the hand gripping the joy stick didn't even tremble, and his eyes were still fixed on the enemy Fokker.

He was out of position now, but he flew on, straight for the enemy, for Schumacher. He saw the barrel of the gun swing around to meet him, and the thought flashed across his mind that this was going to be one unlucky day all the way around. But still he held his fire, letting himself get closer, his whole body tensed and waiting for the smacking impact of the shredding bullets. He was close enough now to see the face of his enemy; he imagined he could see the lines around Schumacher's pale eyes, the individual hairs of the man's thin blond mustache. He wondered why Schumacher wasn't firing and thought in that same instant that the Fokker's gun must have jammed. He saw Schumacher smile, acknowledging to him this final victory, in the second before his own finger pressed down on the trigger. There was a blinding explosion as the bullets struck the fuel tank and the Fokker disintegrated before his eyes.

He went down then, after Monte, praying, hoping that Monte had somehow brought the wounded Spad safely to

*earth and walked away, just like all those other times, con-
vincing himself that he hadn't seen those flames and believing
it until he saw the greasy smoke billowing up from the field
below.*

*The Spad was still burning when he landed beside it. It
was so hot he couldn't even get close, although he tried. It was
only some kind of instinctive self-preservation that kept him
from throwing himself right into the tower of flames, even
though he knew there was no way Monte could be in there and
still be alive.*

*He clung to the thought that Monte must have jumped,
taken the easier death. But when the flames eventually died
down, he saw Monte still sitting in the Spad, his charred face
staring out at him over the blackened carnage of the cockpit,
his funeral pyre—*

Linc awoke suddenly to the feel of a hand on his
face, and he flinched instinctively. He reached up to
brush the hand away and felt a wetness on his cheeks.
He turned his head away from her.

"You were having a bad dream," she said.

He nodded.

"About Monte?"

"How did you . . . ?"

"You were crying his name."

He felt weak and cowardly, and bitterly ashamed of
his tears. He wanted to ask her to go away; he was
afraid she would.

"Tell me," she said.

"I can't."

She kissed him, a gentle, undemanding kiss. And
the kiss was like a key, unlocking the pain.

"The real horror of it, Cassie," he said when he got
to the part about seeing Monte's burned body in the
plane, "the real, gut-wrenching horror was that Monte
had always been so terrified of burning up. We weren't
allowed to wear parachutes, you see. They were afraid
we'd bail out too soon if we got hit, instead of trying to
bring the machine down." His lips twisted. "Airplanes

being much more valuable than men. So Monte used to take a pistol with him every time he went up. He said it was so he could shoot himself if he ever caught on fire. But that day . . . that day he forgot it. He started to go back for it, but he knew I was impatient to get going so he changed his mind. Because of me he went up without it . . . and he burned to death."

Cassie was sitting beside him, her legs folded beneath her. "Maybe he was already dead, Linc," she said matter-of-factly. "Maybe he was hit by one of the machine-gun bullets. Otherwise, he would have jumped. If he was that frightened of fire."

Linc shook his head. "It's a comforting thought, but I don't really believe it. Human beings are funny when it comes to wanting to live. Jumping meant sure death. No, he would have stuck with the Spad until the very end, hoping, believing he could pull it out." His hand glided over her thigh in an absent caress. "I know Pete has somehow put it into your head that I came back from France feeling guilty about surviving the war, and that might have been true, once. But I meant what I said last night. You have shown me how badly I do want to live. Even knowing we aren't meant to last, even if you walk out that door tomorrow morning and I never see you again, I will never regret loving you, Miss Cassandra Jones."

She came into his arms then, and he made love to her, slowly and gently, as the first light peeked through the moss-draped arms of the tree outside their window and a mockingbird began to sing.

As a result they were late getting out to the airfield, and Cassie worried that they were not taking enough time to check over the *Pegasus* for sabotage. Linc began to lose his temper as she thought of one thing after another that might have been done to the plane overnight.

Finally he slapped his helmet against his thigh in exasperation. "Damn it, Cassie, the *Pegasus* was well guarded last night. We're just going to have to take a calculated risk."

She faced him with her hands on her hips, her chin in the air. "You are so maddening, Linc Cameron. Don't you even care that somebody's trying to kill us? Or are you going to have to be dead before you do something about it?"

Then the absurdity of what she had just said struck Cassie. She opened her mouth to take it back, but Linc as usual was too quick for her.

"I can always haunt him from my grave," he scoffed. "Of course I care that somebody's *apparently* trying to kill us, but what do you want me to do about it? Go up to people, tap them on the shoulder, and say, 'Excuse me, but are you trying to kill us? Because if you are, we'd like to know why. We're dying of the suspense, you see'?"

"You don't need to be sarcastic to make your point," she said, looking hurt.

He rubbed the back of his neck. "Hell, I'm as jumpy about it as you are, Cassie. But apart from being careful, I don't know what more we can do besides drop out of the race, and that's assuming that the race is what's at the bottom of this. There are other implications here you're not considering. Suppose the race has nothing to do with it; suppose it's really only one of us who's the target? We haven't been together long enough to have acquired any mutual enemies."

"I haven't acquired any enemies at all."

"You haven't, huh? What about a cigar-store owner whose shop you wrecked? You've been running amok on this planet for twenty years now; you can't tell me there aren't thousands of men out there who dream nightly of wringing your neck!"

"Oh, if that isn't just typical!" She advanced on him, thinking that neck wringing sounded like a very good idea.

"Now, Cassie!" Linc cried, backing up and pretending to be frightened.

Patches darted from beneath the wing and between her legs, barking a cheerful greeting, and she turned around at the sound of laughter. Edward Farrell strolled up, his hands shoved deep in the slash pockets of his leather jacket. Gregory Pearce followed along behind him, intently studying the ground. Probably because he was so used to tripping over things, Cassie thought with an indulgent smile.

"Lord, Cassie, what a shrew you've turned into since you became a wife," Edward said, wearing a self-satisfied smirk. He bent over to give Patches a pat. "Sort of makes you want to remain a bachelor forever, doesn't it, Greg?"

Cassie gave him one of her best glares. "What do you want?"

He shrugged, straightening. "We came by to pass the idle minute or two before the race starts up. We thought we'd see how things are going with you two. In the race department, that is, not the marital department." He chuckled.

"Starting to feel the pressure, are you, Ward?" Linc said, and Cassie turned her head sharply at the strange note she'd heard in his voice. But the expression on Linc's face was one of benign friendliness.

"Oh, I think not. After all, we're in second, with only thirty-seven minutes separating us and the Schmidts, and you're what—fourth?"

"Third."

"Really? Still, there is only one more checkpoint before we get to New York, and this leg should separate the men from the boys, metaphorically speaking, of course. In fact, with luck the eventual winner could have the race practically sewn up by the time we get to Dayton."

"Melodie is going to meet us there," Gregory Pearce

aid in a squeaky voice, his Adam's apple bobbing
bove his collar.

Cassie favored him with one of her brightest smiles.
he was growing to rather like poor Gregory Pearce.

And she, too, was anxious to get to Dayton. Dayton,
Ohio, Leroy Bean's hometown, was the final check-
oint before the finish. It was going to be the longest
eg of the race, covering over eight hundred miles.
Vard was right. Right now the cumulative time be-
ween the three leaders was so close it was anybody's
ace, but a lot could happen in eight hundred miles.

A race official had walked out into the middle of the
irfield to wave a yellow flag. "Well!" Edward said with
n expansive smile. "It's time to warm the Jenny up."
Ie held out his hand to Linc. "I would wish you luck,
ld friend, but you know how it is. . . ."

Linc smiled and shook the men's hands. "Ward.
Greg. Take it easy. And slow. Very slow."

Edward laughed, then his face grew serious. "Just
hink, Linc, if things had worked out differently . . .
ren't you sorry now that you didn't accept my offer?"

"The race isn't over yet, Ward."

"What offer was he talking about?" Cassie asked
inc as soon as the two men were out of earshot.

"What? Oh, to team up with him in the race. A fifty-
ifty split like we've got."

"He offered to team up with you after the *Betsy* blew
p?"

"No, way before then. It was during the time I vis-
ted him in Virginia when you almost flew into me."

Cassie sucked in an indignant breath. "I did not almost fly into you!" Then she saw he was laughing, and
he laughed herself. She started to climb into the cock-
it, then stopped. "It's funny, but I always thought
Vard hadn't decided to enter the race until the last
ninute."

Linc picked up their flying kits, stowing them in the
ocker. "He talked about needing money for his planta-

tion and asked if he could race with me. But when I told him I already had Pete Striker for a copilot, he seemed to lose interest. I think he was hoping for an inheritance or something. Maybe it didn't come through."

"Oh," Cassie mumbled, feeling a sick chill at even this oblique reference to the hateful Lawrence Kingly. Once more she started to climb into the cockpit, then paused again. "Linc, did you remember to check the fuel line?"

"Yeah," he called back, going up to spin the prop.

"Let's check it again."

Linc sighed and assumed his long-suffering look, but they checked it again.

It broke five hundred miles later, while they were flying over the Cumberland mountains of Tennessee.

The fuel gauge on the *Pegasus* was notoriously inaccurate, so when it read next to empty an hour after they had filled the tank, Linc paid it little heed. Not long afterward though, the engine's steady hum changed to an uneven pulse, and they began losing altitude. Linc pulled back the throttle with little response.

He woke Cassie, who had been catching a nap in the front cockpit, shouting over the racket that they were going to have to land. It wasn't going to be easy; below them were heavily timbered mountains. He spotted a small clearing and circled. It was narrow, bordered by a gorge on one side and a rocky stream on the other, and it was short—too short.

It would have to do, he thought as the engine began to sputter and miss. He cut the ignition and banked to land.

He fishtailed in, slipping the aircraft a little sideways to see the ground, easing back on the stick. A steep rise carpeted with thick pines and hedgerows of chokeberry and mountain ash loomed in front of them, and they were coming up on it fast, much too fast. Just then Cassie started to crawl out of the cockpit.

Linc thought she had panicked and decided to jump, but they hadn't even touched down yet, and she was going to dash her brains out. He shouted at her to get back. She waved and flashed him a grin, then stepped out onto the wing just as the *Peg*'s wheels hit the ground with a hard bounce. Her feet flew out from under her, and she slid past him across the wing's slippery, taut fabric. Linc flung out his arm to catch her, but missed.

Cassie hung from the edge of the wing by her fingertips for a couple of endless seconds, then hauled herself back onto the flat surface. Linc let out his breath. She scooted along, walking like a duck, and then to his utter horror she leaped from the wing onto the fuselage in back of him. He twisted around to scream at her to stay still for Chrissakes, and the *Pegasus* hit a rut, swerving toward the gorge. Behind him he heard Cassie scream. He kicked the opposite rudder, the plane swerved back, and Cassie screamed again. He glanced back and saw her inching along on the bouncing fuselage. He understood now—the little fool was going to try to slow the plane down by putting her weight on the tail and forcing it to skid against the ground to act as a brake. It was the stupidest, most dangerous thing she had done yet, and if they didn't run into the side of a mountain within the next five seconds, he was going to have her head for it.

Yet it was working. He felt the sudden drag, and the *Pegasus* began to slow. He aimed the nose toward a tangled screen of blackberry vines and willed the plane to stop.

The vines were thicker than he thought. It was like hitting a wall, albeit a collapsible one, and the *Pegasus* careened to such an abrupt halt that he would have been flung from the cockpit if he hadn't been strapped in. He whipped his head around and saw to his relief that Cassie was still there, clinging by her fingertips to the elevator and draped limply over the tail like a rain-sodden flag.

It was suddenly so quiet that Linc could hear his hammering heart. He pried his numb hands loose from the stick and scrambled from the cockpit. He leaped to the ground, yanking off his helmet and goggles, and ran back to Cassie, grasping her around the waist.

"You can let go now," he said.

She let go, rolling off the tail and into his arms. He set her down, holding her tightly against him.

Then he clasped her by the shoulders and pushed her away from him, shaking her roughly. "What the hell were you doing!"

"I thought—"

He shook her again. "I know what you thought, you little idiot. You were right, and it was the gutsiest thing I've ever seen anybody do in my life, and don't you ever, *ever* do anything like that again!"

"I don't think I will," she said, and gave him a shaky smile.

"Ah, Christ, Cassie . . ."

He brought his mouth down hard on her lips, crushing them against her teeth. She responded hungrily, digging her fingers into his arms, pressing, rubbing her stomach against his sudden, surging hardness. Oh God, but he wanted her, wanted her with such an agony of desire he knew he was going to have to take her right here, right now.

He broke the kiss long enough to tear her helmet and goggles off her head. Then his mouth came back down over hers and he yanked open her coat, his fingers pulling down desperately at the straps of her overalls, dragging them down around her knees along with her underwear. He pushed his fingers inside of her. She was hot and wet and ready for him.

Cupping the soft underside of her bottom, he lifted her, leaning her back against the wing struts and bracing her slight weight easily. She opened his whipcords and, cradling him with both hands, pulled him free, panting against his mouth, saying, "Hurry, hurry, hurry," and he thrust into her, hard and sure. She cried out, arching, throwing her head back. He pressed his lips against the taut column of her throat and pushed deeper inside of her, letting the power of the coming explosion build and build—a hot, consuming fireball that tore through his muscles and blood, seared the air from his lungs, and shattered him into a thousand pieces, hurling them into the universe.

She collapsed against him as the last shudders washed over them both. After a moment, he cradled her face between his palms and raised her head to meet his eyes.

"I love you," he said.

Patches chose that moment to poke his head out of the cockpit and let out a high-pitched, indignant bark.

Cassie laughed shakily. "Poor Patches, he hates bumpy landings."

Linc eased her down, but when he went to help her pull her clothes back together, he saw that his hands were trembling. He gave her a rueful smile. "I don't know whether I'm reacting to the collision I almost had with a mountain or the one I just had with you."

She blushed, dropping her eyes. She took his hand and pressed her lips against his curled fingers. "I love you too."

The *Peg*'s nose, they discovered, was firmly entangled in the blackberry patch.

"I suppose you couldn't help it," she crowed, enjoying this sweet revenge. She plucked a few of the berries off the vine, although none was close to being ripe. "Things were a bit hectic there, and we all make mistakes."

He turned around to glare at her, his hands on his hips. "I'll have you know—"

She popped a couple of the berries into his mouth.

He spat them out, grimacing at their sourness. "I wish you wouldn't do that, Cassie."

"You looked hungry. What are we doing here, by the way? Did you suddenly get a hankering for blackberries, or did we have an emergency?"

"Fuel line broke, I think."

She gave him a meaningful look.

"Oh no, Cassie. I checked it, you checked it, we both checked it at least a dozen times since we left Baton Rouge. It was an accident, pure and simple."

"Maybe."

Linc swore and turned back to the *Pegasus*.

Cassie looked around her at the clearing. There were wildflowers—jack-in-the-pulpit and devil's paintbrush and buttercups—splashes of bright color in the lush grass. In the gorge cinnamon ferns blanketed the ground, and scattered among them like discarded wads of paper were fat, white mushrooms. A soft, fitful breeze brushed against her face. She heard the tap of a woodpecker and the hum of bees flitting back and forth among the flowers. It was peaceful here, yet at the same time there was an untamable quality about this land.

She looked back at Linc. He had taken off his jacket and rolled up his shirtsleeves to repair the fuel line. The sun caught the gold lights in his brown hair and bronzed the tanned skin on his forearms. Patches lay in the shade cast by the *Peg*'s wings, resting his nose on his paws and wearing his cheerful grin.

They had probably lost the race, and she didn't care. She thought it would be nice to stay here a while. They could build a cabin right there, nestle it against the rise of the mountain. They could go down to—where was the nearest large town from here? Knoxville, probably. They could go down to Knoxville and buy a swing to put on the porch. And a cradle too, just in case, because Linc had been in such a big, hot hurry he'd forgotten to put on one of his precautions again, and if they kept forgetting they were going to be needing a cradle pretty soon.

She could still feel the wet tenderness between her thighs. His rough, impetuous passion had surprised her. There were so many different facets to this man. Open or brooding, tender or tempestuous, giving or unyielding—she never knew which side he would show her next. Life as Mrs. Linc Cameron, she thought with a secret smile, would certainly never be boring.

But when she looked back across the clearing and saw the buttercups, she thought of her mother, and an immense sadness overwhelmed her. Surely the young and beautiful Sara Jones had approached Lawrence Kingly on their wedding day filled with the same happiness and dreams of a wonderful future together. Yet it must not have been long at all before the dreams had turned to nightmares, and Sara had sought solace in the arms of another man, dooming herself and, in a sad, twisted way, dooming Lawrence Kingly as well. It was dangerous to dream, Cassie thought, for you could get seduced into believing that your dreams might come true. No, she would end their love, hers and Linc's, while it was still shiny and new, before it had time to molder and decay the way her mother's had. She would leave before he could hurt and disappoint her; that way she would be leaving with her dreams intact.

Which made the few hours they had left together so precious. She would have to savor every moment of them, store up the memories for the future without him.

She went up to Linc, wrapping her arms around his waist and pressing her face into his back. She breathed deeply of the musky, masculine smell of him, rubbing her palms across the hard taut muscles of his chest and stomach.

"This thing's shot all to hell," he said, and she

smiled when she heard the slight catch in his voice as her hands roamed lower. "What we need . . . is a whole new . . . uh, line."

She started to pull his shirttail out of his pants. He grasped her wrist. "Cassie . . ."

"I think you're still hungry," she said.

He turned around, and his arm encircled her waist, pulling her closer against him. He pushed his fingers through her hair, gathering a handful. "I'm always hungry," he said. "For you." And she sighed, closing her eyes as he lifted her up on her toes to meet his descending mouth. . . .

There was a loud click, and Cassie's eyes flew open. She saw the dull gray of metal and the twin gaping maws of a shotgun barrel.

"You move so much as an inch," said a voice that sounded like the growl of a bear, "and I'll blast your brains all over this here mountain."

Chapter 16

"**We** aren't revenuers," Linc said, slowly and distinctly. Cassie felt his breath caress her cheek, for they had done as the gruff voice ordered and hadn't moved an inch.

"That a fact?" the voice drawled.

The grass rustled as it folded beneath the man's boots. He whistled softly under his breath, then Cassie heard a low moaning sound. It was the sound Patches made when someone scratched his belly. Patches was a sucker for anyone who would scratch his belly; that dog had no pride.

"You two come apart now, nice and easy," the man said. "But keep your hands where I can see them."

Linc released her and took a single step back. The man had walked around to where they both could see him, although the shotgun remained pointed at their heads. He was the biggest man Cassie had ever seen, tall and broad, with huge muscles. He had a tangled black beard that came to the middle of his chest, but his huge head was a bald dome. Thick brows, like two black dashes, hung low over his pebble gray eyes. The eyes moved slowly over them, assessing and judging.

"If you ain't revenuers, what are you then?" he said to Linc.

"We were flying—"

"You two were flyin' all right," he said with a sudden growl of laughter, and his eyes shifted over to Cassie, giving her a look that made her blush. He grinned at her, showing two rows of square, white teeth. "Been watchin' you all for some time now. Since you landed, in fact."

Cassie's blush deepened several shades, and the man rumbled another laugh.

"—across the country," Linc went on as if he hadn't been interrupted. "In a race. And our fuel line broke. If you have some spare tubing I'd appreciate the opportunity to buy it from you."

The man opened his eyes wide. "Now, what makes you think I got any tubin' a way out here?"

Linc flashed his easy, charming smile. "Just hoping, I guess."

The man showed his teeth again. "I got to bring you all back to the cabin anyway so's Nora can get a look at you. Otherwise she'd chew my ear off. She took a ride in an airplane once when we lived down in Knoxville, and she got so excited she didn't shut up about it for nigh on two months." The man's voice had turned friendly, however the shotgun hadn't budged.

"We're in a bit of a hurry," Cassie said.

"That a fact?" The man's smile broadened. "But I was under the impression you got to see where you're going to fly one of these things."

"You do," Linc said.

"Well, give it another hour or so, and it's going to be so foggy around here you won't be able to see the ground to spit on."

Cassie glanced up. The sun was shining as brightly as ever; there wasn't even a cloud wisp in the azure sky. She looked at Linc. He cocked one brow at her and raised his shoulder in a slight shrug.

"If you were to have some tubing, would it be back at your cabin?" he asked the man.

"If I did, it would be."

"We wouldn't want you to get on the bad side of your Nora," Linc said. "I'm Linc Cameron, and this is my wife, Cassie. That traitorous mutt is Patches. I'd shake your hand if it didn't have a shotgun growing out the end of it."

The man laughed and broke the gun open. "Wasn't loaded," he said. He held out his hand. "Name's Daniel Boone."

Cassie burst out laughing, then blushed. "I'm sorry. Is that your real . . . I mean, are you a . . ."

"You askin' me if the real Dan'l Boone was my great-great-and-so-on-grandpappy?" He shrugged. "Don't know. Truth to tell, I think my ma just had a funny sense of the ridiculous."

The man led them on a mile's walk up the mountain through some of the wildest country Cassie had ever seen. She began to see what it must have been like all those years ago when the original Daniel Boone had slashed his way through this wilderness, fighting Indians and wrestling with bears.

They broke into a good-sized clearing where a large cabin stood backed up against a stand of red pines. The cabin looked as if it had been added onto at various times over the years. Two sections were made of rough-hewn logs, but two newer rooms had been constructed of processed lumber. A large, screened-in porch wrapped around the front, and in the yard was an old stone well.

The door to the porch banged open, and a young woman came out. She was about Cassie's age. Her hair was the color of cornsilk and she had plaited it into one thick braid that hung down over her shoulder. Tall and very slender, she wore a simple cotton dress the shade of bluebells. She was barefoot, and her large hands and feet gave her an awkward look.

Patches bounded up to meet her. He paused a moment to sniff her legs, while she bent over to give him a pet, then he signaled his approval by dashing around in circles and barking excitedly. Daniel Boone's Nora was obviously not one of those la-di-da misses, Cassie thought with a smile.

Daniel slipped his arm around the girl's waist as she walked up to them. Now that she was closer, Cassie could see that she had eyes the color of pine needles and very fair skin, with a light dusting of freckles across her nose and cheekbones.

"Honey, I was right about thinkin' I heard an airplane," Daniel said. "This is Linc and uh . . . Cassie? . . . Cassie Cameron. My wife, Nora."

The woman gave them each a shy smile, then looked questioningly at her husband. "They're racin' across the country," he said. "Don't know what for."

"Fifty thousand dollars," Cassie said.

Daniel whistled and rubbed his bald head. "That a fact?" He turned to his wife. "Fifty thousand dollars the girl says." Nora pursed her lips together. Cassie wondered how she managed to chew her man's ear off when she hadn't yet opened her mouth.

Nora poked Daniel in the chest and raised her brows.

"Oh, yeah," he said. "Would you all like somethin' to eat or drink?"

"I'd like some water if you wouldn't mind," Cassie said. "And Patches, our dog, could probably use some too."

As Cassie spoke, Daniel's eyes flickered over to her, and Nora whipped her head around to give Cassie a quizzical look.

"She can't hear you," Daniel said. "She was born stone deaf and dumb. But if you wait until she's lookin' directly at you, she can read your lips," he added, a note of pride in his voice.

"I'd like some water, please," Cassie said, feeling self-conscious that Nora was carefully watching her mouth as she spoke.

Nora's face broke into a smile, and she nodded. She took Cassie by the hand and led her over to the well. Handing Cassie a dipper, she drew a bucket of water. The water tasted delicious, and it was so cold it gave Cassie a pinched feeling in her chest.

Nora touched Linc on the arm. She made a flying motion with her hand and then pointed toward the ground.

"She wants to know how come you all landed a way out here," Daniel said.

"Our fuel line broke," Linc explained. "I tried to patch it together, but it's just too far gone. We need some new tubing."

Nora scowled at her husband.

"You know, I've been thinking," Daniel drawled, "that I just might have some tubing I forgot about stuck in the shed out back."

Nora beamed at Cassie and Linc, then gave her husband a slight shove.

"All right, all right. I'm gettin' it," he said. He started to walk off, then turned around. He handed Linc the shotgun. "Here, hold this for me."

Nora made a small, impatient movement, lifting the gun out of Linc's hands. She put her palm down in a staying motion before taking the gun inside the cabin. She was back out a few moments later with a piece of paper and a pencil. She gave the paper to Cassie.

Linc read it over her shoulder. *Tell me all about the race*, Nora had written in a fine copperplate script.

"It's a transcontinental race, from California to New York," Cassie said. "Six legs, this one is the fourth, and the plane that gets to New York with the lowest cumulative time wins fifty thousand dollars. We're third right now, or were. The whole thing's being put on by the man who makes Bean's cola. Have you ever had any of that stuff? It's the most god-awful tasting—"

Linc groaned and rolled his eyes. "Jesus, Cassie."

"Well, it is," Cassie said. "It tastes like tar or something." Nora nodded vigorously in agreement.

Nora made the flapping motion with her hand and pointed at Cassie, cocking her head in a question.

"Of course, I do," Cassie said. "It's my plane. Linc is just along for the ride, and he's been nothing but trouble to me since the day we started."

Linc sputtered at this just as Daniel came around the cabin carrying a coil of flexible copper tubing in his hand. "Will this do?" he asked.

They all went back to the *Pegasus* to install the tubing, Nora dancing ahead like an excited child. She clapped her hands with delight when she saw the *Pegasus*, then laughed silently and pointed to the *Peg*'s nose buried in the blackberry patch.

"I don't need to tell you who's responsible for that," Cassie said.

"She always give you so much trouble?" Daniel asked Linc with a grin, cocking a thumb at Cassie.

Linc sighed. "She doesn't quit."

"You gotta do like I did and find yourself one who can't talk back," Daniel said.

Nora caught this and gave him a glare that was so much like the one on Cassie's face that Linc burst out laughing.

As Linc set about repairing the fuel line, Cassie noticed that the temperature in the clearing had dropped considerably in the last hour. She looked up and saw wisps of fog, like ghostly fingers, creeping over the mountain.

"Why, it *is* getting foggy!" she exclaimed.

Daniel, who was tapping tobacco into his corncob pipe, nodded sagely. "Told you it would. It'll blow away again sometime around dawn, when the wind comes back up."

"There'll be clear skies above though," Linc said. "If we could fly up through it without hitting something first."

"It's already reaching higher than the crest of Red

'ine Mountain here, and she's close to four thousand eet. And it'll be covering the whole ridge, all the way up and down the Cumberland range. You could climb above it eventually, I expect, but you'd be doing it blind."

"It'll be dark in another hour or so anyway," Linc said resignedly.

Cassie pounded on the *Peg*'s wing. "Damn, damn, damn. This means we've lost the race for sure."

Nora cocked her head.

"Between the breakdown and this fog, we'll wind up with a slow time on this leg and we'll never make it up," Cassie explained.

Nora looked sad, then made an eating motion with her hand.

"She wants to feed you supper," Daniel said. "Nora's always wanting to feed people. I used to be five feet tall and weigh one hundred pounds soaking wet before I hooked up with Nora."

Nora reached up and rubbed Daniel's bald head, and he heaved a huge sigh. "I know, I know. I also used to have more hair on me than a bear in winter."

By the time Linc finished with the *Pegasus*, the fog was so thick that Cassie was glad they had Daniel Boone himself to lead them back up the mountain to the cabin.

It was dark when they first stepped inside, and Cassie saw only faint black shadows until Daniel struck a match and held it to the wick of a kerosene lamp that was fastened onto a bracket by the door. Then light flared into the room, and Cassie gasped in surprise, for it was stacked floor to ceiling with shelves of books.

"Nora's the book lover in this family," Daniel said. "I had my letters beaten into me as a boy, and it put me off the activity for life."

Linc and Cassie went over to the shelves to read some of the titles. "My heavens, Linc, look. Some of these books are in Latin and French!" She turned to

Nora. "But how did you ever manage to learn to read and write English, let alone Latin, when you've never heard words spoken aloud?"

Nora smiled shyly and shrugged.

"It's a mystery to me how she did it," Daniel said, the pride back in his voice. "She taught herself. Just like she taught herself to read lips. She's got eight brothers and sisters, and none of them can even write their own names."

Nora beckoned with her hand, and they followed her into the kitchen. She ushered them into cane-bottomed chairs grouped around a table, then tossed a couple of logs into the belly of a big iron stove.

Patches was exploring every cranny of the kitchen with his nose. Nora pointed to him and then to her mouth, cocking her head.

"He'll eat any kind of scraps you have," Linc said.

"Except peas," Cassie put in. "He always eats around the peas."

Daniel left the room and returned with a clay jug tucked under his arm. "I just happened to stumble across this here moonshine when I was out in the shed looking for that tubin'," he said with a grin and a wink. But Cassie noticed that Nora regarded her husband with angry eyes.

Daniel went to a shelf and took down three glasses, carrying them wedged between his thick fingers over to the table. But when he went to put one down in front of Cassie, Linc covered the top of it with his hand. "She doesn't want any."

"Honestly, Linc, just because one time I happened to have a bit too much champagne, you think I can't hold my liquor," Cassie protested.

"You won't like it. Go ahead, try it." Linc handed her his glass after Daniel had filled it.

Cassie took a sip and gasped. Her eyes started to water, and she actually put her hands up to her ears because she thought flames might be shooting out.

"I told you you wouldn't like it," Linc said, laughing. He took a hefty swallow of the whiskey and sighed with pleasure. "You know, Daniel, if a fellow were to stumble on a lot of jugs like this one here in a couple of months when the whole country goes dry, he could make himself a good bit of money."

Nora shook her head vigorously back and forth and scowled at Linc.

Linc looked at Daniel. "What did I say?"

The big man refilled Linc's glass. "Nora don't hold with drinkin' it, and she especially don't hold with makin' and sellin' it. Her daddy was a mean drunk. Used to beat on the younguns and his woman when he'd get a bellyful, which was just about every three days. Put Nora off whiskey for life."

"I don't blame you," Cassie said to Nora.

Daniel grunted. "Doesn't mean I'm going to turn into a lusher like her daddy was just because I got me a still and I take a nip now and then. You can't tell her that though. When we lived down in Knoxville she joined that group of tambourine beaters, that Women's Temperance Union. Went and took an ax to the bar of one of my best customers."

Linc smothered a groan. "Not another one! Seems like all of a sudden the whole damned country is full of angry females on the rampage over something or other."

"Don't pay any attention to him," Cassie said at Nora's quizzical look. "He's always spouting nonsense."

Daniel cocked a brow at Linc. "What's your woman on the rampage about?"

"The vote," Linc said with a sigh. "And places of business that don't want women customers, and race committees who don't favor women pilots, and farmers in Nebraska who take the Bible a little too literally. I could go on, but it would take all night."

"You look like you could use another drink," Danie said.

Cassie decided that the best thing to do with Lin when he got in one of these moods was to ignore him "So you all haven't always lived here on this beautifu mountain then?" she asked Nora.

"I was born and raised right here in this cabin, Daniel answered for her. "But Nora prefers the city life so we tried it for a while down in Knoxville. I got me job sellin' shoes. Had to put on a fancy coat and tie every day. Like to drive me crazy, I kept feeling like was smotherin'. So after a while Nora realized that was pure miserable, and she suggested we come back here." He chuckled. "Let me tell you, I was up here in time to see the next sunrise." He looked at Nora and gave her a tender smile. "I tell her if she gets to want ing it real bad, I'll go back down and give it another try."

Nora smiled at him, shaking her head. She leaned over and kissed him on his shiny head. Then she stood up and, touching Cassie on the shoulder, beckoned her to follow.

She took Cassie into the smaller of the cabin's two bedrooms, and again Cassie gasped in surprise. Quilts covered all four walls, and another, still being made, was spread out on a big table. The quilts weren't just made of haphazard scraps of material sewn together, they were works of art—scenes of the wild and beautiful Cumberland countryside.

Daniel and Linc came as far as the door. They both leaned lazily against the jamb, holding their glasses of whiskey. Judging from the sparkle in Linc's eyes, Cassie thought he had imbibed a bit too much of the powerful homemade brew, but she didn't mind it if he got drunk. This way she would have fresh ammunition to fire back at him whenever he brought up the subject of their wedding night.

"All Nora's books and geegaws," Daniel said, waving the glass of whiskey and spilling some of it down his shirt, "come from money she made from these here quilts. She won't spend a penny on herself of the money I make off my moonshine."

Nora nodded emphatically in agreement.

Cassie was beginning to think that although Daniel was Nora's voice and ears, she was not as dependent on him as she first appeared. Hers was a quiet, interior strength that made her man look strong. But Cassie had the feeling that although Nora obviously loved her husband, she could survive without him, whereas the big brawny Daniel would fade into nothingness without her. Still...Nora and Daniel made a pair that somehow became greater than the sum of its parts.

She remembered what Maisie had said to her that morning in Nebraska: *A man and a woman, they come to settle into a way of living together, and what works for one couple doesn't necessarily work with another.* With a flash of insight she understood Maisie, how Maisie's love for Seth and her children was strong enough to sustain her through poverty and hardship and living with a difficult man. And Tessa. Tessa and Anselm were both born to lead, and neither one was able to follow. And when they tugged in different directions? Cassie smiled at the memories. How the sparks would fly between those two! Yet they adored one another; it was obvious even when they weren't speaking to each other.

Now here was Nora Boone—with her abhorrence of alcohol, her books, and her quilts—married to a rough-spoken moonshiner. Yet together they had found an enviable happiness and harmony on their beautiful mountain. Nora, Maisie, Tessa—how had these women managed to escape the fate of Sara Jones Kingly?

Cassie stared at Nora, confused, wanting to ask her, but she was unsure of how to frame the question, and in that instant of hesitation the flash of insight died.

She opened her mouth instead to ask Nora how long

it took to make one of her quilts when there was loud blast of a shotgun, and bullets twanged through the screened-in porch.

"Git down!" Daniel shouted, rolling to the floor with a heavy thud.

Linc threw himself at Cassie, tackling her around the legs and flinging her down. "Ow!" Cassie cried as she banged her head on one of the table legs. She pushed at Linc's dead weight. "I could have gotten down by myself, you brute. You didn't need to *hurl* me to the floor like a sack of—"

There was another shotgun blast and the sound of shattering glass. Patches gave one frightened howl and dove for a pile of material scraps and bolts of ticking that lay in a corner, burrowing under it until only his tail was visible.

Daniel had crawled out into the front room, going for his gun, which sat beside the fireplace. Linc, crouching along the floor, started to go after him, but he paused long enough to turn around and point a finger at Cassie.

"What have you done now?" he demanded.

Cassie glared at him. She wouldn't even dignify the question with an answer. Just because they were being shot at again was no reason for him to jump to the conclusion that *she* was the cause of it.

"You stay here," Linc ordered. "We're in enough trouble right now without you adding to it."

Daniel had retrieved the shotgun, and he sidled up next to the window while he loaded it. Linc blew out the lamp, and a gray darkness descended on the room.

"Danny! Danny Boone!" a voice cried out from among the pines that surrounded the cabin. "You in there, Danny? We've come to make you real sorry for breakin' the law, Danny boy. Just like we promised."

"Shit," Daniel said, snapping the breech shut.

Linc flung himself against the wall on the other side of the window. "Revenuers?"

"Yeah. I been payin' them a boodle to leave me alone, but they got greedy so I skipped this month. Looks like it was a mistake."

"Where's your still?" Linc asked. "Out back in the shed?"

"No, it's hid real good. These guys could never find it. Hell, they couldn't find their way to the bottom of a flour sack with a map and a compass. It ain't the still I'm worried about, it's your airplane. They stumble across it, and like as not they'll jump to the wrong conclusion and start hackin' it into kindling."

"How much would it take to make them go away?"

"It's too late for that. They're aimin' to teach me a lesson."

"Shit," Linc said.

"Yeah. Let's just wait here a bit until we can think of something. Are you good at thinking of things?"

"Not especially."

Linc began to worry that it was too quiet in the bedroom. He inched back along the wall and poked his head around the corner. He saw a lot of quilts and Patches's tail sticking out the pile of scraps, but not a single strand of blond hair.

He let out the foulest oath he could think of, then added another one in French for good measure.

"What's the matter?" Daniel asked, peering over his shoulder.

"Cassie has disappeared."

Daniel looked around the room. "She's with Nora. They'll be all right."

"You don't know Cassie."

"Is she good at thinkin' of things?" Daniel asked hopefully, but Linc could only grind out another oath.

The revenuers were shouting at Daniel again, telling him to come out with his hands in the air. Daniel and Linc crawled back to the window. It was starting to grow dark, and the fog was lifting a bit. Whereas before the pines had been mere ghostly shadows in the white mist, they were now distinguishable as trees.

"I tell you what," Daniel said after a while. "I'll go out and stall them while you hightail it out back, circle around to the plane, and get her out of here."

Linc shook his head. "It's going to be a tricky enough takeoff as it is without trying to do it in the fog and the dark. And besides, I can't leave Cassie."

"You could come back for her later."

"I'd never make that landing again. I barely made it the first time."

Daniel shrugged. "It was a thought."

It had been a good minute since they had heard from the revenuers. Linc poked his head above the window-sill, hoping they might have given up and gone home. Just then a stark naked woman streaked through the fog across the back end of the clearing. Hard on her heels was a man wearing a pair of rolled up overalls, a bulky jacket, and a floppy, big-brimmed felt hat. Linc had no idea who the man was, but even through the fog he recognized every inch of the woman. He let out an exclamation of surprise that was drowned out by the woman's piercing, terrified scream.

Linc bounded up, heading for the door, but Daniel held him back.

"That other one is Nora," Daniel said, showing all his teeth in a big grin. "That's my hat. I'd recognize it anywhere. She'll lead them so far up the mountain, it'll take 'em a week to find their way back down."

The revenuers had indeed taken the bait. Bellowing cries of outrage or lust, they took off to the rescue or to join in the ravishment, Linc wasn't sure which.

Daniel's bear laugh was rumbling over the cabin. Linc started to laugh as well. He sat back down, leaning against the wall, laughing until his stomach muscles hurt. Now that the danger was over, Patches came creeping out of the back room, snarling and growling ferociously and setting Linc off on another bout of laughter.

Daniel had gone back into the kitchen to retrieve the jug. He pushed it into Linc's hands. "It'll be a while before they get back," he said, still chuckling. "We might as well pass the time pleasantly while we wait."

They finished that jug, sitting against the wall by the window. Daniel went out back for another, and they took it and the lantern and went out on the porch. They passed the jug back and forth between them—having long ago dispensed with the glasses—while Linc talked about flying and Daniel talked about "first shots" and "tails" and how to make fine sippin' whiskey. Linc was beginning to feel numb and the world's edges had blurred when the screen door opened and Nora entered with Cassie hovering behind her like a shadow. Linc was relieved to see that his errant wife was once again modestly clothed.

"Nora, honey!" Daniel bellowed. He belched, then blushed, covering his mouth with his hand. Linc took his feet off the porch rail and straightened up, assuming his sternest face.

Cassie's voice was soft and tentative. "Linc...?"

"Come here," he said.

Cassie sidled around Nora and came slowly toward him, her eyes cast meekly downward. Linc took a swig from the jug to keep from laughing. "I thought you promised me you would stay out of trouble until we got to New York."

Cassie flung her head up, and her eyes flashed. "I wasn't the one in trouble, Daniel was. And I never made any such promise."

"Whooee!" Daniel suddenly exclaimed, slapping his thigh. "I coulda pondered all year and never thought up that idea. Which one of you two female geniuses came up with it?"

Nora smiled broadly and pointed at Cassie.

"Well, actually we came up with it together," Cassie said. "We tossed a nickel to see who would get to be the damsel in distress."

"*Get* to be!" Linc exclaimed.

Cassie grinned at him. "Yes. And I won."

"Cassie, girl," Daniel whooped again, "if you don't got the nicest, roundest, prettiest pair of—ugh!"

A blond braid whipped across Linc's vision, followed by the front door slamming. Daniel lumbered slowly to his feet, rubbing his large belly.

"Now, Nora honey," he pleaded once he had her attention, "you can't blame a man for lookin'. . . ." There was another grunt, then a moan, and then a soft sigh of surrender.

"What are you looking so smug about?" Cassie demanded.

Linc gave her his wide-eyed innocent look. "Who me?"

She widened her eyes back at him. "Yes, you."

He laughed, then shrugged. "I guess it's just nice to know another man admires your woman's, er . . . your woman."

"Your woman, huh?"

Linc set the jug down and shifted slowly to his feet. "Yes . . . well, uh . . ."

She wrapped her hands around his neck, pulling his head down. Her lids descended to hide the smoky shadows in her eyes, and her lips parted into that soft, vulnerable look that never failed to excite him.

"Your woman," she said with a sigh, and then pressed her mouth hungrily to his.

Chapter 17

The morning sun was just peeking out from behind Red Pine Mountain when they entered the clearing. Dew sparkled on the grass and flowers, looking like millions of tiny ice chips. Even the olive fabric of the *Pegasus*'s wings shimmered brightly.

"Oh, look, Linc!" Cassie exclaimed. "What a gorgeous morning!"

Linc pressed his fingers against his throbbing forehead and sighed. "It's very lovely, Cassie. But do you have to shriek about it like a stuck pig?"

Daniel, who stood arm in arm with Nora, practically leaning against her, started to laugh, but the laugh quickly ended in a deep groan.

Cassie cooed at them both with false sweetness, "Poor babies. Aren't you feeling well?" And Nora's eyes danced with silent laughter.

"I'm glad it's you, Linc, who's got to go flying this morning," Daniel said, pulling his favorite felt hat down low to shade his eyes from the piercing, blazing sun. "All that rocking and bumping up and down, that shaking and noisy vibration, my stomach couldn't take—"

"Excuse me," Linc said suddenly, and strode off rapidly toward the pines. At the distressing sounds that

283

were now coming from the trees, Daniel's face turned the color of pea soup. He made a harsh, strangling noise, jerking away from Nora and stumbling into the forest after Linc. Patches saw them go and started to follow, but Cassie whistled him back.

She exchanged looks with Nora. "It serves them right," she said, and Nora nodded in solemn agreement.

Linc and Daniel had continued to share the jug all through supper the night before. Afterward, a third one was fetched, and the two men stumbled out onto the porch to do, in Daniel's words, some "serious sippin'." Cassie stayed behind in the kitchen with Nora. A few minutes later she heard Linc's loud, exuberant voice explaining to Daniel the proper way to go about training a lion. She started to laugh at this and looked over at Nora, who was bent over a piece of paper writing, and she realized that of course Nora could not hear what the men were saying.

Nora handed Cassie the piece of paper. *How did you and Linc meet?* she had written.

Cassie told her about diving on Linc with the *Pegasus* to scare him away from her territory. "I almost flew right into him, only don't ever let on that I've admitted that, because after we landed I was going to apologize to him all nice and humbly. But he had the nerve to sock me right in the jaw."

Nora looked horrified, and Cassie laughed. "He thought I was a man, you see. Because of the way I was dressed. And when I opened my eyes, I found I was looking up into the face of the most incredibly gorgeous man I'd ever seen in my life. Then he opened his mouth, and I found out how downright infuriating he could be, and it's been all downhill ever since."

Nora broke into a fit of silent laughter.

"So what about you?" Cassie asked. "How did you manage to meet Daniel Boone?"

Nora scribbled rapidly on a piece of paper, still silently laughing. She pushed the paper over to Cassie.

I found out Daniel was one of the men selling whiskey to my father, and I smashed up his still. Twice. The third time he lay in wait for me, and you can guess what happened when he caught me!

Nora suddenly seized Cassie's hand and pulled Cassie out of her chair, beckoning at her to follow. She took Cassie into the main bedroom and showed her a cradle beside a big bed made out of rough-hewn logs.

Cassie turned to her in excitement. "Oh, Nora, are you going to have a baby?"

Nora nodded enthusiastically and held up seven fingers.

"In seven months? How wonderful!" Cassie gave her an impulsive hug, suddenly feeling a surprising stab of desire to have a baby of her own, Linc's baby, growing inside of her.

They talked then about babies until Cassie began to feel tired from the day's flying. Nora made up a bed on the floor in the front room, and Cassie drifted off to sleep to the sound of Linc's and Daniel's off-key voices singing a naughty rendition of "The Mademoiselle from Armentiers."

She smiled to herself now at the memory as she watched Linc and Daniel emerge pale and shaken from the forest. "If you're planning on getting sick again after we're aloft," she said to Linc as he walked gingerly up to her, "be sure to stick your head out into the slipstream."

Linc glared at her with bloodshot eyes. "There is going to come a time, Cassie Jones, when you'll need all my sympathy and mercy, and then you are going to rue this day."

Because of the men's condition, it took more time than it should have to get the *Pegasus* untangled from the blackberry patch and rolled out into position for takeoff. Cassie was unhappy about the direction the wind was blowing. They would not be able to go up into it, but would instead have to make a crosswind takeoff. She also worried about the shortness of the field, for she was not as proficient as Linc when it came to tricky takeoffs and landings. Yet it was obvious that she was going to have do the flying today. When she mentioned to him that he might want to at least get the *Peg* up, he had merely patted her on the shoulder and said, "You can do it, Cassie." His reliance and faith in her filled her with pride, but also a confused anger. What if she were to fail him?

They started the engine, letting it warm up. Then she was hugging Nora good-bye, promising to write, and kissing Daniel on his bald head. She climbed into the cockpit after Patches, nervously adjusting her goggles and helmet. She glanced back at Linc and saw that he had already settled down in his seat, with his arms folded across his chest and his eyes shut. Really, he was the most abominable man. She was about to attempt the trickiest takeoff of her life, and he had gone to sleep!

Squeezing her eyes briefly shut to whisper a prayer, she sent the *Pegasus* down the clearing, opening the throttle and holding the nose down, letting the plane build up speed until, at what seemed to her the last possible second, she literally lifted off by applying a slight backward pressure on the stick. She held the plane steady, gaining altitude until they were well clear of the trees, and then when she had achieved sufficient speed, she banked on a slow turn, the shadow of her wings brushing across the mountain in front of her. She laughed out loud. She had done it, and with room to spare.

She passed over the clearing, tilting the *Peg*'s wings in a last good-bye to Nora and Daniel, then turned north, following the Cumberland ridge toward Kentucky. With luck, she thought, they would be landing in Dayton that afternoon.

* * *

Cassie leaned out into the slipstream, wiping at the dust that smeared her goggles to look at the landing field below. Carved out of acres of flat, fertile farmland, the field had been cleared and packed and marked well with painted rocks, even a pair of wind socks. Alongside it were two huge hangar tents and a grandstand decorated with flags that billowed and snapped in the wind. The seats appeared filled to capacity, and hundreds more people swarmed over the field, looking from this distance like confused ants who had just had their hill knocked over.

The people, automobiles, tents, and grandstand all made a colorful tableau, but Cassie couldn't find the one thing she was looking for, and it made her cry out with joy. There was not another airplane in sight.

"We must be the first ones!" Cassie shouted to Linc. "We're first!" And he grinned, giving her a thumbs up sign.

Linc had the controls now, and he took the *Pegasus* down carefully, for thermal updrafts billowing up from the hot ground were causing a fierce, invisible turbulence that made the landing dangerous. In Cassie's mind, however, the truly frightening part came after the *Peg* had rolled to a stop, for the crowd surged around the plane, pulling them from the cockpit before their feet could even touch the ground and passing them overhead from hand to hand.

Then she heard Pete Striker's loud laugh, and she struggled against the hands that clutched her, tumbling down into his arms.

"Hot damn, Cassie!" he exclaimed as she kissed his rough cheeks.

"Oh Pete, are we first?"

They clung to each other as the crowd jostled against them. "Where's Linc?" Pete asked. "He's got to log in."

Cassie turned her head around and got a brief glimpse of Linc surrounded by reporters and talking to an official-looking man with a sheaf of papers and a big gold watch in his hand. "He's doing it now," she said. "Are we really first? What happened to the Schmidt brothers?"

"Them Boche pilots cracked up somewhere outside of Lexington. A cylinder blew out, tearing the engine apart. They sheared off their right wing against a telephone pole coming down and crashed nose first in a backyard chicken coop." He laughed. "Hell, there ain't enough left of that Avro of theirs to make a box kite."

"But what about Hans and Werner, are they all right?" Cassie's chest felt tight; she did not want to hear about any more deaths.

"Hans's arm got peppered with splinters, I heard, but yeah, they walked away from it, so I guess they're all right."

"So we've at least moved up to second," Cassie said, able to smile now with satisfaction, for the rules allowed only one plane per team. The Schmidt brothers were out of it.

Pete looked at his wristwatch. "And if Farrell and that other fellow don't get here within the next thirty-eight minutes, we're in the lead. And it's about goddamn time."

Laughing, Cassie whirled around. She spotted Linc pushing his way through the crowd toward her, and she ran to meet him, throwing her arms around his neck. Then above all the noise her ears picked out the drone of an approaching engine. She waited tensely as the plane came into view. It was Edward Farrell's Curtiss Jenny.

"Oh, no," she sighed, pressing her forehead against Linc's chest as sick disappointment washed over her.

Linc hugged her tightly. "I'm sorry, honey. But it isn't over. There won't be much time separating us, especially once they land and log in. We'll pass them by on the way to New York."

Cassie nodded, fighting off a ridiculous desire to burst into tears as she watched the Jenny land.

She noticed that the pilot was allowing his plane to drift sideways a bit in the crosswind, and she was about to point this out to Linc when the plane hit one of those violent updrafts. It landed hard, skidding along the packed field. Then the undercarriage collapsed and the plane began to cartwheel, shredding fabric and splintering spars and struts.

There were shouts and screams, and the crowd started to spill out onto the runway. "Stay back!" Linc yelled as he pushed through them. "Stay back. The tank could explode!"

Linc, Cassie, Pete, and the race official broke through the crowd. A pair of men carrying a stretcher and another with a black bag came running out of one of the hangar tents. With a relief so sharp it almost made her cry out, Cassie watched Edward Farrell crawl on his hands and knees out of the wreckage. The man with the black bag ran up to him, paused to look him over a moment, then pulled him to his feet and led him away.

Cassie stood back from the plane, feeling useless and shivering with dread, while Linc and the men with the stretcher lifted Gregory Pearce's body from the tangled mess of wood and steel wires. She saw that his face was covered with blood and looked away quickly. Then she heard someone say, "He's alive," and she let out a shaky breath.

Suddenly there was a terrible shrieking noise, and Cassie looked up to see Melodie Farrell stumbling across the field in her tight skirt. But to Cassie's astonishment, Melodie ran right by the doctor and her brother to fling herself weeping hysterically onto Gregory Pearce's unconscious chest.

They carried Gregory off the field on the stretcher with Melodie following behind. She was, to Cassie's intense disgust, still wailing and getting in the way.

"Will he be all right?" she asked as Linc came up to her.

"As near as we can tell he only has a bad gash on his forehead. They were lucky."

She and Linc looked together at the wrecked plane. Edward Farrell's Jenny would not be leaving Dayton in the morning. "I don't think I want to win it this way," Cassie said.

Linc brushed his lips against the top of her head. "We knew in the beginning that this race would be one of endurance and survival. Take the advice of someone who has learned it the hard way—don't feel guilty because you've survived."

He slipped his arm around her waist and led her toward the hangar tents. A man came out to meet them halfway. Cassie recognized the beaked, eaglelike face of Phineas Barlow, Leroy Irving Bean's personal assistant.

"Mr. and Mrs. Cameron?" Barlow said, his rubbery lips stretching into a smile of welcome. "Mr. Bean is waiting to greet you up at the big house."

The "big house" was indeed big. It was brick, with white columns, three wings, and four stories, and topped with a gray slate roof. Cassie counted fourteen chimneys.

Phineas Barlow led them up sweeping gray stone steps, while the double front doors swung silently open before him as if he had whispered a magic word. They went across a black-and-white tile floor and up more stairs, this time made of heavy dark walnut, into a room filled with massive pieces of furniture, velvet drapes, and thick rugs.

"Welcome to Dayton," a dry voice said, and Cassie stiffened with shock as she looked into the face of Lawrence Kingly.

She realized an instant later that she had been mistaken, although Leroy Bean's physical resemblance to her mother's husband was remarkable. They had the same thin hair slicked across a bony skull, the same piercing, hard black eyes. But then Leroy Bean smiled

d the resemblance ended, although Cassie still had to
rce herself to step forward and take the man's hand.

"So, you are winning my race," Leroy Bean said to
nc. "I rather thought you would. Tell me, what are
u going to do with the fifty thousand dollars?"

Linc flashed the man his dazzling smile. "Well, I
n't think I had better spend any of it until I get to
ew York."

Leroy Bean laughed. "Very wise. And you," he said,
rning to Cassie. "Will you think it amiss of me if I
dmit that I had my doubts about allowing you to em-
rk on this adventure? And now that I see you, I
onder . . . you are very small. Yet you must be good,
ry good indeed."

Cassie could think of nothing to say. She knew she
ust appear rude and sullen, but she couldn't help it.
o matter how charming and generous Leroy Bean
as, she couldn't like him; he too closely resembled the
an she hated above all others.

"She is good," Linc finally said as the silence became
vkward.

"Mr. Bean has invited all the pilots to stay here at the
g house tonight," Phineas Barlow put in smoothly.
Please allow me to show you and Mrs. Cameron to
ur room."

He led them up more walnut stairs and into another
om filled with dark, ornate furniture, including a
assive four-poster bed with a blue satin canopy.

"Your flying kits have already been brought up from
e airfield," Barlow said. "Your mechanic is seeing to
ur airplane, and he will also look after your dog. I'm
raid you will not be able to have him with you in the
ouse. Mr. Bean is allergic to animal hair." He paused
 the door. "Refreshments will be served in the
allroom at seven. A servant will be here at five min-
tes before the hour to accompany you there."

"Whew!" Linc exclaimed after the door had closed
ehind Phineas Barlow. "He's even bossier than Tessa

Pernell." When Cassie didn't smile, he put his finger under her chin and tilted her face up to meet his eyes "Is something wrong? You were looking at poor Leroy Bean as if you wanted to stick him on the end of skewer and roast him over a hot fire."

Cassie shivered. "I know it's silly, but he looks like somebody I know—someone hateful."

"Who?"

Cassie longed to tell him, but she couldn't seem to get enough air into her tight lungs to push the words out. So when she said nothing, he let her go and turned away. Picking up his flying kit, he went into the bathroom. After a moment Cassie heard the water running in the sink.

An hour later she was bent over, peering into a mirror to wrap the sequined bandeau around her head when she heard a knock on the door. She thought it was Linc, who had gone down to the airfield to check on the *Pegasus*. She opened the door with a bright smile, hoping to melt some of the chill that had once again, thanks to her, arisen between them.

"Why, Cassie, you've got on that pretty peach frock again!" Melodie Farrell tripped through the door, wearing a shimmering, tasseled tube dress and trailing an ostrich-feathered stole.

Cassie shut the door behind her. "Hello, Melodie. I'm glad to see you've recovered from the shock."

"What shock?"

"Your brother's near death."

"Oh, that." She dismissed it with an elaborate wave of her stole. "Ward's always falling out of the sky in those dreadful machines. He didn't even get a scratch."

"Gregory Pearce did though."

"But that's what I've come to talk to you about, Cassie. How did you guess? It's still a secret, but I did want to tell you, and Ward, of course. Gregory is going to be just fine. Isn't that wonderful?"

"Yes, it is," Cassie said truthfully. "But why is it a secret?"

"What? Oh, silly, that isn't the secret!" She clasped her hands to her breast and whirled around. "The wedding will be next month!"

"Who's getting married?"

Melodie stopped dancing. "My word, Cassie, I think all that flying must be addlin' your poor brain. Gregory and I are getting married."

Cassie stared at her in astonishment. "You and *Gregory!*"

Melodie giggled, blushed, and bobbed her head.

Cassie sat down carefully on the edge of the bed. "How . . . wonderful."

"Isn't it?" Melodie flounced down beside her, seizing her hands. "Oh Cassie, I fell in love with him the moment I first laid eyes on him."

"You did?"

"Yes." She sighed. "Unfortunately he barely noticed that I existed. First I tried to make him jealous by flirting with the Schmidt brothers, but that didn't work."

"It didn't?"

"No, darn him. So finally in Kansas City I swallowed my pride and asked him to marry me."

"You didn't!"

"Only he couldn't give me his answer right away, since it was all such a sudden surprise. He told me he had to think about it. He has his family to consider, and there's a girl back home in Richmond that he was nearly promised to. He told me he would give me his answer when I met him here in Dayton. Oh Cassie, you'll never believe it—I could hardly believe it—but his answer was yes!"

Cassie was trying to match this hard-to-get Gregory Pearce with the love-smitten young man who had fallen into a tub of Bean's cola. She couldn't do it.

"We're going to live in Richmond," Melodie was saying. "His father owns an emporium there, and he's going to take over the business. He thinks it might be a difficult adjustment for me at first, fittin' in with his family and the Richmond society and all, but he believes I'll measure up in time. Oh Cassie, we are perfect for each other, and I'm going to try to be the most perfect wife, even though Gregory has warned me he can be a bit exacting at times."

Cassie found her voice. "I don't believe it!"

Melodie squeezed her eyes shut and hugged herself. "I know, I can't believe it either. Isn't it wonderful?" She opened her eyes and looked earnestly at Cassie. "I have to admit for a time I was so jealous of your bein' married and all, and not because I wanted Linc Cameron for myself, because I could never have been happy married to a man like him. He makes me so nervous, he's always so impulsive. You never know what he's going to say or do next, and I don't like that. It was your happiness I envied, the wonderful happiness you two have together."

"Linc and I seem happy to you?"

Melodie let out a peal of laughter. "My heavens, it sticks out like a rose in a weed patch. You're always laughing and smiling when you're together. And if one of you's alone in a room it's like you're only half there, a shadow, but as soon as the other one comes in, you light up inside. You can see your love. It positively glows in your eyes."

"Linc's eyes too?"

Melodie slapped her lightly on the thigh. "Of course, Linc's eyes too, you ninny. Especially his eyes." She gave Cassie a brisk hug and stood up. "I have to go see to Gregory. He's lyin' down 'cause he has such a dreadful headache from that awful bump on the head, which was all Ward's fault and I told him so."

Stunned, Cassie remained sitting on the bed as Melodie floated out of the room. She was still there ten minutes later when Linc returned. He paused in the doorway, and the sight of him gave her such a funny feeling in the pit of her stomach that she got up and went to look in the mirror to see if her eyes were glowing.

He came up to stand behind her, tracing his finger down the bare skin along her spine. "I thought we jettisoned all our California clothes in that mudhole you landed us in in Louisiana."

She met his eyes in the mirror and smiled. "This dress must have been accidently left on board."

He pressed his lips against the exposed nape of her neck. "I'm glad it was, because you look beautiful in it. It is also one of those dresses that comes right out and begs a man to take it off."

She leaned back against him, delighting in the feel of his caresses, then reluctantly slipped out of his embrace. "I've only just put it on, Linc. And besides, we haven't time. You aren't dressed yet, and it's almost seven o'clock. Unless you're wearing your flying clothes"—she made her voice sound pompous and punctilious like Phineas Barlow's—"to attend the gathering in the ballroom."

Linc turned away from her, unbuttoning and shrugging out of his shirt. "You don't have to worry that I'll embarrass you by looking like a flying bum, because Pete brought my morning coat along on the train with him. He said he figured I would need to be somewhat formally dressed when I accepted that fifty-thousand-dollar check."

She watched him covertly while he dressed, thinking about what Melodie had said. She sighed, trying to hide a smile. "I have some bad news for you, Linc."

He turned to face her, a look of pure horror on his face. "What have you done now?"

"Oh! Why are you always . . . I haven't done a thing! It's what you're going to do that I'm worried about."

"Christ. What's happened?"

"Melodie Farrell is lost to you forever. She's marrying Gregory Pearce."

"Damn it all, my hopes are dashed . . . or is it dash it all, my hopes are damned?"

Cassie laughed.

"My life is in ashes," he exclaimed. "But I wish her only happiness," he added, putting his hand over his heart.

"Stop acting silly." She started to giggle. "Oh Linc, you'll never believe it. *She* proposed to *him!*"

His hand fell to his side, and he stared at her, fascinated. "Is that a new fad, like bobbed hair and smoking cigarettes and drinking cocktails?"

Cassie trailed her hand along the bedstead, avoiding his eyes. "What would you say if a woman proposed to you?"

Linc draped his tie around his neck and went to the mirror. "A hypothetical woman? I would say I'm already married until I get to New York."

She turned around slowly. She could not see his face, only the broad expanse of his back. "And after New York?"

"Not a good time either. I'm going to be embroiled in a very messy, scandalous divorce. I will be committing adultery—"

She let out a shriek of outrage and descended on him with clenched fists, but he whipped around, grasping her wrists.

"How dare you!" she cried. "How dare you threaten to sleep with another woman!"

"One of us has to do the dirty deed. For the divorce. I thought I'd be gentlemanly about it."

"You're doing this deliberately. You're trying to make me jealous so I'll change my mind about this ridiculous marriage."

"No, I'm not," he answered mildly. "That's why I've brought up the subject of our divorce. It has to be confronted and dealt with eventually. In order to end this ridiculous marriage."

She studied his face, but it was impossible to tell

what he was thinking. Was he trying to provoke her into admitting that she wanted the marriage to continue? Or warning her that he still intended to end it once the race was over?

Someone rapped on the door.

"Who will you do it with?" she asked stiffly.

"There's someone at the door . . . do what?"

"You *know* what!"

"Oh, that . . . I don't know yet." He gave her his sudden, dazzling smile. "Perhaps a Ziegfeld chorus girl. I seem to attract that type."

She whirled around and marched toward the door. "Damn you, Linc Cameron, you are so infuriating!" she shouted, flinging open the door to confront a man-servant wearing a dinner jacket and a stone face.

"Mrs. Cameron?" the man said. "Mr. Bean awaits you and your husband in the ballroom."

Chapter 18

∽ ⟋⟍ ∽

Cassie turned around slowly, smiling with delight. She had never seen a ballroom quite like Leroy Bean's. Actually she had never seen a ballroom before, but it was certainly unlike any ballroom she had ever imagined. It was more like a museum, although the artifacts on display were airplanes and automobiles, the earliest inventions to the latest models. They were lined up in rows down the enormous room, as big as a hangar, that ran the entire length of one wing of the house.

She saw what looked to be a very early model of the Wright brothers' pusher biplane, and she started to go examine it more closely when a familiar voice spoke in her ear.

"You look quite lovely in that dress, Cassie. It almost makes me regret I didn't try harder to win you."

She spun around, laughing. "Oh, Ward, I'm so glad! Glad you're all right, I mean. I'm sorry about your plane."

He studied her carefully. "You know, I believe you are sorry. Even if it does mean that all you've got to do is get to New York in one piece and you've won the race. I suppose you've heard about the latest disaster?"

"Is the Jenny completely beyond repair?"

"Yes, but that wasn't the disaster I meant." He gave her a twisted smile. "There have been so many disasters in my life lately, it's hard to keep them straight. But the one I'm talking about is Melodie's disastrous engagement."

"But I thought Gregory Pearce was your friend?"

"Damn it, he is my friend, but that doesn't mean I want my sister to marry him." He ran a finger along the edge of his stiff butterfly collar. Cassie noted with amusement that all these disasters hadn't prevented Edward Farrell from turning up impeccably and most appropriately attired.

"The truth is," he said, "I was rather counting on Melodie to marry someone with bags of money. Greg's family does all right, but his old man has his fist wrapped tight around the purse strings, and he's not about to pry them loose for a brother-in-law with a plantation that swallows dollar bills faster than the mint can print them." He sighed. "I suppose I'll just have to hang on by my fingernails until my nasty, rich Uncle Lawrence descends into the hereafter."

Cassie felt her muscles tense. "Ward ... isn't it strange ... I mean, don't you think Leroy Bean looks like him?"

"Like who? Uncle Lawrence?" He shrugged. "I suppose they do have the same cadaverous appearance now that you mention it. But the resemblance is strictly physical. Can you imagine Lawrence Kingly giving away fifty thousand dollars? Excuse me, Cassie, but here comes Linc bearing glasses of champagne, and I don't think I can face his gloating right now."

"Linc doesn't gloat," said Cassie, indignant, but Edward had already walked off.

Linc put a glass of champagne in her hand.

"Are you sure you can trust me with this?" she teased.

"One glass is all you get." He leaned intimately into her and lowered his voice. "I thought we would make a polite appearance, and then I'm going to drag you up-stairs and ravish you on that big four-poster."

She glanced up and caught him giving her a look so hot she thought her flesh would melt. So hot she couldn't stand its bright intensity, and so her eyes shifted down to his mouth, his firm warm lips, and she felt an irresistible yearning to taste those lips, to press her mouth against his and feel their texture. Sighing, she swayed into him, her lips parting open—then she jerked herself upright.

She waved a shaking hand over her shoulder. "Have you seen that, Linc?" she asked in a squeaky voice. "Mr. Bean has an old Wright pusher plane."

His fingers clasped her arm, sending chills coursing down her spine as he led her over to look at the plane. But he was soon studying it with such intense interest that Cassie felt abandoned, and she laughed at herself for her foolishness.

"The Wright brothers flew a plane like this fourteen years ago right here in Dayton," Linc said. "It was in an old cow pasture called Huffman Prairie not too far from where we landed today. They stayed up for what was then an astonishing thirty-eight minutes, and no one believed it because no one was here to see it. This looks like the original."

"I was here, and it is the original," a dry voice said, and Cassie steeled herself to turn around and look at the familiar, skull-like face of Leroy Bean.

Leroy Bean smiled, and his resemblance to Lawrence Kingly vanished immediately. Cassie had to admit Ward was right. Although the two men might share a similar appearance at first glance, Mr. Bean certainly didn't have Lawrence Kingly's air of evil malevolence.

"You have a remarkable collection here, Mr. Bean," she said, forcing an answering smile.

"Thank you. I must confess," he said to Linc, "I was hoping you would wear your uniform tonight. With your medals."

Linc shifted uncomfortably. "I'm afraid I didn't bring it with me."

"I certainly understand. You have to be conscious of the weight you carry in your machine." He turned slightly as Phineas Barlow came up to them. "Did I tell you, Phinny, that Linc—you don't mind if I call you Linc?—did I mention that Linc scored a hat trick in medals? He earned all three: the Legion of Honor, the Victoria Cross, and the Distinguished Service Cross."

Barlow looked impressed and paid a suitable compliment, and to Cassie's amusement Linc flushed red with embarrassment.

"I have something to show you, Linc," Leroy Bean said, smiling expansively again. "The latest addition to my collection. At the moment it's out on the back lawn, since I haven't yet had it dismantled again to put inside."

Cassie took Linc's arm as they followed the old man past his aeronautical display, out a pair of double doors, and into a terraced garden. She leaned her head against Linc's shoulder and whispered softly, "I didn't know I had such a hero for a copilot."

He frowned at her. "I'm not, Cassie. Don't make a big deal out of it." Then the frown abruptly vanished from his face as they stopped before a single-seater biplane. "Good Lord. It's a Spad, just like the one I used to fly in the Lafayette. It even has the Indian-head insignia."

"It is the one you flew," Bean said, emitting a hoarse chuckle. "The last one. I had it shipped over from France."

Linc laughed. "This must be the only one I managed not to crack up."

Cassie gazed with avid interest at this important piece of Linc's past. It was small and looked very agile; she could easily imagine it swooping down on enemy fighter planes, diving on unsuspecting bombers and observation balloons. She walked around to examine it from the other side, climbing the small stepladder that had been placed nearby so one could view the interior of the cockpit. There was a pair of machine guns mounted in front, and she ran her palm along one of the slick black metal barrels.

"It fires eight hundred rounds a minute, and it can kill someone very dead."

She jumped, whirling around so fast she almost fell off the ladder. "Ward! I wish you would stop sneaking up on me like that."

"Did I frighten you? I'm sorry. Normally you aren't such a nervous Nellie." He held up his hand to help her down. "Has Linc been regaling you with stories about how he won the war?"

"He doesn't like to talk about it, you know that. What's the matter with you, Ward? You're acting as if you're jealous of him."

He looked down at her hand resting in his. He rubbed his thumb across her fingers, then released them. Looking up, he fixed her with brooding, whiskey-colored eyes.

"Is that so surprising, Cassie? He married the woman I love. And now he's going to win the race I had to win. Monte, Linc, and I, we were all three as close as brothers once. But when Monte died I think a part of the friendship died with him. Perhaps it's not jealousy I'm feeling, Cassie, but grief. Maybe I'm simply mourning the death of a friendship."

"But Linc is still your friend."

"I know." He looked at her with eyes as bleak and barren as a desert. "And therein lies the tragedy, if you want to be melodramatic about it."

She clutched his arm. "Ward, why don't you just sell that damned plantation?"

He gave her a twisted smile. "There would be so much grave spinning in the Kingly cemetery, folks would think we were having an earthquake.... You know I can't, Cassie."

"Don't be silly, Ward. They're dead, they'd never know—"

"I would know."

She sucked on her lower lip, thinking how best to phrase her thoughts. "Would you let me help you, Ward? If Linc and I win the race, I could give you a loan from out of my share. With interest, of course," she added hastily for the sake of his pride.

She half expected him to get angry, but instead he gave her a poignant smile. He brushed his fingertips across her cheek. "You could have helped me once, Cassie. But it's too late."

"I don't understand—"

He lifted his shoulders in his elegant shrug. "There's nothing to understand. I'm admitting defeat. I've lost you, and now I'm telling you a polite, gentlemanly good-bye."

"No, wait," she said as he started to turn away. "We're still friends, aren't we? I want us to still be friends."

He paused, lifting his hand as if in a blessing and flashing her a smile, then he turned around once more and walked across the lawn back to the house. Cassie watched him go with a worried frown in her eyes.

"My dear?" A dry, age-spotted hand fell on her arm. Cassie cried out, whirling around and dropping her empty champagne glass. Shuddering, she stared down at the ground, watching it roll along the grass.

"I beg your pardon," Leroy Bean said. "I didn't mean to startle you."

Cassie looked up into his black eyes, glittering from the skeletal hollows of their deep sockets, and she cringed.

Linc stepped forward, taking her arm. "Cassie, what's the matter?"

She squeezed her eyes shut and sucked in a deep breath. "I'm sorry...I don't...sorry..." She pulled away from him to run, blinded by tears, across the lawn.

He found her two hours later, sitting in the dark in their room. She was on the window seat, her knees drawn up under her chin, staring out at the moonlit fields.

"Go away, Linc," she said.

He came up to stand in front of her. He wanted to take her in his arms, but he dared not. "No, I won't go away. I love you, and I want to know what's wrong."

She said nothing.

He sat down beside her on the window seat. "Leroy Bean frightens you. Why?"

She shook her head. "He's a nice, sweet old man."

"But the person he reminds you of must not be. Who does he remind you of?"

"Mr. Bean only looks like him, but it's enough to—" She stopped and turned her head to look at him. Her haunted eyes, glowing silver in the half-light, pierced his heart. "He reminds me of Lawrence Kingly, the most hateful man ever born of woman," she said. "If he was born of woman, that is, and not spawned by the devil."

"Why is he so hateful? What did he do?"

"He was my mother's husband."

"Your mother's husband, but not your father?"

"No." She laughed harshly. "Not that my father was anything to brag about." She pulled her legs tightly against her chest and rested her chin on her knees. "When I was a child I used to pretend my father, my real father, was a deposed prince from one of those tiny European countries who had gone back to claim his throne. I'd imagine that one day he would return for me and take me away from Kingly to live with him on his castle high on a hill. But all that was pure make-believe. I knew it even then, and not because there had never been a prince, deposed or otherwise, within a undred miles of Kingly. I knew it was all make-believe ecause I knew who my father really was, everyone knew. He was a schoolteacher, and he was married with three children. Just like my mother was married. They had an affair. I was conceived in sin, and the sin was committed right there in Kingly. Which is all just a nice polite way of saying that I'm a bastard."

Bastard. That was what Lawrence Kingly had called her whenever he bothered to acknowledge her existence at all. *Your bastard,* he would snarl at her mother. *Your bastard should learn to be seen and not heard. . . . Keep your bastard out of my sight. . . . I don't want to be tripping over your bastard every time I turn around. . . . Your bastard . . .*

Lawrence Kingly had never let his wife forget her sin. Perhaps if she had been a different sort of person, she would have stood up to him or left him. But she'd had a simple spirit. She liked country dances and summer picnics and sing-alongs around the piano. Instead, her life was one of jealous rages, bitter words, hard fists, and cold isolation. Cassie had watched while the hell of that marriage had crushed her mother's will inch by inch. The doctor had said it was pneumonia that killed her, but Cassie knew differently—Sara Jones Kingly had died of a broken spirit.

"I asked her once why she ever married Lawrence Kingly in the first place, and she said she had loved him. Loved him!" Cassie stood up abruptly, pacing the floor. "He was older than she was, and rich. And she must have been lonely, living in that little house—you saw it, Linc—living there with Quigly, who was a wonderful person but so preoccupied and absent-minded. Mother needed people around her to talk and laugh with. She said when Lawrence Kingly came into her life, she thought he was magic, the fairy-tale prince. So they were married, and she was happy at first, but then he changed."

It began with little things at first. He would become

angry with her if he couldn't find her where he expected her to be. She had never had many girlfriends, but the few she did have he soon found fault with, so that one by one they were all driven away. He could not bear to see her talking with another man, no matter how innocently. Once he had come across her in the rose garden speaking to the gardener, and he had flown into a rage, firing the man on the spot. He was even jealous of her cat, an old tabby that she had grown up with. One day the cat disappeared, and she knew Lawrence had had it destroyed. She would feel eyes watching her, hear footsteps following her around the house, and know that it was Lawrence stalking her, waiting to pounce on her and accuse her of betraying him, of no longer loving him. . . .

One day she escaped to visit her brother; Quigly was the only person left of either sex that Lawrence could still tolerate her seeing. There was a man there, sitting on the front stoop. He told her Quigly was in the barn fixing a bicycle that he had brought by. They started chatting, about nothing really important, but somehow they got onto the subject of the Civil War. He mentioned he was a teacher at the high school, and the Civil War had always held special interest for him because his father had been a young private in Lee's army. He had smiled and said, "There are a lot of well-preserved battle sites right around Kingly. I could give you a tour." And she had known then that she was standing on the edge of a cliff, that all she had to do was take one step, one tiny step, and she would be doomed.

She looked up into his smiling gray eyes . . . and she took that step.

"It was the scandal of the century. The great and mighty Lawrence Kingly's pretty young wife had taken a lover barely a year after their marriage," Cassie said. She was leaning against the window casement, looking out at the dark. Linc stood beside her, not touching her because she did not want that yet. To hear his steady breathing, to turn her head every now and then and see the chiseled profile of his face in the moonlight was enough.

"When the scandal broke," she went on, "the schoolteacher slunk out of town in the middle of the night, so it all might have been forgotten after a while, forgotten at least by everybody but Lawrence Kingly. Except that nine months later my dark-haired, brown-eyed mother gave birth to a baby girl with the blond hair and gray eyes of her lover. Every time he looked at me, Lawrence Kingly saw my mother's failure, her sin. And he tormented her with it. He tormented her into her grave."

He covered her hands with his own. She raised her eyes and looked into his. "So you see, my darling Linc, that's why I don't believe in marriage. I've seen what it does to love—it destroys it. And the people who love, it destroys them as well."

He brushed a stray curl that had escaped from her bandeau back off her forehead. Then his fingers moved down the side of her face, tracing the line of her jaw. "You saw one marriage that went bad," he said softly. "One failure. You're not predestined to relive your mother's life. You aren't Sara Jones, and I'm not Lawrence Kingly, and our love isn't doomed. Of course, there will be times when we hurt and disappoint each other." He gave her a lopsided smile. "Times when you'll cause all sorts of trouble, and I'll dearly want to wring your neck. But I can't envision a time when I won't love you, Cassie."

She looked at him out of dull and hopeless eyes. "I can envision it easily. Because we're wrong for each other. You've said so often enough."

"Maybe we are. But I know I would be miserable without you, so I'm willing to try to make it work. Cassie—"

She pressed her fingers against his lips. "And if we

fail? I can't bear to take that risk, Linc. Not in this."

He was still for a moment, then he let his fingers trail down and away from her face. "Then there's no hope for us."

"But I love you!" she cried, despair in her voice.

"Then stay with me, damn it! Live with me. Be my wife."

She pressed trembling hands to her mouth, tears glistening on her face. She shook her head back and forth. "I can't."

He stared at her in silence a moment. Then he turned and started for the door.

"Linc wait!" She took a step to follow him, then stopped. She clenched her hands together into a fist in front of her. "Where . . . where are you going?"

He stood beside the door, his hand on the knob. "I promised you your freedom when this is over, and you'll have it. But I'm not going to torment myself now with wanting something I can't have."

Then the door shut behind him, and she was alone.

Pete Striker was sitting on an oil can next to the *Pegasus*, rubbing Patches's belly with the toe of his boot, when Cassie entered the hangar.

Pete stood up when he saw her, and Patches trotted over for a pet. "You and Linc have a fight last night?" Pete asked.

Cassie tossed her flying kit into the locker, ignoring them both.

"I only ask," Pete said, "because I was wondering why a man would choose to spend the night on the floor of a hangar when he could sleep in a soft bed instead."

"Linc doesn't tell me his reasons for doing things," Cassie said testily.

"He doesn't, huh? Look, Cassie, honey, every marriage has its rough spots—"

She turned on him. "Let's just get one thing straight.

Linc and I only got married because the race committee was making a ridiculous stink about it being immoral for us to fly together. The whole thing is a farce, and it ends the minute we collect the prize in New York. There's no law that says we have to get along together in the meantime."

Patches's ears perked up, and he let out a happy bark. Cassie turned around. Linc stood by the *Peg*'s tail, his hands shoved deep into the pockets of his leather jacket. His face wore its shuttered look.

"Is what she just said true?" Pete asked.

"Yes."

"Then you two don't love each other?"

Linc said nothing.

Pete struck a match with a greasy fingernail, lighting a cigarette. "What a pair of fools," he said to the air, and walked stiff-legged out the hangar door.

Cassie felt Linc's eyes on her, but she refused to look at him. "How much of a lead do we have?" she asked coolly.

"Enough. Over seventy-five minutes. If the *Pegasus* holds together another two days, we'll win it. I thought I'd do the piloting the first part of this leg. That way you'll be the one flying her when we finish the race."

"No, I want you to be the one to land the *Pegasus* in New York."

"But—"

"It's what I want, Linc."

"Fine. If it's what you want."

She ran her hands over the bracing cables on the wings, pretending to test their tautness. She tried the words out in her mind before she said them. "I've decided I'm definitely going to make Quigly's engine with my share . . . will you be manufacturing airplanes with yours?"

When he said nothing, she looked up at him. It was impossible to tell by his face what he was thinking, yet there was something in his eyes, and it wasn't sadness this time. She couldn't be sure, but she thought it was plain old-fashioned worry.

Seeing that she was staring at him, he shrugged. "I haven't made any definite plans yet."

"Oh." She wiped her hands on the seat of her overalls. "Well, I probably shouldn't be doing that anyway, making plans to spend the money before we've won it." She started for the hangar door. "We better get the *Peg* rolled out onto the field and the engine warming up or we—"

He reached out a hand to stop her as she walked by him. "Cassie."

"What?"

Linc looked as if he had something important to say, but instead he let her go. "Never mind. As you said, we've got to win the race first. If we lose it a lot of things aren't going to matter anyway."

Linc thought later, as he crossed the airfield heading back toward the hangar, that he should have gone ahead and told Cassie about the Black Hand's claim on the prize money. Not that he had any intention of letting Bartinelli get away with one penny of Cassie's share. Still, he should have told her about it, and long before now. He laughed grimly to himself. The joke was that he hadn't wanted to ruin things between them by telling her about it earlier, and now that things *were* ruined between them, he couldn't tell her because they were barely speaking to each other. . . .

"Linc! Mr. Cameron!"

Linc turned around as an automobile pulled up beside him. It was Phineas Barlow, and he had a worried look on his face. "Mr. Bean wants to see you. Up at the big house."

Linc looked at his watch. "Now? But the race—"

"Won't start without Mr. Bean." Barlow opened the passenger door. "Please . . ."

Phineas Barlow didn't drive up to the front of the house, but instead went around back to where the Spad had been displayed yesterday. It was no longer there.

Leroy Bean was at the spot where it had been, however, along with a pair of Dayton policemen. They all turned and approached Linc as he climbed out of the car.

"Linc, the most distressing thing has occurred," Leroy Bean said. "Your Spad has disappeared."

The older of the two cops was studying Linc carefully. "You wouldn't happen to know anything about it, would you, sir?" he asked.

Linc returned the man's hard look with one of his own. "I'm two days away from winning fifty thousand dollars. What would I want with the Spad, and what the hell would I do with it if I had taken it?"

"Of course he didn't take it, you fool!" Leroy Bean snapped. "We were only wondering, Linc, if you saw or heard anything unusual last night."

Linc was loath to admit that he hadn't spent the night in the house with his new bride, but in the hangar sleeping on the hard, cold floor instead. He shook his head. "No, nothing. Sorry."

Then it occurred to him just who might have taken the Spad, and he frowned at the thought. But he also thought he could understand the motivation behind the impulsive action, so he said nothing. There were some loyalties that went deeper than right or wrong.

Leroy Bean sighed loudly. "What a pity. Perhaps whoever's taken it only did so for a lark, or as a joke. In any event, there's nothing we can do about it right now. The race is the important thing."

He gestured toward the automobile where Phineas Barlow waited patiently behind the wheel. "Phinny will drive you back to the airfield, Linc. I'll be following behind in the carriage." He held out his hand. "I suppose it would be unfair of me to wish you extra luck above the other contestants," he said, then smiled and winked. "But you well know where my sentiments lie."

Sunlight glinted off the doped fabric, and the wind whistled through the flying wires of the planes as they waited on the runway. Cassie ran her hand along the edge of the *Pegasus's* wing, feeling the vibrating drum of the engine on the taut fabric.

Pete Striker's face peered at her from between the struts. He had to shout a bit to be heard above the noise of the engine. "I'm sorry I butted my nose into your business."

Cassie smiled to show him it was all right.

"The race won't start for another fifteen minutes yet," he said. "There's coffee and doughnuts back in the hangar. Why don't you go get a bite?"

Cassie glanced back at the hangar.

"Linc ain't there," Pete added perceptively. "He's up at the big house."

She set off for the hangar then, wondering idly what had sent Linc up to the big house. Phineas Barlow and Leroy Bean had both been down here at the field earlier to see the start of the race, but then they had left in a big hurry, and now Linc had chased after them. She only hoped he got back in time.

Gregory Pearce, with Melodie in tow, came up to Cassie as she emerged from the hangar swallowing the last of her doughnut. Gregory had a huge piece of sticking plaster on his forehead, and Melodie clung possessively to his arm.

"Hi, Melodie," Cassie said, wiping the sugar off her mouth with her sleeve.

"I wanted to wish you all luck," Melodie said. "Now that Gregory isn't competing in the race anymore I'm hopin' that you all will be the winners." Then her brow furrowed with worry and she glanced apprehensively at her fiancé. "That is all right with you, isn't it, darling?"

Gregory smiled indulgently. "Of course it is."

"Are you sure, darling? I don't want you to think..."

"It's quite all right. Really."

Cassie's fingers itched to box Melodie's ears. Was the silly woman going to spend her entire married life deferring to her "darling" Gregory?

"Where's Ward?" Cassie asked. She had hoped Ward would be here this morning, if not to wish them luck then at least to see them off.

Melodie's face clouded with confusion, then brightened. "Oh, I remember now. He left last night. He said he was going to arrange a welcoming party. Isn't that nice?"

"A welcoming party? For us?"

Melodie chewed her lip and looked at Gregory. "Well, I suppose so."

He patted her hand. "I think he was making a joke, Melodie."

"Oh... but he wasn't laughing."

"It wasn't that kind of joke."

A voice through a megaphone announced that the race was to start in five minutes.

"I've got to go," Cassie said. Impulsively, she stepped up and kissed Melodie on the cheek. "I'm so happy for you and Gregory."

Melodie hugged her hard. "Oh thank you, Cassie. Oh dear, I was so excited last night I forgot to tell you the most important thing. I consider you my very best friend in the whole wide world—"

"You do?" Cassie asked, truly surprised.

"Of course, silly." Melodie's mouth turned down. "Why, Cassie, aren't I your best friend?"

"Well, uh... sure," Cassie said, realizing now that

she thought of it that Melodie was probably her *only* girlfriend.

"Of course I am," Melodie said. "Which is why you've just got to be my maid of honor."

"Darling," Gregory put in. "My sister's going to be your maid of honor, remember?"

Melodie's face fell. Then she stuck out a rebellious lip. "It's my wedding, Greg. I think I should be able to decide who to have for my maid of honor."

"But, Melodie. Sweetheart—"

"I'm not arguin' with you about it, Gregory. My mind is made up."

Cassie cleared her throat. "Uh, excuse me. The race is about to start." She waved her hand in the direction of the airfield. "I've got to go."

Melodie gave her another bruising hug. "Good luck. And be careful." She tossed a stubborn look at her fiancé. "I'll let you know more about the wedding later, Cassie. I've got a lot of planning to do first. Dresses and flowers and all."

Cassie hurried off, smiling to herself. Gregory Pearce was about to discover that he wasn't the only one who could be a bit exacting at times.

Linc was standing beside the *Pegasus* waiting for her, and her feet slowed as she saw him. She felt a terrible ache in her chest and wondered if it was possible to die of love.

And I do love you, Linc, she wanted to cry out to him. *But I'm still so afraid.*

Since she couldn't say that, she asked him instead why he had gone back up to the big house.

"I'll tell you later," he said, helping her into the cockpit. "It isn't anything that affects us or the race."

She paused and looked down at him. "Linc, when we get there, when we land in New York, you won't just walk away while my back is turned? You'll at least tell me good-bye, won't you?"

His face tightened, and his voice turned hard. "You

might not want anything to do with marriage, but I do.
I want a wife and children, and I won't be able to have
that until I disentangle myself from you. So you'll be
seeing me, if only to sign the divorce papers."

Two days later Linc Cameron looked down through
scattered, smoke-tinged clouds at the densely packed
hotels, mansions, and tenements of Manhattan. He
picked out the green expanse of Central Park, the
bridges cutting across the metallic blue Hudson, and
the distinctive, wedge-shaped Flatiron Building poking
through a particularly low-lying cloud like a spike
through a tuft of cotton.

Before long they would land at Curtiss Field on Long
Island. A flunky from Bean's cola would hand him a
check for fifty thousand dollars, and he would feel rich
for all of thirty seconds. Then half would go to Cassie,
part would go to Pete, and the rest would go to Bartinelli's boys, and he would go back to being poor again.
He laughed to himself. He had flown over four thousand miles, zigzagging across a continent from ocean to
ocean, surviving busted propellers, revenuers, and ber-
serk cigar store owners, and he was going to wind up
with nothing to show for it but calluses on his rump
and the love of a girl who refused to stay married to
him.

As New York Harbor passed beneath them, a ray of
sunlight shone down on the copper torch of the Statue
of Liberty, setting it afire. Linc started to point it out to
Cassie at the same time that she turned around to show
it to him. He smiled at her—and saw horror wash over
her face.

And then he heard the sudden, familiar hacking of
machine-gun fire. The *Pegasus* shuddered and shook
like a wet dog, and Linc felt a searing pain in his leg.
Patches, who was in the front cockpit with Cassie,
began to howl.

For a few seconds Linc thought his mind had become completely unhinged, that he had somehow flown into one of his own nightmares. Then more bullets, real bullets, whizzed over his head, and his mind bolted back to reality. He wasn't flying over France in his Spad; he was over Long Island, New York, in the *Pegasus* with Cassie, but . . .

Somebody sure as hell was shooting at them!

Chapter 19

Linc flung his head around to see a Spad coming down fast on their tail, firing as it dove and filling their fuselage with tracer bullets.

Instinctively he threw the *Pegasus* into a tailspin. It was an old fighter-pilot trick, "playing possum" they had called it. The tailspin not only made your machine a difficult target to hit, but it just might persuade the enemy that you were doomed and going down, fooling him into giving up the pursuit.

He stared at the back of Cassie's head, motionless in front of him. With a sick dread that almost made him gag, he wondered if she had been hit. He could feel a wetness on his own thigh, but numbness had taken the place of the pain, and he could still move it. Patches had quit howling.

The enemy—he was thinking of the Spad as the enemy now—hadn't bought the trick of the tailspin. He was sticking with them but keeping the advantage of height, and for the moment he was holding back his fire.

The nose of the *Pegasus* punched into a cloud, and Linc began to pull out of the spin. He reversed direction and pulled the stick back in his lap, climbing sharply. When they popped out of the cloud, he spotted the Spad to the left and below him. The Spad saw him and immediately gave chase. Linc opened the throttle wide, turning the nose down, running now for Curtiss Field the way he had run for the airfield in France when he was outnumbered and outgunned by the enemy. The ironic thought flashed across his mind that this was certainly a race, but the prize was no longer fifty thousand dollars. They were racing for their lives.

A part of his mind also registered the fact that he was losing a lot of blood, too much blood. He could feel the growing nausea and dizziness, but he fought it off, tightening his hands on the controls.

The air crackled around him, and tracer bullets whipped past the *Peg*'s wings. The Spad was closing in again; he could not shake it off. He gave up on the idea of trying to outrun it and decided to outmaneuver it instead. He changed direction, coming up into the sun to force the enemy to fire directly into its blinding brightness and swerving erratically from side to side to deny the guns a steady target. When he sensed that the Spad was getting too close again, he plunged into another steep dive.

They were almost directly over the airfield now. He could see the grandstands and the hangars and a sea of people undulating in waves over the landing field. He swore in exasperation. There was no way he could put the *Pegasus* down in that crowd of people with another airplane hot on his tail spitting death.

The steepness of the dive was beginning to affect the *Peg*. He could feel her straining against the controls, could almost hear her moaning in protest. Glancing to the side, he saw the fabric was starting to peel off her wing edges from the pressure and the stress. He again heard the machine gun's noisy rattle.

He pulled out of the dive, pitching the *Pegasus* up, zooming up so sharply that he was dancing on the edge of a stall. He plunged into a cloud, threw the machine over onto one wing, and kicked the tail to the rear, abruptly reversing his direction. But the cloud wasn't deep enough and the enemy had for once outguessed him. He ran out of the cover too soon, and the Spad was waiting for him, lurking. As he flew out of the cloud, it pounced.

Bullets slammed into the fuselage. He heard Cassie scream, and his mind screamed her name in response. He felt a flash of white-hot pain, then blackness.

Cassie screamed. A sharp pain pierced through her head, and for a second the spinning blue sky turned black. She flung her hands up to her face, thinking she had been shot. In that next instant she knew with a primeval instinct that it was not she who was hurt—it was Linc.

She touched the controls, felt their slackness. *"Linc!"* she screamed against the cold, rushing air.

Terrified that he was dead, she stood halfway up in the cockpit to look back. He was slumped over sideways, his face a mask of blood. His hand, still resting on the stick, was white and lifeless.

An explosion of grief slammed into her. It was so powerful that she almost blacked out. In one sweeping, blinding instant she saw her life without him spread before her like a desert, barren and useless.

"Linc!" she screamed again, as if she could call him back to life. Then she saw holes appear in the *Peg*'s tail and heard the spit of the machine gun as the Spad swooped down on her, pouring streams of fire.

"Oh God," she prayed, scrambling back down into the cockpit. "Oh dear God, please . . ."

The Spad had circled and was coming in for another attack, still toying with her. She felt numb with shock, as if she had died with Linc. But part of her brain still functioned as a separate entity, and that part reasoned: The *Pegasus* was slower and less maneuverable than the Spad, and without guns they couldn't fight back. Even with Linc's expert aerobatics, they should have been shot out of the sky a long time ago. Unless the enemy had wanted to torment them first. So there was a chance, a small chance, he had not yet tired of the game.

She heard Linc's voice so clearly that she jumped, thinking for one heartbreaking moment that he was leaning over her shoulder, speaking into her ear. She even twisted around, expecting to see him breathing and alive, smiling behind her. He was not there, but the voice inside of her head was still his.

If the enemy dives on you, don't try to evade his assault— fly straight at him to meet it. . . . I remembered the rule . . . I flew right at the enemy and rammed him with my undercarriage.

She looked around for the Spad, saw it below her, maneuvering into position so that it could come zooming up under her to pepper her wings with the deadly fire. And she turned the *Pegasus* wide around and headed right toward him.

Nearer and nearer she came, swooping down on him, her nose centered right on his fuselage. He had not expected this, had not expected to be attacked, and he was out of position now, unable to turn his guns on her. He wasn't trying to maneuver out of her way. It was as if he was letting it happen, *wanting* it to happen. Only a few hundred feet separated them now, only a few seconds before impact, and she lifted the *Pegasus's* nose, veering sharply upward.

And she saw, in the instant before she rammed him, who he was.

There was a splintering crash, and the *Pegasus* heaved and shuddered as the two airplanes collided. Her hands tensed on the controls as she waited for the plunge to earth, but to her astonishment the machine flew steadily on. If was as if the *Pegasus* had shaken off the smaller plane like a lion flinging a monkey off its back.

She looked around for the Spad and saw it going
own in a tailspin, its right wing tattered and crumpled
a upon itself. She leaned out to assess her own dam-
ge. There was a gaping hole in the fuselage and the
wheels had been ripped off—she would have to make
belly landing—but she had survived. She had met
he enemy head-on and destroyed him.

She took the *Pegasus* down, chasing the Spad to
arth. She was cold inside, cold and angry, with not a
hred of mercy. She wanted to see the Spad crash; she
wanted to watch the enemy die, horribly and painfully,
he way Linc had died.

But fate, or the pilot's skill, denied her. At the last
ossible minute he was able to straighten the Spad out.
He grazed the tops of the hangars and, with his engine
till running wide open, pancaked on the field,
ounced up a dozen feet, and after a half somersault,
mashed his nose in the ground.

Strong hands embraced her, lifting her from the
ockpit. They took her helmet and goggles off.

"Are you all right?" a voice asked, sounding far
way. She nodded. She felt nothing now; even the
nger was gone. "She's all right," the voice said.

"Hey, there's a dog in here," someone said.

Other hands were taking Linc's body from the plane.
here was blood all over him, so much blood that Cas-
ie thought he must have bled to death before she got
he *Pegasus* on the ground. It horrified her that Linc
might have lived a bit longer after he was shot. She
ould have told him one last time how much she loved
im, she could have, could have . . . she sucked in a
eep breath and pressed her eyes shut. She was going
o start crying for Linc soon, and when she did she was
ot going to be able to stop. Her life would seep away
a tears, the way Linc's had seeped away. It didn't mat-
er; she no longer wanted to live.

They laid him gently on the ground. Patches tried to

lick Linc's face, but he was pushed away. Cassie took a
tentative step, realized her legs were working, and then
went to him, kneeling beside him. She picked up his
limp hand and was surprised at how warm it felt.

"There's a doctor on the way," somebody said. "And
an ambulance."

Hope blazed up within her with such violence that
she gasped and bent over, clutching at her stomach. "Is
he . . . is he still alive?"

"Yes, but he's lost a lot of blood. Here's the doctor."
The same strong hands lifted her back out of the way. A
man knelt beside Linc, taking her place. More men ran
up, bearing a stretcher.

Cassie shivered, looking down the airfield where the
wreckage of the Spad lay. Several men surrounded the
pilot, who was on his feet, cradling a broken arm. Cassie started to go to him.

"Miss . . ." Someone reached out to stop her, but she
brushed the hand away. She had to know why.

He stood, her enemy, facing her unflinchingly as she
came up to him. He was surrounded by policemen,
who had been on the field to control the crowd, although none for the moment touched him. His face
was streaked with cuts and scorch marks; his clothes
were ripped. He still managed to maintain his air of
casual elegance.

"Why?" she asked him, and all the cold rage came
back, the merciless fury. "Why did you want to kill
him? What has he ever done to you? He thought of you
as his friend."

He looked away from her at Linc being lifted onto
the stretcher. His eyes darkened. "Is he dead then? I
never wanted to kill him. It was just his bad luck to
marry you."

"But that—"

Edward Farrell laughed harshly. "Christ! It was *you* I
wanted to kill, Cassie. Not Linc. If Linc had had the
sense to stay away from you, none of this would have

appened. I would have convinced you to marry me, ecause the final bitter irony in all of this is that I do, in ome crazy way I can't begin to understand, love you, assie. If you had married me, I wouldn't have needed kill you. Or if you and Linc hadn't been such good ilots, such *lucky* pilots, even then I might not have eeded to kill you. That was your one chance to live, ou see—if I could have won the fifty thousand dol- rs." He laughed again. "I did every damned thing I uld think of to slow you down, to stop you, yet you ept showing up at every checkpoint, as perennial as eas in summer and just as pesky."

She stared at him, confused and angry. "None of this akes any sense. How can you claim to love me in one reath, then admit trying to kill me in the next?"

His lips twisted. "Normally you aren't so dense. ncle Lawrence is going to die any day now, and as ure as the sun rises in the east, he's going to leave you verything, all of his holdings in Kingly and two mil- on dollars. Two million dollars that belong to me, assie, that I *need*, Cassie. It's an old, old story. If I had arried you, the money would have been mine any- ay, and we would have been happy together, I know . But you fell in love with Linc instead. I told you that as a mistake, for I couldn't let you inherit then. So I ad to kill you." He turned to the policeman at his side. If you're going to arrest me, do it. Or let me go."

"Oh, we're arrestin' you, laddie," the policeman said a thick Irish brogue, and he grabbed Edward by his ood arm.

She stepped in front of them. "No, wait!" She looked t him, tears pressing hard against her lids. "Oh Ward . . what made you think Lawrence Kingly will ever eave his money to me? He's always hated me. He'll oss it all in a river before he sees one penny of it go to e."

"Hate has nothing to do with it." He shrugged, then inced slightly as the movement pulled on his broken

arm. "Or perhaps hate has everything to do with it
Nasty, rich Uncle Lawrence is dying, and he wants to
buy forgiveness."

Cassie stiffened and unconsciously thrust out her
chin. "My forgiveness isn't for sale."

The policeman tugged on Edward's arm, leading him
away. Edward turned back to look at her, and there was
a strange, bitter laughter in his eyes. "You still haven't
figured it out, have you? It's not your forgiveness
Lawrence Kingly wants. It's your mother's."

"But that's crazy!" she called after him.

He gave her his sad, poignant smile. "I guess it must
run in the family."

More policemen surrounded Edward Farrell and led
him away. The cold rage that had sustained Cassie
since the Spad had burst upon them, firing death,
started to fade. She put her hand up to her cheek and
felt the tears. But she was not sure if she was grieving
for Ward or rejoicing that Linc still lived, that there was
still time to tell him how much she loved him. Still
time, even if just a few hours more, for them to be
together.

She hurried then to catch up with the stretcher. "Is
he going to live?" she asked the man walking beside it,
whom she took to be the doctor.

"He's lost a lot of blood," was all the man would say

The ambulance hadn't arrived, so the worried doctor
had Linc put in the backseat of somebody's touring car
The nearest hospital was in Valley Stream, just a few
miles away. Cassie held his head on her lap. They had
removed his helmet and cleaned a lot of the blood
away. There was a large, open gash along his ear running up into his hair. His face was very white, and his
eyelids looked almost transparent. A tourniquet had
been tied above the wound in his thigh.

The car pulled out onto the road with a squeal of
tires. Linc's lids fluttered open, and his eyes focused on
her. His lips parted as she leaned over him.

". . . love you," he breathed, and then slipped back into unconsciousness.

She pressed her lips against his open mouth.

Cassie slowly pushed the door open, grimacing at the loud squeal it made. She expected to hear harsh voices demanding at any minute to know what she was doing, and she glanced nervously back down the hall but saw no one.

Cautiously she poked her head around the door. Linc lay in bed, looking romantically handsome with a white bandage around his head. His pajama shirt was unbuttoned, and the moonlight shone on his glistening chest. There was a small electric fan on the window edge, but it did little to dispel the room's sticky heat.

She opened the door wider and slipped in, shutting it behind her with a soft click. "Linc," she whispered. "Are you awake?"

She saw the gleam of his teeth as he smiled. "What are you doing here at this time of night?" he said in a normal voice.

"Shhh, you noisy idiot," she hissed at him. "Be quiet or they'll toss me out." She stood at the end of his bed. "I wanted to be alone with you. There were too many doctors and nurses hovering around you this afternoon."

It was the loss of blood from the wound in his leg, not the wound in his head, that had almost killed him. Linc had been unconscious for three days. Cassie had waited beside his bed through every interminable hour, wanting to be there when he awoke. But when he finally did, she had only been able to exchange a few words with him before the doctor ordered her to leave, insisting that what his patient needed was a lot of uninterrupted rest.

Linc clicked on the light and pushed himself upright, wincing a bit. His eyes softened as they looked at her.

"You're all dressed up," he said. "Come over here where I can see you better."

Cassie did as he asked, feeling shy for some inexplicable reason. She stood before him in the new evening dress that she had bought that morning at an outrageously expensive boutique in New York City. It was a smoky purple chiffon, with a high waist and a gold girdle with tassels ending in heavy acorns. It had daring slits up the side of the skirt, almost to her knees, and a décolletage so low she kept having to resist the urge to tug it up.

Linc's eyes went immediately to her exposed cleavage. "I like it," he said.

She grinned at him. "I thought you would. Bean's cola had a banquet tonight to celebrate the end of the race. They gave me the check." She fumbled in her beaded evening bag and handed it to him. He looked the check over but said nothing, and after a moment he gave it back to her.

"I'll put it in a bank tomorrow," she said. "I'll probably have to bring some papers for you to sign."

"Whatever."

She rummaged around in her purse again. "Look, they've put our pictures on a postcard. I look downright awful, but you look very dashing and handsome."

He took it, smiling. "We'll be on cigar boxes next."

She smiled with him, and then her smile faded. "If only Quigly were here. To be a part of all this."

"At least now you'll be able to build his engine."

"Yes . . . yes, I will." She twisted her hands nervously and looked around the room. "You'll never guess who was at the banquet tonight. It was that Ziegfeld person, the one with the chorus girls." She laughed suddenly. "He told me I was the quintessential American girl, and he wants to put me in his *Follies* revue. Then he asked me to go to bed with him practically all in the same breath. He wasn't at all bad looking, either. Rather natty and poised. He wears his hair parted down the middle.

It fact, he looks a little bit like Ward—" She cut herself off.

Linc stared at her. "It was Ward in the Spad."

She nodded.

"Why?"

She felt a sudden rush of tears, and she squeezed her eyes shut to hold them back. Taking her hand, he pulled her down beside him on the bed. Up close she could see that his eyes were glowing a bit feverishly. She looked down, following his ragged breathing with the uneven rise and fall of his naked chest.

"Why?" he said again. "Was he jealous of me because of our marriage? Did you forget to explain it to Ward when you were telling the rest of the world that it was all just a farce?"

She started to pull away from him, but he held her down. "I'm sorry," he said. "That came out sounding bitter, and I didn't mean it to."

She lifted her chin and met his eyes. "Lawrence Kingly is Ward's uncle, and Ward got this ridiculous idea in his head that that evil old man, who hates me almost as much as I hate him, is going to leave me all his millions. So in order not to lose the inheritance, which he was in no danger of losing in the first place, Ward tried to get me to marry him. But I told him I wanted nothing to do with marriage, just like I told—" She stopped and bit her lip.

"Me," he finished for her, giving her a rueful smile. "None of us poor, besotted fools can claim he wasn't fairly warned."

"So in the meantime the race came up," she went on rapidly. "And Ward thought he could stave off bankruptcy with the fifty-thousand-dollar prize. But then you and I got married and entered the race together, and he saw both the inheritance and the fifty thousand dollars going into your pocket instead." She drew an indignant breath. "As if I would just turn over all my money to my husband, willy-nilly, even if I were to get an inheritance—"

"Or a husband."

She glared at him. "So Ward tried to kill us by sabotaging our plane," she finished. She was quiet a moment, then she sighed. "He said at first he was only trying to stop us from winning the race, but I think he meant to kill us all along. Otherwise he would have sabotaged the Schmidt brothers' Avro, too, since they were in the lead all the way until Dayton."

Linc idly ran his fingers up the inside of her bare arm, sending chills down her spine. "And when he lost all hope of winning the race," he said, "Ward attacked us with the Spad to ensure he would get the inheritance." He shook his head and heaved a huge sigh. "God, poor Ward."

Cassie nodded, and her eyes filled with fresh tears. "They've arrested him for attempted murder, Linc, and they've put him in a place for crazy people."

"Cassie, that war affected all of us in some terrible ways. At least maybe where he is, Ward can be helped."

"I suppose you're right. It's just so hard to think of him being locked up. . . ."

"They can't lock him up without a trial. Maybe if we testify on his behalf, the judge'll take that into consideration—at least send him to a hospital instead of prison. After all, we're the ones he tried to kill."

He interlaced his fingers with hers, squeezing her hand. "It's funny, I knew Ward had taken that plane, but I just never—"

"You knew!" Cassie exclaimed.

"Uh-huh. Remember all that commotion going on up at the big house that morning we left Dayton? It was because Leroy Bean had discovered somebody had stolen the Spad during the night. And I figured Ward had done it." His lips lifted slightly into a sad smile. "I thought he had taken it for sentimental reasons. The only mystery left is why he didn't finish us off when he had the chance, why he quit and gave up."

"He didn't quit. We got him before he could get us. We rammed him with our undercarriage."

Linc stared at her in astonishment. Then he burst into laughter. "Christ, Cassie! You are incredible. You brought down an enemy plane—who just happened to be shooting at you—by *ramming* into him?"

"Yes. You told me what to do, and I did it."

"I told you what to do? Cassie, that is the most ridiculous nonsense you've come up with yet."

"You can scoff all you like, Linc Cameron, but I was here and you weren't—well, not really. And I know what happened. I heard your voice telling me what to do, and I felt your hands guiding mine on the controls. You don't seriously think I'd ever have been able to do such a thing by myself?"

"Yes, I do. You're the best—"

She shook her head stubbornly. "I know what happened."

He laughed and shrugged. "All right, I give up."

She looked into his eyes. They were so incredibly blue, and so sad in spite of the smile that still hovered around his mouth. He reached up to caress her shoulder, rubbing his thumb along her collarbone, and she felt a spasm of physical desire so strong she had to clench her teeth against a moan.

She pulled away from him and stood up. Clasping her hands together in front of her, she sucked in a deep breath. "Linc, we have to talk."

He turned his head away from her, and his face took on that shuttered look. "If you insist."

"Remember that new fad—"

His head whipped around. "You aren't going to cut your hair!" he exclaimed, so appalled he forgot he was angry.

She waved her hand impatiently. "Not that fad."

"You've taken up smoking?"

"Oh, will you stop being so infuriating! Will you marry me? I mean, will you stay married to me?" He opened his mouth, but she hurried on before he could speak. "I know you think we're wrong for each other and you're right, but you're also wrong...oh, damn!" Her mouth twisted into a funny smile. "This is coming out stupid. What I'm trying to say is...we did it, Linc. We won the race, and we managed to keep poor Ward from killing us, and we did it together. So we must be doing something right in spite of being so wrong for each other. And I've been thinking about what you said about our love not having to be doomed. Look at Maisie and Tessa and Nora. Their love isn't doomed. Their marriages are working out fine, even when you wouldn't expect them to. So maybe the secret is love, Linc. If we love each other hard enough, we can make it last—and why won't you say something?"

Linc opened his mouth.

"Because I *do* love you, Linc," Cassie said. "I would die without you. I almost died when you died...I mean, when I thought you had died. Damn it, Linc, will you say something?"

"Yes."

She stared at him, a look of worried confusion on her face. "Yes? What is that supposed to mean?"

"It means yes, I'll stay married to you, or yes I'll marry you again, or I'll divorce you and live with you in sin. Whatever you want, Cassie, as long as we stay together."

"Then you do love me?" she asked tremulously.

He patted the bed. "Come here so I don't have to drag my wounded leg out of bed to come and get you."

She sat down beside him. He grasped her arms with his strong, sensitive hands. He held her still a moment, then his hands moved up her arms and over her shoulders to stroke her neck. He captured her eyes with his own dark blue ones, blue as the ocean depths, and she thought she would drown in them.

"I love you," he said. "I love you today, and I'll love you all our forever-afters. It seems as if I've been in love with you all my life." His eyes gleamed with wicked laughter. "But I suppose I really fell in love with you that day in Virginia when I got so careless and almost flew my plane right into yours."

Her lips curved up. "And did you love me that day in Billings when you got us shot at by outlaws?"

"Uh-huh. And I loved you that day in Kansas City when I caused all that trouble by stupidly getting in the way of that policeman's club." His face grew serious. "I even loved you that night in Dayton when you told me I was going to have to endure life without you."

"Oh Linc, don't bring that up. I was acting like such a scared little fool—"

He pressed his fingers over her lips to stop her words, then he pulled her head down to meet his mouth. His lips moved over hers in a demanding kiss, and she felt herself losing control, being turned inside out and upside down, as if she was spinning through the sky in the *Pegasus*, and she surrendered with a deep, trembling groan.

Breaking the kiss at last, she leaned back in his arms, toying with his hair where it curled down over the edge of the bandage. "Did they have to shave off any of your hair?" she asked, wearing a frown.

"I don't know. Aren't you going to love me if I grow bald?"

"I'm not sure. I promised for better or for worse, in sickness and in health. Nobody mentioned anything about baldness." She rubbed her palm across his bare chest. "Linc . . . do you still have any of those precautions left?" she asked casually.

"A few." His face took on a comic leer. "Why?"

"You might as well toss them out."

The leer was replaced by a look of incredulous joy. "My God, Cassie, are we going to have a baby?"

"No. But I want to, Linc. Can we?"

He laughed. "I'll do my best." His fingers traveled down her neck to her breasts. He cupped one in his hand, rubbing his thumb against the hardening nipple through the thin material of her dress. "So... hadn't we better get started?"

Her hand covered his, stilling it. "Linc, we shouldn't start something we won't be able to finish. If you aren't careful your leg will be bleeding again before you know it. You're certainly in no condition to—"

"Cassie..." He sighed and lay back against the headboard, his eyelids fluttering closed. He mumbled something else she couldn't hear.

"Linc?" Worried, she leaned over him, putting her face next to his.

"I am in excellent condition," he whispered against the corner of her mouth. And he grasped her hand, pushing it beneath the sheet, pressing it against the proof of his desire.

"Linc!" Cassie exclaimed, genuinely shocked. "This is a *hospital*. What if someone—"

As if in answer the door swung open on its squeaky hinges, and Cassie leaped off the bed, blushing guiltily.

"Damn it, Pete," Linc growled. "Did anyone ever tell you that your timing stinks?"

Pete Striker poked his head around the door, beaming at him. "I see you're feeling better," he said. He shut the door behind him and limped stiffly into the room.

Cassie thought there was something not quite right about Pete. For one thing it had to be eighty degrees outside, and yet he was wearing his heavy leather jacket. He also appeared to have acquired a huge potbelly since she had last seen him, a squirming potbelly.

"Pete, what the hell—" Linc began.

Pete's stomach emitted a muffled whine, and Cassie giggled. He opened his jacket and Patches fell out.

Patches raced across the floor and bounded onto Linc's bed, jostling his wounded leg, and Linc swore around gritted teeth. "Jesus, you mutt. You're drowning me," he groused as Patches bathed his face with his tongue.

"He was worried about you," Pete said. "I had to show him you were going to be all right." He grinned and winked at Cassie. "I see he wasn't the only one who was worried."

"Linc and I are staying married," Cassie announced.

Pete's grin stretched even wider. "You hear that, Patches? These two practically had to get shot outta the sky before they got some sense." He leveled a hard look at Cassie. "Patches was afraid you were turning into one of them la-di-da misses."

"Linc was the one being stubborn about it," Cassie said, and Linc's mouth fell open. "I had to wind up proposing to him."

Pete removed his cap and rubbed at his sparse, ginger-colored hair. "Well, Patches and me talked about it. And we figured it had to be Linc causing all the trouble. He got this ridiculous idea into his head of what kind of wife he thought he wanted, and no one could tell him different."

Linc let out a cry of outrage that was muffled by Patches's tongue.

Cassie slipped her arm through Pete's and kissed his ruddy cheek. "He finally got some sense. So now that that's settled and we've won the race, the three of us can get started on our business."

"Huh?" Pete said, as Linc's eyebrows soared.

"We're going to be manufacturing airplane engines," Cassie said matter-of-factly.

"We're what!" Pete exclaimed, and Linc laughed.

She flashed them each an indignant glare. "Surely you aren't planning to compete in any more of these ridiculous races? There's no future in them, and we're going to have lots of responsibilities pretty soon. Children and things."

"Hot damn!" Pete whooped. "Are you two going to have a—"

"Not yet," Linc put in quickly. Then he looked at Cassie. Smiling, he shook his head. "You are the most incredible woman. Absolutely incredible."

"You're a lucky bastard, Linc, and I hope you realize how lucky," Pete Striker stated emphatically. "You came damned close to losing the best thing that ever happened to you."

"I'm the lucky one," Cassie said turning to Pete, smiling and blushing both at the same time.

And so she missed seeing the worried frown on Linc's face and the sadness that stole back into his eyes.

Chapter 20

The driver expertly wove the shiny red taxi in between the peddler's carts, trolleys, and pedestrians that thronged the crowded street. Cassie leaned forward in the leather seat and peered over Linc's shoulder as they inched past the music halls, nickel movie theaters, and short-order restaurants of the lively Bowery. Arc lamps and pulsing neon glowed in the smoke-colored evening sky. There was a bustling excitement in the air, like electricity sizzling across a hot wire.

It was six days since the finish of the race, and Linc had at last been released from the hospital. As their taxicab turned onto Fourth Avenue, a policeman blew on his whistle, holding up his hand, and the car rolled to a stop. A group of three young women crossed in front of them. They were decked out in the latest fashion: lips painted fiery red, finely arched brows, bobbed hair tucked into close-fitting hats, and long-waisted dresses with draped skirts that rose a shocking five inches above their slender pumps.

Linc eyed their shapely ankles and calves encased in sheer, flesh-colored silk. "Now this," he said, "is one fad of which I think I'm going to heartily approve."

"Amen," the driver replied with a sigh.

Cassie said nothing. She merely put her palm against Linc's cheek and turned his head around to meet her lips, and he soon lost all interest in the scenery.

"Hey!" the driver said for the third time several long minutes later.

Linc reluctantly released Cassie's warm lips and looked around to see what was the cause of this unwelcome intrusion.

"We're here," the driver said, giving Linc a knowing wink. "The Waldorf-Astoria."

"We're on our honeymoon," Linc explained, coloring slightly.

"You don't say," the man replied with a laugh.

A doorman, resplendent in gold braid, opened the cab's door. Cassie paused before passing beneath the red awning to look up at the hotel's impressive edifice, which housed one thousand bedrooms. "Don't gawk," Linc said in her ear as he took her arm. "Otherwise they'll guess you're from out of town."

The lobby was a repository of everything old and expensive—oak paneling, crystal chandeliers, and painted ceilings. Everyone seemed to speak in refined whispers that could barely be heard above the rustle of silk and the swish of furs.

"Your baggage, sir?" a bellhop inquired politely of Linc as he registered their names. Linc pointed to the flying kits lying at his feet. Cassie saw the bellhop give their bags the look of disdain they no doubt deserved, but when he looked back up at Linc again his face wore a look of bland politeness. "If you'll follow me, sir," he said.

Linc caught Cassie's eyes, gave her a devilish smile, and then to her utter shock scooped her up into his arms. Her hat fell off her head and rolled out into the middle of the lobby floor.

"Linc!" Cassie gasped. She struggled against him, but he only tightened his embrace. "What are you doing? Put me down. Everybody's *looking* at us!" Indeed, all eyes in the crowded, cavernous lobby seemed to be turned in their direction.

"They're only looking because you're squawking like a chicken. Am I going to have to kiss you quiet?" And the look he gave her convinced Cassie that he was exercising all his willpower not to ravish her on the spot.

Cassie pressed her lips tight together just in case he decided to make good on his threat. But she couldn't prevent a muffled sound of outrage from escaping.

Grinning broadly, the bellboy picked up their flying kits and Cassie's hat. With Cassie in his arms, Linc followed the young man to the bank of elevators that lined the far wall, a distance Cassie felt was as long as Fifth Avenue itself.

She thought he would put her down once the elevator doors clanged shut, but he did not. The bellhop and the elevator operator exhanged leers and snickers. Cassie pressed her hot face against Linc's shoulder, vowing silently to wring his neck. Everyone in all of New York City now knew what he intended to do to her once they got to their room. And he was always accusing *her* of causing trouble!

The elevator bumped to a stop, the operator slid the door open, and Linc, with Cassie still in his arms, began to follow the bellhop down a long, carpeted hall. He was limping noticeably now. He had probably ripped out the stitches on his leg. It would serve him right, she thought, angry with him for not taking care of himself.

She lightly touched the edge of the bandage where it curved up over his ear. "Linc, you promised the doctor you would take it easy."

He gave her a wicked grin. "That was only so I could get out of that damned place. I have no intention of taking it easy. I am going," he said, raising his voice

loud enough for the whole world to hear, "to mak‹
mad and passionate love to you until it kills me."

An older couple dressed for the theater passed b›
them, hugging the wall and eyeing them as if they wer‹
escapees from a vaudeville hall who had somehov
wandered into the upper-crusty hotel by mistake.

The bellhop threw open the door to their suite with
majestic gesture. Cassie got a glimpse of oriental rug‹
and silk-cushioned settees before Linc carried he›
across the threshold and headed unerringly for the bed‹
room. He kicked the door shut behind them.

Laughing, Cassie plucked Linc's straw boater off hi›
head and sent it sailing across the room. They looke‹
down together at the bed, with its satin-covered head‹
board and matching pillows, then he laid her gentl›
down upon it and stretched out beside her.

He took the pins out of her hair, spreading it in a fa›
over the satin pillows, pressing his face into the thic‹
gold tresses. Then he raised his head and fixed her witl
his intense blue eyes.

"I don't know whether this is the biggest or the soft
est bed in all of New York City," he said with a teasin‹
smile, "but it's got to come pretty damned close. An‹
now, my tempting, temperamental, and most *permanen*
wife"—he lowered his mouth until their lips almos›
touched, and she sighed in expectation of his kiss—"
am going to make good on my promise and wear thi›
bed out making love to you."

And his lips crushed down on hers in a hard‹
hungry kiss.

She clasped the back of his head, pressing his mouth
tighter to hers as the kiss deepened and gentled. Hi›
hands stroked the length of her, their rough calluse›
snagging on the sheer material of her dress. Breakin‹
the kiss, he pulled her upright and slowly began t‹
undo the dozens of tiny hooks that ran up in a row
along her back, stopping now and then to plant soft›
teasing kisses on her neck and shoulders. He eased th‹

dress down over her arms and then removed her modern, new brassiere with a suspicious expertise that would have aroused her jealousy if he weren't already rousing other parts of her to such a degree that she couldn't keep a thought in her head from one second to the next.

He stopped long enough to impatiently tear off his coat and kick off his shoes. Then he threaded his hand through her hair, pulling her head back to expose the sensitive pulse on her neck to his lips and tongue. With his fingers he traced the outline of one breast, then enveloped it in his palm, flattening, massaging, rolling the hard point of her nipple between his fingers.

"Oh, Linc, please," she said between clenched teeth, and he laughed softly, his warm breath caressing the taut skin of her throat.

"Please what? Please stop? Or please don't stop?"

"Don't . . . stop," she answered with a sigh, as he pressed her back down on the bed.

He raised her buttocks, pulling her dress and drawers down over her hips. One shoe had already fallen off; he removed the other and then her stockings. He licked her instep and then between her toes, and she squirmed, trying to pull her foot out of his grasp.

"Oh, Linc, please," she begged again. "That tickles."

"Does this tickle?" He moved his fingers and lips up her calf, following the smooth curve of muscle.

"Well . . ."

"And this?" He licked the back of her knee. She moaned, and her skin quivered beneath his lips. "Or do you like this better?" he said, and his lips roamed up the inside of her thigh. Her legs spread apart, and she tangled her fingers in his hair, inviting his lips to venture farther upward.

She melted and writhed beneath the onslaught of his mouth, as if his panting breaths were flames, his lips a brand. Her skin was on fire, her blood boiling. Just when she thought she would surely go mad from the intensity of the sensations that consumed her, his mouth left off its exquisite torment and searched out her kiss again. His tongue slipped between her teeth to meet hers in an intimate embrace, while below his fingers penetrated her gently, preparing her for his welcome invasion.

He ended the kiss by holding her face steady between his two hands and staring deep into her eyes. Then he rolled off the bed and stood up to look down at her naked body stretched out flat on the bed. He kept his eyes locked on hers as he finished undressing and stood before her, unashamed in his need and desire for her, and she welcomed him back into her arms.

His hands fastened around her waist and he rolled over, pulling her on top of him. He cupped her breasts in his hands as she eased down on him, encasing his swollen hardness with her tight softness. She moved slowly, up and down, up and down, along the length of him, letting the friction build and build, riding the rhythm, spinning through the air, spinning, spinning, spinning . . . until their bodies arched together in one long, shuddering spasm, and he filled her with his love.

Cassie pulled the curtain aside to gaze down at busy and bustling Fifth Avenue. Businessmen and office girls strode purposefully down the sidewalk, glancing up with worried faces at the big round face of the clock on the bank at the corner. Ladies and gentlemen of leisure in their silk suits strolled more slowly, stopping to peer into the windows of Altman's and Tiffany's. Taxicabs, automobiles, and double-decker buses converged on each other, blaring their horns and sending oily smoke into the air.

Sighing happily, she turned and looked back at Linc lying asleep on the bed with the sheet tangled around his brown, naked body. She went to him and, leaning over, woke him with a long, lingering kiss. He grasped the lapels of her cotton wrapper, pulling her down beside him.

"It's time to get up, you lazy thing," she teased.

"I am up," he said, giving her a meaningful look. He pushed her wrapper open, searching out a nipple with his lips. He sucked on it gently a moment, then released it. "It's time I performed my conjugal duties and made love to my wife," he intoned with a serious expression.

"You are most diligent in your conjugal duties, Mr. Cameron," she said, gasping as his fingers drifted down between her thighs.

He made love to her again with tenderness and laughter. And this time when he told her he loved her more today than he had yesterday, and would love her even more tomorrow, she believed him.

Later, as they were dressing, he asked her what she would like to do that day.

"Eat," she answered immediately. "I think we forgot to eat supper last night. And if we don't hurry up, we'll have missed breakfast, and Pete and Patches will be here soon, and we talked about going to the beach for a picnic, remember? And then I must go shopping, Linc. We haven't a thing to wear."

"I'll order some food brought up," he said, going into the sitting room. "And since *we* don't have a thing to wear, we can discuss all the fancy duds you are going to buy me."

She put on her single day outfit, a simple cotton dress with a dropped waist and a big square collar that she had bought in a small Mississippi town where they'd stopped for fuel the day after they had ditched their things in Louisiana. She rolled her long hair into a loose bun on the back of her head. She was tempted to get it bobbed as so many girls were doing this summer, but Linc had already begged her not to. Remembering the way he would stop to bury his face in it and run his hands through it when they made love, she decided she didn't want to cut it after all.

She entered the sitting room and paused on the threshold to look at Linc. Her husband. He sat in a chair, his wounded leg stretched out stiffly in front of him, reading yesterday's newspaper with a scowl on his usually incredibly gorgeous face. The thought of being permanently tied to this man no longer frightened her the way it once had. She trusted him now with her happiness to such an extent that she could no longer imagine a life without him. She loved him with every fiber of her being, every facet of her mind. And she believed, truly believed, that it would last forever.

As she opened her mouth to tell him this, there was a knock on the door. "I'll get it," she said instead, and went to answer it, hoping it was a waiter with their breakfast, for she was starving. But when she opened the door it was to see two friendly, familiar faces smiling down at her.

"Hans, Werner!" she exclaimed. "How nice to see you. Come in." She started to pull the door open wider, and then she looked down to see the revolver in Werner Schmidt's hand. But the even bigger shock was when she turned instinctively around to Linc and saw the total lack of surprise on his face.

"Back into the room, kid. And don't scream," Werner said, waving the gun at her.

"I wasn't going to scream," she said indignantly, although she obeyed his order. There was something strange about his voice, and after a moment it struck her what it was. "What happened to your German accent?"

"It was part of our disguise," Hans said, following Werner and the gun into the room and grinning at her. "Pretty good, huh?" He had his arm in a sling, and there was a raw scar running along his cheek, evidently souvenirs from the plane crash in Kentucky a few weeks before.

Cassie stared at him in confusion. "What disguise? Why are you—"

Werner brought the pistol so close to Cassie's face, pointing it to the spot right between her brows, that she felt herself going cross-eyed. She was so used to thinking of the Schmidt brothers as friendly rivals that she was having a hard time believing herself in danger even now.

"You know what we've come for," Werner said to Linc, who still sat immobile in the chair. "Just cooperate nicely and your pretty little wife won't get hurt."

Linc got calmly to his feet. "There's no need for the gun. I promised Tommy I would pay off his debt if I won the race, and I will. Most of it, at least. I can only give you my share of the prize money."

"What debt? What is going on?" Cassie demanded.

"Now there's the rub," Hans said to Linc. "Mr. Bartinelli doesn't know from shares. All he knows is you got a check from Bean's cola last week for fifty thousand dollars, and he figures it's time your family paid our family the debt you owe us. Those markers Tommy dropped are worth over thirty-three thousand, and Mr. Bartinelli figures what with interest and expenses—that Avro we cracked up in Lexington cost him a pretty penny—fifty thousand give or take a few bucks should just about clear the books."

"What!" Cassie turned to glower at Linc in spite of the gun pointing between her eyes. "What is going—"

"Be quiet, Cassie. Please. I can't give you what isn't mine," he said to the Schmidt brothers. "You'll get my share and that's it, and waving that gun in Cassie's face isn't going to change things."

Cassie gave them all a sweeping glare. "Who are you people? If somebody doesn't tell me what's going on in the next two seconds—"

"You ever hear of the Black Hand, Cassie?" Hans said, thrusting his chest out proudly and earning a scowl from his more serious brother.

Cassie's eyes got huge. "The Black Hand! But I thought you were from Dubuque?"

Hans laughed. "We are. But our ma was from Sicily, and her brother works for Mr. Bartinelli. He got us a job with the family when we came to New York. We're what Mr. Bartinelli calls his 'collectors.' Your husband's brother was stupid enough to play poker with some people he shouldn't have, and to make matters worse, he played with money he didn't have." He shrugged. "We're collecting."

"And she had nothing to do with it," Linc said, anger showing in his voice for the first time. "So leave her out of it."

"Okay, Linc." Werner lowered the gun and stuffed it in his waistband beneath his coat. "I guess you're a better poker player than your brother. We admit we ain't gonna hurt Cassie." He gave her a fond smile. "We got to kinda liking the kid while we were racing, and this ain't her ball game anyway. But Mr. Bartinelli figured you'd turn stubborn once you got your mitts on the cash. He told us to remind you what's gonna happen to your brother should you decide to weasel outta the deal. And your brother we don't know from Adam. If Mr. Bartinelli tells us to arrange an accident, the accident's gonna get arranged. You get my drift?"

Linc said nothing, but Cassie had no trouble recognizing the look of implacable stubbornness on his face.

"What's going to happen to Tommy if this Mr. Barti-whatsit doesn't get his money?" she asked.

Hans chuckled. "Let's just say he won't be flyin' through the air with the greatest of ease anymore."

Cassie stared at Linc. He met her eyes, but his face now wore that maddening shuttered look. "Give it to them," she said. "Whatever they want."

"No."

"Then I'll give it to them." She started for the door. Linc grabbed her arm. "Cassie—"

"Let go of me."

"This isn't your affair. Stay out of it."

She jerked her arm free. "It's been my affair since Salt Lake, hasn't it? You just neglected to tell me about it." She turned to Werner. "Mr. Schmidt—if that's your name—will a bank draft do?"

"Well... Mr. Bartinelli's not a very trusting sort. Maybe you'd better make it cash."

Linc stepped in front of her. "Cassie, I'm not going to let you do this. I mean it."

"You can't stop me, Linc Cameron. It's my money. I can do with it whatever I like."

He glared at her, and she glared back.

"Get out of my way," she said.

"Cassie, if you don't stay out of this, I'll never—"

"I don't give a damn what you do. Now get out of my way, or do I have to ask the Schmidt brothers to remove you?"

Werner took the hint. He pulled out his gun and slammed the butt solidly and expertly into the back of Linc's head. Linc's knees buckled, and he slid gracefully to the floor, unconscious.

Cassie stared down at him, and her eyes darkened with worry. "You didn't hurt him, did you? He just got out of the hospital."

"He'll only be out a half hour or so, and he'll wake up with a headache, is all," Hans said. "Can you really give us the money? All of it?"

"Yes," she said.

The brothers traded glances. "Fair enough," Werner said. "Alls we care about is that the money gets collected." He nodded his head at Linc. "He's gonna be smokin' mad when he comes to. He won't clobber you or anything like that, will he, kid?"

"If he does, I'll clobber him back."

The Schmidt brothers went with her. She had deposited the money in the bank just down the avenue from the hotel, the one with the large clock above its doors. Luckily, Linc had never bothered to sign the account papers, so the money was solely in her name.

The cashier could not handle a withdrawal of such size, so they were ushered into the manager's office. He was a pinch-mouthed man of indeterminate age, with stiff, jerky movements. He seemed to have a strange, dry aura about him, like the smell of money, thought Cassie, although she doubted he ever dirtied his hands touching the real stuff.

They had already spent some of the money on Pete's share for being the advance man, the evening gown for the banquet, and the week's stay at the expensive Waldorf-Astoria, which was to have been their honeymoon. Even so, what was left made a considerable pile on the bank manager's desk, and Hans had to jog across the street to Altman's to purchase a carpetbag to carry it in.

While the men were stuffing the money in the bag, the bank manager drew Cassie aside. "Is this some sort of blackmail?" he asked her sotto voce. "Perhaps I should summon the police."

"No. I'm merely paying off a debt."

He glanced apprehensively at the Schmidt brothers. "I see. If you are quite sure?"

"I'm quite sure."

The bank manager gave her a dubious look, but he let it go.

Out on the sidewalk Hans Schmidt started to hold out his hand, then dropped it as he got a look at her face. "You want my advice," he said to her. "You keep your brother-in-law away from the poker table. He doesn't know a full house from a royal flush, and he doesn't know when to quit."

"And I'll give you some advice as well, kid," Werner said. "Don't get to mournin' this money. You ain't ever gonna get it back, and there's no such thing as getting revenge against the Black Hand. You'd only wind up real dead."

"You just tell that Mr. Barti-whatsit to leave Tommy
lone," Cassie said fiercely.

Hans opened his mouth to laugh, then thought bet-
er of it. "Yeah. Sure. We'll, uh, tell him."

Cassie started to leave, then she turned back. "If you
neant to collect the prize money from Linc all along,
hen why did you bother to compete in the race?"

"Mr. Bartinelli sent us along to keep an eye on his
nvestment," Hans said.

"But you almost won. If you hadn't smashed up in
exington, you probably would have won."

Hans shrugged and gave her a weak smile. "It was
nybody's race. And Mr. Bartinelli just likes to hedge
.is bets."

Cassie walked slowly back to the hotel. The same
.an who had been there yesterday when Linc had car-
ied her up to their room was operating the elevator,
nd now he gave her a leering smile. She scowled at
.im. She stood outside the suite's door a long time be-
ore she opened it.

Linc was in front of the window when she entered;
.e didn't bother to turn around. She wondered how
.ng it had been since he'd regained consciousness and
f he had watched her leave the bank with the Schmidt
rothers. She said nothing to him, but went into the
.edroom and began to gather her things together.

"What are you doing?" Linc said from the doorway.

She stuffed the dress she had worn the evening be-
.ore into her flying kit. "What does it look like I'm
.oing? I'm leaving."

She waited for him to speak, to order her not to go,
.o beg her to stay. He said nothing.

She straightened and turned to face him. He leaned
.gainst the doorjamb, his hands stuffed into his
.ockets, his face expressionless. She looked into his
.yes and let all the anger and disappointment she was
.eeling show in her own.

"Oh God, I think I hate you now, Linc. I really do. I

trusted you. I let myself fall in love with you. I let my
self believe"—her voice caught, and she had to suck in
a deep, ragged breath before she could go on—"believe
that you were different, that *we* would be different
when all along you were lying to me."

He pushed away from the wall and took a step to
ward her, but stopped as she backed toward the bed. "I
never lied to you, Cassie."

She turned away from him and stuffed the rest of
her clothes into the sack. "It was worse than a lie, what
you did. You found out about Tommy's debt and these
Black Hand people in Salt Lake, and you said nothing.
You knew they were watching us, that they were going
to come after the money if we won, yet you never
bothered to mention it to me, the person who just hap
pened to be your copilot, whom you just happened to
have married, for God's sake." She looked up at him
and tears blurred her vision. "The person who just
happened to fall in love with you."

A muscle ticked in his jaw, and his eyes shifted away
from her. "It was my brother's debt, which made it
my problem, not yours. I had no intention of giving
them a cent of your money. If you hadn't as usual made
matters worse by impulsively jumping in where you
don't—"

"Oh, to hell with the money! It's not about the
money, Linc. It's about the way you treated me. Instead
of relying on me, expecting me to help and support
you, you treated me as if what I thought and felt didn't
even matter. We should have faced this *together*, Linc.
But you didn't even bother to tell me about it!"

"I thought I could handle it myself—and that you
were better off not knowing."

She took a deep, shaky breath. "Better off! After all
we've been through together, you still weren't able to
trust me to react like a normal, adult human being.
What did you think I would do, Linc? Have hysterics
and chase you around the airfield with a rolling pin, fall

to a swoon and beg for the smelling salts?"

He flushed and spread his hands in a supplicating
gesture. "Damn it, Cassie, I wanted to tell you, and I
almost did. Even that first night at Salt Lake. But I've
never had much practice sharing my problems with
other people."

"I wasn't just any other person, Linc! You slept with
me that night. You made love with me for the first time
knowing—"

"That's the point. I was falling in love with you, and
I didn't like the fact that I was. All I knew was that I
wasn't ready to lose you, and I didn't know you well
enough to guess how you'd react. I didn't want to spoil
that little happiness I thought we would have together."

"Then what about later, when you knew me better?
What about the day I told you that I loved you? Or the
day you first said you loved me? What about the night I
asked you to marry me?" She dashed the tears from her
eyes with the back of her hand, disgusted with herself
this show of weakness when she had vowed that she
would be strong, that she would never let Linc Cameron hurt her again. "What about *last* night, Linc?"

"Because by then it was too late. Because I knew that
if I told you, *this* would happen," he said, waving his
arm in an arc.

She turned away from him. "I really thought you
were different than most men. I thought I was of some
value to you, as a helpmate, as a *woman*, Linc. Not just
some . . . some stupid object to keep by your side—"

"Damn it, I don't think of you in that way and you
know it. For God's sake, Cassie, we've been through
hell to get to this point. Don't throw it all away because
I made one little mistake."

"It wasn't a little mistake."

"All right, a big mistake. You have a right to be
angry. And if I have to grovel for forgiveness, I will, but

don't give up on me. Don't give up on us. We love eac
other too much to—"

"You should have thought of that sooner, Linc." Sh
snatched up her flying kit and headed for the doo
"You should have thought of that before you decided
lie to me. Before you decided to treat me like some .
some *wife* who has to be protected and coddled and *li*
to for her own good."

He grabbed her by the arm and jerked her aroun
hard, pulling her against him. "You walk out on m
Cassie, and you had better mean it. You'd better thir
really hard about what you're giving up, what you'
going to be living without. Because I won't take yo
back."

"I know exactly what I'm giving up," she said, h
voice brittle and cold. "And I'm better off without it."

"Are you, Cassie? Are you going to be able to liv
without this?" And he crushed his mouth down o
hers in a savage, ruthless kiss.

Her body betrayed her immediately, respondin
against her will to the power of his passion. She gav
up struggling, let herself be carried away by the fee
ings that tore through her, ravaging her like a hurrican
battering against a helpless coast.

He released her so abruptly that she stumbled bacl
ward and had to clutch the bedpost to keep from fal
ing. His blue eyes glittered brightly at her, filled wit
anger and passion. And triumph.

She looked at him for a long time, wanting even a
she was leaving him to take with her a memory, like
talisman of love, to sustain her during the endless year
without him.

"Good-bye, Linc," she said finally, and this time h
let her leave.

Chapter 21

R ia stood on the edge of a dusty pasture outside of Kingly, Virginia. She tilted her head back and put er hand up to shade her eyes, squinting into the glare s the airplane passed overhead. She thought it was oing to fly off, disappear into the sun, but at the last moment it turned around and descended to earth in a mooth, graceful glide. The wheels touched down in ne pasture, sending up a cloud of dust. The plane undled down the length of the field, bouncing a bit ver the ruts before rolling to a stop.

The pilot climbed out of the cockpit, looking small nd fragile. The slight figure seemed to hesitate, and or a moment Ria thought it was going to climb back in ne plane and fly off again. Instead the pilot strode pur- osefully, perhaps angrily, toward her, and Ria smiled.

The pilot stopped and pulled off her helmet with an npatient gesture. Tangled blond hair fell down around er shoulders. "What do you want?" she said to Ria. What are you doing here?"

Ria looked into smoky, enigmatic eyes and laughed. Your bluntness is refreshing, Cassandra. But I must dmit it is always a bit disconcerting to meet it head-on. Je are on our way to Florida, Tommy and I. We have

quit Bartinelli and joined a new troupe. I left Tommy
the train station, however. I did not think you woul
care to see him, but I wanted to—"

"Did Linc send you here?"

Ria shivered and widened her eyes. "Good heaven
no. He was acting perfectly dreadful and refusing to te
me where you were. It was all I could do not to thrott
him. I had to pry the information out of that loud ar
nosy redheaded friend of his. But I felt I had to con
here personally to thank you for what you did f
Tommy and me."

Cassie shrugged, a faint blush coloring her cheeks.

"Linc did at least tell me that much," Ria went on. '
telephoned him long distance as soon as Bart—M
Bartinelli—got the wire that the debt had been settle
and Linc told us that they had made you give up yo
share of the prize money as well. I want you to kno
we intend to pay you back."

"Don't. I mean, it doesn't matter. So please . .
don't. . . ." She shifted nervously and looked awa
back across the field toward the *Pegasus*.

A silence grew between them, and Ria let it buil
until Cassie's eyes turned back to her, then she smile
"Are you going to make me stand out here in this h
field, or will you invite me into your house and off
me something cool to drink?"

Cassie laughed, although she still held herself r
gidly, as if expecting to be dealt a blow at any minut
Ria smiled to herself. Cassandra Jones Cameron wa
about to be given a blow all right. A sly, tricky blov
and she wasn't even going to know what had hit her.

"I don't have any of that Russian drink," Cassie sai
as she led Ria toward a ramshackle house that leane
against a big barn. "What was it called?"

"Vodka," Ria said.

It was only slightly cooler inside the house. Ria too
off her hat and fanned it against her face. "Perhaps
glass of water?"

Cassie opened a cupboard door, then shut it. She
ked distractedly around the kitchen and brushed the
 out of her face with an angry gesture. "I haven't
 clean glasses. Did Linc tell you we were no longer
ether?"

Ria went to the cupboard and took out a coffee cup.
is will do fine," she said, filling it with water from
 sink. She sat down in one of the chairs by the table
 took a sip of the water. "What was I saying? Oh
 ... no, Linc would not tell me a thing over the tele-
ne. Those long-distance wires are impossible for
 but the most rudimentary conversations. But I saw
 in New York before we got on the train—he was
ving next week himself for Hammondsport, some-
g to do with the movies, I believe—and I asked
ut you. He explained the whole thing to me. Or
er, he was about as forthcoming as a rock, and I
 to chisel it out of him in bits and pieces."

Cassie leaned back stiffly against the sink and her
 paled. "He explained the whole thing?"

"Well, he said that you and he had only married so
t you could race together." Ria took a quick drink of
ter to hide a smile. "I told him I thought it was a
her drastic thing to do, but he said it had seemed a
d idea at the time. Well, that much I can under-
nd, since you two were obviously mad about each
er." She glanced casually around the room, then
d her eyes on Cassie's face. "I don't suppose you
sidered staying together?"

Cassie jumped as if someone had just poked her
m behind. "We decided ... decided it wouldn't
rk."

Ria nodded seriously. "That was probably a wise
ision on your part. One should be careful not to
fuse passion with love." Then she shrugged. "Al-
ugh I am probably not the one to be giving you ad-
e on the matter. I regret to say this, but while I

have had considerable experience with passion, I ha
had little with love."

Cassie jerked upright. She seized a chair and
down at the table across from Ria. "Haven't you ev
been in love?" she asked. Her whole body was tense,
if the world depended on Ria's answer.

Ria sighed, and her eyes filled with tears "Once
was seventeen and he was a trick rider from t
Ukraine, half-Tartar and all wild. Oh, I was mad w
passion for him, true enough, but I loved him as w
—with all my heart. He, of course, was mad about n
We planned to marry, but my parents wanted us
wait. They were afraid I was too young, and he had
terrible reputation. He was a womanizer—before
met me, of course—and he gambled and drank a
much at times."

"Vodka?"

"Vodka." She gave Cassie a mischievous smile. "N
family tried to keep us apart, but they didn't alwa
succeed, and I must confess I allowed passion to ov
whelm me during the times we were together, for r
Tartar was irresistible." She sighed softly, and her ey
focused on the distance as if she were watching t
past on a movie screen.

Cassie leaned forward. "What happened? Did
leave you?"

Ria shook herself as if waking from a trance. "O
no. At least not in the way you mean. No, eventua
my parents relented and a wedding date was set. B
my Tartar, my wild and passionate Tartar, was kill
the week before. He fell off his horse while practicing
triple somersault and broke his neck."

"Oh, no!" Cassie exclaimed, her eyes filling wi
tears. "How awful!"

"It was awful at the time. I thought, in fact, tha
would die from it, from the awfulness of it. But ther
discovered that I was with child, and that child gave r
a reason to go on living."

"And the child . . . was Linc?"

"Yes."

Cassie sniffed and wiped at her nose with the back her sleeve. "And you never fell in love again? You ver found anyone to take his place?"

Ria set the cup of water down and looked at Cassie, r eyes glowing wetly. "I never found anyone to take s place because I made his place impossible to fill. He d not live long enough to hurt or disappoint me; he as the perfect man. No one else was ever able to mea- re up to him." She smiled wistfully. "But life, and rtainly men, are never perfect. Yet I wasted my best ars yearning for a dream, a perfect man who never ally existed except in my dreams, and I rejected all e flesh-and-blood men who offered me their love. h, I would let them love me for a time, but then there ould be a little misunderstanding, a little argument, d I would think, Ah, but my Tartar would never ve treated me in such a way. My Tartar would never ve shouted at me in a such an angry voice, and— of! I would show them the door."

Cassie was quiet, chewing on her lip in thought. Ria ve her a minute, and then she jumped abruptly to r feet. "My heavens, look at the time! I must be get- g back to the station."

"I'd give you a ride, but I no longer have a car. uigly and I sold it before we left for California."

"Oh, I don't mind walking, I enjoy exercise. But I ust leave you now, or else I shall miss my train."

"I'll walk with you," Cassie said. "I need to stop off town anyway and get some more fuel for the *Peg*. nd besides"—she grinned suddenly—"I want to see at Tommy of yours and give him a piece of my ind."

Cassie entertained Ria with anecdotes about the race uring the two-mile walk into Kingly. Ria laughed roariously, pretending that she had not heard them once already. Tommy was pleased to see Cassie and

relieved to find that she didn't hate him for being t
reason she'd had to give up all her prize money to t
Black Hand.

As the train pulled away from the station, I
watched Cassie's small figure diminish into a tiny c
and then disappear, and she laughed out loud.

"What's so funny?" her younger son asked, looki:
up from the racing form he had been studying. T
Black Hand had cured him of poker; unfortunately,
had recently developed an avid interest in the horses.

"Oh, Tommy!" Ria exclaimed, laughing until tea
started in her eyes. "I just told poor Cassandra the b:
gest pack of lies. It was a marvelous performance, i
do say so myself, and if Linc ever finds out about it,
shall *kill* me."

"I told you, Linc, that as soon as Mr. Weinraub go:
look at that mug of yours, he'd wanta make you tl
lead."

"I don't know how to act," Linc said for wh
seemed the hundredth time.

Theodore Bunstin rolled his eyes heavenward, as
ing for divine assistance. "So who said you need
know anything about acting? All you gotta do is sm:
that fourteen-karat smile of yours for the camera, ar
no one's gonna give a rat's behind whether you c:
act."

Linc grimaced. "I thought all I was going to have
do was fly the plane. You said you would get me a j:
flying stunts for the movies, not being *in* the damn:
things, for Chrissakes!"

"You get fifty a week to do stunts, compared to fi
hundred bucks to smile pretty for the camera. Now y:
tell me what you wanna do, huh?"

Linc sighed, disgusted with the whole idea. F
knew that he had no choice. He owed his soon-to-l
ex-wife twenty-five thousand dollars. It would take
lot of weeks earning fifty dollars per to remove th

aggravating millstone from around his neck.

"All right, Mr. Bunstin. Where do I sign?"

"Ted! Ted! How many times do I hafta tell ya to call me Ted." He pushed around the pile of papers on his desk, seizing one and waving it triumphantly in the air. "I knew you couldn't re—that you'd see reason. And who knows? Things work out and you could be heading for the big time. Mary Pickford makes ten thousand a week. Can you imagine that? Ten goddamned thousand bucks a week. Say, that reminds me. I saw a picture of that little wife of yours the other day, and she sure as hell could give America's Little Sweetheart a run for her money. You wouldn't consider letting her—"

"You'd have to ask her," Linc said, plucking the pen from Ted Bunstin's fat fingers and scrawling his signature on the contract. "You could probably find her in a small town called Kingly, Virginia. Rural delivery. Is that all?"

"Huh? Oh, yeah. You got to be in Hammondsport a day earlier now. Next Wednesday?"

"Fine."

Linc left Bunstin's office feeling as if he had just sold a piece of himself. Then he had to laugh. What the hell difference did it matter how he made a living? At least it was honest work. Well, legal work anyway. Just because he wasn't going to be doing what he really wanted to do.... Most things in life never work out quite the way you want them to, he thought grimly. Take marriage, for instance. And love.

As he crossed the street into Washington Square, he spotted Pete Striker sitting on a bench gazing up at the sky. Patches lay at his feet.

Patches wagged his tail listlessly as Linc walked up. Pete's eyes popped open and he blushed guiltily, as if he had been caught with his fingers in the till instead of simply sneaking a catnap.

"Did we get the job?" Pete growled to cover his em
barrassment.

"*I* got the job."

Pete got to his feet, grumbling. "Yeah, well, yo
need somebody along to take care of you. Those time
you and—uh, you overhauled the *Peg*'s engine durin
the race, it looked like a bloody amateur had been :
it."

They strolled slowly through the park. It was a rar
summer's day in the city. Warm, but not too humic
The air was light and so clear it seemed to shimmer. /
squirrel ran across their path. Patches stared after it ir
differently.

Linc tilted his head in Patches's direction and raise
his shoulders at Pete. "What's the matter with him?"

"He misses—he's, uh, lonely."

Linc let it pass. "I won't be flying the stunts in tha
movie," he said. "I mean, I will be, but I'll also be ac
ing in it. I know, I know, I can't act. But they offered t
pay me a lot more money, so I thought, What the hell.

Pete squinted up at him. "You also thought you'd b
able to pay—uh, to pay off your debts just that muc
quicker."

Linc stopped abruptly. "Will you quit it, for Chris
sakes?"

Pete tried to look innocent. "Quit what."

"Quit tiptoeing around her name as if I can't bear t
hear it mentioned. Her name is Cassie. I was in lov
with her, and I thought she loved me, but she didn
and now I'm not. See? I can say it without wanting t
run and jump off the Brooklyn Bridge."

Pete sighed. "Yeah."

"I swear, you're taking this harder than I am. She'
gone. It didn't work out, and now she's gone. That's n
reason for the three of us to sink into a decline like
bunch of Victorian virgins."

"Patches and me trusted her," Pete said, watchin

Linc carefully. "We never took her to be one of them
la-di-da misses."

Linc laughed with bitter amusement. "You're as bad
as she is. The two of you need to learn that people are
going to disappoint you in this life."

"And what do you do, Linc, when people disappoint
you?"

"I forget it and go on. If the war taught me nothing
else, it taught me that. Life's too precious to waste it
bearing grudges and mourning over missed opportuni-
ies."

"So what're you saying, Linc? That you got to forgive, right? Forget and *forgive*, is that your motto?"

Linc gave him an oblique look. "You are more transparent than glass, Pete. If you think you're going to
trick me into admitting that I still feel something for
that obstinate, unforgiving, aggravating little troublemaker—" He clenched his jaw shut and spoke through
his teeth. "And if you think that when she *does* come
waltzing back into my life, I'm going to take her
back—"

"I ain't thinking nothin'. Except that I could go for a
big, juicy steak right about now. Me an' Patches, we
both been feeling a bit peckish lately."

Linc continued to scowl at Pete a moment, then he
relaxed, laughing. "Hell. I'll take you both to Delmon-
co's. My treat."

Pete let out his pent-up breath. He and Ria Cameron
had had themselves a little talk and out of that talk had
come a plan. Nothing fancy, just raising a few questions and sowing some doubts. Maybe laying the
groundwork in case those two young idiots—who
were obviously crazy about each other—ever managed
to swallow their pride and come together, and *stay* together, long enough to make it work for a change. It
made him nervous though, what he and Ria were
doing, because they were taking a big chance. It was

asking for trouble to go interfering in other people'
lives.

But sometimes fate needed a kick in the pants.

Cassie walked down the dusty road, sweltering in
the fierce heat of a Virginia summer afternoon. The
sweet scent of tobacco drifted over from the nearby
fields, and their bronze-yellow leaves made the countryside look as if it had caught on fire. She waved at a
pair of men walking down the rows, stooping over
every now and then to pull at weeds.

The milk can filled with gasoline dragged on her arm
even though it was only half-full. She had wanted to fill
the can up, but she hadn't been able to afford it. She
had all of two dollars and thirteen cents left in her
pocket, and nothing but a few tins of that hateful boiled
beef on the shelf in the kitchen. She was going to have
to take the *Pegasus* on the road soon and earn some
money giving rides and exhibitions. The trouble was
that the skies were now crowded with pilots and
planes, the war having dumped a surplus of men and
machines onto an unprepared country. And there
weren't too many people left who would still be awed
by the sight of a flying machine anyway.

Still, she wouldn't be sorry to leave Kingly. She
hated the place now; it was too full of memories. The
memories of her mother, dying inch by inch in
Lawrence Kingly's gloomy old mansion, and those of
Ward, swimming with her in the river, sticking up for
her when the other kids tormented her and called her
"bastard." And the sweet ones in the later years, of
Quigly and the day he first took her up in his flying
machine, of the day he gave her the perfume and called
her a "woman."

The crushing loneliness now was like a load of rocks
on her shoulders. Everything reminded her of Quigly,
especially the house and the barn, with its engine that
would never get built. And as for the other memories,

f a man she thought had loved her, those memories he couldn't bear at all.

Cassie set the can down and paused to rest a moment and wipe her hot, wet face with a bandanna. She felt a sharp pain in her chest, like a stitch from running so hard, but it didn't come from the hot walk. The visit that morning from Linc's mother had disturbed her more than she dared admit. She had tried to shut her mind to all memories, all thoughts, of that dreadful day when she had so impulsively stormed out of the Waldorf-Astoria. Now Ria had come and stirred up terrible doubts, terrifying fears, and they beat against her closed mind like moths' wings against a window at night. What if . . . ? For several long seconds she forgot to breathe.

What if she had made a mistake?

She shuddered, slamming the doors closed again, pulling herself back to the present with a wrench that was physical. She picked up the milk can and resumed walking down the rutted lane toward the house.

As she rounded the bend, she noticed that there was a man sitting on the front stoop, and her heart stopped for the two seconds it took for her to realize that he was a stranger. Then she forced a smile and put a jauntiness into her step as she approached him. It wasn't good business to let a potential customer realize that you were desperate.

The young man sat on the sagging step, elbows on his knees, studying the ground. His head jerked up at the sound of her footsteps on the gravel. He stared at her for a long moment and then got slowly to his feet. He was tall and lanky, with a gaunt, long-jawed face and sleepy-lidded eyes. He smiled at her, revealing a small gap between his two front teeth that gave him a boyish look.

She smiled back. "It's really too late to go up for a ride this evening. It's going to be dark soon. Why don't you come back in the morning?"

"Ride?" He looked around, spotting the *Pegasus* tie
down in the field and the faded banner on the bar
wall. "Oh, I see. Actually, half of me has alway
wanted to go for an airplane ride. The other half quake
with dread at the thought. So far the other half ha
prevailed, but a ride does sort of sound like fun." H
raised his fedora a couple of inches, dipping his head i
a polite nod. "I'm Nathan Spranger of Spranger an
Spranger."

"Cassie Cam—Jones... Spranger and Spranger?"

He smiled self-consciously. "A bit awkward sound
ing, I know. My father wanted to make it Spranger an
Son, but I thought that sounded even worse. Sort o
like a feed-and-grain store rather than a law practice
He paused to smile again. "I confess, I didn't come fo
an airplane ride. I'm here on a legal matter."

A bleak chill spread over Cassie in spite of the hars
summer heat radiating from the road and withere
fields, and she had to clench her teeth together to kee
them from chattering. The divorce. Linc had sent th
man to get the divorce, and once that happened the ri
between them would be permanent. He would marr
someone else, have children, buy a house with a swin
... he would be lost to her forever.

She realized that the man had said something to he
"I'm sorry?"

"I said that this could take some time. I was wonder
ing if we couldn't..." He gestured back toward th
door of the house.

"Oh yes, of course. I'm sorry. Please, come in."

Cassie ushered Nathan Spranger into the kitcher
He paused just inside the door, removing his hat, an
surveyed the room by turning around in a slow circle.

"It's a bit messy," Cassie said, coloring slightly. "I'r
afraid I'm not much of a housekeeper."

"To tell you the truth, neither am I. It's one of th
nice things about living alone, I think. You're allowe
to be as sloppy as you want, and when it gets so ba

at even you can't stand it anymore, you just sweep it
ll out and start creating a new mess." He bent over
nd picked up a stack of Quigly's engine designs,
which were lying on one of the chairs shoved at hap-
azard angles around the table. "If we could just put
his somewhere..."

Cassie hurried to take the papers out of his hand.
he looked around the kitchen for somewhere to put
hem, finally settling for the top of the icebox, already
iled high with newspaper clippings about airplanes.

"Would you like something to drink?" she asked.

Nathan sat down, placing his hat on the table in
ront of him. "Uh...yes, please."

She covered her mouth with her hand to smother a
ugh. "This is terrible, but I really haven't anything to
ive you. Except water. Or I could make some coffee?"

"Coffee would be fine. If it's not too much trouble."

She could feel his eyes on her while she made the
offee. She glanced back at him over her shoulder once,
nd he smiled at her.

She cleared her throat, addressing her reflection in
he window above the sink. "Has he committed the
dultery, or do I have to do it?"

"I beg your pardon?"

She turned around, bringing coffee cups and spoons
o the table and setting them down so hard they rattled.
I don't see the need for it, frankly. If he wants a di-
orce that badly, why can't we just all agree that it's
een committed, without someone actually having to
o out and *do* it?"

"I'm afraid I don't—"

"Or does the judge demand proof? Like photographs
r something?"

"Actually—"

"You can tell him from me when you see him—are
ou going to see him? Tell him that if he's in such an
ll-fired hurry to get the divorce, he can go do the dirty
eed himself. Why is he in such a hurry? Has he found

someone else already, or is he just being—"

Nathan held up his hand. "Stop a moment . . . the
uh, coffee's boiling over."

Cassie whipped around, letting out a small cry of
dismay. She yanked the pot off the stove, burning her
hand and swearing out loud.

Nathan laughed. "I haven't come about a divorce.
Are you getting a divorce?"

She turned around to glare at him so ferociously that
he blinked. "What are you doing here then? Besides
pretending you want a plane ride when you don't and
inviting yourself in my house only to criticize my
housework. And then insisting upon having coffee so
that I go and burn my hand!"

He stared at her openmouthed, then laughed again.
"Are you always like this?"

"Like what?"

"Never mind." He stood up and gestured at his
chair. "Come here and sit down."

Cassie hesitated a moment, then did as he asked.
Nathan looked around for another chair. He spotted
one beneath Cassie's flying coat and helmet. He hung
them on the hook by the door, then he brought the
chair over and placed it opposite hers, easing his lanky
frame down on its sagging cane seat. The laughter had
gone out of his face, and a sharpness glimmered in his
eyes beneath their heavy lids.

"Now, are you prepared to listen to me without in-
terrupting?"

Cassie nodded stiffly.

"Your, uh . . . Lawrence Kingly died in his sleep the
day before yesterday." He paused, but Cassie said
nothing. "Naturally a man of his eminence and wealth
left a will. I prepared it, or rather, Spranger and
Spranger prepared it. He's left the bulk of his estate to
you, including two million dollars in the bank and a lot
of assets worth even more."

"I don't want it."

Nathan's lips twitched. "Somehow I thought you would say that. Nevertheless, the fact remains that you have been given it, whether you want it or not."

"It can just molder and rot in the bank then, because wouldn't touch a penny of Lawrence Kingly's money if I were starving, dressed in rags, and sleeping in the gutter!" Which is—she thought with an urge to burst into wild laughter—not too far from exactly where I am right now.

Nathan was nodding seriously. "You could do that, of course. Unfortunately, money can't seem to just sit quietly on its own. It needs to be invested, managed, and so on. And certainly the textile mill and the quarry and tobacco plant can't operate without direction."

"I'll give it away then," Cassie said. "To orphans and people like that."

Nathan sighed. "That is an alternative, true. And a most generous one. However, I must caution you. As soon as word gets out that you've inherited the Kingly fortune, you are going to be inundated with requests for donations to charitable causes. Some will be quite worthy and legitimate organizations, others ... not so legitimate. You'll need to exercise caution if you want to see the money—"

Cassie jerked to her feet, pacing the floor and pushing her hands through her tousled blond curls. "Oh, this is so infuriating! This is the meanest thing Lawrence Kingly has done to me yet. He knew I wouldn't want his money, he knew it would bring me nothing but trouble. He's done this deliberately just to try to ruin my life!"

"It doesn't have to ruin it."

Cassie stopped pacing.

"They say that money can't buy happiness, but it can buy a lot of things. Comfort for one. An easy life for your children and grandchildren. The realization of your dreams, or at least those on the material level. . . ."

Cassie thought about Quigly's engine. She had been

to every bank around, even over to Richmond. Few were willing to discuss lending a woman the money to start her own business. One banker, after looking at Quigly's designs and patents, had said he would consider it, but only if she hired a man to be in charge of the operation. But with two million dollars of her own, Quigly's dream wouldn't have to die with him.

She bit her lower lip. "I just hate to give Lawrence Kingly the satisfaction of thinking he has managed to buy my forgiveness."

Nathan gave her a tiny smile. "He isn't thinking anything now; he's dead. Whatever satisfaction giving you his fortune brought him, that has already been experienced. Denying yourself the inheritance now won't change that. You can't spite a dead man."

"No ... no, I guess you can't. But what about Ward Farrell? Didn't that evil monster leave his own nephew anything at all?"

"Several substantial loans made to Mr. Farrell by the estate were forgiven. Other than that, nothing. However ... haven't you heard? Edward Farrell committed suicide two days ago."

"No ... I hadn't heard."

Ward's thin face, the way she had seen it last, with its sad and twisted smile, appeared before her, and she squeezed her eyes shut. She felt an immense sadness. Edward Farrell had been the closest thing she would ever have to a brother. They had shared their childhood, and he had befriended her when no one else in Kingly had dared. At first, when she had thought Linc would die, she had hated Ward for what he'd done, but the hatred had soon turned to pity. The war had changed Ward, warped him in some way. She could understand why he had taken his life. At least now he wouldn't spend the rest of his years locked up in some prison or asylum.

Ward Farrell had given her so much, and at a time when she had needed him the most. If only there had been something she could have done for him, some way to convince him... but then, his fears had had substance all along. Lawrence Kingly—mad, frightened, and dying—had tried to erase the past by paying for his sins with gold instead of suffering. And Edward Farrell had suffered in his stead.

"A mental breakdown, I understand," Nathan was saying. "He was going to go on trial soon for attempting to murder—" Nathan stopped himself, embarrassed. "But I guess you know that."

Cassie had forgotten about the trial. And this time her feelings of sick disappointment were all for herself. She realized she had been counting on Ward's trial as a chance to see Linc again, a chance perhaps to undo the mistake she had made in leaving him.

Nathan Spranger got to his feet, picking up his fedora. "You don't need to decide anything definite tonight. The idea of sudden wealth can be a bit intimidating." He flashed her his gap-toothed smile. "But most people find themselves adjusting to the thought before too long. I'll leave you now and give you some time to think."

He paused on his way to the door. "By the way... Lawrence Kingly's funeral is tomorrow."

"I'm not going. And I don't care what people think."

He laughed. "No, I'm sure you don't." He looked down at the hat he held in his hands, twisting the brim. When he looked up at her, his face was serious again. "You're probably going to think this is strange—no, not strange, suspicious. I come to your house to tell you you've just inherited a pile of money, and then on the way out the door I... I'm going to do it anyway." He took a deep breath. "Cassie, I've never run across a woman quite like you before, and I'd like to get to know you better. Would you consider having dinner with me tomorrow evening?"

Cassie smiled shyly. "That's very kind of you to ask, Mr. Spranger, but I thought you knew... I'm married."

"Yes, I know, but I thought when you talked about divorce..."

Cassie could only shake her head, unable to speak around the ridiculous lump that had become lodged in her throat.

He stopped on the threshold to give her a sad crooked smile. "I suppose it's because I'm a lawyer, but I like to get all the facts on the table right from the start. Will you tell me just one thing? Can I ask you out again next week, next month, or never?"

"Never... I'm sorry."

"I was afraid of that." The heavy lids lowered to shield his eyes. "This isn't any of my business, but you obviously still love your husband very much. Why don't you and he...?"

Cassie shook her head, fighting back hateful, humiliating tears. "We can't. We're wrong for each other."

"How do you know?"

"What?"

"How do you know you're wrong for each other? What's right? Maybe love is just like sudden riches. Maybe all you need is time to adjust to the idea of it." He tipped his hat in a cocky salute. "Good evening, Cassie Jones."

Cassie stood speechless in the middle of the kitchen floor while the door closed behind the lawyer. Then she groped for a chair and sank down into it.

"I'm rich," she whispered. The idea meant nothing to her. She felt no different now than she had an hour ago, before Nathan Spranger had shown up on her front stoop and turned her life inside out. No, she did feel different. She felt confused, afraid, and excited all at the same time.

I'm rich, she thought. She giggled, pressing the back of her hand against her mouth. An hour ago she was worried about where she was going to find the money for her next tank of gasoline, and now she had two million dollars. Not to mention a textile mill, a quarry nd a tobacco plant. Suddenly she yearned with a erceness that was physical to share this extraordinary ews with someone. No, not just with anyone, with—

Abruptly she got up and went outside to stand on he stoop. The sun was setting, its fading light giving a olden edge to the trees, the fields, the few cottonlike uffs of clouds in the sky. The *Pegasus* sat in the middle f the pasture, looking as lonely as she felt. She hought about all the small moments of triumph and isappointment, of laughter and anger, of excitement nd danger—all those moments that she and Linc Ca-meron had shared during those days and nights, flying cross the continent. And she thought that in later ears it would not be the victory she would remember, o much as that struggle. The struggle they had faced nd conquered together.

The struggle and the victory. Something of the tex-ure of life is lost, she thought, if you can't share it with he man you love.

A flesh-and-blood man, not a dream.

Chapter 22

⌒○○⌒

She flew. And the blue sky spread wide before her blue like his eyes. And infinite.

It was also empty, and this worried her. She had been told he would go up today, to practice stunts for the movie they were going to start making tomorrow. She had planned it all out carefully; she was only going to have one chance at this. It was the scariest thing she had ever attempted in her life, and she could not bear the thought of failing.

The movie was being filmed at the Glenn Curtiss flying facilities at Hammondsport, New York. Yesterday Cassie had hidden in a grove of trees near the hangars, waiting until the camera crew, the directors, and the actors had all left for the day. Until only Pete Strike remained, tinkering on the Sopwith Camel fighter plane that Linc Cameron would use in his acting debut as a daring British ace.

Pete was swearing under his breath as she approached the open hangar door. He was bent over his toolbox, looking for a particular bolt tightener that he was sure he had and muttering damnations against people who borrowed a man's tools and then didn't bother to put them back.

Patches was curled up asleep on the pilot's seat. He eard her footsteps and his ears pricked up, then the reeze carried her smell to him. He poked his head out 1e cockpit and let out a joyful bark.

Pete's head whipped around, then he straightened lowly. Cassie swallowed hard, for he did not look at all appy to see her.

Patches bounded up to her, beaming his idiotic grin. he knelt on the packed-dirt floor and hugged him ght against her chest, burying her face into his smelly ir. He slobbered all over her face, letting her know 1at he, at least, was glad to see her.

"So it's you," Pete said.

She gave Patches a final squeeze and stood up. "It's 1e. I've come to beg him to take me back . . . sort of."

Pete said nothing. He took his box of cigarettes out f his shirt pocket and occupied his eyes and hands vith lighting one up. She waited until he was finished, ntil he no longer had an excuse not to look at her.

"Pete," she said.

He took a deep drag on the cigarette, held it a long noment, then exhaled the smoke at his feet.

"Pete."

He looked up.

"What do you think my chances are?"

Now that he was looking at her, she suddenly vished he wouldn't. Her courage was starting to crum- le. She had a sudden yearning to be up in the *Pegasus*, lying back to Kingly, Virginia.

"You want me to be honest?" Pete finally said.

Cassie took a deep breath and held it, nodding.

"Not good," he said. "You know what a stubborn astard he can be. He's back to thinking he was right about you the first time, and once he gets an idea into his head, it takes a stick of dynamite to blast it out."

She let the breath out, smiling for some inexplicable eason, since she certainly hadn't been given encourag- ng news. Maybe she had been afraid that Linc had

somehow changed during the past weeks. At least no
she knew she would be facing the same man she ha
left, instead of a stranger.

"I know, Pete," she said, and actually laughed. "Lir
Cameron has got to be the most infuriating man aliv
But he's my man, or was. And I want him back. I hav
to try. All I've got to lose at this point is a little pride."

Pete grinned back at her. "He'll be out here by him
self early tomorrow morning to practice the stunt
Why don't you try then?"

"Thanks, Pete." She stretched up and kissed him o
the cheek. Then she knelt and gave Patches a big hu;
"Put in a good word for me tonight, will you, boy?" sh
whispered.

She started to leave when Pete called her name.

"It might help to know," Pete said, "he's been mise
able without you. Even if he won't admit it."

"I'm miserable without him, Pete."

He pinched the cigarette butt dead between h
fingers, then flipped it out the hangar door. "I've neve
in my life run across a bigger pair of fools. Patches he
has got more sense than the two of you put together."

At the sound of his name, Patches barked as if h
heartily agreed with everything Pete had said. Cass
and Pete started laughing, which made Patches rac
around in circles trying to catch his tail, an antic tha
always got a lot of laughs. Patches loved more tha
anything to make people laugh.

She saw the shadow first, black wings floating ove
the rolling acres of vineyards below. Then she saw th
plane, two thousand feet lower and in front of her. H
was doing a chandelle—an upward, corkscrew climb.

She flew straight at him, slashing and wheeling lik
a barracuda, close enough for him to see her, but not s
close this time that they were in danger of colliding. H
did not stay up in the sky to play with her, but took th
Camel down immediately. She wondered if that was

good or bad sign. She thought it was probably bad.

She let him land first. He stood beside his plane watching her come in, a tall slender figure in whipcords and a brown leather jacket, looking the same as on the first day she saw him. Again she stopped at the far end of the field and waited nervously for him to come to her.

He came.

She took off her helmet and goggles and swung out of the cockpit to meet him. The hard, unforgiving look of fury on his face was even worse than she had expected, and it took all the courage she possessed to stay and face him.

He stopped while there were still ten feet separating them. "What are you doing here?" he demanded, fury in his voice as well.

She put her hands on her hips and summoned up her best glare. "You don't need to snap my head off, Linc Cameron. Although I suppose it's an improvement over the first time we met, when you tried to knock it off."

"I told you—"

"That you wouldn't take me back, and you meant it. I told myself I wasn't coming back, and I meant that too. Yet I'm here." She took a couple steps, cutting the distance between them by half. She was close enough now to see the muscle ticking in his jaw. She took another step; his eyes narrowed and darkened.

"We're both making a big mistake, Linc," she said, lowering her voice into an intimate caress. "I thought one of us should admit it, and it seemed to be my turn."

He looked off into the distance, then his head swiveled back to her, and he pinned her with his eyes. "And the next time something like this happens, Cassie? How many mistakes do we both have to make before we realize that—"

"That we are meant to be together? If you expect me

to promise that we'll never fight again, I can't. Because we both know you can be so infuriating at times. . . ." She took another step. He tensed, but she thought she detected a slight softening around his mouth. "So we'll yell and scream at each other, and I'll probably do something impulsive and get into trouble, or have a temper tantrum and storm out of the house. But I won't go far, and I'll come back, Linc. I'll always come back."

"Will you?"

She took another step. "Oh, I'll come back. Because I've learned something from all this, and so have you, even if you are too stubborn to admit it. And it's not that I can't live without you, because I can."

"That's good, Cassie," he said. "Because you are going to have to."

She took two more steps. They were close enough now that she could have reached out and touched him, but she stood straight before him, her arms loose at her sides. She had come this far, but the final step was now his to take. Or not.

"But I don't want to live without you, Linc," she said, her voice breaking. "We might be wrong for each other, but we are meant to be together. It's our fate, our luck both good and bad. We are meant to bring to each other all our greatest joy, and all our greatest pain. Because you can only be hurt if you care, Linc. If you love."

She could see the rise and fall of his breathing, even though he still wore the leather jacket. There was a slight film of sweat on his face; dark tendrils of his hair clung damply to his forehead. It took all her willpower not to reach up and brush them aside. The immensity of her love for him was almost too intense to be borne.

"Oh, Linc . . ." She breathed his name again and swayed into him.

He crushed her against him, tangling his fingers in her hair and pulling her head back, bringing his mouth down hard on hers in a kiss full of anger, pain, and surrender. And her lips parted under his with a long, shuddering sigh.

At last he released her lips, but he did not let her go. He held her face against his shoulder, rubbing his cheek in her hair, pressing his mouth to her head, his hands moving restlessly over her back, as if suddenly he could not get enough of touching her. Then he grabbed another handful of her hair and yanked her head back.

"Christ, I must be crazy. Why do I let you *do* this to me?"

She laughed, feeling suddenly weightless with joy, for she knew now that she had won. "Because I'm trouble," she said. "And you thrive on trouble. You'd be miserable without it, and without me. You might as well admit it, Linc."

"Like hell," he growled. "I'll admit I love you, and I'll admit I need you. But you are never going to get me to admit that I like all the trouble you're always causing." He encircled her waist with his arm, pulling her against him, smiling down at her at last with carefree and joyful eyes. "We are going to settle down and have a nice normal *quiet* life, Cassie—"

Cassie gulped in sudden alarm. "Oh, no. Linc?"

"Unfortunately, thanks to that damned Tommy, it's going to be a while now before we can get the airplane engine business going, so we'll start by having children—that should go a long way toward keeping you out of trouble. Then—"

"But, Linc—"

"—we'll buy a house. Nothing too big or fancy." He gave a small laugh. "Because I can't afford anything big or fancy. But at least we'll have each other, and you can pick where you want to live. I don't care where it is, as long as it's someplace and as long as it's with you."

"Linc!"

"What?"

"I have something important to tell you, and I don't think you're going to like it. In fact, you're probably going to hate it, because you are always so proud and stubborn when it isn't necessary to be that way with *me*, so you have to promise you won't get mad."

He had grasped her shoulders, pushing her back at arm's length. "I knew it! You're starting it already, aren't you? What have you done now?"

"Nothing. It's not my fault."

"You can't imagine how much it relieves me to hear you say that, Cassie. What have you done that's nothing and isn't your fault?"

She bit her lip and gazed up at him with big gray eyes. "You won't lose your temper?"

"I never lose my temper."

Her eyes widened even farther at this outrageous statement.

"Well, almost never," he amended. "Anyway, I won't this time."

"Even if you don't like it? And you won't like it, Linc. I know it. But it isn't my fault. I had nothing—"

"Cassie, you are driving me even crazier than I already am! For the love of God, will you tell me what it is and put me out of my misery?"

"Promise, first," she said stubbornly.

"Cassie . . ."

"Promise."

He laughed suddenly and gave her a hard, swift kiss. "Ah, Christ, but I do love you . . . and I promise I won't lose my temper. No matter what this thing is that you had nothing to do with and isn't your fault."

So she took a deep breath—and told him about the two million dollars.